Knowing God
The Ultimate Meaningfulness of the Universe

Related titles by Anthony Mansueto

Knowing God series:

Restoring Reason in an Age of Doubt, Volume 1 (Ashgate 2002)

The Journey of the Dialectic, Volume 3

Doing Justice, Volume 4

In the Theopolitical Visions series
(Cascade Books):

*The Death of Secular Messianism:
Religion and Politics in an Age of Civilizational Crisis*

Knowing God
The Ultimate Meaningfulness of the Universe

VOLUME 2

Anthony E. Mansueto

☙PICKWICK *Publications* • Eugene, Oregon

THE ULTIMATE MEANINGFULNESS OF THE UNIVERSE: KNOWING GOD, VOLUME 2

Copyright © 2012 Anthony E. Mansueto. All rights reserved. Except for brief quotations in critical publications or reviews, no part of this book may be reproduced in any manner without prior written permission from the publisher. Write: Permissions, Wipf and Stock Publishers, 199 W. 8th Ave., Suite 3, Eugene, OR 97401.

Pickwick Publications
An Imprint of Wipf and Stock Publishers
199 W. 8th Ave., Suite 3
Eugene, OR 97401

www.wipfandstock.com

ISBN 13: 978–1-55635–986–6

Cataloguing-in-Publication data:

Mansueto, Anthony E.

    Knowing God / Anthony E. Mansueto.

    xxiv + 408 p. ; 23 cm. Includes bibliographical references.

    Contents: 1. Restoring Reason in an Age of Doubt. 2. The Ultimate Meaningfulness of the Universe 3. The Journey of the Dialectic. 4. Doing Justice.

    ISBN 13: 978-0-75460-853-0 (v. 1)
    ISBN 13: 978-1-55635-986-6 (v. 2)
    ISBN 13: 978-1-55635-987-3 (v. 3)
    ISBN 13: 978-1-55635-985-9 (v. 4)

    1. Metaphysics. 2. Philosophy — Modern. I. Title.

BT50 .M265 2002

Manufactured in the U.S.A.

Contents

Introduction / vii

1. Empirical Lore, Cosmological Mythology, Mathematical Physics, and Science / 1
2. The Foundations of Mathematical Physics / 88
3. The Development of Mathematical Physics / 122
4. The End of Mathematical Physics / 207
5. The Principles of Scientific Explanation / 279
6. Physical Organization / 305
7. Biological Organization / 340
8. Social Organization / 358

Conclusion / 373

Bibliography / 399

Introduction

STATEMENT OF THE PROBLEM

To be human is to search for meaning—for some principle in terms of which we can understand the universe and our place therein, and from the standpoint of which we can order our action and organize our lives together. And in so far as our knowledge begins with the senses and terminates in concrete practical activity, we seek this meaning first and foremost in the world around us, even if we find that that world ultimately points beyond itself to an *arche* and *telos* which transcends what can be known by the senses and which is infinite rather finite and necessary rather than contingent. It is this search for meaning in the universe which forms the basis for the cosmological mythologies of band, tribal, and communitarian societies. It is also principal font of science, which until the nineteenth century was the ally, not the adversary, of both rational metaphysics and of religion.

It has not, to be sure, been obvious to all human societies that the universe is ultimately meaningful. On the contrary, some cosmological mythologies, such as those of the Aztecs, the Aryans, and other societies dominated by warfare and exploitation, see the universe as grounded in violence—in a primordial act of self-sacrifice—and as in perpetual danger of collapsing into chaos and destruction (Brundage 1985, *Rig Veda*). Similarly, both ancient atomism and modern mathematical physics have called cosmic teleology and even the principle of causality radically into question in favor of doctrines which see the universe as governed by (at best) an order without a purpose or (at worst) by chaos and contingency. Indeed, by the middle of the twentieth century, it had become the common wisdom of the scientifically literate public that the universe had come into being for no good reason out of vast cosmic explosion and that it would eventually either collapse into a final singularity like the one from which it had emerged, or else expand endlessly, as energy dissipates and matter becomes increasingly uniform, so that the tentative and local movement in the direction of increased complexity and organization which characterizes the small region of space-time which we occupy, and which itself is merely the result of random variation and natural selection, disappears forever in a night darker and colder than the pit of Dante's Hell.

The scientific results which are taken to point in this direction are, in fact, quite numerous. Beginning with Laplace's claim that God is an hypothesis of which he had no need (Laplace 1819/1951, 1799–1825), up through the development of Darwinian evolutionary theory (1859/1970) and the discovery of the Second Law of Thermodynamics, which resulted in bleak predictions of impending cosmic heat death (von Helmholtz 1854/1961), and continuing in the present period with quantum cosmologies which undermine the principle of causality (Hartle and Hawking 1983, Halliwell 1991, Linde 1994, Bucher, Goldhaber, and Turok 1995, Bucher and Spergel 1999) and inflationary big bang theories which leave little room to hope in the long term survival of life and intelligence in the universe (Davies 1994), the tendency of mathematical physics and its daughter disciplines[1] has been to render claims for the ultimate meaningfulness of the universe less and for the existence of God and less credible. This mobilization of mathematical physics against rational metaphysics and religion we call the "cosmological critique."

There have been a number of responses to this situation. The two most important ideological trends in the present period: neoliberalism (Hayek 1988) and postmodernism (Derrida 1967/1978, Lyotard 1979/1984) accept it and in fact glory in it, regarding it not as a loss of meaning, but rather as a liberation from political and religious authorities which had been legitimated, at least in part, by the older teleological cosmology.

Among believers the dominant tendency has been to abandon rational metaphysics altogether in favor of what amounts to fideism—the notion that we can attain knowledge of God only by means of faith or some

---

1. By mathematical physics we mean any physics that seeks not so much to explain the universe in terms of a rationally transparent principle (as did Aristotelian physics) but rather to produce mathematical formalism which describe it very precisely. This has, we will argue, been the focus of almost all physics since the seventeenth century. We regard as daughter disciplines of mathematical physics those for which rigorous formal (mathematical) description remains the epistemological ideal. This includes almost all of chemistry and the applied physical disciplines (astrophysics, geophysics), as well as much of biology and the social sciences (e.g. neoclassical economics).

other nonrational means. A much smaller group, centered mostly but not exclusively within the Catholic Church, which condemned fideism at the First Vatican Council (Vatican I, *Dei Filius* II, Canon 2:1; John Paul II 1998: 53), has attempted to find other ways to demonstrate the existence of God, which evade rather than confronting the critique emerging out of mathematical physics.[2]

These alternative strategies for finding God are seriously flawed. As we will show later in this work, none of them actually succeeds in proving the existence of God. And because they evade the question of the ultimate meaningfulness of the universe, the sort of spirituality they encourage is so otherworldly as to be vulnerable to critiques of the sort advanced by Feuerbach, Marx, Nietzsche, and Freud. If knowledge of God is possible only on the basis of something other than rational inference from sensory experience, then we cut a chasm between our ordinary sensual appetites and any possible love of God. Love of God is not just higher than love of objects we know through the senses—it is radically different. And this is, of course, precisely the position of the whole tradition, beginning with Augustine, which grounded knowledge of God in this way. A whole host of evils follows in train—hatred of matter, of women, of sensuality, and ultimately of the universe itself. It is difficult to see how, from this point of view, "natural" humanity, still submerged in sensation and the sensual appetites, is not radically depraved, or how such a "natural" humanity would ascend to even civilized behavior, without benefit of divine intervention—which is, of course, precisely what the religious right argues.

Clearly "theism" of this kind has nothing to do with the ultimate meaningfulness of the universe. On the contrary, it is, as Marx suggested, an opium for those who, living under conditions of brutal oppression, have lost faith in the world (Marx 1843/1978: 54). What he failed add is that it is also a practical atheism—a conviction that the universe, if it is indeed the handiwork of some great power, is shoddy work indeed, showing nothing of divine majesty, and pointing not towards God but towards a cosmic tyrant.

---

2. These include the "purely metaphysical" forms of the cosmological argument favored by Gilsonian or "historical" Thomists (Gilson 1936, von Steenberghen 1980, Tweeten 1996), the transcendental arguments put forward by Rahner (1958, 1976) and the Transcendental Thomists, and also, in somewhat different form, by Hartshorne and his followers (Gamwell 1990), and intuitionist or illuminationist arguments which lead back towards the ontological proof (Seifert 1981). These and other attempts to find God by going around, rather than through cosmology, will be discussed in depth in a later chapter.

A third response to cosmological nihilism has been to argue that mathematical physics and the disciplines based on that physics, do not in fact show that the universe is without meaning and purpose, but rather, at least when properly understood, provide as solid a ground for an intellectual ascent to God as the earlier Aristotelian physics. Generally this sort of argument has been favored by scientists rather than philosophers, who attempt to move directly from physics to claims about the ultimate meaningfulness of the universe and the existence of God, without benefit of an intervening rational metaphysics. It is also generally associated with attempts to develop a unified physical theory under which all of the sciences can be integrated—an enterprise which in practice always involves privileged claims regarding one or another specific discipline—e.g., relativity (Tipler 1994; Gal-Or 1987), quantum mechanics (Bohm 1980, Smolin 1997), nonlinear thermodynamics (Prigogine 1977, 1979, 1984, 1989), developmental biology (Sheldrake 1981, 1989), or evolutionary biology (Margulis and Fester 1991). Of particular importance to this line of reasoning are such findings as quantum nonlocality, which suggests that the entire universe is one vast interconnected system, and cosmological fine-tuning, which suggests that certain physical constants are fixed at just precisely the levels necessary to permit the development of complex organization. In some cases there have been attempts to rework the hegemonic information theoretical neoliberalism to accommodate cosmohistorical progress (Smolin 1997) and even the existence of God (Barrow and Tipler 1986, Tipler 1994). In other cases an attempt is made to argue, on the basis of mathematical physics, for an outlook which is sharply in contradiction with neoliberalism, and which is broadly holistic (Bohm 1980), dialectical (Prigogine 1984; Gal-Or 1986; Harris 1990, 1991) or even teleological (Swimme and Berry 1992; Sheldrake and Fox 1996). Others, meanwhile, are merely suggestive and fail to take a well-defined position on key scientific or philosophical questions (Davies 1988, 1992). All of these attempts, however, are marked by profound internal inconsistencies, so that they fail to show that contemporary mathematical physics is really compatible with strong claims for the ultimate meaningfulness of the universe. And none of these thinkers come to terms adequately with the deep-seated contradictions between the principal theoretical streams within mathematical physics (relativity and quantum mechanics, dynamics and thermodynamics, thermodynamics and evolutionary theory), or with the growing body of empirical evidence that calls many aspects of these theories into question.

The result has been the triumph of nihilism: either a radical, secular nihilism which rejects the search for meaning and value altogether, or an otherworldly religious nihilism which drains the world of meaning even as it proclaims the transcendent sovereignty of a god who, we can only imagine, must hate his own creation.

The impact of this nihilism, whether in secular or religious form, has been disastrous. If we reject the search for meaning altogether we lose any basis for hope and any possible way of grounding moral discourse. The highest objects of our love dissolve like mirages. Lacking any criterion by which to judge, people become incapable of seeing injustice. Lacking any reason to hope, they become incapable of action on behalf of the Good. If, on the other hand, ignoring the apparent evidence of reason and experience, we invest all our faith and hope and love in a principle so radically transcendent that it drains the world of meaning, then we can hardly be expected to act effectively to promote human development or to conserve the integrity of the ecosystem and the social fabric.

Cosmological nihilism is not simply a spontaneous ideology of the marketplace; it is the product of a conscious polemic which, by undermining claims about the ultimate meaningfulness of the universe, also undermines rational metaphysics and thus the metaphysical foundations of any possible substantive doctrine of the Good from the standpoint of which the market allocation of resources might be contested and an alternative justified. The early, liberal forms of cosmological nihilism critique provided the bourgeoisie with a kind of direct apologetic, portraying it as a champion of liberty and an ally in the struggle against superstition and clerical hegemony. The clerical variants, meanwhile, provided an indirect apologetic, arguing that partisans of the *via dialectica*, even when they claimed to prove the existence of God, ultimately undermined divine sovereignty with their "rationalist hermeneutics." Eventually these two strains flowed together into postmodern nihilism, which argues that "totalizing metanarratives," religious or secular, which make claims about the ultimate meaningfulness of the universe, in fact legitimate totalitarian domination and an oppression far worse than that of the market order (Mansueto and Mansueto 2005).

What nihilism does is to undermine the possibility of any criticism of the market order and to make the search for ultimate meaning in terms of which criteria for judgment might be formulated into an object of ridicule, a neurotic obsession of those who are too weak to face the darkness of the abyss, to risk themselves in action in the knowledge that everything ends in absolute loss. And it glorifies the capitalist and the imperialist warlord who stops at nothing to make his mark on the world, knowing full well that with the rapidly shifting sands of time it will soon be eroded.

THESES

This book is an attempt to answer the physical or cosmological critique of rational metaphysics, and to mount an argument for cosmic teleology. It forms an integral part of a much larger project which aims at restoring rational metaphysics in the dialectical tradition, and thus at regrounding a substantive doctrine of the Good from the standpoint of which the market order and other social structures can be subjected to moral scrutiny. An earlier book, *Knowing God: Restoring Reason in an Age of Doubt*, answers the epistemological critique of metaphysics advanced by Kant and Hume and given new significance by the development of the sociology of knowledge. Later books address the claim, advanced by existential and postmodern theorists, that metaphysics (or ontology or "ontotheology") is, in fact, at the very root of a plethora of social evils, from technological domination through imperialism and totalitarianism to atheism and despair, and will elaborate a radically historicized natural law ethics which demonstrates, among other things, that the market order is morally indefensible.

The book operates at two distinct but integrally interrelated levels. It is, first of all a work of ideological criticism, which analyzes the social basis and political valence of various scientific paradigms, and more specifically of the Aristotelian physics which grew up in ancient Greece and which was dominant until the seventeenth century, and the mathematical physics which had always existed alongside it but which became the dominant paradigm just as the market order finally gained hegemony in the seventeenth century. It is, second, itself a work of metaphysics, making an argument about the proper aims and methods of the sciences, and the relative merits of various scientific paradigms,[3] and making at least a preliminary argument about the ultimate meaningfulness of the universe.

---

3. This sort of argument would generally be regarded today as part of the "philosophy of science." I prefer the term metaphysics for two reasons. On the one hand, the ancient

More specifically, I advance the following theses:

1. Aristotelian physics first emerged as an integral part of a fundamentally political project: a critique of the emerging petty commodity society of the ancient Mediterranean basin. Aristotelian physics provided a cosmological infrastructure for a rational metaphysics and a substantive doctrine of the Good from the standpoint of which the emerging market order could be contested and an alternative justified. This cosmology was scientifically superior to the rationalist (Pythagorean), empiricist (Democritan), and idealist (Platonic and Neo-Platonic) alternatives in the sense that it offered a more complete and comprehensive explanation of the available empirical data. It nonetheless had significant scientific flaws. The details of the Aristotelian cosmological model, with its perfect concentric spheres, was never entirely in accord with the available astronomical evidence, something which opened up a gulf between observational astronomy and Aristotelian astrophysics long before the time of Copernicus and Kepler. Second, Aristotelian physics was unable to advance a unified theory of motion which could account in teleological terms for such terrestrial phenomena as decay and disintegration, or even for that matter what came to be called "forced motion," such as the flight of a javelin. These were not, however, insuperable difficulties, and might have been overcome within the context of a teleological paradigm.

2. Second, I will show that

    2.1 the turn to mathematical physics as a solution to the difficulties of the Aristotelian paradigm was driven not so much by scientific considerations as by a complex of forces including:

    2.1.1 the emancipation of *techē* from the rule of science and metaphysics which accompanied the gradual dissolution of the craft guilds and the publication by means of the emerging print media of the whole complex of emerging technologies which had previously been the property of a

---

meaning of the term—i.e., any discipline which comes after physics, captures the fact that this sort of argument depends on principles which arise out of, but transcend the conclusions of purely physical research. At the same time, the modern use of the prefix "meta" to mark any discourse the formal object of which is another discourse, captures, when joined with the term "physics" the very nature of the argument in question: it is an argument about the aims, methods, conclusions, and limits of physics.

relatively small community of master artisans and practitioners of scholarly magic,[4]

2.1.2 the spontaneous effects of the market order on the way in which people experienced and understood the world around them, and

2.1.3 conscious polemics mounted by intellectuals attached to the clerical hierarchy and the emerging bourgeoisie.

2.2 What passes for "science" today, while incorporating much authentic knowledge, is first and foremost, an element in the ideological strategy of Capital. "Scientists" are actually subaltern ideological agents of the market order. This is why what is often called the "modern scientific worldview" has turned out to be so resilient in spite of mounting contradictions both between the dominant physical theories and the empirical evidence and between the principal physical theories themselves. Of these difficulties the following are the most important.

2.2.1 Mathematical physics has, first of all, shown itself unable to unify:

2.2.1.1 relativity, which depends on the notion of a space-time continuum and a concept of signaling which implies strict causal relations, and quantum mechanics, which theorizes the universe as a discrete order and which calls into question certain aspects of strict causal relatedness (Bohm 1980),

---

4. This process, which has been traced in detail by William Eamon (Eamon 1994) whose *Science and The Secrets of Nature* shows that at least a very significant part of the content of the esoteric texts and traditions of late antiquity and the middle ages in fact amounted to a bundle of emerging technologies, including many which were important to the later development of metallurgy and medicine, and indirectly of chemistry and biology. These "secrets of nature" were closely guarded not only for economic reasons, but also because it was thought that they might be dangerous in the hands of those who had not yet traveled the road of wisdom, mastering the liberal arts, the sciences, and metaphysics. The publication of this material in the late Middle Ages contributed to the development of capitalism directly by helping to break down the power of the craft guilds, and indirectly by creating what amounted to a market in technical knowledge unregulated by any sort of moral discourse regarding the proper use of these new techniques.

Introduction

2.2.1.2 dynamics (understood to include both relativistic and quantum theory), which treat reversible processes, and thermodynamics, which treats irreversible change (Prigogine et al. 1979, 1984), and

2.2.1.3 thermodynamics, which points to a global tendency towards disorder, and evolutionary theory (biological and social) which points to at least local and possibly cosmic movement towards increasing degrees of organization.

2.2 Furthermore, just as the geocentric models of the universe borrowed by Aristotle from Eudoxus and refined by Ptolemy had growing difficulties accommodating improved empirical data regarding planetary motions, the scientific disciplines which are based on mathematical physics are confronting growing empirical difficulties. The standard "Big Bang" cosmology, for example, has given rise to the following empirical problems:

2.2.2.1 the existence of large scale structure which contradicts assumptions of cosmic homogeneity,

2.2.2.2 missing dark matter,

2.2.2.3 stars older than the universe itself is supposed to be, and

2.2.2.4 incorrect predictions regarding the basic ratios of such elements as Deuterium, Helium, and Lithium (Lerner 1991).

Indeed, even where mathematical physics is able to patch together an authentically powerful explanation of a range of natural phenomena, it does so only with theories which ultimately contradict each other. Thus, one of the triumphs of mathematical physics is the explanation of chemical organization using quantum mechanics and thermodynamics—but these two theories have fundamentally different understandings of such basic concepts as "time."

2.3 Finally, mathematical physics is not only fraught with internal contradictions; it also fails the test of true science. The aim of science is to explain; mathematical physics merely describes. Sometimes these descriptions imply explanations indirectly. Thus the discovery of the quantum nature of energy transfer explains why there are discrete chemical elements rather than a continuum of forms of matter with properties which gradually shade into each other. The quantum description of atomic structure, together with thermodynamics explains why the various elements interact with each other the way they do. But neither quantum mechanics nor any other theory in mathematical physics can explain why energy transfer is quantum rather than continuous, nor is there any theory in mathematical physics which can explain why the laws discovered by relativity, quantum mechanics, or thermodynamics are the way they are and not some other way. Nor can there be such a theory in mathematical physics. Mathematical formalisms are, in the final analysis, just very rigorous descriptions of the systems they formalize; they explain only when they limit logically what is possible. We will argue that the only way to develop complete explanations is through a teleological strategy, a strategy which explains in terms of final cause.

3. Third, I show that it is not only possible to make a case for the ultimate meaningfulness of the universe, but that a teleological approach in fact has far greater explanatory power than a purely formal or mathematical approach. I will outline a new teleological research program and suggest what such a restored teleological science might look like, addressing important issues in physics, biology, and the social sciences. This new program does not exclude mathematical formalization, but subordinates it to teleological explanation as a way of specifying rigorously just what must be explained. Integral to this proposal, therefore, is an argument about the proper relationship between not only science and metaphysics, but also between science and what I will argue is essentially the art (τχvη) of mathematical formalization.

METHOD

An argument of this sort, embracing as it does over 2500 years of scientific history, and making claims at both the ideological-critical and metaphysical levels, poses some extraordinary methodological challenges. The first problem concerns sources. It would simply not be possible to master all of the relevant scientific texts. I have thus relied on existing

Introduction xvii

scholarship in the history and philosophy of science as my principal raw material, sometimes using their conclusions as the building blocks of my own argument, and sometimes subjecting their data to secondary analysis. I have returned to the original sources only when it seemed necessary in order to settle disputed questions, or when the texts themselves had such a pivotal impact as to make them really essential to my argument. Aristotle's *Physics* and *Metaphysics*, Galileo's *Two Discourses on a New Science*, and Marx's *Capital* are cases in point. Among the secondary sources which have been most influential in shaping my understanding of the history of science, Pierre Duhem's *Le System du Monde*, William Eamon's *Science and the Secrets of Nature*, and Eric Lerner's *The Big Bang Never Happened* each contributed enough to the main outlines of my argument to be singled out for special mention. In other cases, such as that of David Lindberg's *The Beginnings of Western Science*, I am indebted to the author for the wealth of data compiled even though I reject many of the conclusions.

More needs to be said about my method of analysis. My aim here is not to write a history of science, but rather to make an argument concerning science on the one hand and the ultimate meaningfulness of the universe on the other. I do this by (re)constructing and then subjecting to ideological-critical and metaphysical evaluation three scientific paradigms: that of Aristotelian physics, that of mathematical physics, and that of the new teleological physics I am proposing. Reconstructing a paradigm means specifying its material and formal objects as well as its aim or purpose. By the material object of an intellectual discipline we mean what it studies in the simple and straightforward sense of what it is about—e.g. stars or economic systems. By the formal object of an intellectual discipline we mean the aspect under which its subject matter is studied. Thus astronomy, astrophysics, and astrology all have the same material object: i.e. the stars, but they consider them under different aspects, and thus have different formal objects. Astronomy considers the motion of the stars, which it models mathematically. Astrophysics considers the origin, nature, and development of the stars, which it attempts either to model mathematically, to explain, or both. Astrology considers the stars as an influence (or in more modern formulations as an indicator of other influences) on human affairs. Both neoclassical and dialectical (Marxist) economics study economic systems, but the first considers them as systems of exchange and the latter as systems of production.

In addition to the material and formal object of a discipline, it is also necessary to specify its aim or purpose. This includes not just its immediate purpose—to describe and/or explain—but also the "mediate" ends to which it is ordered as part of a larger ideological and social system. Thus we will show that Aristotelian physics was ordered to and ultimately governed by a metaphysics which formed part of a larger political project: resistance to the emerging market order. Mathematical physics, on the other hand, is ordered to *techne* and more specifically to the manipulation of the physical, biological, and social universe for human purposes generally and (in the context in which it actually became hegemonic) to the service of the market order.

It must be pointed out that our reconstruction of a scientific paradigm will inevitably look rather different from the work and ideas of any given particular scientist, no matter how critical that scientist was in the development of the paradigm. This is because individual scientists, whatever their ideological limitations, are for the most part seriously committed to the pursuit of truth, and will generally pursue this aim well beyond the boundaries of the paradigm in which they generally work. As a result they trade internal consistency for explanatory power and the ability to accommodate the empirical evidence. Even theoretically oriented scientists, furthermore, are rarely system builders. Think of Newton and Kepler or Einstein and Bohr. The result is a failure to draw out systematically all of the implications of their ideas.

The reconstruction of an intellectual paradigm thus turns out from the very beginning to be inseparable from an ideological-critical analysis. Identifying the aims and purposes of a discipline means, among other things, situating it in a definite social context. This in turn requires that we specify its social basis and political valence. By the social basis of an intellectual paradigm we mean not just the social location of those who created it and/or supported its creators, though this is certainly important, but more broadly the social structures which gave rise to the paradigm and made it (at least seem to) make sense. Thus, we have already noted (and will argue in greater depth) for the role of both residual communitarian structures and the conscious ideological leadership of dialecticians in creating Aristotelian physics and of both spontaneous market forces and conscious ideological polemics in displacing this physics and securing the hegemony of mathematical formalization in physical, and to a lesser extent in biological and social research. By the political valence of a paradigm we mean its impact on the development of human society: e.g., to legitimate or to undermine the legitimacy of some social structure.

From here, our next step is to consider the scientific adequacy of the paradigm in question. This means considering both internal coherence and explanatory power, i.e. the capacity of the paradigm in question to explain as much of the empirical data as possible using as few independent principles as possible (Occam's Razor) while remembering that the most economical explanation is not necessarily the most reductive (Mansueto's Switchblade) and avoiding internal contradictions, especially between core explanatory principles. In the case of the new dialectical and teleological paradigm we are proposing the task is somewhat different. On the one hand we need to show that the approach we are proposing can do a better job than the hegemonic mathematical physics of explaining the existing empirical evidence. At the same time, we will need to outline an interdisciplinary research program in terms of which our approach can be further tested.

Finally, we need to draw out and evaluate the metaphysical implications of the paradigm. What metaphysical principles, if any, does it presuppose? To what metaphysical principles, if any, does it conclude? What, if anything does it imply about the ultimate meaningfulness of the universe? Here the dialectical method comes into its own. We begin with the highest order principles to which the various special sciences themselves have concluded and draw out the presuppositions, implications, limitations of these principles, and the contradictions between them, in search of higher order principles in terms of which the various special sciences can be unified and their various principles rendered no longer presuppositions, but rather "hypotheses in the literal sense, things laid down like a flight of steps up which it may mount all the way to something that is not hypothetical, the first principle of all; and having grasped this, may turn back and, holding on to the consequences which depend on it, descent at last to a conclusion (Plato. *Republic* 511b)." This is, of course, the movement formal to transcendental abstraction (Thomas. *In Boethius de Trinitate*), and from *Verstand,* which comprehends only the external relations between phenomena, to *Vernunft* which shows those phenomena to be rationally necessary (Hegel, *Encyclopaedia of the Philosophical Sciences: Outline* 212, *Encyclopaedia of the Philosophical Sciences* 467). It is the same movement, which Marx attempted in a more limited way, in the field of political economy, from a formal description of the movement of commodities to an explanation of the origin, development, and eventual demise of the commodity system itself (Marx 1971: 500).

Indeed, it should by this point be apparent that what I am proposing to do is nothing less than to extend to the whole of mathematical physics, including its dependent and derivative disciplines, the sort of critique which Marx himself carried out in the limited realm of political economy. Marx's critique of political economy will in fact turn out to be merely a special case of the more general critique that I elaborate in this work. This is true in spite of the fact that we conclude to certain principles which Marx himself would have rejected: i.e. to God. On the basis of his partial critique Marx could rise only to the first principle of political economy: i.e. to labor which, by increasing the level of organization of the raw material on which it works, increases their value. Engels attempted to situate this result in the context of a larger cosmohistorical evolutionary process by means of which matter develops from lower to higher levels of organization (Engels 1880/1940). For reasons we will analyze in some detail he failed, with the result that dialectical materialism as it actually developed tended to regard human history as an island of meaning within an otherwise meaningless universe (the tendency in Western, humanistic Marxism), or else as the story of the gradual triumph of human labor over a hostile and unforgiving natural world (the tendency if Soviet Marxism). In either case there is no basis on which to conclude to a metaphysical first principle of any kind, much less to God.[5] Things will look different once we have subjected bourgeois science as a whole to a critique, and shown that many of the results which Engels accepted as fact were in fact an integral part of the ideological strategy of the bourgeoisie, of which he became an unwitting agent.

It will, no doubt, be objected that the method I am proposing joins two fundamentally disconnected lines of argument which are themselves in contradiction with each other: i.e. an argument that scientific paradigms are the product of, and serve to legitimate or contest, definite social structures, and an argument that it is possible not only to achieve authentic knowledge of the way in which the universe is organized, but even to rise to a metaphysical first principle. Metaphysical realism and sociological relativism, it will be argued, just don't mix. This criticism will be ad-

---

5. Nor does either approach, incidentally, support development strategies which are concerned to conserve the integrity of the ecosystem as well as promoting human development. The results are apparent in the effective poisoning of much of Eastern Europe.

vanced, albeit with differing agendas, both by relativistic postmodernists and by defenders of traditional (e.g., Platonic or Thomistic) realism. If you are going to claim that mathematical physics is a reflex of the market order and an ideological weapon of Capital, then you must acknowledge that all ideas are similarly contextual and also serve interests which are irreducibly particular. The standpoint of totality, to which Lukaçs aspired, is out of reach, at least for finite human reason. If, on the other hand, you are going to make strong claims about the truth value of scientific and philosophical statements, you must sacrifice the ideological-critical dimension of your argument which treats ideas as political weapons rather than as more or less adequate attempts to understand the Truth.

We have responded in depth to these criticisms elsewhere (Mansueto 2002b, Mansueto and Mansueto 2005). Here it is possible only to explain and justify briefly the theory of knowledge on which the validity of our whole argument admittedly turns. Knowledge begins with the senses. Data collected by the external senses creates topographical and dispositional representations in the human nervous system (Damasio 1995), what the Aristotelian and Thomistic tradition historically called the phantasm or image. While it would be difficult to demonstrate that the relationship between image and object is "onto," i.e., that the image is a copy of the object,[6] and while clearly sensory knowledge is limited by our location and perspective, as well as by the particular way in which our senses have developed, we have good reason to believe that the senses do produce real knowledge about the outside world. Otherwise our sensory knowledge would not be so useful in helping us to survive.

The complexity of the human nervous system makes possible the creation of complex links between stored images and, at a neurological level, it is in precisely these links that the intellect consists. It is impossible, however, to explain in purely neurological terms why, out of all the many logical possibilities, some links develop and others don't. This is why attempts to theorize the human intellect as an information processing machine (Tipler 1994) are so inadequate and why Aristotle developed the notion of the Agent Intellect, which illuminates the images formed by the internal senses and reveals intelligible structure of objects they represent. From this point of view the human nervous system corre-

---

6. Damasio (Damasio 1995), however, reports that when monkeys are exposed to visual images of geometric forms, the result is a topographical representation in the brain that actually resembles the object seen.

sponds to what Aristotle and Thomas called the "possible" or "potential" intellect. Most of the medieval commentators on Aristotle, including Ibn Sina, Maimonides, and Ibn Rusd believed that because the Agent Intellect revealed intelligible and thus immaterial principles, and was thus itself immaterial, it was also unique. Matter is the principle of individuation in the Aristotelian tradition and if something is immaterial there can only be one individual in each species. The result was the notion of the unity of the Agent Intellect—one single Agent Intellect for all of humanity. This, however, made it difficult to explain why different people process similar sense data in such different ways. It also created various theological problems. Thomas thus defended the idea that each individual has his or her own agent intellect which illuminates the images s/he garners from sense experience.

The development of the social sciences has both complicated this problem and suggested a solution—one which turns out to be deeply in accord with another aspect of the Thomistic epistemology: i.e. the theory of connatural knowledge. We now know that not only do individuals process similar sense data differently, but that people from different societies exhibit often fundamental differences in outlook. This suggests that the "agent intellect" is in fact both one and many, neither purely material nor purely immaterial, but rather social—i.e., society itself. Living within a definite social formation, people actually *live* its structure. Thus people who live in tribal societies develop systems of classification which mirror the kinship structure which organizes their societies, while people who live in market societies governed by complex market relationships organize their experience using complex quantitative formalisms which reflect actual structure of the marketplace. Living a structure, people become connatural with it. They gain a preconceptual knowledge of the structure in question so that their sensory experience is illuminated by it. People who lack such a connatural knowledge have grave difficulties mastering concepts for which they lack a real basis in experience. Thus the Uzbek villagers studied by Alexandr Luria (Luria 1974/1976) during the early 1930s refused to solve simple classification problems in a way which most people in market societies would consider reasonable, insisting, for example, that all the elements in the sequence "log, axe, saw, boy" go together—because you need tools, raw material, and a helper to assist you with your work. People in market societies, on the other hand, have difficulty thinking teleologically because they have so little experience of participation in structures which are ordered to some global purpose.

None of this implies an irreducible relativism. That our ideas are generated by, and thus shaped and limited by, definite social structures, does not mean that the ideas have no truth value or that we cannot test that truth value against experience. On the contrary, just as with the images we garner from sense experience, so too with our ideas: some help us survive and others do not. And this difference cannot help but have something to do with the adequacy with which they capture the way the world is organized. Whatever else one may say about Newton's theory of gravity—and it will come in for some stiff criticism later on in this work—it must have some bearing on reality otherwise it would have turned out to be so useful in technological applications.

Incorrect ideas, in other words, simply don't work. There can be no doubt that human societies, like the sensory systems of various animal species, are finite and can reveal only part of the systems which they perceive. There is, furthermore, no doubt that the part of reality which is revealed by these structures is selected by the needs of the social systems in question, just as animals develop those senses which serve their adaptive strategies. But abstractions which help a society to survive and flourish must disclose something important about the way the universe really works, just as well adapted sensory systems disclose something important about an animal's environment. Ideas and systems of ideas which lead to stagnation and decline are probably flawed in some way. Ideas, in other words, develop on definite material bases (the human nervous system) and are formed by definite structural principles (those of the society in which they are produced). They are, nonetheless, ordered to the Truth, even if they also serve particular social interests. Indeed, their ability to serve those interests, and the viability of those interests themselves, is constrained by their relationship to the Truth.

From this vantage point it becomes clear that the practice of ideological criticism is by no means opposed to the agenda of epistemological and metaphysical realism—even to a strong realism which claims to be able to rise to the idea of God and of the transcendental principles of value. Ideological criticism is, rather, an integral part of the dialectic of ascent by which we discover what the Truth is and indeed that it Is. Demonstrating that a particular set of ideas (e.g., the Aztec belief that the universe came into being through divine self-sacrifice and had to be sustained by continuing human sacrifice) legitimates particular social interests (that of the Aztec warlords and their priestly allies) does not by itself demonstrate that the ideas in question are wrong. But when we understand that the Aztec empire fell, and how, including the ways in which Aztec religion was implicated in the fall, we are at least one step closer to knowing that the Aztecs were (at least partly) wrong after all, as well as to gaining some insight into what does in fact create and sustain organization (social or cosmic). An argument linking mathematical physics with long-term stagnation under the market system would have similar force.

It might be objected that this already presupposes a principle of value: i.e., that it is a good thing that civilizations survive and continue to grow and develop. But this is not really true. The principle of value is implicit in the practice of science, or of producing cosmological mythologies, and indeed in the whole practice of living; our argument merely makes it explicit. Whether or not we share their ideology, the Aztecs were, in fact, trying to survive and they were helped and hindered in this struggle by various aspects of their ideology. The same is true of other civilizations. Indeed, everything in the universe struggles after its own manner to persist in being—a point even Nietzsche would accept. Certain ideas, those which have a relatively larger share in the truth, help us in this struggle; others, those which have a lesser share, hold us back. This suggests that Being is indeed a transcendental principle of value. A definitive judgment, of course, is possible only at the End, and which we can never know with certainty and in advance. But the cumulative judgments of history, harvested by ideological criticism, do in fact gradually give shape to at least a rough and ready knowledge of what Is, and thus to some criterion for judgment.

Ideas, in other words, including scientific ideas, *are* weapons in the class struggle, but the class struggle is also a struggle for knowledge, a scientific and ultimately a metaphysical struggle in which (as we hope to show over the course of the whole four-volume work of which this book forms an integral part) one side—the side of the working classes, which participate in the development of the universe towards ever higher degrees of organization, are able to demonstrate their epistemological, ontological, and moral superiority over the exploiting classes which siphon off surplus which might be used to promote development for warfare and luxury consumption. The much vaunted "hermeneutical circle" within which ideological criticism and indeed most philosophy since Kant has been caught is revealed to be in fact a dialectical spiral in which the partial viewpoints of finite human beings and human societies are able to engage in a real contest over their relative merits and not simply a political contest for hegemony, and thus show themselves to be real participations in the one Truth which does indeed transcend all finite understanding.

A second criticism which will likely be raised against our method is that it makes philosophy (and specifically metaphysics) the arbiter of scientific truth, and thus undermines the legitimate autonomy of the sciences, something which has been regarded as sacrosanct since the seventeenth century. To this charge I offer two responses. First, the relationship which I envision between science and philosophy, while not entirely symmetric, is, however, more nearly reciprocal than the charge allows. The whole design of this study takes for granted that the resolution of key philosophical questions in fact depends on certain scientific results. One cannot answer the question about the ultimate meaningfulness of the universe apart from the results of empirical scientific investigation. Any claim for cosmic teleology must meet the standards of scientific demonstration. And this demonstration can only be carried out by the sciences themselves. In this sense the argument we will make here can only be preliminary and provisional—which is why we conclude with an outline for a new teleological research program. At the same time, the nature of science and of scientific explanation are not subjects for science itself, but rather for philosophy. This is because science claims to be a road to Truth, and the task of discerning just what sort of thing Truth is, and how we might arrive at it are matters not for explanation, which is the task of science, but rather of rising to principles (i.e., wisdom). Good science can be done only by scientists, but judgments regarding what constitutes good science can be made only by philosophers. The relationship between philosopher and scientist is thus always that between ruler and ruled, but this rule is not a despotism. Rather the ruler supplies the principles needed for the work of the ruled, for the benefit of the ruled, on the basis of what s/he learns by consulting the ruled.

This said, we are ready to begin work. Our first task will be an analysis of the social basis, principal concepts, methods, and conclusions and internal contradictions of Aristotelian physics. We will then turn to a much more extended and detailed consideration of mathematical physics, before we begin to build the case for a new dialectical paradigm which extends the old Aristotelian teleology and allows to make at least a preliminary case for the ultimate meaningfulness of the universe.

1

Empirical Lore, Cosmological Mythology, Mathematical Physics, and Science

Human beings have always struggled to understand the world around them. Indeed, the evolutionary passage from the merely animal state to the human might well be defined by the emergence of a survival strategy centered less on fixed, specialized adaptations oriented towards exploiting a particular ecological niche and more and more on the ability to understand the dynamics of a variety of different niches and to develop a whole repertoire of technologies which make it possible to survive and prosper under widely differing ecological conditions. The very act of tool making presupposes an ability to grasp the latent potential of some raw material, to reason in terms of purpose, and to discover a way to relate the raw material to that purpose. From the very first time a hunter used a stone to fell prey, or a gatherer used a stick to uproot a plant, human beings have been reasoning about the organization of the universe and their place therein. This struggle to understand the universe has not, furthermore, functioned merely as a survival strategy. On the contrary, human beings have from the very beginning sought to understand why the universe is the way it is, and to locate themselves within this larger structure, in order to discover what they might about the meaning of their lives, and so they might better order their lives to the ends which their inquiry disclosed.

It must, at the same time, be acknowledged, that there are many different ways of exploring and struggling to understand the world around us. Each approach has a distinctive social basis out of which it emerges, each has a unique epistemological status, and each is ordered to distinctive ends. It is the aim of this chapter to analyze the emergence of these various disciplines. Our principal focus will be on Aristotelian physics, but in order to understand the significance of this discipline we need to set it against the background of the other disciplines which emerged before or alongside it: the empirical lore and cosmological mythologies of tribal, communitarian, archaic, and tributary societies, and the early mathematical physics which emerged in Greece and which in fact predated Aristotelian physics and the larger dialectical project of which Aristotle's work formed an integral part.

Our method, as we noted in the previous chapter, will be to situate each discipline in the social context out of which it emerged, to specify its material and formal objects and the end or purpose to which it was ordered, something which will lead us quite naturally to a consideration of political valence of the discipline in question, and then to mount an immanent, dialectical critique, which identifies both the truth which the discipline achieves and its epistemological limitations. This approach necessitates a discussion of the history of human society which is rather more extended and more theoretically driven than readers might expect. This discussion is, however, quite necessary to my argument, which depends on a reading of history which departs in important ways from prevailing accounts, including those of other dialectical sociologists.

EMPIRICAL LORE AND COSMOLOGICAL MYTHOLOGY

The Emergence of Human Civilization

Human society emerged when bands of sophisticated primates began to make tools and to engage in complex linguistic communication which made it possible for them not only to survive and reproduce, but to create new forms of organization, whether physical (e.g., by the act of tool making itself), biological (by consciously or unconsciously selecting for some plant or animal traits over others, and thus beginning to affect the course of the evolutionary process) or social (by creating increasingly complex relationships among themselves). This advance in and of itself entailed a quantum leap in the cosmohistorical evolutionary process, from mere reproduction (characteristic of biological organization) to creative innovation.

The nature of any human society (indeed of any natural system) can be defined in terms of its material basis, the structural principle by which

Empirical Lore, Cosmological Mythology, Mathematical Physics, and Science

it is ordered and regulated, and the end to which it is ordered. The material basis of the earliest human societies was simply the ecosystem itself, or rather the diverse ecosystem into which humans gradually migrated, all of which were at least initially capable of supporting growing populations on the basis of a relatively simple hunter gatherer technology. Surplus in such societies consists primarily in the free time which is left over after basic needs have been met, and if surviving hunter gatherer societies are any indication, this surplus was very significant. Most hunter gatherers appear to "work" only about 15 hours per week; the remainder of their time is devoted to complex socioreligious activities. The allocation of this surplus is, in turn, regulated by a socioreligious structure which varies considerably even among surviving hunter-gatherer societies, but which generally centers on the kinship system and an associated totemic religion. Gradually the amorphous bands of subsocial primate society give way to a complex system of distinctions between clan and clan, phratry and phratry, tribe and tribe. The result is that the entire social world is subjected to a rigorous classificatory scheme. Complex rules emergence specifying who is permitted—or required—to marry whom. This system of social classification also serves as the basis for a classification of the entire universe. Each group—tribe, phratry, clan, and in some cases each individual—has its own totem, a plant or animal that serves at once as its emblem, its guardian, and its animating spirit. The totem appears on the artifacts produced by the clan and the totemic animal or plant, usually taboo is consumed in a communion sacrifice at the annual feast of the clan. What is most striking, however, is the fact that the members of the clan actually think of themselves as being, in some sense, the totemic plant or animal. Whole groups of objects, furthermore, which we would never associate with the totem, are included within its *taxon*. The complex structure of the tribe provides a basis in experience for the emergence of the idea of structure in general, an idea which is then applied to the universe as a whole. There is, furthermore, a kind of "category of totality," the existence of which Durkheim attributes to the experience of inter-tribal relationships, which is represented in a kind of vague and remote "Great Spirit (Durkheim 1911/1965)."[1] Tribal societies generally see

---

1. There has been some effort, most notably on the part of Levi-Strauss—to argue that the taxonomic schemes of tribal societies are, in fact, universal and independent of social structure. Specifically, Levi-Strauss argues that the mythic systems of tribal societies—and indeed all human thought—is based on what he calls dual classification. Kinship

systems which divide tribes into exogamous clans and then require marriage outside the clan are simply an example of this classificatory strategy. Anyone who reads Levi-Strauss, however, cannot help but marvel at the facility with which he has reduced the most diverse social structural and mythic content to the simplest and most universal formulae. Apparently, for example, both the Oedipus cycle and all known versions of the Zuni emergence myth—and indeed all other myths—can be reduced to the following formula:

$$f_x(a):f_y(b) \sim f_x(b):f_{a-1}(y)$$

Levi-Strauss arrives at this conclusion by dividing myths into what he calls their "gross constituent units." These units are not, furthermore, simply episodes, but rather relationships, or rather bundles of relationships, such as that between Oedipus and his mother, summed across all variants of the myth. Levi-Strauss includes here not only different versions of an oral or literary tradition, but also modern reinterpretations such as that of Freud. And the "relationships" are characterized in starkly simple terms as "opposition" or "negation." In this way the opposition between autochthony and bisexual reproduction, which Levi-Strauss sees as the heart of the Oedipus cycle is identified with the opposition between agriculture and hunting in the Zuni emergence myth (Levi-Strauss 1958/1963: 206–231).

What is happening here is that Levi-Strauss reduces the myths he analyzes to such simple elements that they cannot help but appear identical. We have entered Hegel's "night in which all cows are black (Hegel 1807/1967)." What Levi-Strauss discovers is nothing more than the logical limits on any possible system of classification: i.e. that it involve difference or distinction, and thus binary oppositions. While the more complex formalisms he develops to describe the myths may well hold, he does not show that these are the only possible way to formalize the myths nor even that they are the most economical. He merely shows that all classification, in so far as it depends on difference, involves binary opposition, and that this in turn imposes certain constraints on the form and pattern of classification. Any conclusion that this very thin universality of patterns of classification is based in universal structures of the human mind, neurological or otherwise, is entirely unwarranted.

The fact is that the evidence for diversity in systems of classification is every bit as strong as the evidence for similarity, if not stronger. And this evidence also points to a social basis not only for the act of classification generally, but also for a more specific determination of systems of classification by the structure of the society which produces them. The Inuit, for example, have far more names for snow than do Europeans, and appear to see these various forms of matter as distinctly as we might see rain and snow or sand and rock. The fact languages like Inuit have far more names for snow than does English, for example, does not simply reflect environmental differences—i.e. the fact that snow and its many varieties are far more important to the Inuit than they are to us. It also reflects a fundamentally different linguistic strategy and thus a different way of thinking. Primitive languages often have far richer nomenclatures than more advanced languages, coupled with less sophisticated paradigmatic structures (hierarchies grouping similar classes into higher categories). Complex languages, rather than having a separate name for each genus or species, use category names and modifiers—wet, icy snow, dry, powdery snow, etc. We will see that this reflects a trend towards rationalization, or rather "formalization" of the culture's categorical scheme, something which comes with increasing complexity of social organization.

their existence on earth as ordered in some way both by and to this Great Spirit, who put them here to take care of the earth as they progressed in their own process of spiritual development.

The presence of human encampments in any given ecosystem produces profound changes. Gradually expanding population puts growing pressure on most (though by no means all) ecosystems inhabited by hunter-gatherers. The great megafauna of the Paleolithic are hunted to extinction, and smaller prey becomes increasingly scarce. Some species, on the other hand, learn to adapt to the human presence and to benefit from it (Budiansky 1992). Those plants with significant food value and relatively little in the way of waste and hulls and thorns were eaten most frequently—and most frequently deposited in waste piles, where unconsumed seeds soon grew, creating, essentially by accident, the first fields. Neotenous animals—those retaining the juvenile characteristics of curiosity and "cuteness" (big heads, big eyes) were more often fed and soon began to frequent human encampments, the presence of which selected for these features, leading to the "self-domestication" of dogs, sheep, goats, etc.

The result was the gradual development of settled village communities. This involved a new way of centralizing and allocating surplus. Land was generally controlled by the village, even when it was parceled out to individual families for cultivation—though collective cultivation was by no means uncommon (Mandel 1968). The village provided, in a way that clan and tribal organization could not, for both a rational division of labor and for the centralization of surplus to be invested in activities promoting the development of human social capacities—e.g. the focused study of the virtues of various roots and seeds and herbs, or the study of the stars, which helped fix the proper dates for planting and harvesting.

The experience of life in the village community created for the first time the basis in experience for the idea that the universe is not only a structured but also an organized system. This is apparent from the fabric of human language itself. The Hellenic word *kosmos* means "right order for the community," in the sense of the traditional order of the village, and the Slavic *mir* means "village community." Both mean "universe," in the sense of the organized totality of being (Bogdanov 1928/1980, Mandel 1968: 30–36, Wolf 1969: 58–63, Hayek 1973: 37). The earliest human societies, which were predominantly matriarchal and communitarian (Stone 1976), recognized the universe itself as one vast interconnected system, regulated by the "perfect pattern of creation" (Waters 1968) which was less something imposed on the world by a transcendent creator god than something implicit in each and every thing, and above all in the harmonious relationships of all things with each other. This view of the world found its most typical (and most profound) symbolic expression in the cult of the *Magna Mater* who is at once, in the form of Demeter or Tonantzi, the profoundly material goddess of the earth and of its fruits and, as Isis, Sophia, or Sussistinako, the goddess of wisdom, the latent pattern from which all complex organization emerges.[2] Masculine high gods, however, like the Hopi Taiowa or the Semitic El, were not unknown. Generally they co-existed with the Great Mother, with little interest shown in rigorously defining their relationship.

The progressive potential of this mode of social organization is well documented. Gordon Childe has shown that the vast majority of the scientific and technological advances on which humanity's great agrarian civilizations depended in fact took place prior to the emergence of the great warlord states around 3000 BCE and that little new progress took place in the entire period between 3000 BCE and advent of European feudalism (Childe 1951, Anderson 1974, Lerner 1991). Clearly much of this progress is the result of effective but noncoercive mechanisms for centralizing surplus for development, and the absence of and exploiting class which could drain that surplus off into warfare and luxury consumption. But technological progress does, in fact, depend on a real, if not necessarily complete grasp of natural processes, and we have already seen that centralization of surplus presupposes some sense of a *telos* or

---

2. We should keep in mind that the word matter derives from the Latin *mater*, or mother. Originally matter referred simply to the *potential* for being, and thus for complex organization. It was only later, as patriarchy and the warlord state gained hold that this potentiality was transformed into simply a passive capacity to receive form from the outside—from the Father God, or his philosophical reflex: the Idea. In this sense, the communitarian worldview was profoundly materialist, not in the modern sense of denying spirituality, but in the archaic sense of locating the capacity for spirituality within, rather than outside, the self-organizing universe. Mary Daly's *Pure Lust* (1984) is particularly useful in clarifying this distinction.

Demeter, of course was the great grain goddess of the Mediterranean world and Tonantzi her counterpart among the Nahuatl of Mesoamerica. Isis was the Great Cosmic Librarian of the Egyptians and both in her own right and as the rather more abstract Sophia became the great Mediterranean goddess of wisdom. Sussistinako is the Keres "thinking woman," she who "thought outward into space and what she thought became reality (Tyler 1964: 89)." On the cult of the Magna Mater, cf. Stone 1976, Matthews 1991).

purpose, and thus a criterion of value by which allocation decisions can be made. This suggests that we need to take seriously the specifically cognitive claims of both the empirical lore and the religious symbolism of these communitarian societies.

Eventually growing population once again began to place a strain on the ecosystem. Access to water was a particularly vexing problem for cultivators. As more and more people were forced out into dryer areas, pressure developed to build irrigation systems which could carry water to them, something which required the ability to centralize resources and organize labor from several villages. But even without this pressure there was a drive towards centralization. Human beings crave knowledge and thus value the services of those who can provide it. Those villages with the best priests and teachers, and with the finest animal breeders, herbalists and metallurgists, soon became centers of activity which attracted resources from the surrounding countryside. The idea of a high god or organized and directed the universe as a whole, ordering it to some end, which had always been present but which had previously been vague and amorphous, began to gain force. The result was the formation of urban centers with temples and observatories, something which we see evidence of in places like Chaco Canyon and Cattal Huyuk. This level of development we call the "archaic" because it is characterized by the systematic ordering of all human activity to an *arche* or first principle. Here surplus extraction is noncoercive and resources are channeled overwhelmingly into activities which promote the development of human capacities. The priests who run the centralized temple complexes function more as an elite stratum of a population which is itself engaged in increasingly creative activity, and not as a true exploiting class.

In most places, however, development to this level was cut short by invaders from societies occupying less favorable ecological niches long before it reached this point. The advent of metal technology, itself one of the principal achievements of the high communitarian and archaic epochs, opened up for such societies a new pathway of development: conquest and exploitation. Instead of investing resources in activities which might gradually increase agrarian productivity and increase the total surplus available to support human development, these societies began to raid their more prosperous and often more developed neighbors, and eventually to subject them to tribute in the form of rents, taxes, and/or forced labor. This "tributary" more of production (Amin 1979/1980) became the dominant mode of social organization on the planet for nearly 5000 years, from 3000 BCE until roughly 1500 CE. The result was a sharp decline in the rate of innovation, as resources were increasingly channeled into warfare and luxury consumption (Childe 1951, Lenski 1982, Lerner 1991). This was reflected in the development of much darker and pessimistic mythologies, which we will have occasion to examine shortly.

Cosmos and Society

Empirical Lore

Throughout this period, it is possible to identify two principal modes of intellectual engagement with the natural world. The first is empirical lore. By empirical lore we mean the accumulation on the basis of either long experience or systematic observation, of concrete knowledge of the properties, behavior, and uses of various mineral, plant, and animal species, as well as similar knowledge about human beings and human societies. Empirical lore would thus include knowledge of which types of stone, metal, and wood are best for making various kinds of tools, which types of plants were useful for food or medicine and how to cultivate and prepare them, and how animals behave and how to hunt them or raise them for food or labor. It would also include the accumulated practical wisdom of a society about child rearing, the proper organization of local communities and how to lead them, knowledge of other communities and how to relate to them, etc., up to and including the high prudence involved in statecraft and diplomacy. This knowledge can be quite in-depth and often involves the elaboration of complex taxonomies and the formulation of broad empirical principles that attempt to sum up concisely what a society knows about the behavior of a whole class of phenomena. What we do not see in empirical lore, and what sets it apart from the sort of investigation of the natural world which is carried out under the auspices of mathematical physics or Aristotelian science, is the attempt to generate formal, mathematical descriptions of empirical phenomena or to explain why the universe is organized the way it is.

The social basis of empirical lore is not difficult to specify: it is the human labor process itself. Human beings do not bring to the task of survival either the capacity for rapid reproduction characteristic of most lower animals, or the sort of anatomy which is necessary effective predation, like most carnivores. Rather, we have large brains and agile hands which allow us to understand our environment in a way no other animal on this planet can, and to develop ways to tap into sources of energy which are not available to other species. Human beings have, from the beginning, been engaged in observing the world around them in order to identify properties and patterns that might be useful to them. Layered over this fundamentally biological reality is the fact that all human beings live in communities which themselves have some sort of structure. Thus the division of a tribe into clans and phratries provides a basis in experience for the act of classification; the regularities in the patterns of social behavior on which all societies depend creates a basis in experience for the ideas of force and law (Durkheim 1911/1965).

The discipline or disciplines of empirical lore that arise on this basis have for their material object minerals, plants, animals, human beings, societies, etc. They have for their formal object the sensible properties of these phenomena and any empirically visible patterns in their regular behavior, especially those which suggest some use from the standpoint of human communities. In this sense empirical lore must be said to operate at the lowest degree of abstraction: i.e., that of totalization, which abstracts from the individual to the logical whole of which it is a part, arriving at a rudimentary and informal definition which is usually little more than a collection of distinctions, while making little or no effort to develop formal, logically consistent descriptions, or to explain why things are they way they are.[3] This is why the systems of classification developed by pre-market societies often seem a bit disjointed or out of kilter to us, something which Luria noted in his study of Uzbek peasants in the 1930s, on the eve of Stalin's forced collectivization (Luria 1974/1976).

Empirical lore is always ordered to the survival, reproduction, and further growth and development of those human communities, though

---

3. In accord with the Thomistic tradition, we distinguish three degrees of abstraction:
   1) totalization,
   2) formalization, which abstracts from the individual to its underlying structure, which it attempts to model using mathematical formalisms or similar tools, arriving at a rigorous definition from which conclusions may be drawn analytically, and
   3) transcendental abstraction, which abstracts from the structure of a thing to its underlying organizing principle—the reason for its being and for its being the way it is. For a more complete discussion, see Mansueto 2002b, Maritain 1938 and Maurer 1962.

especially in its more advanced forms, the accumulation of this lore may well become an end in itself. In this sense the political valence of empirical lore is unambiguously progressive. The accumulation of this sort of knowledge, to the extent that it actually identifies the useful properties of minerals, plants, and animals, and helps a community to understand how human communities actually function, can only serve to promote social progress.

The question, of course, is to what extent empirical lore actually generates authentic knowledge of the natural world—a question which has once again come to the fore with the renewal of interest in herbalism, acupuncture, and other medical disciplines which do not depend on a mathematical-physical description of human physiology. Indeed, the resurgence of non-allopathic[4] medical disciplines provides a good test of the epistemic status of empirical lore.

It is important to point out, to begin with, that both traditional and allopathic medicine are empirically based, but where traditional medical disciplines rely on thousands of years of accumulated experience, and careful clinical judgments regarding the impact of a particular treatment on a particular patient, allopathic medicine relies on controlled clinical trials which lead to statistical predictions regarding effectiveness. Traditional medical disciplines, asked to explain how their treatments work, use broad qualitative formulations: e.g., by balancing "hot," "cold," "dry," and "moist" principles in the body, or by influencing the functioning of energy meridians. Allopathic physicians, on the other hand can often trace in detail the mechanical or biochemical process by which a particular treatment works, though this is by no means always the case.

It is, of course, true that many traditional treatments don't always work, but the same is true of many allopathic treatments—which often have far worse side effects. Many of the most effective treatments in allopathic medicine work in ways we understand no better than the acupunc-

---

4. The term "allopathic" refers to the conviction, on which most "modern medicine" is based, that the source of disease comes from outside the body (e.g., by infection) and is best treated by agents which destroy or hinder the operation of the pathogen (e.g., antibiotics). The term was originally used in distinction to "homeopathy," which treats illness by using minute quantities of agents which are known to cause the principal symptoms of the illness. Here we use to term "allopathic" to describe the official medicine of the American Medical Association, by preference to the more cumbersome "medicine based on a mathematical-physical description of human physiology." We use the term "traditional" to describe medical disciplines based on empirical lore.

turist understands the workings of her needles. And modern medicine, even if it understands fully *how* a treatment works (in the sense of tracing mechanisms) rarely understands *why* it works, in the sense of what is being done for the body in a global sense or why the body needs this.

What are the relative merits of these approaches? Clearly in terms of sheer contribution to technical prowess knowing how something works is of enormous help in making it work for us in new and better ways. And it is certainly nice to know roughly how often we can expect a particular treatment to work. On the other hand, there is something to be said for thousands of years of accumulated experience. People don't do things for that long if they don't work. There is also good reason to believe that controlled experiments, by focusing narrowly on the interaction of a few well defined phenomena, may well fundamentally distort our picture of reality, especially when dealing with complex systems such as the human body. Thus, having identified a statistically significant relationship between heavy drinking and diets high in saturated fat on the one hand, and the incidence of heart disease on the other, allopathic physicians began encouraging their patients to restrict alcohol consumption and to cut out all fatty foods. As it turns out, however, some alcoholic beverages, such as red wine, have significant health benefits, as do certain foods high in saturated fat, such as avocados and chocolate, which turn out to prevent cholesterol from forming plaques on arterial walls. It is possible that the various cuisines developed by peoples around the world and the old dietary theories which call for balancing hot, cold, wet, and dry foods, may turn out to be finely tuned medical prescriptions which are based on long experience, and which in fact give people better advice than the allopaths.

Our analysis of the nature of empirical lore also provides a useful reminder of the enduring importance of empirical pattern recognition in scientific research—something which is often forgotten by theorists who value the formalism above all else. It was Kepler's ability to see patterns in Tycho Brahe's data which made his formulation of the laws of planetary motion possible. The foundation of scientific chemistry is the periodic table of elements, a masterpiece of pattern recognition, which defines just what precisely such formal theories as quantum mechanics must explain. Similarly, the basic empirical insight which grounds evolutionary biology—the existence of phylogenetic relationships between various species—is uncontested by serious scientists in a time when the theoretical core of Darwinism—the idea that random variation is the sole source of variations which have survival value—is very much under attack. More attention to empirical pattern recognition might be useful to scientists who are wrestling with fundamental contradictions in existing theory or attempting to explain phenomena which existing theory cannot accommodate. When reasoning in and between theories doesn't yield a solution it may help to return to a more naive level of observation. And yet very little of this seems to be taking place. When a small domesticated rabbit came to live with us a few years ago I began to do research on rabbits and other members of the order *Lagomorphidae*. I was struck by how little we know. Most of the books that I could find were technical manuals which included enough physiology to enable one to raise rabbits on an industrial scale. There were also a few suggestive articles justifying the classification of rabbits in a separate order (they used to be regarded as Rodents), which pointed out the rabbits' unique digestive system which produces a special kind of feces which are eaten in order to supply needed proteins and vitamins not contained in the rabbits' ordinary diet, but rather produced by bacteria in its digestive tract, as well as such taxonomic anomalies: e.g. a morphology like that of the rodents and a blood chemistry which is suspiciously bovine. But I found no ongoing body of research directed at solving these mysteries. Why the unusual digestive system? Why the taxonomic anomalies? The answer of course is simple enough. We know enough about rabbits to exploit them effectively, and the unsolved questions, while interesting, do not have obvious theoretical or technological implications. But who knows what theoretical possibilities are missed because we fail to accumulate the "empirical lore" which might point us towards interesting patterns and eventually towards new explanations?

Cosmological Mythology

The second way in which human beings in tribal, communitarian, archaic, and tributary societies engaged with the universe was through what we have called cosmological mythology. Cosmological mythology is a type of fine art. A cosmological myth is a complex of stories through which a people expresses its vision of the universe—where it came from, how it works, and where they stand within it. The capacity to generate such stories is rooted first and foremost in the imagination: the ability, which we share with other higher animals, to organize the data we garner from the senses into images, and then to store these images in our memory and later recall them. What sets the human imagination apart from that of other animals is the fact that we can also analyze these images into their component parts and recombine them in new and more interesting ways, so that we can form images of things which do not in fact exist, but which articulate in some way a meaning or value which is important to us. This ability to "imagine" as well as to simply form, store, and recall images, is a result of the fact that the human imagination is ordered to and formed by the intellect, and in particular by the acts of totalization and transcendental abstraction. Totalization allows us to sort and classify images for recombination. This may be done in a way which is relatively realistic, as when a novelist combines elements from the personalities of many different people to create a unique but entirely believable character, or it may be done in a way which is utterly fantastic. We know that feathers and wings and horns are parts of the bodies of animals, and are able to combine them with other body parts with which they do not naturally occur in nature. Adding feathers and wings to a serpent we get Quetzalcoatl. Added to the body of a horse, wings give us the great Pegasus and a horn gives the magical Unicorn. The *way* in which images are analyzed and recombined, however, is driven by the act of transcendental abstraction. The artist rises to some principle or meaning which s/he hopes to communicate, and creates images with that end in mind.

The material object of a cosmological myth is, in other words, the universe as a whole; its formal object is the image or complex of images through which some meaning or value is expressed. It is this meaning or value which is the end to which the myth is ordered.

What sets a cosmological myth apart from the other works of fine art which have the universe as a whole for their object—say Dante's *Commedia* or the novels of Doris Lessing's *Canopus in Argos* cycle? A myth expresses a collectively held vision of the universe; the poem or novel an individual artist's transformation of that vision, a transformation which, in really great art, aims at a larger transformation of the social order as well. The role of a particular myth in a society may be guaranteed or reinforced by more or less widespread literalism, though this is by no means essential, and it is only in tributary societies in which a centralized priestly elite has gained a monopoly on ritual activities that we begin to see an effort to promote anything like adherence to a single, uniform, mythic cycle, and even this trend is by no means universal. Matters are complicated, furthermore, by the figure of the imaginative prophet, who like the individual artist transforms the dominant mythology, or at least the meanings inherent in it, in some way, but who is recognized as a central figure in the larger religious system, even if s/he is also frequently subject to marginalization or persecution. In a very real sense, what sets the prophet apart from the individual socially critical artist of the modern era is the absence in bourgeois societies of a widely shared mythos with which to interact, and thus radically diminished opportunities for the sort of global socioreligious impact of the sort enjoyed by an Isaiah or a Jeremiah. In this sense, someone like Dante stands somewhere in the borderlands between imaginative prophecy and literature in the modern sense.

None of this should be taken to imply, however, that all cosmological mythology somehow has a uniform social basis or political valence. Rather, it arises within very different societies and serves very different political ends. The form of the myth, furthermore, more or less transparently reflects the social order, something of which Durkheim was already aware when he showed that religious symbols are "collective representations" of the social structure (Durkheim 1911/1965). Thus, in hunter-gather societies, which are generally organized on a tribal basis, the principal symbolic forms are totems, animals, plants or minerals, which serve as a sort of emblem for the clan and other social groupings. In communitarian societies, which were often also matriarchal (Stone 1976) we see the emergence of a nearly universal cult of the *Magna Mater*, who is at once a goddess of fertility and the divine wisdom which lies behind the teleological ordering of the universe which communitarian societies were rapidly discovering. This cult was almost never exclusive however. Of particular importance in communitarian societies are culture heroes such as the Pueblo *katchina* (Waters 1963) or the Chinese Shen-nung (Chang 1963) who teach humanity the arts of civilization. Here the dominant cosmological myths at once reflect and reinforce a social order in which the efforts of each are ordered to the development of all, in a way which remains in at least rough harmony with the larger ecosystem.

The picture looks very different with the advent of warlord states or tributary social formations after 3000 BCE. There is, first of all, a growing sense that the universe is at best unpredictable, and at worst downright hostile to human life. Partly, no doubt, this reflects the movement of human beings into less hospitable ecosystems as population expanded and warm, fertile valleys became overcrowded. The reality is, however, that communitarian peoples also, often occupied hostile ecosystems, and nonetheless seemed to feel very much at home in the universe. There is nothing, for example, in the myths of the desert dwelling Hopi that compares with the Aztec or Hindu myths of cyclical cosmic destruction or the Semitic myths of the flood. Furthermore, even regular, highly predictable patterns in nature began to appear fragile and in need of active support. Partly this is reflected in the expanded role of high gods, who no longer "think outward into space creating hard beings," as Sussistinako had, but rather are engaged in a constant battle with the forces of chaos and destruction—forces often represented as violent and unpredictable transforms of the old mother-goddess. Order in a tributary society is not a manifestation of the self-organizing potential of matter itself, but rather the work of a mighty warrior who conquers and contains the forces of chaos and destruction. Thus the high god is also a war god. Deities of earth and fertility, wisdom and craftsmanship are pushed aside. This growing sense of fragility is also reflected in the growing cult of sacrifice. Indeed, many warrior societies—the Aryans, the Aztecs—regard creation itself as a form of self-sacrifice, as the cosmic man Purusha is dismembered to provide the parts of the world, or the high gods of the successive cosmic epochs of the Aztec calendar throw themselves on the sacrificial pyre, bringing into being the "sun" of that epoch. Animal, or in some cases human sacrifice is required to sustain the gods in their enormous creative effort.

There are, finally, cosmological myths produced by movements of resistance to the warlord state and the tributary social formation which it helped sustain. These myths generally take as their raw materials what remains of the old communitarian/archaic religion, or else certain aspects of the tributary cosmology itself. Thus, in many societies, the cult of the *Magna Mater* or its local equivalent became a means by which the peasantry and intelligentsia gave voice to their resistance to the oppression and stagnation characteristic of the tributary regime.

One of the clearest examples of the first dynamic, which mobilizes communitarian or archaic survivals and a form of resistance, is the story of the rape of Persephone, which is said to have taken place beside Lake Pergusa, in the Province of Enna, in the parched grain growing uplands of the Sicilian interior. This myth is usually told as a story explaining the origin of the seasons. Demeter, distraught by the abduction of her daughter by Hades, deprives the earth of her graces, and it becomes dry and barren. The people, threatened with famine, beseech Zeus for assistance. After the intervention of Hermes, sent by Zeus as an emissary, Hades agrees to release his prisoner, provided she has eaten nothing during her stay with him. Persephone, however, has swallowed six pomegranate seeds, and is thus condemned to pass six months of every year with Hades in the gloomy nether regions of Dis. It is during these six months that Demeter, ever distraught at the absence of her daughter, is mourning, and that the earth becomes dry and barren.

But this reading of the myth conceals another, more profound, and intensely political meaning. Demeter is the grain mother, and Parthenia/Persephone the new and the ripe, harvested grain. Hades, the god of the underworld, is so called because he is the god of the great underground storehouses where the grain was held. Thus the identification with Pluto, the God of wealth. The half year that Persephone spends with Hades is the half of the grain—the halfyear's surplus labor—which customarily belonged to the landlord. The pomegranate seeds represent the loan of seed grain, the interest on which indebted the peasant to the landlord, a debt which was often used to justify the extraction of rents, taxes, or forced labor.

The cult of the *Magna Mater* was not, however, exclusively a fertility cult. The Great Mother was the Goddess of wisdom as well as of fertility and her cult may well have served one of the contexts for the emergence Hellenic philosophical tradition. Au Set, or Isis as she was called by the Greeks, was first and foremost the cosmic librarian, and the cosmic writer whose pen directed the course of human history. In most forms of the myth of Isis and Osiris, it is not the death and dismemberment of Osiris which is regarded as salvific, but rather his reintegration. And this reintegration is the work of Isis, in her capacity as goddess of wisdom.

> What then is the task of Isis? Plutarch tells us "(Typhon or Set) tears to pieces and scatters to the winds the sacred writings, which the Goddess collects and puts together and gives into the keeping of these that are initiated into the sacred rites." Isis is, then the re-assembler of lost knowledge. (Matthews 1991:74)

This sort of resistance, because it represents a reaffirmation—against the tributary cult of death and destruction—of the underlying dynamism of matter and its drive towards ever higher degrees of organization, and because its principal symbolic form is the *Magna Mater*, we call *mater/ia*.

The second dynamic, which draws on elements of the tributary mythology and transform them into a form of resistance is best illustrated by ancient Judaism. Product of successful peasant resistance to the Canaan warlords and their Egyptian overlords during the late bronze age (Gottwald 1979), this cult took the Canaanite high god (El, the father of *ba'al*, and a rather remote and insignificant figure in most Canaanite religious practice) and transformed him into *El yahwi sabaoth yisrael*—El who brings into being the armies of Israel. Gradually this form of El is recognized not only as liberator but also as creator of heaven and earth, the causative power of Being which grounds all things.

We should note here that in many respects the cosmology and theology remain that of the warlord state. Israel retained the Semitic creation story, the myth of the flood, etc., all of which suggest a sense of the universe as a system always on the edge of chaos. Yahweh's interventions on behalf of his peasants are of a piece with his larger creative activity. Both are represented as containing a tide—be it that of the ocean with its great sea monsters or that of the Philistine flank on the west. And militant Yahwism was always hostile to the residual cult of the Great Mother, particularly the cult of Astarte, which it did not really distinguish (whether through patriarchal blindness or because the two were in fact intimately intertwined). This has given feminist theology reason to look at Yahwism with some caution. At the same time, Yahwism gave birth to a cult which put the struggle for justice against overwhelming odds at the very center of religious life.

Like empirical lore, cosmological mythology can make an authentic claim to truth—not, to be sure, as a description—even a very informal description—of the universe, but rather as a *window on its meaning*. This should not be taken to imply that all myths are of equal value, any more than all traditional healing disciplines or modern scientific theories are of equal value. On the contrary, it should be clear that the mythologies of communitarian and archaic societies, and of the movements of resistance to the warlord state, have a greater share in the truth than the mythologies of tributary social formations. This is apparent from the practical impact of these various mythologies. Where the communitarian and revolutionary communitarian mythologies mobilized human societies effectively for social progress, tributary mythologies reinforced social structures which contributed to social stagnation. It thus stands to reason that the former were more nearly based on a correct reading of reality than were the latter. But even the myths of tributary social formations capture something of human experience. Warfare and exploitation *are* sometimes the only road forward for societies trapped in a difficult ecosystem. And predation is a widespread survival strategy within most ecosystems. Indeed, we not only admire predators, but keep their neotenized cousins as household pets.

Where cosmological mythology of all varieties falls short is in the capacity to generate an argument capable of persuading someone whose experience is different from our own. Thus, the peasants who worshipped YHWH in preference to *ba'al* were quite unable to persuade the Canaanite warlords of the superiority of their God, because the whole way of life of the warlords formed them intellectually and morally as devotees of the *ba'alim*. And the Mediterranean and Mexican peasants who articulated their enduring faith in the ultimate meaningfulness of the universe in their preference for the cult of the *Magna Mater* or of *Tonantzi* over that of Zeus or *Tezcatlipoca* were never able to persuade members of the ruling classes of their societies that matter is in fact ordered to organization and does not need to be formed from the outside. In tributary societies, where the persistence of the village community conserved a basis in experience for the conviction that the universe is ultimately meaningful, this was not an insuperable problem. The peasantry always knew the truth, even if it was also sometimes susceptible to seduction by the death-cult of the warlord elite. But with the emergence of markets and of a social structure organized by the market system, things changed. As we noted above, people experience a market society as a system of only externally related atoms governed, perhaps, by some formal law, but with out a real end or purpose, and soon begin to think about the universe in much the same way. Against the background of this experience cosmological myths lost their power and nihilism gradually took hold. Thus the need for the dialectic—and thus the need for the teleological physics which formed an integral part of the *via dialectica*.

THE UNIVERSE OF NUMBERS AND ATOMS

The Emergence of the Market System

Afro-Eurasia as a whole seems to have undergone a rather protracted period of civilizational decline between 1400 and 800 BCE as tributary structures went into crisis and gradually retrenched. By around 800 BCE, however, there were real signs of a revival. It is, specifically, just precisely around this period that we see the beginnings of specialized agriculture and crafts production. In the Mediterranean Basin this meant, above all, oil, wine, and the pottery in which to store and transport these agrarian products (Anderson 1974, Ste. Croix 1982), though there is some evidence that the Greeks also exported the occasional sophist for the amusement of Indian rulers (Thapar 2002: 178). The West generally suffered a significant balance of trade deficit with both India and China, something which is reflected in the accumulation of vast hordes of Greek and Roman coins in both regions (Frank 1998, Thapar 2002: 242). China exported silk (Frank 1998), India pepper and other spices, teak and ebony, and cotton textiles (Thapar 2002). Southeast Asia entered the system largely as an exporter of spices and specialty woods. Peripheries such as the Horn of Africa and Southern Arabia exported frankincense. Gold and textiles came from West Africa. Porcelain and tea entered the system later from India and China.

Initially the development of specialized agriculture seems to have taken place under the sponsorship of archaic or tributary structures. In Greece, for example, civilization seems to have revived around tribal and inter-tribal sanctuaries which, because they drew pilgrims for seasonal festivals, also became important market centers (Snodgrass 1980). Elsewhere, where civilization had not collapsed altogether, tributary states sponsored investment in these new products (Thapar 2002: 137–279). But in the long run specialized agriculture meant the emergence of markets –first local, then regional, and eventually "global" (i.e. Afro-Eurasian) in scope. Increasingly investment decisions were dictated by the complex interplay of supply and demand. Thales of Miletus, for example, who is generally credited with taking the first steps towards the development of an abstract mathematics, also discovered the law of supply and demand. Foreseeing an unusually good crop of olives on year, he secured control of every olive press in his region, and then demanded monopoly prices for their use—though at least one story suggests that having made his theoretical point he relented and let the presses at their "fair" or "natural" price (Turnbull 1956: 79–82). Archaic and tributary structures became subordinated to what eventually, with the completion of the Silk Road around 200 BCE, became a global petty commodity system in which resources were allocated, at least in large measure, by a global market in luxury goods.[5]

Politically this was a period of fragmentation. The Hellenic *polis* were, first and foremost, sanctuaries become market towns which extracted surplus from their hinterlands by religious means or later by means of exchange rather than by coercion. Debt servitude and chattel slavery were later developments, which depended in part, at least, on the absence of a state structure which could provide effective economic regulation (Snodgrass 1980, Anderson 1974, de Ste. Croix 1982). Small states prevailed in areas which, like China and the fertile crescent, had previously been dominated by large empires. Northern India was just undergoing what seems to have been a primary process of state formation, largely independent of the earlier Indus Valley or Harrapan Civilization, which in any case did not extend east into the Gangetic Plain, north in to the Himalayan foothills, or south into the Deccan or the peninsula. Some of these states were *gana-sanghas*, a sort of republic in which power

---

5. There is a vigorous debate regarding the point at which an integrated "world economy" or "world system" first emerged (Frank and Gills 1993). In its original form "world systems theory" attributed the formation of a world economy to the European conquest of Africa, the Americas, and Asia (Wallerstein 1974, 1980, 1989), a conquest which was regarded as the origin of the current poverty and underdevelopment of the "Third World." Gradually, however, as scholars began to overcome their Eurocentrism, it became apparent that a world system incorporating all of Eurasia and much of Africa already existed long before the European conquests (Abu-Lughod 1989). Andre Gunder Frank, originally a proponent of the view that the creation of a unified world system was a result of the European conquests in the sixteenth century, now argues that the existence of global (i.e., Eurasian) trade networks can be traced back some 5000 years (Frank and Gills 1992) and has argued that the Chinese in fact retained a dominant role in the system until roughly the time of the Industrial Revolution (Frank 1993). He also rejects the notion of "capitalism" as a useful way of distinguishing the modern world system from its predecessors. While I think Frank does a good job of showing the long history of global trade, I also believe that he misses three important transitions. First, beginning around 800 BCE we see the development of local and regional trade networks which actually begin to shape what is produced. This is apparent in the recognition of the laws of supply and demand by thinkers such as Thales of Miletus. By around 200 BCE these networks have effectively linked together all of Afro-Eurasia, from Mali, Iberia, and Britain all the way to China (Bentley 1993). These two transitions represent the advent of local and regional petty commodity production: i.e. a system in which resource allocation is shaped by the existence of a global market in luxury goods. Finally, between 1500 and 1800 we witness the gradual emergence of a new system, capitalism, in which not only goods and services but also labor power itself has become a commodity. The construction of capitalism cannot be said to be complete, however, until the full development of capital markets in the twentieth century, which makes capital a commodity as well.

was held by the senior lineages of what was still in part a tribally organized pastoral-raiding society which had only partly adopted agriculture. Others were small kingdoms (Thapar 2002: 98–173). Where larger tributary structures persisted they gradually altered their economic strategies, seeking to tax trade rather than direct production and thus to capture for themselves a portion of what was becoming a very healthy commerce.

The emergence of specialized agriculture and crafts production and of petty commodity production offered to humanity an extraordinary new opportunity. By using the principle of comparative advantage it was possible for distant regions to profit from trade with each other, and thus grow rich without the systematic exploitation of either their own populations or their trade partners. Such an outcome, however, required conscious leadership and intervention into the marketplace. The spontaneous tendency was towards rapid economic differentiation, as those with better land and better access to markets grew rich and those less well endowed grew poor. Peasants, who in many places had just been emancipated from tributary exploitation, found themselves falling into debt peonage and losing access to their land altogether. *Nouveau riche* elements who cared nothing for the traditional obligations between classes challenged sacral monarchs and priestly elites for power, so that political structures lost their integrity altogether.

This was also a period of profound ideological upheaval. Specifically, in all of the principal civilizational centers of Africa and Eurasia we witness a problematization of meanings which were previously taken for granted, as well as an incipient process of religious rationalization and democratization. Concepts and arguments partially displace images and stories in the way humanity thinks about God and the universe and speculation around such questions is opened to up to a much wider public, beyond the priestly castes whose unique privilege it had previously been. This is the period which Karl Jaspers called the axial age (Jaspers 1953).

Axial Age Science

Changes in the way humanity thought about the universe were an integral part of this process. In an emerging market society, where everyone has his or her own particular purpose, it becomes increasingly difficult to think in terms of a single organizing principle and thus in transcendental principles of value. People experience society in one of three ways. Viewed from the standpoint not only of the direct producer, it appears as a raw material to be worked on. From the standpoint of the active entrepreneur, small or large, it is a system of individuals engaged in complex, but largely external interactions. From "without" or "above," as it were, from the standpoint of an investor who is involved in neither production nor the day to day management of an enterprise, society appears as a system of quantities—specifically as a system of prices in which once task is to minimize costs and maximize profits.

Element Theories

These three vantage points in turn constituted three different traditions in natural philosophy: element theories, atomism, and an incipient mathematical physics. Element theories attempted to reduce universe to four or five basic substances, the combination of which is then understood to produce the entire phenomenal world. In Greece and India, these elements were earth, air, water, and fire; in China they included wood, fire, earth, metal, and water. Often there was an attempt to identify one element as primary –water in the case of Thales, air in the case of Anaximander, and fire in the case of Heraclitus.

What these theories fail to do, of course, is to explain where the elements themselves come from. The next step in rationalization was the emergence of atomistic theories, which treat the phenomenal world as a composite of atoms, or indestructible particles. Again, we find such theories in the Mediterranean Basin (Democritus and Epicurus), in India (the Caravakas and, with some modification, the Vaisheshika) and in China (the Mohists) (Collins 1998). Different forms of matter, including the elements, are the result either of differently shaped atoms (the position in Plato's *Timeaus*, for example) or of atoms combining in different structures, densities, etc.

Atomism

Similar, but perhaps more serious issues arise when we analyze the second spontaneous natural philosophy produced by the axial age civilizations: the atomistic tradition represented by Democritus and Epicurus in Greece, In all such theories atoms are regarded as moving about randomly in an absolute space—i.e., a space which exists independently of matter. The atoms themselves are indestructible and thus eternal, but combine to form more complex forms of organization: the four basic elements (earth, water, air, and fire), the earth, and ultimately plants, animals, human beings—and even the gods. In the more radical forms of atomism (Hellenic atomism, the Caravaka and early Vaisheshika school), thought is simply the result of an effluence of atoms from the object perceived into the soul, which is itself composed of atoms. Even the gods are taken to be the product of atomic interactions. More moderate atomisms (Mohism and later Vaisheshika doctrines) posit a sovereign god who orders atoms to create a structured universe.

This doctrine has proven extraordinarily resilient and many lay people today confuse it with modern atomic theory, which is really quite different. And it did make important contributions to the development of science and philosophy. Of particular importance in this regard is the notion that more complex and highly organized systems can develop out of the less complex, without the ordering action of a rational agent external to the process. This insight is at the foundation of all theories of self-organization, and it is no doubt for this reason that Marx and Engels saw in the atomists the precursors of materialist science and philosophy.

Once again, however, the limitations are very real. Within this system there is no place for underlying structure or design. Explanation is thus limited to an economical description of our experience. Systems of only externally related atoms, furthermore, have no immanent purpose. The gods, if they exist, are either themselves systems of atoms and thus in no sense ontologically superior to any other physical system. Or else there is a transcendent creator God who orders things by fiat. The result is that ethics is reduced to the pursuit of pleasure or submission to divine will. That some atomists—especially Epicurus and his followers—may have developed a rather refined concept of pleasure and others (the Mohists, for example) developed egalitarian doctrines of justice makes little difference. Without some criterion which transcends individual desire (ours or God's), the doctrine cannot help but serve as a rationale for either the market system or for arbitrary imperial power (which is exactly what it did).

Axial Age Rationalism

Rationalistic tendencies were also apparent in all of the principal Afro-Eurasian civilizational centers. At the center of these tendencies was the development of an abstract mathematics, i.e. one which goes beyond the solution of concrete problems to the creation of formal models or, better still, to the thematization of such questions as "What is a number?" and "What makes a mathematical proposition valid?"

The reason for this development is not hard to understand. It lies in the development of market system and the resulting experience of the universe as a system of quantities. Indeed, we should not be surprised to find that the first of the great Hellenic mathematicians was a merchant, and a retired one at that—Thales of Miletus (640–550 BCE). Indeed, Thales seems to have gone so far as to have had rudimentary grasp of the laws governing the marketplace. Foreseeing an unusually good crop of olives on year, he secured control of every olive press in his region, and then demanded monopoly prices for the their use—though at least one story suggests that having made his theoretical point he relented and let the presses at their "fair" or "natural" price (Turnbull 1951: 79–82).

Thales, perhaps, spent too much of his life engaged in traveling over rough terrain and deep seas, and was too deeply engaged with the empirical world to retreat completely into mathematical formalisms. For him the universe was made of water. It was left to his student, Pythagoras, a member of the next generation, which had inherited wealth and which managed money rather than merchandise, to develop the idea that it is fact number itself which is the basis of reality, and that the world we experience with our senses is just a reflection of this purely formal system which lies behind it.

Similar developments took place in India and China. In India the development of mathematics was driven in part by the complex requirements of Vedic ritual, which involved the construction of fire altars composed of 200 clay bricks in five layers, such that no two adjacent layers of brick were arranged in a congruent manner (Stahl 1999, Hayashi 2003). Formalization of this and similar problems led to what some scholars claim is actually the first formulation of the Pythagorean Theorem:

> The diagonal rope (*akṣnayā-rajju*) of an oblong (rectangle) produces both which the flank (*pārśvamāni*) and the horizontal (*tiryaṇmāni*) <ropes> produce separately. (*Sulba Sutra* in Hayashi 2003: 363)

Chinese mathematicians developed a decimal system and the concept of negative numbers early on and were solving systems of linear equations in multiple variables by no later than the end of the Axial Age, though the exact dates are difficult to fix given the fact that behind the earliest extant texts of key mathematical treatises, such as the *Nine Chapters on the Mathematical Art,* dated around 179 BCE, lie long oral traditions (Martzloff 1996, Dauben 2007).

It is, at the same time, the *petty* commodity character of these economies which lies behind what to us seem some rather strange doctrines, such as the notion that each thing has its own number (another Pythagorean claim) and the "failure" of Hellenic, Indian, and Chinese mathematicians to develop a complete theory of algebraic and topological systems. In a petty commodity economy trade forms only a small sector of a system which in which patterns of production and consumption are still largely determined by nonmarket forces—ecological and technological constraints on the development of the productive forces, custom, or imperial decree. One imagines that if Thales had actually exacted a monopoly price for his olive presses that he might well have been killed by a mob or called up before the public authorities to account for his actions—a fate which awaited many a price gouging merchant well into the seventeenth century, even in such mercantile societies as New England (Hatch 1974). In such a system prices change so little that the notion develops of a natural price—a "number" corresponding to a thing. This is the likely basis in experience for what is otherwise a rather obscure doctrine. Similarly, it requires a more profound sense of the mutual determination of things—the idea that relations between things are prior to the things themselves—for an authentic algebra to emerge and to be applied to geometric forms which otherwise seem to be more fundamental than and thus prior to the formalisms used to describe them. This is why algebra developed only slowly in the petty commodity societies of the Mediterranean basin, largely among the Arabs, and was completed only with the advent of European capitalism and why topology developed only as finance capital was beginning its domination of the global market in the nineteenth century.

Towards an Explanatory Theory

Clearly element theories, atomism, and rationalism were all incapable of either *explaining* the universe, or answering fundamental questions of meaning and value.

A major advance in this project occurred when philosophers stopped asking what things are made of and began to ask how they come to be what they are. This shift first becomes apparent with Heraclitus (Ephesus fl. 504–501 BCE)—who was, interestingly enough, one of the last representatives of the old priestly intelligentsia which had been dominant during Archaic era (Collins 1988: 83). At first Heraclitus seems merely to be counterpoising an argument for the primacy of fire (the element of ritual sacrifice *par excellence*) to Thales' argument for the primacy of water (the natural element of the merchant in a sea-going society). But when Heraclitus says that the universe is an "ever-living" fire, he is really saying that it is a constant process of change or flux that at once consumes and produces, as fire consumes fuel and produces smoke and embers. This flux is, furthermore, rational, Fire being identified with the One, or God, and with the Soul. It at once unites and orders all things. The constant struggle and strife that we see in the world is in fact just a complex interplay of opposites, a finely tuned tension through which a higher order is produced. Here Heraclitus comes close to Hegel, and to Engels' doctrine of the unity and struggle of opposites.

The difficulty, of course, is that Heraclitus does not really explain change; instead he merely posits a process of rational change in order to explain the contradictory phenomena of order and chaos in the universe. The existence of the flux itself remains unexplained. It was this limitation in the Heraclitan doctrine that led Parmenides (Elea, fl. 480 BCE) to carry out a more exhaustive analysis of what it means for something to exist in the first place. What Parmenides realized is that unlike other attributes, Being is absolute—either something exists or it doesn't. Change, fundamentally, involves a coming into being or a passing out of being. But in order for something to come into being it must come either from something or from nothing. But "nothing can come from nothing." Forms or qualities that do not exist at one point in time cannot, therefore, simply appear at a later point in time. If, however, they come from something, then it is difficult to understand in what sense they are actually coming into being. Being is, simply and absolutely; all else is mere appearance. Parmenides concluded that the universe is a material, spherical, motionless plenum, eternal and uncreated, beyond which there is nothing (Stumpf 1994: 16–18).

From a certain point of view the analysis is brilliant. If Heraclitus was the first to penetrate the nature of change, and to reconcile the existence of order and chaos in the universe, Parmenides is the first philosopher to penetrate the still more profound mystery of Being—indeed the to show any real awareness of the idea of Being as such. On the other hand, his reasoning betrays the limits of formal abstraction. He seems entirely unaware of ideas—such as the idea of the Good—which can reconcile being and becoming and ends up carrying an important insight—that there is a reality behind what we perceive with our senses, a reality which is fundamental—to the point of absurdity. This tendency is even more apparent in the work of Parmenides' student Zeno, who used similar reasoning to prove that, for example it is impossible for a runner to complete a race because he would have to traverse an infinite number of points (Stumpf 1994: 18–21).

Later pre-Socratic philosophy—especially the work of Empedocles (Agrigentum, 490–430 BCE) and Anaxagoras (500–428 BCE)—can be read as an attempt to effect a synthesis of the Parmenidean and Heraclitan doctrines. Empedocles, for example, argues for the existence of four fundamental material elements: earth, water, air, and fire, but argues that their motion can be explained only by the forces of Love and Hate or Harmony and Discord which, respectively, cause the aggregation and disintegration of the various elements in different proportions, resulting in the multitude of different phenomena which we experience (Stumpf 1994: 21–23). Here we lose something, I think, by comparison with both Heraclitus and Parmenides. Empedocles' doctrine of matter falls short of the Parmenidean realization of the absolute and transcendent character of Being, while his claim that there is a perpetual struggle between Love and Discord lacks Heraclitus' insight into the ultimately rational character of all change. Anaxagoras attempts to remedy this latter failure by suggesting that it is νους or intellect which orders and directs the unending combination of elements.

A similar stage in development is represented in India by doctrines which introduce a rational principle (the *jiva* of the Jaina or the *purusa* of the Samkya school) which interacts with matter (*ajiva* or *prakriti*), setting in motion a complex evolutionary process, and in China by the fusion of the five elements school with Taoism, which also brings a rational if to fully formalizable principle into play to explain their interaction with each other (Collins 1998).

In both all cases, however, the system as a whole, the motion of matter in accord with some ordering principle or principles, remains unexplained. Formalization is incapable of advancing beyond description to explanation. For this it would be necessary to advance to transcendental abstraction—something which, we will see, is intimately bound up with practice, and specifically with a radically transformative practice, be it revolutionary, spiritual, or both.

TELEOLOGICAL COSMOLOGIES

The dominant view of the physics which developed at the end of the Axial Age and which dominated the great Silk Road Era, whether Aristotelian, Vedic, Buddhist, or Taoist and indeed of the larger metaphysical project of which this physics formed a principal support (Amin 1988), is of a static worldview resistant to change developed—according to some historians (Wood 1978) quite intentionally—in order to shore up the interests of the landed elites during a period of democratic upheaval. Our first task will be to demonstrate that this represents a profound misreading of the Socratic project generally and of Aristotelian physics in particular. We will show that, on the contrary, the rational metaphysics project represents an attempt to reground ethics as part of a comprehensive movement of resistance to the emerging market order and that the physical doctrines on which rational metaphysics rests carries this project further precisely by supplying it with a more dynamic and progressivist cosmology. The effort is, however, flawed by an inability to grasp fully the self-organizing dynamism of matter, a failure which is rooted partly in the low level of development of human organizing capacities and in part by an alliance with patriarchal and tributary elements also arrayed against the emerging market order.

Our focus will be primarily on Aristotelian physics, since it is in reaction to this physics that modern mathematical physics first developed, but we will refer to comparable developments in India and China in order to indicate that the dynamics we have identified are in fact global in nature.

Towards an Axiological Space-Time

Aristotelian Physics

The immediate roots of Aristotelian physics lie not in a scientific or technological, but rather in a metaphysical and ultimately in a political problem. We have already noted that Ancient Greece was among the planet's first true petty commodity societies. This development was rooted in powerful new agricultural technologies, which vastly increased human productivity and which made possible the liberation of ever-larger sectors of the population from agricultural labor. At the same time, the incursion of market relations brought with it profound social contradictions. Differences in the quality of the soil, access to markets, and a myriad other factors led to rapid economic differentiation and to the equally rapid disintegration of the village communities. Those who became impoverished were forced to borrow from those who prospered and when they could not pay back what they owed the lost their land. The result was the formation of large landed estates on the one hand and a rapidly growing class of debtor servants on the other hand.

At the political level this economic differentiation led to a dual movement. On the one hand, the emerging *nouveau riches* elements, which can only be regarded as a sort of bourgeoisie,[6] began to push aside the old order of the *archontes*[7] and establish an oligarchic regime. At the same time, beginning in the sixth century before the Common Era, there was a series of peasant revolts directed at restoring and protecting the land rights of the peasantry and at gaining for the peasantry admission into the political arena. These struggles were resolved in different ways throughout Greece. In Sparta, for example, the landed elites co-opted the masses by enserfing the surrounding Messenians and transforming the whole population of the polis into a "mass" warrior aristocracy. In other places the uprisings were suppressed with only a few concessions and an oligarchic constitution predominated. What interests us here is the Athenian settlement,

6. The term bourgeoisie is taken here to apply to any social class which drives its revenue from the exploitation of the labor of others and the sale of the resulting goods and services in the marketplace, even if the exploitation in question is not strictly capitalist in character (i.e., based on wage labor), but depends rather on coercion of some kind, in this case on chattel slavery.

7. The precise social character of this regime is itself open to debate. The Mycenean and Minoan civilizations which dominated Greece in the second millennium before the common era had clearly defined tributary features—i.e., a standing military which engaged in conquest and which appears to have exacted tribute. At the same time the Minoan civilization at least appear also to have conserved significant communitarian or archaic features. It was, among other things, matriarchal. The long "dark ages" which followed the collapse of these civilizations witnessed a return to more nearly communitarian or archaic forms, though it appears that in each city there was a group of hereditary ruling families (the *dynasts* or *archontes*) which exercised combined political and sacerdotal functions. In this sense Iron Age Greece resembled Europe during the Middle Ages, combining communitarian and tributary features in a way which made possible unusual freedom of movement and innovation (Anderson 1974).

since it is this settlement that provides the immediate background to the ideological developments we are trying to understand. On the one hand, Solon and Pericles carried out a moderate agrarian reform, guaranteeing credits and other protections for the peasantry in order to stem the tide of latifundialization. And while the terms of the constitution were constantly changing, those Athenian peasants who retained property also acquired the right to vote and in general to participate in public life. At the same time, the lands of the rich were not redistributed, with the result that they had to acquire a new labor force for their estates. This they found in the prisoners of war who were already pouring into Attica as a result of Athens' military exploits (something which also secured for the city a growing commercial empire.) The result was a structure which integrated broad political participation with sharp economic inequalities and profound social contradictions.

It is in this context that the emergence of the Sophists must be understood. We have already noted in the previous chapter the impact of emerging market relations on the ideological sphere. A market society has no global purpose, but only individual ends which themselves are subject to constant change. People thus lack a basis in experience for thinking about the universe as an organized system. The result was the emergence of an increasingly skeptical worldview. This effect was compounded, however, by the operation of the new "democratic" political arena. The rich were now forced to obtain the consent of the poor (or at the least of the property owning poor) in the midst of the assembly, and for this they required *rhetors* capable of making particular interests appear universal. Schools grew up to teach this art, and those who ran them began to produce a relativistic doctrine that legitimated their activity. The spectrum of sophistic opinion was diverse. Some, like Protagoras were quite moderate, arguing that "man is the measure of all things," that morals were a product of convention and thus subject to revision by law or custom. Others, like Gorgias were more radical, eventually calling into question the very existence of objective reality (Plato. *Protagoras, Gorgias*).

There has been a tendency, especially on the left, to regard the Sophists as the spearhead of a fundamentally progressive, if historically premature, attempt by protobourgeois elements to lead a democratic revolution (Wood 1980). But this is only a half-truth. That the sophists, along with the Pythagoreans, the Atomists, and the Skeptics do represent a broadly "bourgeois" trend cannot be doubted. But their function was not progressive. On the contrary, their effect was to undermine further the already fragile foundations of public morality and to legitimate policies that made the πολις an instrument of private interests—those of the agrarian bourgeoisie and the emerging class of merchant capitalists. This is because, in the absence of anything that is Beautiful, True or Good in itself, moral judgment and thus any judgment regarding the justice of social structures or public policies, becomes impossible. The market system has no better defender than the relativist or nihilist who denies the existence of any criterion which might be used to find the market allocation of resources wanting or to ground some alternative allocation or method of allocation.

It is in this context that the Socratic tradition must be understood. Socrates, and Plato and Aristotle after him, were concerned first and foremost to reground ethics and thus rescue the public arena from the Sophists and the bourgeois interests they represented. This project was carried out in three distinct stages. Socrates himself developed what was primarily a logical, immanent critique of Sophism, drawing out the implications and internal contradictions of sophistic ideas and demonstrating the need for an ascent to first principles. The result was the dialectical method, the most important instrument of the philosophical tradition. But it is difficult to find anything like a consistent cosmology or metaphysics in those of Plato's dialogues that represent more nearly Socrates own position. Indeed, even his ethics is rather spare.

It is only with Plato that the Socratic project progresses beyond purely methodological issues to begin to trace the outlines of a systematic answer to the sophists. The two most important texts in this regard are, without question, the *Republic* and the *Timaeus*. Let us examine them in detail. Plato opens the *Republic* with a scene that situates the dialogue in its concrete political context. Socrates is returning from the feast of the Goddess at Piraeus (a suggestive reference to the cult of the *Magna Mater* with which Socratic philosophy has a profound affinity) when he is detained by a group of rich young men who insist that he accompany them home (a reference to the arbitrary power of the rich in Athenian society). Once there he engages his host, a rich man of the older generation, and several of the young men who had detained him in a debate regarding the nature of justice. He disposes handily of the traditional view, represented by his host Cephalus, that justice is merely a matter of paying one's debts, a view which reflects the *mores* of a society in which market relations have begun to emerge but have not yet eroded traditional norms of reciprocity. Socrates rejects this position, showing that it fails to address the vitally important question of what people actually *ought* to have. Thus, it is hardly just to give a mad man a weapon, even if it was borrowed from him before he went mad and would ordinarily have been returned as a matter of course (Plato. *Republic* 327a 331d).

This insistence on a substantive ethics already challenges market norms. He then goes on to answer three positions which were quite common in Athens at the time: the idea that justice means helping your friends and hurting your enemies, and the radical and moderate sophistic positions—that justice is just the will of the stronger and that it is merely a (necessary) social convention (Plato. *Republic* 331e–354c). His argument in all three cases involves drawing out the internal contradictions of each position in a way which points ever more insistently towards the conclusion that any adequate theory of justice presupposes a substantive doctrine of the Good, and that a just society is one governed by those who know what is Good, i.e. by philosophers, whom he calls Guardians, who undergo a long period of political-military and theoretical training, and who themselves hold no private property and thus have no particular interests to defend (Plato. *Republic* 471c–541b). Throughout this discussion Plato does not so much make his argument as outline it, setting forth a philosophical program that would still need to be fleshed out in other works, or perhaps by other thinkers.

Having set forth this program, Plato then does something odd. He engages in an extended argument aimed at showing that were a just city to exist, it would inevitably degenerate. Aristocracies, societies governed by the intellectually and morally most advanced elements degenerate into timocracies, societies governed by the courageous and proud (i.e., warriors). Timocracies degenerate into oligarchies, governed by the rich, oligarchies into democracies, governed by the people as a whole, who do not know the Good, and democracies into tyrannies, which transform the state into an instrument for satisfying the rapacious desires of a single individual. Errors in the training and selection of the Guardians would bring to power leaders more interested in wealth and honor than in truth and justice. Eventually these decadent elements would force a restoration of private property not unlike the *nomenklatura* privatization we have witnessed in the former Soviet bloc. Even if at first the property holders were persons formed under the old system and concerned at least for their own honor, if not for the highest values of truth and justice, gradually, from one generation to the next, the growing opportunities for making money would encourage its pursuit and the "timocracy," rule by lovers of honor, would degenerate into an oligarchy or a plutocracy—rule by the wealthy. But the degeneration does not stop there. The people see that the rich are able to indulge in the most various pleasures without negative consequences, and they too become infected with greed, rising up at the first possible moment to seize the wealth of the few and share it out among themselves. The rich respond with force, and the result is inevitably tyranny, as the most unscrupulous, playing one class off against the other, make the state their private plaything (*Republic* 543a–576b).

Plato takes up this same theme in the *Timaeus*, but goes further, arguing that social disintegration is part of a larger and inevitable cosmic dynamic. This dialogue, like the *Republic*, takes place at a feast of the goddess—this time the festival of Athena, two months after that of Bendis. The topic, however, is still the just social order. The question arises as to whether or not such an order is possible. A story is told, which Solon learned while traveling in Egypt of an "earlier Athens," founded by the goddess herself, the laws of which were not unlike those of the just society described by Socrates. This society was, however destroyed in a conflict with Atlantis, which is now submerged in the oceans.

The cosmology of the *Timaeus* is then presented as if to explain this tendency towards disintegration which appears to be written into the very fabric of the universe. It is interesting to note that Plato has Timaeus (a Pythagorean), and not Socrates, present the theory, suggesting that he regards it as a "best effort" regarding which he has, however, serious reservations. This is not surprising, since the theory has little which is specifically Platonic, but represents, rather, an unstable synthesis of Pythagorean and atomist elements (Cleary 1995:25).

The principal thesis advanced by Timaeus is that the universe was forged by the Demiurge, a kind of cosmic craftsman, on the basis of an eternal model which Timaeus calls a "living being," indicating a sense of organic unity and completeness. The forms of things are impressed on a "receptacle," which is identified as space and called the "matrix," the "nurse of all becoming." The resonance between the concept of matter and the doctrine of the *Magna Mater* should be apparent.

The principles by which the matrix is ordered a rigorously mathematical, and reflect the influence of the Pythagorean doctrine. Thus the universe as a whole, intended as a copy of the perfect model, is spherical because this is the most perfectly symmetrical shape. The World Soul, which moves all things, is self-moved: it rotates in a manner dictated by the interaction of the Same and the Different: the Celestial Equator and the Zodiac or Ecliptic. Even the properties of the various physical forms of matter are explained in mathematical terms. Timaeus accepts the notion of four elements, as well as the atomist gloss that they are in fact composed of distinct particles. For Timaeus, however, these particles are the result of the impression of mathematical forms on the matrix of space itself—forms which are ultimately reducible to the simplest: that of the triangle. As triangles combine to form solids, one gets the cube, the icosahedron, the octahedron, and the tetrahedron, the particles of earth, water, air, and fire respectively. The dodecahedron, the regular solid which most nearly approximates the sphere, is the sign of the cosmos itself.

The creative activity of the Demiurge extends only to those aspects of the universe which are eternal: the heavens and the world soul, and the stars and planets, which are identified with the gods of mythology. To these in turn is allotted the work of creating the plants, animals, and human beings, whose soul is mixed from the same ingredients as the world soul, but is not so pure.

This ordering work is not, however, all there is to the nature of the universe. The receptacle, Timaeus suggests, is resistant to the work of the Demiurge. Matter, far from being potential organization, in fact resists form, and even when formed begins to disintegrate. Necessity, in this sense, constrains the work of Reason. Here we encounter the atomist element in Plato's cosmology, the sense that the random and probabilistic motion of matter continually reasserts itself, leading even the best works of the Demiurge to disintegrate. This is the basis, for Plato, of the irreversible time that we experience—as distinct from the cyclical time defined by the self-motion of the world soul and marked by the movements of the heavenly bodies. Because of this, while we are able to provide a rational account of the work of the Demiurge, we can offer only a "likely story" to describe the phenomenal universe, which is governed as much by randomness as by reason.

What is going on here? What are we to make of this rupture in the middle of the *Republic* and the turn towards radical cosmological pessimism in the *Timaeus*? The answer is to be found not in the text or even the philosophical context, but in the larger social reality to which Plato was responding. If Plato is pessimistic about politics then it is because he has reason to be. The history of Greece in his time was one of rapid social disintegration. His own life was marked by the execution of his mentor, Socrates, and by the failure of his own political projects both at home in Athens and in Syracuse where he attempted to persuade the tyrant Dionysius to implement is political program (Wood 1980). And pessimism in politics tends, as we will see, to produce pessimism in cosmology.

There is, however, a more subtle process at work here as well. While Socrates and Plato clearly advance, by means of the dialectic, beyond the merely formal abstraction of the Pythagoreans to a higher, transcendental abstraction capable of grasping the first principle and its transcendental properties, the dialectic itself still depends on formalization and in particular on the distinction between the form or underlying structure and the appearance. And in a period of social disintegration "form" or "structure" are generally regarded as something static—there is no progress towards more complex forms of organization—while the appearance is identified with the matter or the "receptacle" to use Plato's term, which is constantly changing, which resists form, and which leads to cosmohistorical disintegration. Plato's failure to distinguish clearly between formal and transcendental abstraction leads him to revert to the spontaneous ideology of his time and to regard the first principle in increasingly formal rather than transcendental or teleological terms.

The resulting doctrine is problematic on scientific, metaphysical, and political grounds. Plato is unable to explain growth and development—something which ought to have been apparent to him in the plant an animal world if not in human society. Indeed, more broadly he is unable to achieve a unified theory that comprehends both celestial and terrestrial motion, and both reversible and irreversible phenomena. Indeed, our analysis of the *Timaeus* suggests that the obstacles to unification along these two dimensions may be more closely connected that historians and philosophers of science have thus far realized. We will see that when Newton unified celestial and terrestrial mechanics he did so only at the expense of any theorization of irreversible processes, which became an object of scientific investigation only with the advent of thermodynamics in the nineteenth century—a science which, at least in its first formulation, reproduced and even radicalized Plato's—or Timaeus'—doctrine.

Even more serious is the fact that Plato's cosmology fails to support the metaphysics that he sets forth in the *Republic*. There is no sense in the *Timaeus* that the Good draws all things towards itself, awakening in matter a latent potential for organization. On the contrary, matter is not only inert but chaotic, not only threatening, but actually working disintegration. Order comes from on high, from a sort of celestial monarch—or rather from his vice-regents—who impose it ever some imperfectly on a universe which tends towards chaos and destruction. It is hardly surprising that in his later years Plato should have drifted even further into political pessimism, arguing that philosophers could rule only secretly and from behind the scenes, through a Nocturnal Council which intervenes into what is otherwise an essentially oligarchic regime (*Statesman*), and eventually conceding the inevitability of rule by a (nonphilosophical) landed elite (*Laws*).

It is these difficulties in Plato's system which Aristotelian physics attempts to resolve. Physics is, for Aristotle, a science or *episteme*, and science is first and foremost knowledge of the principles of things (Aristotle. *Metaphysics* 1025b). Aristotle means by this that when we understand something scientifically, and thus grasp the principle which governs it, we can deduce from that principle all of its particular features or characteristics thus explaining what we observe with our senses. Each science has its own object, and physics is no exception. Aristotle's explicit attempts to specify this object are, however, a bit misleading. One the one hand, he makes a distinction between physics, ethics, and poetics. Physics, he says, is concerned with things that have their source of motion or rest in themselves (Aristotle. *Physics* 192–93), while the other disciplines are concerned, respectively, with things which have their cause of motion or rest in action or in making. The difficulty is that according to this definition, mathematics and metaphysics would both be branches of physics, something which Aristotle clearly does not intend. Physics, mathematics, and metaphysics are all theoretical sciences, which aim at knowledge for its own sake, but they are not to be identified with each other.

It is necessary, therefore, to supplement this first distinction with a second one, which pertains to the degree of abstraction proper to each of the theoretical sciences. Physics, he says, abstracts only from individuating matter, that is from the matter which distinguishes Fido from Fifi or Spica from Vega; it does not consider things as if they had no matter at all. Mathematics, on the other hand, makes just precisely this move, considering the form of things apart from the matter in which that form is emerging or disintegrating. Arithmetic, for example abstracts not only

Empirical Lore, Cosmological Mythology, Mathematical Physics, and Science

from these particular rabbits, but from the matter which makes them capable of nutrition, growth, reproduction, sensation, and locomotion. It does not attempt to explain how they reproduce. Rather, it abstracts only their number, and abstracts from the fact that it is *their* number, and considers only operations on and relationships between the numbers thus abstracted. And even a mathematics applied to rabbits (what we would call mathematical biology or mathematical population biology) would seek only a formalism describing their rate of reproduction in terms of other quantities—i.e., the so-called logistic equation. Geometry abstracts not only from the motions of this particular heavenly body, but also from the motion of the heavenly bodies in general. It does not attempt to explain their motion. Rather, it considers only the form of the mathematical object traced out by said motion, and its difference from and similarity to other forms. Even a mathematics applied to the heavenly bodies (astronomy) would seek only a formalism describing the motion, and not an explanation of it. Metaphysics, finally, abstracts from matter altogether, considering things that, because they are immaterial, are also changeless and eternal (Aristotle. *Metaphysics* 1025b–1026a).

What this means is that physics, for Aristotle, is fundamentally the science of material systems considered as material or, what is the same thing, it is the science of motion and its causes, course, and effects. As the science of motion, physics attempts to explain how and why motion is possible, in terms of universal, necessary principles. The physicist, for example, wants not merely to describe the laws that govern the heavenly bodies, but to understand why they are in motion, and ultimately why they are, and are as they are in the first place.

These strictures against the conflation of physics with mathematics notwithstanding, Aristotle is critical of philosophers such as Democritus who conceive physics in entirely materialistic terms, the result of which is to reduce change to local motion and to neglect the problem of form entirely (*Physics* 194a). This means that his understanding of form must be rather different from that of the Pythagoreans or of the Plato of the *Timaeus*, and this does in fact, turn out to be the case.

> The form is indeed *physis* (nature) rather than the matter; for a thing is more properly said to be what it is when it has attained to fulfillment than when it exists potentially . . .
>
> We also speak of a thing's nature as being exhibited in the process of growth by which its nature is attained. (*Physics* 193b)

> Again, "that for the sake of which" or the end, belongs to the same department of knowledge as the means. But the nature is the end or "that for the sake of which." For if a thing undergoes a continuous change and there is a stage which is last, this stage is the end or "that for the sake of which." (*Physics* 194a)

What this suggests is that "motion" or "change" for Aristotle is *first and foremost* growth and development, and that this is conceived of as at once the perfection of a form which is latent in something and the realization of the end for which the thing exists. Aware that not everything realizes its latent potential in this way, Aristotle is careful to add that "privation too is in a way form (*Physics* 193b)." If we are to understand the world as it is we must be able to accommodate decay and disintegration as well as growth and development.

From here, Aristotle goes on to treat causation, or that in terms of which motion can be explained. Aristotle distinguishes between

1. material cause, or that out of which something comes to be,
2. its formal cause, which Aristotle identifies with the essence, or what a thing is,
3. the efficient cause, that by which it comes to be, and
4. the final cause, or "that for the sake of which" a thing exists. (Aristotle. *Physics* 194b, *Metaphysics* 988a–b)

A few points of clarification are in order here. First, material cause may be understood either relatively or absolutely. Understood relatively it refers to the already-partially-formed matter that undergoes a change of form or receives still further formation, as when rock becomes molten into lava or an embryo develops into a fully-grown organism. Absolutely speaking, material cause refers to prime matter that, for Aristotle, is merely the possibility of receiving form—it is not itself anything real or actual. In Aristotle's physics, it is, *immediately* at least, the form that actualizes matter and thus brings something into being. Motion for Aristotle is primarily motion from materiality to formality, from potency to act. This motion is driven ultimately, we will see, by the teleological attraction of the unmoved mover which acts, through the medium of the heavenly bodies, to give rise to forms of various kinds in the sublunar realm.

There are, for Aristotle, four primary qualities, hot, cold, dry, and wet which represent the lowest degree of formality of which any physical system is capable. These qualities, in various combinations, in turn yield the four fundamental elements of which everything in the sublunar realm is composed:

1. fire, which is hot and dry,
2. air, which is hot and wet,
3. earth, which is cold and dry, and
4. water, which is cold and wet.

It is the fact that these four fundamental elements are themselves composites, and the all actual physical systems are further composites, which makes it difficult for things to retain their form and which consigns everything in the sublunar realm to eventual decay and disintegration. The heavenly bodies, on the other hand, which do not undergo corruption and which have only a perfect spherical motion are composed of a fifth incorruptible element not composed of contraries, what Aristotle calls "quintessence" (Multhauf 1978, Lindberg 1992: 55).[8]

From here, Aristotle defines a whole hierarchy of degrees of organization. The form of a body he identifies with its "soul" or *psyche*. Things that have the capacity to retain their form have what he calls a mineral soul. Add the capacity for growth, nutrition, and reproduction, and the thing in question acquires a vegetative soul. Animals have the additional capacities of sensation and locomotion—they can, that is, sense material goods and pursue them. Human beings are rational animals that, in addition to sensing and pursuing material goods, are also capable of discerning intelligible goods with the intellect, and of willing them with the intellectual appetite.

At each level of this hierarchy, motion takes place primarily through the acquisition of a new, and generally higher, form. Thus the mineral, in crystallizing, acquires a still higher capacity to hold its form. The plant, in taking in nutrients, is able to grow and realize its latent potential and eventually to reproduce its form through its seeds. The animal, in the act of sensation, actually takes on intentionally, the form of the thing sensed, even if this form is still embedded in an image. The rational animal goes

---

8. It is interesting to note here that Aristotle understands quite well the role of contradiction in change but unlike later dialecticians—Hegel, Marx, Engels, Lenin—he is unable to see how it could lead to the emergence of higher degrees of organization rather than merely degrading existing forms.

further, as the Agent intellect abstracts this form from the image garnered by the senses, so that we actually become the thing known. This is why Aristotle is able to say that the soul is, in a sense, all things (Aristotle. *De Anima* passim). Far from being static, Aristotle's vision was dynamic and progressive, and leaves scope at least for a fully evolutionary theory of cosmic and social development.

The question, of course, is where form—and thus the motion that seeks the perfection of form—comes from in the first place. Interestingly enough, Aristotle only begins to answer this question, in terms of the perfect spherical motion of the heavenly bodies, and only partially draws out the implications of the theory for the entire sublunar realm. Aristotle borrowed the astronomical model of Plato's student Eudoxus, according to which the heavens surrounded the earth in perfect concentric spheres, beginning with the moon and rising through the planets (including the sun) to the heaven of the fixed stars. It is the perfect, spherical motion of these heavens which moves the stars and planets along their changeless paths.

The text in which Aristotle provides his most complete treatment of this question, the *Metaphysics* is notably obscure at this point. In some places Aristotle seems to imply that in order to explain the complex motions of the heavenly bodies, we must posit fully 55 spheres, each with its own unmoved mover (Aristotle. *Metaphysics* 1073a–1074a), which he then goes on to identify with the astral deities of paganism (Aristotle. *Metaphysics* 1074b). Still, Aristotle insists that the whole system is ultimately unified and is driven by a first unmoved mover which is one both in definite and number (Aristotle. *Metaphysics* 1074b).

> It is clear, not only in argument but also in fact, that there is something (i.e. the heavens) which is moved with unceasing and cyclical motion. Consequently, the first heaven must be eternal. There is therefore also something which moves it. And since a moved mover is intermediate, there is, therefore, also an unmoved mover being eternal, primary, and in act. (*Metaphysics* 1072a)

This first unmoved mover, Aristotle argues, if it is truly unmoved,

> must impart movement as do the desirable and the intelligible which impel movement without themselves undergoing movement. But what is primary for desire and for intelligibility is the same; for what is desired is what appears good, and the primary object of rational choice is what is good. (*Metaphysics* 1072a)

It is, in other words, the teleological attractiveness of the unmoved mover, which imparts to the heavens their perfect spherical motion, by inspiring in them a love of its own infinite goodness. Contrary to the claims of Gilson (Gilson 1949) and others, who give form the primacy of place in Aristotle's system, it is actually finalism that is fundamental. To be, for Aristotle, is indeed to have form, but the power to bring into being is first and foremost the power of teleological attraction.

It was an attempt to complete this system by extending teleological causation into the sublunar realm that led to the emergence of astrology and alchemy. It is the attractive, teleological effect of the planets on prime matter which brings into being the four fundamental qualities and which leads them to become combined in the four fundamental elements. This same influence also affects the combination of the elements in the various material substances we encounter in the sublunar world. Aristotle focused mostly on the role of the Sun in this regard, which he regarded as, in effect, "cooking" raw materials in the earth first into minerals and then into plants and animals (McGee 1985: 19). His medieval followers, especially Abumasar, whose *Introduction to the Science of Astrology* became the foundation for the discipline. argued that the planets and the geometric "aspects" or relationships between them played a role as well—adding spices as it were the great stew of the cosmos and modifying the way in which things in various times and places evolved.[9]

Alchemy follows fairly naturally from this doctrine. If the forms of things are ultimately just combinations of four fundamental qualities (hot, cold, dry, and wet), then shouldn't it be possible to change things by heating them, drying them, cooling them, or wetting them? More specifi-

---

9. This focus on cooking as the primal process of cosmogenesis marks the social basis of Aristotelian cosmology. A physician and the son of a physician Aristotle came from the ranks of the artisanate—albeit from its most privileged stratum, serving, like his father before him, the Macedonian royal family. Medicine during this period, and indeed right up through the middle ages, was closely allied with cooking. Health was understood the depend on maintaining the proper balance between the four fundamental qualities—hot, cold wet, and dry. Human were regarded as naturally a little to the warm and moist side. It was the job of the cook to prepare meals which could maintain this balance or if necessary restore it (Laudan 2000: 76–81). This orientation contrasts sharply with the ideologies of the tributary aristocracy which, we have seen, regarded warfare and sacrifice as the foundational cosmic processes.

Just how cosmic cooking is related to the underlying dynamic of teleological attraction is unclear. Perhaps it is ultimately the heat of our desire for God, a desire which is shared in some degree by all forms of matter, which drives the process.

cally, shouldn't it be possible to help along the process by which things evolve towards the perfection of form, thus participating in the creative work of God? This, and not the manufacture of gold, was the true dream of the alchemist, and it is something about which we will have more to say later on.

The result of Aristotle's efforts was the development of a complete, systematic physics, which explained a great deal of the observable universe in terms of a single principle—the power of the unmoved mover, by its incredible attractive power, to draw things from potency into act, to give rise to form, to organization, to finite teleological orderings where before there had been only possibility. This system at once allowed for diverse forms of motion: crystallization, vegetative growth and reproduction, animal sensuality, human intelligence and will, and the perfect spherical motion of the heavenly bodies, while reducing all to one common cause.

Aristotle's system, furthermore, remedied the defects of Plato's Timaean cosmology. Indeed, it is possible to read the *Physics* and the *Metaphysics* as an extension of Plato's doctrine in the *Republic* which makes the Good the principle of all things. In Aristotle's universe it is not only possible to rise to a first principle on the basis of which action can be ordered and judged; this same principle explains how the universe works, why it is they way it is, and gives us some reason to hope that progressive change in possible.

The resulting vision of the universe is governed by what we will call an Aristotelian space-time. In contrast to the later Newtonian space-time with its concept of an absolute and neutral space which is independent of matter, Aristotelian space is a function of the presence of matter. Time, similarly, is simply the measure of motion. The most striking feature of this space-time, however, is its irreducibly axiological character. Motion is either up or down a scale of values which is fixed in reference to God, the first unmoved mover, the Good which draws all things to itself. If the heavenly bodies provide a fitting measure for motion it is not because they constitute a fixed frame of reference on the Newtonian model against which all other motion can be gauged. Rather, it is because they are closer to God and their motion more divine. As we progress towards the Good, after all, we gradually come to rest and the circular motion of the stars and planets is an image of the perfect rest that the Good has in its knowledge of itself. In this way physics provides an infrastructure for the fundamentally metaphysical, ethical, and political project to which

Aristotle had dedicated himself: a critique of the agnosticism of the marketplace with its mechanistic cosmology and its value-neutral science.

The synthesis that Aristotle developed was unable to take hold even, as it turns out, among his own followers. Indeed, the period after the death of Alexander witnessed the global collapse of the whole Socratic project, with both its Platonic and Aristotelian wings largely abandoning the doctrines of their teachers. The Academy under Speusippus drifted back towards Pythagoreanism, increasingly identifying Plato's Forms or Ideas with mathematical objects. Eudoxus established a school at Cyzicus which taught a similar doctrine, but attached to it a hedonistic ethics. Eventually, under Xenocrates, this numerological trend was layered over with a full-blown cult of the stars imported from Babylon. This, in turn, eventually gave way to a radical Skepticism which revived the critical emphasis of the Socratic dialectic but detached it even further from the ethical project of which it had originally been a part (Collins 1998: 100–101). Aristotle's followers, on the other hand, adopted a radical materialism, with Theophrastus, Aristotle's successor at the Lyceum, attacking the doctrine of the Unmoved Mover, and Strato, the third *scholarch*, rejecting teleological explanation altogether in favor of a physics of weight and motion. In this sense they joined the Epicureans, who had elaborated the atomistic doctrines of Democritus, on the empiricist and materialist left.

What is behind this collapse? The answer to this question must be sought in the global political defeat of the whole Socratic project. Both Plato and Aristotle had hoped to significantly transform the πολισ, and pursued a two pronged strategy, establishing schools in Athens where they trained leaders and plotted strategy, while at the same time allying themselves with sympathetic tyrants and monarchs in other cities. In both cases this meant joining forces with antidemocratic elements—in the case of Plato the *rentier* elite of Athens and the other cities where he worked, in the case of Aristotle the tributary dynasts of Macedon who were his family's traditional patrons. It was, of course, the latter who eventually triumphed, establishing a regime which secured the economic interests of the rentierized landed elite by creating a relatively pacified οικομενε in which market forces could operated undisturbed, while dispossessing both them and the popular classes politically. It should not be surprising, under these circumstances, to see the Academy moving sharply to the right, returning first to what amounts to a Neo-Pythagorean position and eventually to an idealist skepticism along the lines of Berkeley and Hume—who, we will argue at length in another context, also represented rentierized landed elites. The vision of a universe dominated by numbers or by stellar deities accessible only by means of a mathematized astronomy, and then only very partially and imperfectly, is a reflex of the market system seen from the standpoint of the *rentier* elite which alone can penetrate the mysteries of the market order, and then only in a partial and incomplete manner. The turn to Skepticism reflects the retreat of this stratum from active participation in public life into private consumption, with an attendant focus on the subjectivity of sensation and perception and a growing recognition of its inability to transcend this position.

Rather more difficult to understand is the turn of the Aristotelians to radical materialism. Randall Collins explains this development in microsociological terms. Platonists and Aristotelians defined themselves in relationship to each other, he argues, a dynamic that pushed each to adopt more radical positions than their founders had held. Another school, meanwhile (the Stoics), took up the philosophical middle ground between idealism and materialism that Aristotle had formerly occupied (Collins 1998: 107–108). While this thesis undoubtedly has some merit, it does not explain the larger context in which this jostling for position took place, and more specifically it does not explain why the Stoics were able to seize the middle ground from the Aristotelians, and why the Aristotelians so willingly yielded it.

In order to make sense out of this situation we need to understand a little bit about Stoicism. The Stoics saw the universe as a material system infused by a rational World Soul or Logos which organized and directed its activity in a more or less deterministic fashion. What this doctrine did was to conserve the Aristotelian distinction between matter and form, and thus Aristotle's "centrism" in the struggle between idealism and materialism, while at the same time eliminating the teleological element that was fundamental to Aristotelian science and metaphysics. This was a reflex of a social order in which people, at least in the larger cities, no longer had a day to day experience of participation in a whole ordered to a common end, and thus were no longer able to think of the universe on this model. Order, rather, came from the outside, from the state, which brought some measure of form to an increasingly chaotic social system governed by the operation of market forces. This identification between the state, at first Republican and later Imperial, on the one hand, and the Logos on the other, actually becomes explicit in Cicero and Marcus Aurelius.

At the same time, the Aristotelian turn towards empiricism and materialism reflects the original social base of the school in the privileged stratum of the artisanate. Its political ambitions defeated this stratum now settles down to focus on the scientific research which can support its principle activity, which is tecnη. Rejection of the doctrine of the unmoved mover reflects this political acquiescence. Without a metaphysical principle to ground it, the dialectical critique of the market order, as well as any potential critique of the Macedonian Empire, cannot stand. At the same time, the Aristotelians resist any impulse to directly or indirectly legitimate the imperial order by adopting something like the Stoic position. In this sense Aristotelianism ceases to be a global ideology and becomes a partial stance proper to a social stratum with no prospects for hegemony.[10]

Eventually, after the Roman conquest, philosophical alignments shift once again. Stoics begin the pick up elements of the discarded Platonic metaphysics and move to an increasingly idealist position. The Academy abandons Skepticism and returns gradually to idealism. At first this meant simply a focus on the capacity of the intellect to make up for the fallibility of the senses. Gradually, however, perhaps as a result or cross fertilization with the Stoics, the intellectual descendants of Plato began once again to regard intellect as the fundamental principle of reality, and began increasingly to see material objects as results of an act of the transcendent intellect. It was at this stage that the idea of the divine *logos*, so important for the later development of Christianity, and which marks the distinctiveness of Middle Platonism, first emerged. Eventually this vision of the universe as product of the acts of the divine intellect gave way to an emmanationist cosmology quite different from that originally advocated by Plato. According to this view the material universe is neither drawn out of prime matter by teleological attraction, nor imposed on it by a Demiurge following a kind of perfect pattern of creation but, rather, emerges out of the first principle, eventually identified by Plotinus as the One, through a process which was sometimes understood as a kind of rationally necessary differentiation and sometimes as a kind of cosmic fall

---

10. The distinction between global and partial stances is due to Antonio Gramsci, who distinguished between fundamental classes which are able to offer a global vision for the reorganization of human society, and are thus able to mount a credible contest for hegemony, and nonfundamental classes, which develop political and ideological forms which simply advance their interests within the context of existing social structures and existing class alliances (Gramsci 1949b).

into plurality and finitude. Humanity's task is, by one means or another, to recover our lost divinity and return to the One from whence we came (Collins 1998: 109–33).

The means of this return are important. Neoplatonism, as the doctrine came to be called, was associated, sometimes loosely and sometimes very closely, with the mystery cults that revived and at least partially rationalized the old pagan religions of the Mediterranean Basin. Of particular interest to us, however, is the association between Neoplatonism and the Hermetic tradition—a group of texts, believed at the time to have come from Egypt, which purported to disclose the "secrets of nature." At issue here was a mixture of purely practical techniques for preparing medicines, perfumes, metals, jewelry, ceramics, etc. with what is generally called theurgic magic, i.e., magic which attempts to release the latent divinity present within each person. Sometimes the line between the two types of tecnη is difficult to define. Consider for example the attempt to produce an incorruptible substance, generally identified as the quintessence, or fifth substance, of which the heavenly bodies were composed, or to prepare an elixir which might confer immortality. Is this metallurgy and medicine or theurgic magic? The answer, of course, is that it is both.

These texts were, variously, regarded as gifts of the god Hermes or Mercury or as the esoteric teachings of Aristotle, who shared this knowledge only with those who had undergone the intellectual and moral formation necessary to insure that it would not be abused for profit or power. In either case, they represent the realignment of the high order tecnη cultivated above all in Aristotelian circles with the religious idealism of the Platonists. Aristotelian philosophy more or less disappears during this period as an independent force, but Aristotelian concepts are increasingly appropriated by Neoplatonists. If emanation is the underlying creative process, teleological attraction—the incredible Beauty of God—is nonetheless the motor of salvation.

What was the social basis and political valence of this trend? On the one hand, it there can be little doubt that Neo-Platonism played a central role in the legitimation strategy of the late Empire. The notion that all order—indeed Being itself—comes from on high, coupled with the ornate hierarchical schemes worked out by Neo-Platonic philosophers are a more or less transparent reflection of the structure of Imperial society after the reforms of Diocletian. And Neo-Platonism played a role both in efforts to shore up the old Pagan religion as a means of legitimation and then to replace it with Christianity when it became apparent that it could no longer carry out this function. At the same time, we must remember that the Empire was not the only or indeed the principal exploitative institution in this period. Rather, it had grown up as a means of securing a kind of "free trade zone" in which commerce could proceed unimpeded and the large producers of grain, oil, and wine who at least initially controlled the system could expand their margin of profit. It was only gradually that the Empire took on the trappings of a fully developed tributary state, and even then it served as a means of upward mobility for those who entered its service. Pagan restorationism, with which Neo-Platonism was closely connected, had a significant, if far from revolutionary, social reform agenda. Recognizing that they needed to re-ignite faith in the human civilizational project if they were to face down the Christian challenge, under Julian the Apostate the pagan party simultaneously carried out significant land reforms, canceled debts, and reduced taxes, while investing significant resources in promoting Neo-Platonic philosophy and reforming the pagan priesthood (Collins 1998: 199–33, Rubenstein 1999: 194–210). The Hermetic element in the tradition, furthermore, reflects the artisanal character of Aristotelian philosophy, even if it has also undergone transformation in an aristocratic and priestly direction. It would probably be most accurate to say that Neo-Platonism reflects the historic commitment of the dialectical tradition to resistance to the market order, as well as its alliance in this struggle with patriarchal and tributary elements, but that these latter elements have in fact become dominant in a way they were not in the philosophy of Plato and Aristotle themselves.

It is necessary in order to understand this period to consider as well the influence of the prophetic religions—Judaism, Christianity, and (towards the end of the period) of Islam on the development of cosmological thinking. Here as well the impact is complex and contradictory. On the one hand, all three traditions shared a commitment (stronger in Christianity than in the other religions) to the doctrine of creation *ex nihilo*, something which tended to promote a view of the universe as dead matter which is radically dependent on God, and to undermine any sense of natural teleological ordering. This is particularly evident in the work of Augustine, who developed the doctrine of the *rationes seminales* to explain how growth and development and even evolution can occur without recourse to either spontaneous self-organization or teleological attraction. According to this doctrine, when God created the universe, he planted in matter the seeds of all the many forms of organization which he intended to bring into being. It is the growth of these seeds planted by God, and not anything in matter itself, which drives development. At the same time, the doctrine of creation implied, against the more otherworldly forms of Gnosticism and Neo-Platonism, that the material universe must in some sense be good and not merely the consequence of a fall. This sense of the radical goodness of matter was most fully developed in Judaism and Islam. Philo of Alexandria, for example, drawing on a mixture of Jewish, Stoic, and Middle Platonic ideas, argued that the ideas, or the forms of things, exist in the mind of God as a kind of intelligible world. In their latent form Philo called these ideas σοφια or the divine wisdom. In their active, creative form, they became the λογος, the word through which all things came into being. Unlike the Hellenic tradition, however, Philo rejects the eternity of matter, and teaches that matter itself was the product of divine creative activity. Thus, while he retains the form/matter dualism that is characteristic of philosophy in all pre-industrial societies he takes an important step towards the recognition of the material world as a realization of, rather than a falling away from, the divine will.

According to Philo, the Law of Moses is nothing other than the law of the cosmos itself, fully accessible to reason and binding on all humanity. On this basis, Philo develops a harmonizing ethics which integrates Jewish and Greek elements, arguing that authentic freedom consists not in citizenship in Rome or some reconstituted Greek city state, but rather in service to the one true God who alone is authentically self-existent. It is the Jews, who know and follow this law, and not the Greeks and Romans, with their devotion to wealth and earthly political power who are the true cosmopolitans. Knowledge of the law flows out from the Jews to the other peoples of the earth who will eventually be united as in a single city, under the one law of the living God.

The movement to rehabilitate matter from Neo-Platonic otherworldliness was not limited to Judaism. Islam, at times at least, actually saw itself as bringing into being a universal just social order which was subject to divine law. And even Christianity made some contribution to the cause of matter. The doctrine of the resurrection of the body, when it was not eclipsed by the hope of eternity in an immaterial heaven, implies that it is in fact better, at least for human beings, to be with a body than to be without one, even after they have been afforded a direct vision of the essence of God.

Coupled with this sense that the material universe has a real value and purpose came a growing recognition of the ultimate meaningfulness of human history. This insight also came from Judaism, with its potent sense of movement from past oppression to future liberation. Christianity was far more circumspect in this regard but even the pessimistic Augustinian vision presents history as a battleground between good and evil, something which invests history with meaning even as it argues that salvation is radically otherworldly.

On the whole, however, the social dynamics of the Hellenistic and Roman periods could not sustain a progressivist cosmology. On the contrary, the overwhelming stagnation of the period, a result of the combined action of market forces and the widespread dependence of chattel slavery, tended to promote cosmological pessimism and otherworldliness. This was only accentuated as the system moved towards crisis and the Empire collapsed throughout the West and yielded to Islam in much of the East. It would be in the new civilizations that grew up in Northwestern Europe and in the Islamic lands that the full potential of the Aristotelian vision would come closest to being realized.

It is among the foundational myths of the "modern" era that the middle ages were a period of backwardness and stagnation in which brutal warlords ran roughshod over dependent peasant communities, which they subjected to the most intense forms of exploitation, and that this whole system was shored up by a Catholic Church which legitimated feudal power both directly, by helping to sacralize it and indirectly by focusing the attention of the people on otherworldly redemption, all the while fighting tooth and nail to contain the development of both rational criticism and empirical research which it saw as a threat to its ideological monopoly. Such a view of the middle ages is, to be sure, no longer given serious credence by historians, who recognize both the complexity and internal diversity of medieval society and its enormous creativity, at least in certain times and places. But it continues to affect assessments of the period even where this creativity is recognized. Nowhere is this more apparent than in recent Marxist analyses, which attempt to explain the rapid progress of Europe during the middle ages largely in terms of the fragmented character of the ruling class and the incomplete character of the tributary state which they were in the process of building (Amin 1979/1980). By the time this state was complete in the seventeenth or eighteenth century, "feudalism" was already giving way to the early stages of capitalist development, and the absolutist state was either quickly overthrown or gradually transformed into an instrument of specifically capitalist interests (Anderson 1974b).

This analysis of "feudalism" as an immature variant on the tributary mode of exploitation, first advanced by Samir Amin (Amin 1980) is fundamentally correct. Under feudalism, as under other variants of the tributary mode, warlords exploit peasants through rents, taxes, and/or forced labor. The difference is the fragmented and decentralized character of the system, in which a centralized tributary apparatus presided over by a full-fledged sacral king has not yet emerged. What is not correct is the claim that medieval Europe was exclusively or principally feudal. On the contrary, feudal institutions co-existed and sometimes competed with other forms of organization which are best described as neo-archaic and protosocialist.

We will recall that by archaic social formations we mean those in which a groups of villages cluster around a temple complex to which they voluntarily contribute a part of their surplus product in order to support the priests of the place who in turn provide to them services which promote the development of human capacities, both by opening a window on the divine, and by improving knowledge of the motion of the heavenly bodies, the action of various roots and herbs, etc., which help advance technical progress and expand agrarian production. Archaic societies seem to have yielded to tributary societies soon after the development of metal weaponry, but there is some evidence for such systems at places like Cattal Huyuk and Chaco Canyon. The memory of such societies is also very powerful, and is reflected in the stories about Atlantis and other myths of a "golden age." The political project of Plato and Aristotle is best described as neoarchaic in so far as it aimed at restoring this golden age by returning to power those who were intellectually and morally most advanced.

The neoarchaic element in medieval society is, of course, provided by the Church and especially by the monastic movement which played such an important role in the economic development of parts of Northwestern Europe. Surplus extraction on monastery lands was at least partly noncoercive, based on the social prestige of the monks, and was used largely in ways which helped to advance the human civilizational project, by conserving ancient learning and helping to develop new agricultural and other techniques. That many of the monasteries were corrupt and infected by a degree of luxury consumption contrary to their mission does not alter the fact that the structure itself cannot properly be described as feudal or tributary—any more than the existence of a few philanthropists in the ranks of the bourgeoisie renders capitalism as a system nonexploitative or progressive.

The protosocialist element in the system was provided by the guilds, which were organizations of skilled workers, including both artisans and intellectuals, which regulated training, standards, and prices and which in many cities actually came to power in the twelfth and thirteenth century, albeit generally under the overall rule of a bishop or feudal lord, or in some cases of the Holy Roman Emperor.

Amin and Anderson are quite correct that the break-up of the Roman Empire unleashed new possibilities for social progress in Europe, because it led to a fragmentation of the ruling class and that the Church contributed to this process in part, at least, by stalemating the drive towards unification of the system by the Holy Roman Empire. What they miss, however, is that progress requires not just reduced exploitation but also institutions which can centralize resources and invest them in a way which actually encourages human development. What the fragmentation of authority during the so-called Dark Ages allowed was not just the formation of a more prosperous peasantry with more incentive to produce and innovate but also the development of new forms of organization—the monastery and the guild—which could channel surplus in a productive way. The result was the first significant period of technical innovation since the development of iron technology and advent of specialized agriculture in the period between 1000 and 700 BCE. The three field system, new kinds of plows better suited to northern and alpine climates, and the increased use of water and animal power all served to increase productivity as agrarian yields jumped from 4:1, where they had been for more than 1500 years, to 9:1.

This complex of fragmented tributary structures combined with protosocialist and neoarchaic elements created some unusual ideological dynamics. On the one hand, as the pace of technological innovation quickened and productivity increased human beings began, perhaps for the first time in more than a millennium, to regard their own labor as a significant force in the universe and a real participation in the life of God. This was reflected both in the neoarchaic monastic economy, as Benedictine theologians developed a sophisticated theology of work—

including manual labor—which treated it as a form of prayer, and in the cities, where progress in handicrafts and the growing power of the guilds created a basis in experience for a more optimistic cosmology. On the other hand, the feudal element in the social formation was very real and people conserved a powerful sense of the underlying lawlessness of the universe generally and of human society in particular—an outlook which did much to encourage the persistence of pessimistic Augustinian ideas. And even as production expanded and social progress resumed, market forces began to regain their strength, spontaneously reproducing the ideological trends which we have already noted everywhere accompany the development of commodity production: mathematical formalism and atomistic empiricism.

The Catholic hierarchy occupied an ambiguous position in this larger complex. On the one hand, they benefited by comparison with the secular warlords and, at least in the West, had encouraged the Augustinian political theology which regards all purely secular power as little more than rape and plunder. It was only the ordering of the secular lords to the hierarchy, or rather their anointing by the hierarchy, which could confer on them even a semblance of legitimacy. On the other hand, this political theology severely restricted the scope of clerical intervention into the secular arena. Lawless warlords could hardly be expected to become agents of the Common Good, and as civilizational progress resumed, forward thinking hierarchs such as Gregory VII and Innocent the III began to envision a much larger role for the Church in the public arena. It is thus not surprising that some of them began to turn towards Aristotle, who had seen the poliς as a school of virtue, in their search for a theology that might help them to theorize the role of the Church in a period of rapid civilizational progress. Still, anything which suggested that the universe generally, and human beings in particular, were *naturally* ordered to God, threatened to call into question the very necessity of the hierarchy and its sacramental system . . .

The social and ideological dynamics of the Islamic empires were rather different. The social formations which came into being as a result of the Arab conquest of an enormous empire reaching from Spain to Persia and eventually to India were, in fact, tributary empires which extracted rents, taxes, and forced labor from dependent peasant communities. They differed, however, from other empires in their characteristically lower rates of taxation and the much greater scope their afforded for the artisans, intellectuals, and the petty bourgeoisie. Many Islamic rulers invested heavily in the arts, sciences, and philosophy and the Islamic capitals rapidly emerged as important centers of learning. The result was, as in Europe but perhaps even more markedly so, a tremendous optimism regarding the universe and human civilization, something which was reinforced by Islamic doctrine generally which, we have seen, focused attention on the task of realizing God's will on earth rather than on otherworldly salvation. This was a favorable environment for Aristotelian science, and indeed the environment in which it would find its most radical formulations. At the same time, the Islamic rulers and the Islamic clergy were not at all immune to the concerns which affected their Christian counterparts. If the world is naturally ordered to God, then it needs not nearly so much external direction, secular or clerical, as would otherwise be the case. Powerful tendencies in Islam stressed the absolute, arbitrary sovereignty of God, a reflex of the sovereignty of the caliphs and sultans who had come to power as military commanders, and were suspicious of Aristotelian doctrines which might call this into question.

It was in these contexts that Aristotelian science experienced a resurgence, and finally achieved its most complete expression, serving as the ideology of a rising class of urban artisans and intellectuals who were (along side the monks and peasants in the countryside) the principal carriers of civilizational progress during this period. This development was driven by a number of debates, some of which reflected internal difficulties or ambiguities in the work of Aristotle himself, others of which reflected a need to integrate Aristotelian philosophy with Christian doctrine or the developing struggle between the Aristotelian and Augustinian parties. The issues addressed in this period included:

- a cluster of issues related to the origin and end of the world, its perfection and corruptibility, which brought to the fore the tension between the Aristotelian doctrine of the eternity of the world and the Christian doctrine of creation *ex nihilo*,
- a cluster of issues related to the nature and structure of the heavens, including what they are made of, the number and nature of the celestial orbs, the role of angels, intelligences, and the Unmoved Mover, together with the vitally important question of whether or not the heavens can be said to be alive,

- questions related to celestial influence and the possibility of alchemical transformations, brought to the fore by the incorporation of the Hermetic tradition into the larger body of Aristotelian science,
- the question of the Agent Intellect, the power by which we abstract the intelligible essence of things from the images we form of them based on sense experience, and
- a cluster of issues forced by Augustinian defenders of arbitrary divine sovereignty, including the question of whether or not the universe can be moved rectilinearly and whether or not God could have created other worlds.

The most serious question that divided Aristotelian and Augustinian philosophy concerned the origin and age of the universe. Aristotle had taught that the universe is eternal, something which follows from his underlying cosmology and metaphysics which see the universe as drawn into being by the attractive power of God. If God is eternal, then so is the universe, which arises naturally as a necessary result of the existence of God. Indeed, the pull within Aristotelian science was towards a sort of panentheism, as followers of the great commentator Ibn Rusd argued that God is the formal cause of the universe or even is material cause, as well as its αρχη and τελος.

These claims contradicted, of course, the manifest sense of the Jewish, Christian, and Islamic scriptures as well as a long tradition of reasoning regarding the origin of the universe and the existence of God which had grown up independently in Judaism and Islam, more or less independent of Greek philosophy —the so called *kalam* (Collins 1998: 395–401). This tradition argued for the existence of God from the principle of efficient causation, reasoning that everything, in order to come into being must have some antecedent cause. But an infinite regress of causes is rationally abhorrent, since without some first cause none of the other links in the causal chain would have been possible. In the *kalam* tradition the order of causation is understood as temporal rather than as merely logical, as it is in the Thomistic version of this proof (Thomas. *Summa Theologiae* I.1.3). The implication is not only that there must be a first efficient cause, but that the universe is temporally finite and began with a divine creative act.

As Maimonides, Thomas, and others showed, this argument was far from conclusive.

> the efficient cause which acts by motion ... of necessity precedes its effect in time.... But if the action is instantaneous and not successive, it is not necessary for the maker to be prior to the thing made in duration.... Hence ... it does not follow necessarily that if God is the active cause of the world, that He should be prior to the world in duration, because creation, by which He produced the world, is not a successive change.... (Thomas *Summa Theologiae* I.46.2)

At the same time, they insisted, Aristotle's arguments and those of his Arabic commentators, were no more conclusive. Thomas argued that God brought the world into being through an act of will, and that

> in agents acting by will, what is conceived and preordained is taken as the form, which is the principle of action. Therefore from the eternal action of God an eternal effect does not follow, but such an effect as God willed, an effect that is which has being after not being. (Thomas *Summa Theologiae* I.46.1)

> It was possible, of course, for God to have willed the universe to exist from all eternity. The will of God, except where it was constrained by logical necessity, could be known only through revelation, and the creation of the universe *ex nihilo* was an article of faith and not a conclusion of philosophy. (Thomas *Summa Theologiae* I.46.2)

Thomas' rather inelegant solution to the cosmological question was bound up with a radical innovation in the sphere of metaphysics—namely a distinction between the essence of a thing and its act of existence. This allowed him to avoid the pull within Radical Aristotelianism towards thinking of God as either the material or formal cause of the universe and thus towards a materialist or spiritualist pantheism. God is the power of Being itself, from whom all finite systems derive their power of being as well as their particular form or essence. God is thus radically transcendent, though all things participate in His Being to the extent and in the specific way that their essence permits. Divine creative activity is nothing other than a sharing of the divine Being with the creature, In so far as Thomas recognizes the convertibility of Being with the Beautiful, the True, the Good, and the One, this strategy is not incompatible with Aristotelian finalism, but it does open itself to other interpretations as well.

The result was a rather muddled cosmogony in which an Augustinian doctrine of creation by divine will was grafted onto Aristotelian stock. Two different theories of causality operated alongside each other, without any real attempt to address the tension between them or to argue that superior explanatory power compensated for the resulting loss of economy. This situation was not really satisfactory to either side. Averroists continued to argue that reason was on the side of the eternity of the world while Augustinians magnified still further the role of the divine will, developing further Augustine's doctrine of the *rationes seminales*, with the explicit aim of reducing the role of secondary causes in the operation of the universe.

The struggle between Radical Aristotelians and Augustinians extended as well into the debates over the nature and structure of the heavens. Aristotle first advanced the idea that there were in fact orbs which account for each motion of the heavenly bodies, transforming the mathematical model of Eudoxus into a physical one. His model included some 55 such orbs. By the middle ages, drawing on the work of Ptolemy and others, astronomers had adopted a rather different model, assigning one orb to each of the planets, including the sun, and then adding eccentrics and epicycles to account for the full complexity of celestial motion. They also generally added at least two more orbs to account for the daily motion of the stars, the procession of the equinoxes, and the progressive and regressive motion of the stars, an approach suggested by the Arab astronomer Thabit ibn Qura in the ninth century (Grant 1996: 280–81, 315, Duhem 1913–1959: 3:404). Christians also generally added an immobile orb, the Empyrean heaven, outside of space and time, which was the true abode of God and the blessed (Grant 1996: 372ff.). Thus the vision of the heavens popularized by Dante in the *Commedia*.

Aristotle, we will remember, had argued that the spheres and the heavenly bodies they carried were made of a fifth incorruptible element—the quintessence—and that each sphere or orb had its own intelligence, which he identified with the astral deities of Greece and the surrounding societies. Jewish, Christian, and Islamic commentators and scientists identified these intelligences with the angels mentioned in the scriptures, continuing a tradition which was already well established in both the Neo-Platonic and Jewish mystical traditions. Radical Aristotelians, following Ibn Sina, tended to regard the intelligences as joined to their orbs as soul to body, and to regard each sphere, or even the heavens as a whole, as living organism—as in fact a perfect animal (Grant 1996: 427). This was, indeed, the only tenable view once one assumed an Aristotelian cosmology and metaphysics, in which all motion is ultimately driven by the love of God. The spheres move because, with the direct, intellectual intuition which characterizes the angelic intellect, they have a vision of the divine nature and seek to emulate it with their perfect, regular, spherical motion. The higher the sphere the closer its intelligence is to the divine, the more perfect its love, and the more divine its motion.

Augustinians found this view abhorrent because it tended to sacralize the created universe, tended toward pantheism or polytheism, and seemed to diminish divine sovereignty. They could not entirely extricate themselves from the underlying cosmological models, but insisted that the spheres themselves were in no sense alive and that the intelligences were not their souls—a position formally defined by the Condemnations of 1277. Thomas' position, that it is indeed separate intelligences that move the heavens but that they do so only by virtual contact with them, and not as a soul moves its body (Grant 1996: 475–76), seems also to have been condemned, when Stephen Tempier also rejected the view that the angels move the spheres by will alone (Grant 1996: 529). The result was a tendency was to see the heavens as moved by some kind of impressed force, and to stress the direct involvement of God in moving them (Grant 1996: 533). Augustinians in particular, as we will see, emphasized that God could, in fact, move the heavens in whatever manner he pleased, something which contributed in no small measure to the development of a purely mechanistic physics.

Closely related to the question of the structure of the heavens was the question of celestial influence. We have seen that Aristotle laid the groundwork for the disciplines of astrology and alchemy by arguing that it was the influence of the heavenly bodies, especially the Sun, which set in motion changes in the sublunar regions. This was merely an inference from the obvious role of the Sun in producing meteorological changes or in promoting the growth of plants and thus indirectly of animals, or of the moon in producing tides. Gradually incorporating the Hermetic disciplines into the larger body of Aristotelian science, medieval thinkers associated each heavenly body with a particular influence. Saturn was associated with the element earth, the Moon with water, Mercury with air, and Mars with fire. The sun was said to produce gold, the moon silver, Mercury the metal of the same name, Venus copper, Mars iron, Jupiter tin, and Saturn lead. The influence of Mars was said to produce yellow bile, Saturn black bile, the Moon phlegm, and the Sun and Jupiter blood. And acting through these humors, which were thought to govern the activity of the body, the planets influenced body type and physical disposition, including our passions, which in turn affected the conditions under which our intellect and will developed (Grant 1996: 573–77).

It must be pointed out that this sort to astrological speculation did no more to compromise freedom of the will than does belief in the force of gravity today. Astrological influences were considered physical forces that apply external constraints, working through the mediation of physical substances such as bodily humors. Those which affect the passions might make it more difficult to do certain things and easier to do others, much the way a certain balance of hormones or neurotransmitters might be thought to affect human action and human development today. But the underlying capacity of the intellect to know the good, and of the intellectual appetite to will it, remains. This, at least, was the opinion of most Aristotelians, and plays a central role, for example, Dante's vision in the *Commedia*, where astrological factors affect the physical dispositions of individuals while leaving the intellect and will free and capable of rising above material constraint (Dante, *Commedia* III.2, 4; Sinclair 1939: III: 43–46, 69–72).

> With in the heaven of the divine peace spins a body in whose virtue lies the being of all that it contains; the next heaven, which has so many sights, distributes that being among different existences, distinct from it and contained in it; the other spheres, by various differences, direct the distinctive qualities which they have in themselves to their ends and fruitful working. These organs of the universe proceed thus, as though seest now, grade by grade, each receiving from above and operating below. Observe well now how I pass by this way to the thought thou seekest, so that then though mayest know how to take the road alone. The motion and the virtue of the holy wheels must derive from the blessed movers, as the craft of the hammer from the smith; and the heaven that so many lights make fair takes its stamp from the profound mind that turns it, and of that stamp becomes itself the seal; and as the soul within your dust is diffused through different members that are adapted to various faculties, so the Intelligence unfolds its bounty, multiplied through the stars, intellect wheeling on its own unity. Diverse virtue makes diverse alloy with the precious body which it quickens and with which, even as life in you, it is bound, but the

joyous nature when it springs the mingled virtue shines through the body as joy through the living pupil. (Dante *Commedia* III.2)

Alchemy is nothing more or less than an attempt to understand and reproduce the process by which the heavenly bodies exercise their influence so as to be able to produce changes in material systems. In this sense alchemy is more *techne* than science, and in some ways it is the very prototype for the sort of *techne* that we today call technology, i.e., a *techne* based on a scientific understanding of how natural process work, as opposed to arts which have developed on the basis of a purely empirical lore uninformed by any explanatory-deductive theory. What sets alchemy part from modern technology, however, is not simply a different understanding of particular natural processes, but rather the larger teleological system in which it understood its activity to be situated. As James Elkins points out

> Alchemy rehearses and often speeds up process that the earth does naturally by brewing metals underground. The work was God's and it was the ongoing perfection of the world. (Elkins 1999: 73)

The drive to produce gold, with which alchemy is traditionally associated, while it was certainly not unaffected by the promise of material gain for those who might succeed, was in reality simply a part of this drive towards perfection, gold being regarded as more perfect than the other metals in virtue of its relative immunity to corrosion or other corruption. The real aim of most scholarly alchemists was to create the Philosopher's Stone,

> a certain pure matter which, being discovered and brought by Art to perfection, converts to itself proportionally all imperfect bodies that it touches. (Arnold of Villanova in Read 1957: 28)

From the Philosopher's Stone could be prepared the Elixir of Life, which conferred on those who partook of it true immortality and incorruptibility.

The Philosopher's Stone was, according to most alchemists, widely diffused throughout the natural world, and was present in greater concentration in those substances that were less corruptible. The task of the "Great Work" was simply to purify ordinary matter in order to obtain a sufficient quantity of it. In doing this, alchemists began with materials were themselves relatively incorruptible, such as gold and silver. These were placed in a sealed pear-shaped vessel known as the Philosopher's

Egg and subjected to various processes which were intended to purify them, resulting first in sophic sulfur and mercury (not to be confused with the modern chemical elements of the same name), and eventually the Stone itself. These processes included many, such as calcination or heating in air, solution, distillation, and sublimation which continue to play a significant role in contemporary chemistry. Others, such as fermentation and "mortification" or "putrefaction" are today applied only to organic matter, but were seen by the alchemists to operate on mineral as well as plant or animal species. The mortification of a metal generally meant its oxidation, something that was necessary in order for its "seed" to germinate. The process could be reversed by reduction, something that was said to produce the "resurrection" of the substance in question. Most of these processes involved the application or withdrawal of heat or the addition or removal of water, thus changing the balance of the four primary qualities, hot, cold, wet, and dry. Often alchemical processes were seen as corresponding to and accentuating the influence of a particular planet and were best carried out only when that planet's influence was strong. Some alchemists also believed that music could help their work along. No manner of technical skill was, however, sufficient, if the operator himself was not of pure heart. The alchemist had to be a just man and a man of prayer if he hoped to succeed at all in the perfection of the material universe (Read 1961: 28–40).

This brings us, of course, to the reason why astrology and alchemy were long held in suspicion by the religious authorities. The image of the alchemist that has come down to us is heavily mediated by the legend of Faust, based on an historical practitioner of the hermetic arts who was said to have cut a deal with the devil in order to advance his own quest for knowledge. In the original Lutheran version of the story—the version that still exercises the greatest influence over the popular mind—Faust is eventually damned. Thus the title of one early edition:

> The History of Doctor Johann Faustus the notorious magician and necromancer, how he sold himself to the devil for an appointed time, what strange adventures he saw meanwhile, bringing about some and living through others, until at last he received his well deserved wages. For the greater part collected and prepared for the printer out of his own posthumous writings as a horrible precedent, abominable example and sincere warning to all conceited, inquisitive and godless persons. (in Watt 1996: 19)

Faust represents everything which the Reformation eventually rejected: the struggle of humanity to achieve salvation under its own power, by cultivation of the intellect and the will, and if need by the manipulation of the physical universe in order to allow the time necessary for mind the complete its long journey towards God.

Catholic attitudes towards the hermetic disciplines were more complex and varied. Albertus Magnus had a significant interest in the subject, and regarded it as well founded in the principles of Aristotelian science, but was suspicious about the possibility of transmuting metals—as he was about the possibility of casting horoscopes sufficiently accurate to provide real guidance for decision-making. Augustinians, on the other hand, tended to be more skeptical. At issue here was the very real danger that the alchemists, if successful, could obviate the need for the priestly hierarchy and the sacramental system, and indeed for the whole of salvation history. Thomas himself held that had we an infinite period of time we could in fact advance to knowledge of God, including knowledge of the divine essence, on our own power. This is, of course, just precisely what alchemy, in its search for incorruptibility and immortality, sought to provide us, and it was something even Catholic Augustinians regarded as demonic.

We are faced here with two opposing visions of sin and salvation. On the one side, the Aristotelians argue that human beings grow towards God through knowledge, and that sin is largely a result of ignorance or of habituation to acts formed in ignorance. Anything that advances the cause of knowledge also advances the cause of redemption. The Augustinians, on the other hand, believed that it was just precisely human grasping at the divine, of which alchemy was a typical example, which lay at the root of sin. It was only by abandoning the struggle to become like God under our own power, and by turning in humility towards the crucified savior, that we could ever hope for redemption. Each vision of salvation is sustained by its own distinctive cosmology. On the one side we have the Aristotelian vision of a universe drawn into being by the attractive power of God, in which every partial system struggles towards God to the full extent of its ability. Understanding how this process of development works allows us to participate in advancing it and thus hastens our own journey towards God. On the other side we have the Augustinian vision, which was increasingly a vision of a purely mechanical universe composed of dead matter created and sustained by God and subject to arbitrary divine intervention. The political valence of each of these lines is not hard to work out. On the one side we have the friends of human development, who see spirituality as merely an extension of human moral and intellectual development generally. On the other side, we have the friends of reaction who counsel submission to the authorities who represent the crucified messiah—and the warlords who now rule in his name.

The fourth great issue that divided the Aristotelians from Augustinian orthodoxy was the question of the Agent Intellect. Augustine had taught that while we know sensible things by means of the senses, that we know intelligibles, including both mathematicals and natural and revealed truth about God by means of divine illumination. This had the effect of undermining the distinction between natural and revealed knowledge and making all knowledge quasi-revealed—an implication which was drawn out fully only by the Traditionalists of the eighteenth and nineteenth centuries and certain extreme advocates of Reformed epistemology, such as Dooyeweerd. Closely associated with this was a tendency to distinguish radically between the body and the rational soul, which was supposed to be capable of existing separately from the body and by its very nature partook more fully of the divine. Any tendency of this doctrine to "divinize" human faculties, however, was mitigated by the central importance which Augustinians assigned to the will, so that it was regarded as quite possible to know a higher Good and still turn away from it. Indeed, once human beings had turned from God in original sin, it became quite impossible for them to return without the assistance of divine grace. The net effect was to make human beings mere objects of divine action, holding them accountable for their divergence from the divine will while denying any autonomous intellectual or moral movement towards God.

The Aristotelian approach to the problem was very different. Aristotle taught that the soul was the form of the body, but also that intelligible, immaterial truths could be known only by an immaterial principle. This implied that there had to be such a principle involved in human knowledge. At the same time, it is matter that is the principle of individuation for Aristotle. Immaterial principles differ only in kind, not in number, so that there can be only one such principle for all of humanity. Some commentators, such as Ibn Sina, allowed the existence of an individual "potential intellect" which receives the forms abstracted by the single Agent Intellect, which functions in effect as the lowest member of an angelic hierarchy of finite but immaterial substances. Others, such as

Ibn Rushd and his Latin followers, insisted that the potential intellect as well was one, so that human beings functioned, in effect, as data collectors for the single human intellect. We have different ideas simply because our internal senses register different images based on differing sensory experience.

Claims regarding the unity of the human intellect were problematic for two reasons. First of all, they made it difficult to theorize personal immortality. There was no difficulty in regarding the intellect as immortal, because it was immaterial, but there was only one intellect. After death the human animal souls that had been joined to it simply died and other "data collectors" replaced them. Clearly this was in conflict with Christian doctrine. Second, the doctrine conflicted with psychological experience. We do not merely experience ourselves sensing, but actually think individually, something that Averroist doctrine in particular seems to rule out.

Situated in the larger context of Aristotelian cosmology and metaphysics, furthermore, monopsychism tended to undermine serious Christian claims regarding the transcendental aim of human life. Medieval Aristotelianism presented the universe as an organized, teleological system in which everything is, in a sense ordered toward God, which draws things from the pure potency of matter in to act. But each thing is ordered to God in a different way, corresponding to its nature. In one sense Aristotelianism seemed to exalt humanity by comparison with the Augustinian orthodoxy, by endowing it with an autonomous ordering to God which was not dependent on revelation or grace, and which therefore had no need of the clerical hierarchy. On the other hand, the possibility of knowing and loving God in essence seems to be excluded. Human beings are "just a little lower than the angels," and will remain there, unable to transcend their finitude.

The effect of this sort of doctrine is to focus energy on the human civilizational project—on technology and institution building, and on the fine arts, the sciences, and philosophy. The highest human authorities are the state, which in the Middle Ages meant the Emperor, and the Philosopher who guides him in the paths of wisdom and justice. The task of the state is to create the conditions for the fully development of human capacities. The actual work of developing human capacities, meanwhile was entrusted to the new institution of the guilds, which cultivated the arts and sciences and which, increasingly, played the leading role in governing the emerging urban communes. Indeed, the "*Universitas*" was simply the chief of these guilds which taught the liberal arts which were necessary for making arguments about the Beautiful, the True, the Good, and the One, and thus for the governance of the state. Religion, in this context, is reduce to a sort of "philosophy for the masses" which presents roughly the same truths as philosophy, but in imaginative form, which at once makes it more accessible but also introduces inevitable distortions. The clergy are reduced to the status of second-rate, ersatz philosophers whose activities serve, and must be regulated by, the state.[11]

There were, to be sure, ways around this impasse. The most important were those offered by Thomas Aquinas and Dante Alighieri. Thomas's approach to the problem depends on the metaphysical innovation we noted above, which distinguishes the act of being from the essence or formal cause of a thing. While Thomas never explicitly breaks the Aristotelian teaching that matter is the principle of individuation, which continues to affect his angelology, his anthropology generally and his psychology in particular build on the notion that human beings are composites not

---

11. This, at least, is the political-theological valence of Radical Aristotelianism as it was understood by its Augustinian critics and as it has been understood by most commentators. It is probably a fairly accurate picture of the direction in which urban Radical Aristotelianism was headed by the end of the thirteenth century. It must be noted, however, that Latin Averroism had a profound relationship with two trends that, while not Christian, cannot be properly regarded as secular. The doctrines of Amalric of Bena, which held that God is the form of the universe, and which implicitly made knowledge of the divine form accessible to human reason through the medium of the sciences, inspired a radically anticlerical but powerfully religious movement which, rather like Joachism, taught the advent of a new knowledge of God *in plenitudo intellectus*, without mediation of revelation or the clergy. The doctrines of David of Dinant, whose name suggests that he came from Dinant in Belgium, an ancient sanctuary of the Goddess, suggest a way of thinking about God that is deeply connected with this cult. The word *materia*, we should remember, derives from the word *mater*, or mother. Understanding God as prime matter is understanding God as the mother of all things, the womb out of which all forms emerge and from which they are nourished.

The problem of the survival of the cult of the *Magna Mater* and its relationship with both the Catholic Church and apparently secularist trends deriving from Radical Aristotelianism is an important one and merits further investigation. My own research among militantly secularist Italian immigrant socialists and communists suggests the persistence of an undercurrent of spirituality centered on the *Magna Mater* and organized through the guilds and the rural *società*. Whether or not the priesthood of the goddess survives, and if so in what form, remains unclear. Similarly the relationship between Amalricianism and Joachism merits further investigation. The links between Joachism and the rural left in Southern Europe is already well established (Mansueto unpublished, Mansueto 1995).

only of form and matter but also of essence (and the essence of humanity or human nature for Thomas include form and matter together) and existence. In effect, we are individuated by the separate act of existence which we are granted by God, something which makes it possible to ascribe to each individual their own unique agent intellect, overcome the difficulties of the Averroist doctrine form the standpoint of both psychological experience and theological implications (Gilson 1949, von Steenberghen 1980).

Thomas' cosmological, metaphysical, and psychological innovations also permit him to reconcile a commitment to revealed Truth with Aristotelian doctrine. What the Agent Intellect does, for Thomas, is to abstract the intelligible principle of a thing from the image garner from the senses. This can mean any one of three things. It may mean just abstracting a logical whole from its parts—the *abstractio totalis* which we all use when we abstract from Fido, Fifi, Rufus and Rover to the logical whole "dog." It may mean abstracting form from matter, the *abstractio formae* used by mathematicians when they form the concept of a triangle based on observation of triangular objects. But it may also mean abstracting the existence of something from its essence, something we do implicitly when we judge that something *is* and *is* such and such a thing in such and such a way. This form of abstraction Thomas calls the *separatio* since it separates Being from essence. It is this degree of abstraction that permits us to rise to the idea of God, Being itself, and its convertibility with the other transcendentals. But we do not gain any real insight into what Being is. This for Thomas, is the mystery of the divine nature, which can be known (initially) only through revelation and later, for us by faith perfected by the gifts of the Holy Spirit. Ultimately for Thomas, this perfected mystical knowledge depends on the gift of caritative wisdom, which we acquire connaturally. By loving God with God's own love we come to know God experientially and connaturally in a wordless wisdom that transcends both philosophy and the words of doctrine.

Thomas's solution at once validated the dialectics practiced by the emerging secular intelligentsia and ordered it to the revealed truth of which the Church was the custodian. At the same time, it stressed radical interdependence of dialectics and revelation. Dialectics terminates in knowledge of the divine act of Being; revelation discloses that act of Being as it really is, at least to those whose faith is perfected by the caritative wisdom and thus by infused mystical contemplation. This solution is embodied institutionally in the Dominican order that at once practices dialectics and seeks the perfection of the mystical union.

The Thomistic synthesis presented the Church with a very attractive solution to the political-theological question. On the one hand, as the Aristotelians taught, everything in the universe is ordered to God. The proper scope of ecclesiastical activity is, therefore, in principle unlimited. Human beings, furthermore, because they can rise rationally to knowledge of the divine act of Being are in fact ordered to not only this natural, but also to a supernatural knowledge of God which they can achieve only through revelation and through the spiritual discipline of the Church. The role of the Church is not only safeguarded, but in fact expanded by comparison with the Augustinian approach. This is a point that the Church, however, recognized only belatedly, and only incompletely, when the full implications of Augustinianism became apparent in the Reformation. This is, no doubt, because while Thomism exalts the Church, it also challenges it to change. While Thomas is quite clear that there is a perfection in the Episcopal state, because the bishop is ordered to the care of the whole community, there is also an perfection in the religious state, which seeks the perfection of infused contemplation. And if the life of the pure contemplative is, in a certain sense the most perfect, then there is another sense in which the Dominican way, which integrates action with contemplation—participating in the Episcopal task from the standpoint of a personal commitment to perfection—is nobler still. Thomas is always modest in his claims for himself and his order and does not draw out the full implications of his doctrine, but there is little question that it points to a Church which looks less and less like a sacerdotal hierarchy and more and more like a *universitas* composed of various "guilds" (the orders) which cultivate both religious perfection and the skills necessary to carry out really effective pastoral work. It is little wonder that bishops like Stephen Tempier, as well as orders less committed to intellectual excellence (the Franciscans) might have felt threatened.

Dante's solution, which comes a full half-century later, differs from Thomas in its effort to conserve more of the contribution of the Radical Aristotelians while still safeguarding the transcendental teleological ordering of humanity and the autonomy of the Church. Dante's cosmology is more clearly teleological than Thomas'. It is love which moves the sun and all the stars and indeed everything in the universe. Dante avoids materialist and spiritualist pantheism not by reference to the Divine act of

Being but rather by theorizing God as the final, rather than the material or formal cause of the universe. At the same time, he puts the Averroist Siger de Brabant in the same heaven as Thomas, along with Bonaventure and Joachim, implying that the insights of the Averroist left—both the affinity with the old cult of the *Magna Mater* and the call to a knowledge of God *in plenitudo intellectus*—must be conserved in the context of the larger Catholic synthesis. And Dante stakes out a middle position on the question of the Agent Intellect, accepting Thomistic doctrine but insisting that human intellectual potential is realized only collectively, something which grounds his insistence on the importance of human institutions—the Empire and the Church—which are the guarantors of human development, natural and supernatural, respectively (Dante. *de Monarchia*).

The final issue which divided Aristotelians and Augustinians had to do with the relationship between the divine will and the structure of the universe. Increasingly, as the Augustinian reaction of the thirteenth century gained strength, thinkers of this latter tradition began to press ever more forcefully their claims for the absolute sovereignty of God. This led them to advance a number of positions which may seem a bit odd to us today but which lead to debates which in fact played a major role in the eventual emergence of a purely mathematical physics. Could God, for example have created other universes? Can God move the universe rectilinearly?

Both of these possibilities were excluded on principal for Aristotelians. The universe is, from an Aristotelian point of view, a necessary consequence of the existence of God, who draws it into being naturally by teleological attraction. As there can be only one God (it being impossible for there to be more than one infinite being) there can be only one universe. Space, similarly, is a function of existence of matter. There can be no space outside the material universe in which God might move the universe around. From an Augustinian view both of these positions represented an infringement on divine sovereignty, and both were condemned by Stephen Tempier, Bishop of Paris, in 1277.

Throughout the Middle Ages, the development of Aristotelian science tended towards the construction of what we will call a completed teleological or Aristotelian space-time. In such a space-time matter appears as the pure possibility of organization, a possibility that is only and always actualized by the teleological attraction of the unmoved mover or, to put the matter differently, by the incredible beauty of God, who draws all things to herself. Change or motion is first and foremost the development of more complex levels of organization under the attractive power of this principle. First the fundamental qualities of hot and cold wet and dry, then the four elements, and eventually the entire scale of forms, mineral, vegetable, animal, and mineral emerge out of pure possibility and into the light of Being. The resulting space-time is axiological, in the sense that all movement is also growth or decay, progress or regress on a scale of values as matter evolves towards God or retreats backwards into the night of nonbeing. Evil is simply nonbeing, or more broadly the failure of matter to realize its latent potential for growth and development.

The "completion" of this space-time was held back by a number of factors. The most significant is the long-standing alliance between the dialectical tradition, which had its social basis in the intelligentsia and artisans of the cities, with patriarchal-tributary elites in a mutual struggle against the emerging market order. It was this alliance, motivated by the relative weakness of the intelligentsia and artisanate, which deformed Aristotle's original synthesis so that he from time to time seemed to conceive the universe as a sort of cosmic monarchy, celestial image of the earthly domain of his Macedonian patrons. Throughout the course of the middle ages, however, as the intelligentsia and artisanate grew in strength, this alliance gradually came unraveled. This had two results. On the one hand, the tributary elites and their allies in the clergy increasingly disengaged themselves from the alliance and developed their own ideological forms, a process represented by the Augustinian reaction which we have already described briefly and which we will have cause to examine in greater detail in the next chapter. Second, this left the intelligentsia and the artisanate to draw out the full implications of their position without concern for the interests of their erstwhile allies. The result was ideological polarization. As Augustinians pressed ever more forcefully their claims of absolute divine sovereignty (in a way Augustine himself never would have done) Radical Aristotelians emphasized more and more the role of teleological attraction and the operation of secondary causes in the cosmohistorical evolutionary process. As Augustinians inched closer and closer to the pessimistic anthropology which eventually found expression in the doctrine of the Reformers, Radical Aristotelians put forward a vision of human beings as rational and social, authentic partners in God's creative power. Nowhere did this find more powerful expression than in the work of the alchemists, which sought to bring the whole creation to perfection. At the political level this vision found expression in Dante's *de Monarchia* that sought, in creating an authentic world government, to create the optimum conditions for the progress of human civilization.

That the development of this Aristotelian science and the political project associated with it was cut short was, at least, in part, a result of brutal ideological repression which accompanied the Augustinian reaction of the thirteenth century, which we will examine in depth in the next chapter. There were, however, *internal* contradictions in Aristotelian physics as well. Specifically, Aristotelian physics remained, throughout this period, unable to advance a unified theory of motion. This contradiction takes a number of forms. First of all, according to Aristotle, the local motion of objects ought to be to their "natural" place—i.e., the place which most perfects the form of the whole to which they are ordered. Thus fire rises above air, which rises above water, which rises above earth. Thus the natural motion of plants towards sources of water and light and the motion of animals towards food and towards their mates. Thus the motion of human beings towards both material and spiritual goods. The difficulty is that not all motion is of this kind. Even minerals can be crushed or eroded and thus lose their form. Organisms suffer disease, death, and decay as well as experiencing growth and development. Animals are sometimes drawn to things which are dangerous for them, and human beings often choose what can only seem like evil options. Much of this unnatural motion, furthermore, occurs as a by-product of motion that is natural. One rock, falling to its natural place, crushes another. One organism lives by consuming another. Human beings do evil in the pursuit of perceived or authentic good. The universe is a place of struggle and tension as well as growth and development.

It is not that Aristotle failed to acknowledge these phenomena. On the contrary, we have already noted that he ascribes corruption in the sublunar realm to the fact that everything is composed of contrary qualities. The mediation of animal and human behavior through the processes of finite sensation and intellect, furthermore, means that there is no real contradiction between an underlying teleological ordering and action that is disordered as the result of sensory or intellectual error. The problem is that these "solutions" to the contradictions of Aristotelian physics seriously undermine the adequacy of Aristotle's answer to Plato, pushing his system back towards Platonic pessimism regarding matter—and thus regarding the possibilities of social progress. Claiming that things disintegrate because the very elements of which they are composed are unstable, contrary combinations is simply a more complex and elegant way of saying that matter, even though it is the potential for form, also resists it.

This has, furthermore, definite political consequences. Aristotle, no less than Plato, seems to believe that some people are constitutionally better fit to be "formed" for leadership and Aristotle, no less than Plato, remains skeptical about the possibility of actually building a just society. Indeed, in some places Aristotle seems to abandon entirely his teleological vision in favor of a political metaphysics driven by *taxis*, but the imposition of order from the outside, a notion with profound authoritarian potential (Aristotle. *Metaphysics* 1075a–1076a).

But the difficulties do not stop here. One of the aims of science is a unified explanation of the universe and it is one of the great appeals of Aristotle's system that he makes so much progress in this direction. For Aristotle perhaps even more than for Plato, however, motion in the celestial and the sublunar realms really doesn't follow the same laws. In the celestial realm the operation of teleology is perfect and its effect a changeless cyclical motion driven by love of the unmoved mover. In the terrestrial realm natural, teleologically driven motion competes with disintegration driven by the internal contradictions of matter and violent motion driven by error. Aristotle has, in effect, reproduced the Platonic distinction between the invisible idea and the visible thing that imperfectly reflects it *inside* the physical universe, in a division between the celestial and terrestrial realms.

Finally, Aristotle's account of celestial motion itself turns out to be in profound contradiction with observational evidence. This was not, furthermore, something which became obvious only with the discoveries of Copernicus, Kepler, Galileo, and Newton. On the contrary, alongside the Aristotelian enterprise directed at *explaining* the movements of the heavenly bodies, there was a vigorous tradition in Greece and later throughout the Mediterranean of observational and mathematical astronomy directed at describing that motion as accurately as possible. And while the motions of the heavenly bodies may seem regular by comparison with those of humans or dormice, they are by no means simple. As better data became available, and better mathematical models were developed, in became increasingly obvious that spherical geocentric orbits were not the most economical means of describing the motions of the heavenly bodies.

We have seen that Aristotle himself, following Eudoxus and Callippus, had to posit as many as 55 spheres to account for stellar and planetary motion (*Metaphysics* 1074a). Ptolemy was obliged to introduce eccentric orbits and epicycles. The efforts of the militant Aristotelian al-Bitruji to develop a concentric-spherical alternative in the 13th century failed, and eventually, of course, concentric geocentric spheres gave way altogether to heliocentric ellipsoids (Lindberg 1992).

More is at issue here than aesthetics. On the contrary, it was the perfect beauty of the spherical form that was supposed by Aristotle and his followers to inspire the movement of the spheres—on which the motion of everything else depended. Long before the attacks of Copernicus and Kepler, Aristotelian cosmology had succumbed to Ptolemaic eccentrics and epicycles that made the Aristotelian account of motion unworkable.

It would, to be sure, have been possible to resolve these problems within the context of the larger Aristotelian problematic. What would have been required, specifically, was a generalization of the concept of teleology to embrace contradiction and disintegration, along something like the lines that would later be proposed by Hegel and Marx. According to such a view, change is indeed driven by teleological attraction, and is therefore fundamentally a process of progressive development towards ever-higher degrees of organization. But it occurs under definite material conditions that may not make available the energy necessary to sustain any given process of development. Systems may, furthermore, develop in ways that lead them to come into conflict with each other in the pursuit of what is objectively a common Good. And the structures which these systems develop in order to tap into available energy and allocate it to various functions may well itself become an obstacle to further growth and development. Such an approach would not only have made it possible to advance a unified theory of motion. It would also have liberated Aristotelian astrophysics from the specific astronomical models to which it had become attached, allowing the stars and planets to be studied as particular physical systems which had achieved a definite level of organization under particular material conditions, their motions governed by the laws of that mode of organization, but subject both to further growth and to instability and degradation. This would have obviated the need for perfect spherical orbits and made it possible to accommodate the finds of mathematical astronomy in the sixteenth and seventeenth centuries.

That such a road was not taken simply reflects the limited conditions under which the Radical Aristotelians themselves labored. A classical Marxist analysis would describe these limitations in terms of the low level of development of the productive forces which did not yet make it possible to transcend the market order, the petty-bourgeois character of the Radical Aristotelians themselves, and their still incomplete emancipation from the hegemony of the tributary elites and their clerical ideologues. According to this view, a correct understanding of the processes of the natural world goes hand in hand with the development of modern industry. And it is modern industry, with its advanced division of labor, which makes both possible and necessary the socialization of the means of production. The petty bourgeois artisans and intellectuals were indeed in a position to grasp the enormous potential for technological and social progress, something which is reflected in their optimistic cosmology and anthropology and in their emphasis on the role of secondary causes, including human labor, in the operations of nature and society, but they also clung jealously to their own independence and the rights and privileges they had won for themselves from their feudal overlords. They were not in a position to understand the role of *contradiction* as a progressive social force because they had not yet experienced a successful social revolution, the transition form feudalism to capitalism itself being incomplete and the possibility of socialist revolution still centuries away. Indeed, the full realization of human potential remained even for them an otherworldly dream, represented by the Unmoved Mover who ultimately still governed the motion of all things in a vision which was still far from being completely secularized.

Such an explanation, I would like to suggest, while it points to a number of important factors, is well off the mark. Most important, it reflects the degree to which dialectical and historical materialism is itself hegemonized by bourgeois ideology, with its idolatry of mathematical physics and modern industry and its determination to banish from science every vestige of the teleological and the divine. This is a point that we will elaborate at much greater length in a later chapter. For now it will suffice to point out that it is precisely the purgation of the teleological from the dialectical vision of Marx, Engels, and their interpreters which at once left their ethical claims ungrounded and required the creation of an earthly equivalent for the missing divine principle in the form of the Leninist party and its General Secretary, organizer and director of the human historical process and aspirant to leadership of the whole process of cosmic evolution. And nonmarket forms of social organization long predate the advent of modern industry which, contrary to Marx's claims, makes the problems of centralized economic planning far more complex and difficult and thus if anything favors the market order.

What the artisans and intellectuals of the medieval communes did indeed lack was the political weight necessary in order to win their battles with the warlords and their clerical ideologues. They constituted a growing, progressive stratum within a dynamic and changing social order, but they were still a small minority. The penetration of market relations into the countryside had not yet proceeded far enough for their philosophical pre-occupations and dialectical disputations to make any sense to the peasantry. Oppressed peasants saw no need for subtle dialectics to prove the justice of their cause and were more likely to be attracted to Joachism or other prophetic movements that articulated with vivid images God's promise to redeem the land. And the dispossessed weavers and other incipient proletarians of the cities were not only few in number; they were also likely to resent the relatively privileged position of the guild-masters and intellectuals who alone fully enjoyed the freedom of the city. The result was a tendency to abandon the larger project of Radical Aristotelianism in favor of a narrower attempt to defend intellectual liberty against the repression unleashed by the clergy, advancing what amounted to an incipient liberal theory of the state (Marsilius of Padua. *Defensor Pacis*) a move which obviated the political need for a teleological cosmology or a metaphysics capable of grounding a natural law ethics, and which thus paved the way for an abandonment of Aristotelian science when empirical evidence against some of its particular formulations began to mount. Alternatively, those intent on defending a teleological worldview made their peace with the Church and provided the intellectual shock-troops for the Counter-Reformation, melding their Aristotle with Augustine in a very conservative reading of the Thomist synthesis (Thibault 1971) designed to defend rather than to undermine clerical authority. As a result promising solutions to the internal contradictions of Aristotelian science when unexplored and possible avenues of development were abandoned. The future, it seemed belonged to the market order and the mathematical physicists who alone seemed unable to unlock the secrets of nature and make the accessible to all who would exploit them.

Hindu Cosmologies[12]

Because it is an attempt to re-assert a teleological cosmology in the face of challenges from modern Euroamerican science, our principal focus in this chapter has been on the Aristotelian physics out of the disintegration of which modern mathematical physics emerged. It is important, however, to note that neither teleological cosmologies and their associated axiological spacetimes nor atomistic and mathematically formal approaches to physics are in any sense uniquely "Western." Both tendencies were also apparent in humanity's other great postaxial civilizational centers, India and China. We have already noted the emergence of atomistic and mathematical approaches to science in these civilizations. Here we will discuss briefly the emergence of teleological cosmologies and axiological space times.

In India, there were, broadly speaking, two distinct traditions which had the potential to contribute to the development of teleological cosmologies. The first of these was the dualism represented first of all by the Jaina tradition and reincorporated into Vedic orthodoxy by the *Samkya* school. This school, we will recall, regarded the universe as an interaction between two principles: *prakriti* or matter and *purusa* or spirit. *Prakriti* contributed to the evolution of spirit by posing obstacles that gradually forced *purusa* to recognize its autonomy. In the pure *Samkya* tradition this recognition of autonomy was itself the goal of spiritual evolution, but the *Samkya* school doubled as a kind of physics for the Vedanta traditions, which regards the aim of spiritual development not simply as the autonomy of spirit from matter but rather the union of the individual self (*jiva/purusa/atman*) with the creative principle of the universe, *Brahman*, a union which is understood by some (the *advaita* school) as essential and substantive and by others (the *dvaita* school) as a loving devotion, and by still others as something in between.

As in Europe and the Mediterranean Basin, these ideas became bound up in India, with astrological and alchemical ideas. But the planets, in addition to their association with specific elements (the Sun and Mars with fire, Mercury with earth, Venus and the Moon with water, Saturn with air, and Jupiter with ether or the quintessence), are also associated with certain qualities or *gunas* which reflect different levels of spiritual development, The Sun, the Moon, and Jupiter, for example, are regarded

---

12. For a brief introduction to Hindu cosmologies, see Balslev 2005.

as mediating *sattva* or goodness, Venus and Mercury as mediating *rajas* or the energy to overcome obstacles, and Mars and Saturn as mediating *inertia* or impurity. A person's birth chart is seen as reflecting the karmic imprint of previous lives, a specific combination of virtues and vices, potentials and weaknesses which in turn define the evolutionary tasks which an individual must address in this lifetime.

This evolutionary dynamic is articulated across a hierarchical, cyclical, and even pessimistic cosmology inherited from the *Vedas* and the *Puranas*. The universe is periodically created and destroyed with each larger cycle divided into shorter periods each of which is worse than the one that precedes it. Thus the present period, which began roughly 3000 BCE with the death of Krishna (roughly the beginning of the Bronze Age and the emergence of exploitative tributary states), is regarded as the *kaliyuga*, a time of social and spiritual disintegration. Structurally the universe is organized around a central mountain, Mount Meru, which sits in a great ocean above which are ranged visible and invisible planets and then various higher realms, including several which are outside the material universe. Generally speaking, more evolved beings inhabit the higher realms, with those beyond the bounds of matter escaping the period cycles of destruction and rebirth.

This cosmology should be seen as a reflection of the persistence of pre-axial tributary elements in the social order of the Indian subcontinent, structures that, as we have seen, tend to encourage cosmological pessimism. The larger dynamic is towards the spiritual development of individuals from lower to higher levels, towards eventual union with the creative principle, Brahman, which is their source. This is reflected in the overlay that assigns higher planes to more evolved beings and which adds immaterial realms immune to cyclic destruction and rebirth.

Buddhist Cosmologies[13]

The second Indian tradition that produced a teleological cosmology accompanied by an axiological space-time was Buddhism. As with the Hindu tradition, there are currents in Buddhist cosmology that are best described as atomistic. Indeed, this is the tendency of the whole *Abidharma* literature, which draws on the results of meditation to analyze experience into elements, leading to recognition that there is no self or

13. For a good introduction to Buddhist cosmology, with attention to the larger Indian background, see Sadakara and Nakamura 1997.

indeed anything else to which one can become attached. The *Abidharma* is essentially a compendium of these elements—5 *skandas*, 13 sense fields, 18 elements, and between 4 and 24 types of causal relations (Collins 1998: 215, Kalupahana 1992: 144–48). One school of interpretation, the so called Sarvastivadins, argued that "the so called objects of everyday life are not real, for they are mere transitory aggregates, but the elements of which they are composed are real and permanent . . . the one item they are at pains to show does not exist is the subjective self (Collins 1998: 216). The Sautrantikas, on the other hand, "rejected the doctrine of the intentionality of consciousness by which the Sarvastivadins defended their realism. Instead they distinguished between the things of experience, which exist, but only as transitory point-instants of space-time, and non-concrete categories, which do not exist; the latter are permanent and real but only as abstractions. There is a non-referential aspect of mind by which *dharmas* which are not existing substances can be real objects of valid cognition (Collins 1998: 217)." Theravadin cosmologies are the result of the struggle between these two schools, which led to a physics which reduced reality to "evanescent point instances" lacking inherent reality and mental constructs which aggregated these instances into the objects of the phenomenal world—something very different from Hellenistic or even other Indian atomisms. Spiritual development involved recognizing that unreality of the phenomenal world and thus overcoming attachments, but there was no evolution in the material universe as such (Collins 1998: 237–39).

This did not, however, represent the endpoint in the development of Buddhist cosmology. The *Mahayana* drew out the logical implications of the debates are the *Abidharma* and developed them in a way which led ultimately to teleological cosmology and an axiological space-time. There were, broadly speaking, two aspects to this process. On the one hand, *Mahayana* philosophy gradually gave greater and greater emphasis to the role of consciousness in giving shape and form to the universe. First, the *Madyamika* school analyzed the evanescent point instants of the Theravadins into an pure systems of interdependent relationships. The *Yogacara* school., meanwhile, pointed out that the consciousness arising out of these relationships can be of any one of three degrees. It could emphasize the conceptualized or constructed aspect (*parikalpitasvabhava*) in which we perceive the objects of ordinary everyday life, the dependent aspect (*parantrasvabhava*) in which we recognize that these objects don't really exist in any absolute sense, or the perfected aspect, (*parinispannasvabhava*) (Williams 1989: 82–86), in which we see the phenomenon in the context of the interdependent system of which it is a part.

> According to the *Samdhinirmocana Sutra* it is the "Suchness" or "Thusness" (*tathata*), the true nature of things, which is discovered in meditation (6:6). It is said to be the complete absence, in the dependent aspect, of objects –that is, the objects of the conceptualized aspect (*Mahayanasamgraha* 2:4) . . . through meditation we come to know that our flow of perceptions, of experiences, really lacks the fixed enduring subjects and objects which we have constructed out of it. There is only the flow of experiences. The perfect aspect is, therefore, the fact of non-duality, there is neither subject nor object but only a single flow. (Williams 1989: 84–85)

The second link in the development of Mahayana cosmologies was the emergence of the *Bodhisattva* ideal. Rather than seeking individual enlightenment only for themselves, the Mahayana schools urged their followers to seek enlightenment for all. For beginners this might mean ordinary acts of compassion, and especially teaching the *dharma*. But if the universe is really just a system of relationships which is given form and definition by consciousness, then those who understand the real nature of things can use this knowledge to transform the universe or even to bring new worlds—what were called *Buddha-kshetras* (Buddha-fields or Buddha-worlds), into being. The aim was to create worlds more and more conducive to promoting enlightenment and thus to the ripening of being. The world we live in is itself such a world, but is limited by the relative lack of merit of its Buddha, Sakyamuni. There are worlds far more conducive to enlightenment than our own, as well, of course, as worlds which are far less so.

The resulting picture of the universe is of one vast, interconnected system developing endlessly towards universal enlightenment.

> The realm of the Buddhas is inconceivable; no sentient being can fathom it . . . The Buddha constantly emits great beams of light; the Buddha body is pure and always tranquil. The radiance of its light extends throughout the world . . . In all atoms of all lands, Buddha enters, each and every one, producing miracle displays for sentient beings: such is the Way of Vairocana. (*Avatamska Sutra* I.1 and I.4, in Williams 1989: 122 and in Cleary trans. 1984: 6)

This universe, which the sutra calls the *dharmadhatu* or realm of dharma *is* Vairocana Buddha, or in another image, the jewel net of Indra, a system of interdependent causality represented as a unified whole (Cook 1977).

And each and every human being has within them the potential to become a Buddha, seeing the *dharmadhatu* as it really is, bringing forth infinite worlds, ripening an infinite number of beings. In this sense, the doctrine parallels the emerging Western idea that human beings can, through some combination of wisdom and justice action actually *become* divine.

> Clearly to know that all dharmas
> Are without any self-essence at all; To understand the nature of dharmas in this way
> Is to see Vairocana (in Williams 123)

They perceive that the fields full of assemblies, the beings and aeons which are as may as all the dust particles, are all present in every particle of dust. They perceive that the many fields and assembles and the beings and the aeons are all reflected in each particle of dust (in Williams 124 in Gomez 1967: lxxxviii).

As in the case of Hindu cosmologies, this highly rationalized system was articulated across a cyclical and hierarchical cosmology which was essentially an elaboration and rationalization of that inherited from the Vedic tradition. The Buddhist rationalization is, however, quite significant. The various *lokas* or planes of existence (of which 31 are generally identified) are not so much physical places as they are states of consciousness. These are grouped into three realms or *dhatus*. The highest of these, the Aruyadhatu or "formless realm" is inhabited by those *devas* or gods who have achieved the four highest levels of meditative absorption. Next comes the *Rupadhatu*, or realm of form, inhabited by those who have achieved the four lower levels of meditative practice. Finally, the *Kamadhatu* or realm of pleasure, includes various physical heavens inhabited by pleasure seeking *devas*, the various worlds of Mount Meru, inhabited by lesser *devas* and the oceans surrounding it, inhabited by the *asuras*, as well as our own and other earthly realms, the realm of animals capable of suffering, the realm of the *pretas* or hungry ghosts, and the various *narakas* or hells. According to most Buddhist sources, this basic structure is repeated thousands upon thousands of times. Other worlds, in other words, exist parallel to our own, at the same time. The whole structure, furthermore, undergoes periodic cycles of creation and destruction, with higher levels destroyed less frequently and the highest not at all.

As with the Hindu cosmologies described earlier, the hierarchical structure no doubt reflects the residual tributary structures present in India and the other societies into which Buddhism moved. We should also note, however, the higher degree of rationalization, reflecting the specific social basis of Buddhism in those sectors of the population most affected by the emergence of petty commodity production (the artisans and merchants and their associated intelligentsia).

Chinese Cosmologies

Chinese cosmologies developed under influence of both indigenous traditions, which include the Legalist, Mohist, Five Elements, Taoist, and Confucian trends, and Buddhism, which brought a range of concerns and concepts quite different from those of tributary and axial age China. The mutual influence between indigenous Chinese trends and Buddhism was profound. It was, for example, above all the Chinese focus on cosmological questions which transformed Buddhism from an other worldly salvation religion which cautioned against attention to cosmological and metaphysical questions into the doctrine of world-creation which we discussed above. At the same time, the Buddhist claim that the phenomenal world is "empty," lacking inherent existence, forced the indigenous Chinese schools to develop sophisticated arguments for theses they had previously taken for granted. The result was a synthesis that integrated an originally cyclical element cosmology with a powerful progressive and teleological dynamic. At the same time, Chinese cosmologies always linked their analysis of the structure of the universe to ethics and politics.

There were several distinct stages in this process. We have already noted the emergence, during the axial era (800–200 BCE) of both Legalist and Mohist atomism, of the five elements cosmology, and of the quasi-mathematical cosmology of the Taoist tradition, with its focus on the concept of the unlimited and the dialectic between *yin* and *yang*. Early Confucianism focused on moral questions, grounding its claims in a loose metaphysics centered on the concept of *tian* or "heaven," a kind of impersonal first principle.

This early period of ferment eventually came to an end when the Qin dynasty imposed Legalism as a state ideology, slaughtering scholars of all the other trends, but especially the Confucians, and burning many of their works. It was only with the establishment of the Han Dynasty in 206 BCE that the Confucian tradition began to reassert itself and weave into its own fabric elements of the other traditions to create a coherent cosmology. An early stage in this process is reflected in the work Tung Chung-shu (179–104 BCE) (Collins 1985: 155, Yao 2000: 83, 88).

> Heaven is the transcendental reality and the source of human life, and humans must faithfully follow the principles of Heaven and fulfill Heaven's mandate. In this relation, Heaven is the spiritual power and the great grandfather (*zeng zufu*) of humans, and Heaven alone can reward the good and punish the bad. Not only are humans considered to be physically shaped by Heaven but their moral and political ways are similarly determined. Human qualities are endowed and animated by Heaven. Insofar as Heaven loves people they should be human (*ren*); Heaven acts regularly in the progression of the four seasons and day and night, so people should observe the principles of propriety (*li*); Heaven has authority over Earth so the Sovereign has authority over his subjects, a father over his son and a husband over his wife. Human behavior must model the operating forces of Heaven, yang and ying, Yang signifies virtue and is associated with spring, thus symbolizing the giving of life and education; yin completes yang and is thus associated with autumn, the season of destruction, and symbolizes death and punishment. To carry out the will of Heaven, a ruler must rely on education and the propagation of virtue, and not on punishments and killing. (Yao 2000: 84–85, referring to Shyrock 1966: 50–51)

The Confucian effort to at once legitimate and reform political authority by appeal to a complex moral cosmology was countered by the Taoists, who insisted that the first principle, which they called the *tao*, was ineffable and that nonbeing had priority over being.

> Vacuity gave rise to Tao, which gave rise to space and time, which in turn gave rise to material force, and then to the manifestations of the material universe. There was a time before yin and yang, Heaven and Earth, and even before non-being . . . (Collins 1998: 157)

The implication here is that the universe emerges out of nothing and that while it has an order, that order is too subtle to serve as the basis for a public morality. This struggle dominated the Wei, Jin, Southern and

Northern Dynasties (220–581 CE) during which Buddhism was gradually establishing itself in China.

Chinese Buddhism, which became the dominant force in the country during the Sui and Tang dynasties, took the insights of the *Madyamika* and *Yogacara* schools, which we discussed above, and developed them to their logical conclusions. This meant a doctrine which stressed the radical interconnectedness of the universe and its role as a context for ripening being.

> "The principle is the mind of the sentient being. This mind includes in itself all states of being of the phenomenal and transcendental world." According to the commentator Fa-tsang (643–712) this One Mind is the *tathagatagarbha* (p. 32). The *Awakening of Faith* itself takes the *tathagatagarbha* as the substratum of *samsara* and *nirvana* (pp. 77–8). The Mind has two aspects –the Mind as Suchness or Thusness, that is, the Absolute Reality itself, and the Mind as phenomena. . . . Differentiation . . . arises through illusion, fundamental ignorance of one's true nature. (Williams 1989: 109–10)

What this did, of course, was to substantially undercut the centrality of the doctrine of *sunyata* or emptiness, which became an understanding of the *way* in which things exist rather than a claim that all things lack inherent existence and a redefinition of the Chinese ideal of the sage, or rather a new understanding of what it meant to be a sage: i.e., to understand that phenomena are empty and dependent and that it is only on the basis of this knowledge that they can be cultivated or "ripened."

There were many variants of this philosophically sophisticated monastic Buddhism. The two most important, however, were the Tien Tai, which enjoyed the patronage of the Sui and the Hua-yen which enjoyed the patronage of the Tang (Collins 1998: 285). The two schools are quite close, with the latter simply building on and drawing out more explicitly the metaphysical implications of what is essentially a common position.

The Tien Tai school, so called for its mountain home, argued for the centrality of the *Saddharmapundarkia* (Lotus) Sutra as the most complete revelation of *dharma*. Using the technique of *p'an chiao*, in which the teachings of various Buddhist schools are ranked in terms of their relative completeness, with the lower ranked schools treated as skillful means (*upayakausalya*), teachings directed at the less developed, The Tien Tai school essentially argued away centuries of Buddhist seminihilism as a way of helping the less developed get past their attachment to phenomena in order to prepare them for a future as advanced Bodhisattvas or fully developed Buddhas engaged in the work of "ripening being." They taught a complex cosmology of ten worlds, including numerous heavens and hells, as well as the persistence of Buddhas as agents for the cultivation of enlightenment, distinguishing between the eternal, cosmic Buddha and his various manifestations.

The Hua-yen (Collins 1998: 286) carried this process even further. The universe is understood as the "jewel net of Indra," Vairocana, the eternal or cosmic Buddha, is just a symbol of this interdependent network.

> If each part does not wholly cause the whole to be made and only exerts partial power, then each condition would only have partial power. They would consist only of many individual partial powers and would not make one whole, which is annihilationism. ... Also, if the part does not wholly create the whole, then when one part is removed, the whole should remain. However, since the whole is not formed, then you should understand that the whole is not formed by the partial power of a condition but by its total power. (Fa-tsang, *Hua-yen I ch'eng chiao I fen-ch'I chang* 508c in Cook 1977: 12)

> Everything, from an atom to the universe itself, functions as the cause for everything else. In Buddhist terminology, this is the emptiness of things, and if there were anything which is not empty, which is to say anything that is not causal in this manner, then that is really a nonentity. Emptiness does not at all rob existence of its vitality and color, rather the full, round, solid form of the object and its vigorous life of activity are in reality precisely its emptiness. Its concreteness, discreteness, and true individuality are indeed realities of the most vivid kind, and it is the manner in which the object exists that is an issue, not these qualities. (Cook 1977: 73)

The early part of the Tang period would be the last time Buddhism was hegemonic in China. Gradually the deeper dynamic of Chinese civilization, which was centered on the reforming activity of a centralizing state informed by a largely Confucian scholar-gentry reasserted itself. It was in this context, during the Song dynasty, that the Neo-Confucian synthesis, or what contemporaries called *dao xue* finally emerged (Collins 1998: 299ff., Yao 2000: 98ff.). *Dao xue* was, in effect, an elaboration of the earlier synthesis between Confucian ethics and Taoist metaphysics which had first emerged during the Han era modified by the debates of the

Wei, Jin, Northern, and Southern dynasties and above all by the struggle with Buddhism. The foundational text was, in this regard, Zhou Dunyi's (1017–73) *T'ai-chi t'u shuo* or *Explanation of the Diagram of the Great Ultimate* (Yao 2000: 98–101). Given the centrality of this text, it is worth quoting from it extensively.

> The ultimate of nonbeing and also the Great ultimate. The Great ultimate through movement generates yang. When its activity reaches its limit, it becomes tranquil. Through tranquility the Great Ultimate generates yin. When tranquility reaches its limit, activity begins again. . . .
>
> By the transformation of yang and its union with yin, the Five Agents of Water, Fire, Wood, Metal, and Earth arise. When these five material forces are distributed in harmonious order, the four seasons run their course.
>
> The five agents constitute one system of yin and yang and yin and yang constitute one Great Ultimate. The Great Ultimate is fundamentally the non-ultimate. . . .
>
> When the reality of the ultimate of nonbeing and the essence of yin, yang, and the five agents come into mysterious union, integration ensues. *T'ien* (Heaven) constitutes the male element and *K'un* (Earth) constitutes the female element. The interaction of these two material forces engenders and transforms the myriad things. The myriad things produce and reproduce, resulting in an unending transformation.
>
> It is humanity alone which receives the five agents in their highest excellence, and therefore is the most intelligent. The five moral principles of human nature (humanity, righteousness, propriety, wisdom and faithfulness) are aroused by and react to the external world and engage in activity, good and evil and distinguished, and human affairs take place.
>
> The sage settles these affairs by the principles of the mean. . . . Thus he establishes himself as the ultimate standard for humanity. Hence the character of the sage is identical with that of Heaven and Earth; his brilliance is identical with that of the sun and moon; his order is identical with that of the four seasons, and his good and evil fortunes are identical with those of spiritual beings. The superior human cultivates these moral qualities and enjoys good fortune, whereas the inferior man violates them and suffers evil fortune.
>
> Therefore it is said that the yin and the yang are established as the way of Heaven, the weak and the strong as the way of Earth and humanity and righteousness as the way of man. It is also said

that if we investigate the cycle of things we shall understand the concepts of life and death. (Zhou Dunyi. *T'ai-chi t'u shuo* 1, in Fieser and Powers 1998: 170)

This text is, clearly, extraordinarily condensed and obscure. There are, furthermore, debates over the original form of the text. The version quoted above begins, in the Chinese, *Wuji ehr taiji*, but another version of the text beings *Tzu wuji ehr taiji*. The difference is significant. The longer version, which Julia Ching, among others, argues (Ching 2000: 22, 235–41) is original, gives more play to *wuji* as the source of *taiji* and thus emphasizes nonbeing over being.

It was, however, the ambiguity of this text that made it so fruitful as a *locus* for metaphysical speculation. There can be little doubt, however, that it outlines a teleological cosmology in which the entire universe is ordered to the development of humanity and especially of the sage. This happens by means of a complex process in which a transcendent first principle gives rise to a hierarchy of cosmic forces, which in turn give rise to the physical, biological, and social universe. Human beings represent the pinnacle of what amounts to a cosmohistorical evolutionary process, and the sage, who understands and follows the laws which govern this process represents the most evolved form of humanity, and is thus the standard by which all others should be judged.

This said, fundamental ambiguities remain. Of these two were most important. The first was epistemological, and concerned the relative role of investigation and meditation in the search for wisdom. Do we know the *taiji* by means of a kind of rational dialectic which begins with the "investigation of things" and concludes to a transcendental first principle? Or do we know that first principle through a kind of intellectual intuition achieved through meditation? While most of the practitioners of *dao xue* engaged in both scientific investigation and meditation in a broadly Ch'an tradition, the tradition diverged sharply around this question.

Second, what is the relationship between *wuji* and *taiji* and what is the nature of the *taiji* itself. The first question defines one's position in the broad Chinese intellectual spectrum which extends from Buddhism on the one side through Taoism to the more rationalistic and materialist variants of Confucianism. The second divided Confucians between those who emphasized *li* or principle, those who emphasized *xin* or mind/heart, and those who emphasized *qi* or material force.

Within this context a wide range of different positions emerged. Shao Yong (1011–77), for example, identified the *taiji* with *xin* and thus emphasized meditation or intellectual intuition in the understanding it, but opted in is *Huangju Jing shi* or *Cosmic Chronology of the Great Ultimate* for an essentially mathematical or numerological understanding of the Great Ultimate. By reflecting on ourselves we can discern the basic structure of the universe, through a kind of mathematical intuition. The Great Ultimate gives birth to yin and yang, which in turn give birth to the four emblems (the heavenly bodies, the earthly substances, the sense organs and the periods of human history—the ages respectively of the Three Sovereigns, the Five Emperors, the Three Dynasties, and the Five Despots). He argued that if the mathematical structure of the Great Ultimate can be decoded, it is possible to predict the course of events (Yao 2000: 100–101).

At the other end of the spectrum we find thinkers such as Zhang Zai (1020–1077), who advanced a materialistic version of *dao xue*. For Zhang, the supreme ultimate is *qi* or material force. The universe came into being when the Great Void contracted. The light part became yang, and the heavy yin. All things are the result of the interaction between these two types of material force and all things ultimately dissolve into them. Human beings are a combination of the two forces. The more yang one has, the better one is. Zhang cautioned against seeking physical immortality, which is quite impossible in this cosmology and argues that it is better simply to cede to the will of heaven (Yao 2000: 101–3).

Ultimately, however, speculation became focused on an intense two-line struggle, the terms of which were defined, ironically, by two brothers whose work was initially regarded as constituting a single school, the *luo xue*. What the Cheng brothers shared in common was a focus on the complex interaction between *tian li* or heavenly principle and *ren yu* or human desires. The task of human beings was to reduce or extinguish their human desires in order to preserve and realize heavenly principle, a position which reflects enduring Buddhist influence. Cheng Yi (1033–1107) emphasized the importance of principle and logic and laid the groundwork for the development of Zhu Xi's *li xue*; Cheng Hao (1032–85) emphasized humaneness, and extended xin to include heaven, laying the groundwork for the *xin xue* of Lu Jiuyuan and Wang Shouren (Yao 2000: 103–4).

Zhu Xi's (1130–1200) synthesis was simple but profound. Human beings acquire knowledge of first principles by investigation of the world around them. What this realizes is a complex interaction of *li* or principle and *qi* or material force. *Li* orders things to their proper ends; *qi* makes the manifestation of things possible and confers form, but also distorts or limits the way in which *li* is expressed.

Many thinkers have seen the relationship between *li* and *qi* in the thought of Zhu Xi as rather like that of *morphe* and *hyle* in the Aristotelian tradition, and the comparison is not without merit. *Qi*, however, carries rather more internal dynamism that the Aristotelian *hyle*, which is a pure potential for receiving form. *Qi* may even be regarded as containing the seeds of form. In this sense it is closer to the way matter was understood by ibn Rusd and the Latin Averroists. *Li*, on the other hand, is above form. In terms of its origin, this idea probably reflects the influence of Buddhism and Taoism, the first of which tended towards a purely negative definition of the first principle and the second of which allowed that there was such a principle but was always skeptical about defining it. In terms of its function in Zhu Xi's system, however, *li* plays a role rather more like the Platonic Good or the Aristotelian unmoved mover, as the end sought by all things, something which is reflected in his tendency to actually identify it with the *taiji* and with *tian* (Ching 2000: 27–29, 44). Ultimately the best way to understand Zhu Xi's position is this: the material universe is the drive of *qi* towards *li*. *Li* itself is one and indivisible, and identical with *tian*, but the myriad things embody it as they strive for and evolve towards it.

This interaction between *li* and *qi* within the universe is reflected in the tension between *dao xin* and *ren xin*, between the mind of the way of Heaven and our natural human mind, which has a limited grasp of the *dao* and thus narrow and selfish desires. Moral cultivation is a result of study (*xue*) but also of ritual which forms human nature in conformity with heavenly principle.

Lined up in opposition to Zhu Xi was the *xin xue* associated with Lu Jiuyuan (1139–93) and Wang Shouren (1472–1528). Where Zhu had emphasized investigation, this school focused on meditation on humanity's moral nature (Yao 2000: 105–115). Where Zhu said *xing ji li* (human nature is principle) this school said *xin ji li* (mind/heart is principle). *Xin* functions in this system as a monistic universal principle, the source of all things, in such a way that *li* and *qi* cannot really be differentiated. The *xin xue* school sharply attacked Zhu's emphasis on exegetical study and natural science as elitist, and argued that because everyone has *xin*, indeed *is* *xin*, that everyone can become a sage.

✻ ✻ ✻

What should be clear is that by the height of the Silk Road Era essentially all of the principal civilizational centers of Afro-Eurasia had developed teleological cosmologies which transformed the hierarchical models of the universe inherited from the tributary era into dynamic systems in which the universe either itself evolved from lower to higher degrees of organization (clearest in the case of the Chinese *dao xue*) or served as a matrix for the promotion of human spiritual development. What were initially physical planes of existence were rationalized as different degrees of spirituality. What made the West different was the disintegration of this synthesis under the pressure of two new social forces: the formation of sovereign nation states and the process of primitive accumulation which led eventually to the development of the capitalist system and of a new civilizational ideal centered on divinization by means of innerworldly civilizational progress. This new civilization—modernity—would not only require, but was in fact *constituted* by a new physics, one which, rather than explaining why the universe is the way it is, and how human beings fit into, would describe rigorously how it works, in order to subject it to rational human control. It is to the development of that physics that we must now turn.

2

The Foundations of Mathematical Physics

THE DEVELOPMENT OF INTELLECTUAL disciplines is never independent of the social systems out of which they emerge, which nurture them, form them, and which fix the ends they serve. This does not mean that the arts, the sciences, and philosophy, are ever *merely* ideological in the sense of articulating and reinforcing particular social interests. On the contrary, in order to be credible in the first place they have to hold their own as forms of knowledge, and while a very powerful case can be made that some social locations provide a better vantage point for the intellect than others, no location is so deprived as to render those who occupy it wholly incapable of seeing as least a small part of the Truth. Still, if we are to evaluate the claims of an intellectual discipline accurately then we need to take into account its social context. In what ways do the structure of the society in which it emerges spontaneously shape the way people see the world? And what interests—conscious or unconscious—might be at stake in the way questions are posed and the way in which they are answered? What are the real ends served by the discipline and how does this ordering affect its capacity for the Truth?

We have shown that Aristotelian physics, whatever else it may have been (and we have given a very favorable judgment on it as science) played an integral role in a fundamentally political project: the struggle against the progressive marketization of human society which began with the development of specialized agriculture on the Hellenic peninsula and which gradually spread throughout the entire Mediterranean basin until it came to dominate the whole organization of the Hellenistic and Roman social order. By showing that the universe is indeed ordered to a first principle infinite, necessary, and perfect, and thus divine, Aristotelian physics provided the necessary foundation for metaphysics which in turn regrounded ethics and provided criteria in the light of which the market order could be judged and found wanting. The resulting philosophical tradition, which we have called dialectical, then merged with the prophetic religions which had developed out of the struggle of the peasantry against the tributary order which had been dominant since at least the discovery of metal technology. The new order which emerged from this synthesis, while it fell far short of the aims of prophet and dialectician alike, represented a significant advance over both the slave-driven petty commodity order of the Greek and Roman metropoles and the older tributary states of the interior, both of which converted most the surplus extracted from the productive classes to warfare and luxury consumption. The Islamic empires and the feudal domains of Europe were, by comparison, characterized by lower rates of exploitation and a greater capacity to allocate resources to activities which promoted the development of human capacities. To the extent that Aristotelian physics failed as science—i.e., in its inability to develop a unified theory of motion which comprehended the teleological ordering of chaos, contradiction, and decay, as well as of growth and development, it also bore the marks of a specifically ideological deformation—specifically the marks of a profound compromise with patriarchy and with the old warrior aristocracy with which it allied itself in the struggle against the market order. We have also shown more briefly that comparable dynamics characters the development of science in India and China.

The new physics which grew up over the course of the later Middle Ages, and which became dominant as a result of the "scientific revolution" of the seventeenth century is, similarly, a political movement as much as it is scientific. Specifically, we will argue that mathematical physics and the intellectual disciplines which grow out of it (including not only most chemistry, but also much of the biological and social sciences, especially classical political economy), are shaped by and/or contribute to capitalism and the market order in three distinct ways. First, mathematical physics, which is itself more properly understood as *techne* rather than *episteme*, i.e., as mathematical model making than as explanatory-deductive science—is integral to the technologies on which capitalism is founded and develops along side them. It is, to this extent, the organic ideology of the master craftsman (Prigogine 1984) and later the engineer who claims to have unlocked the secrets of Nature (Eamon 1994) and put Her at the service of humanity. At the same time, mathematical physics represents an *emancipation* of *techne* from the higher disciplines to which it had previously been ordered, something which, as we will see, leads to profound deformations. Second, however, mathematical physics is the spontaneous ideology of the market order itself, which appears to its participants as a system of quantities (prices) or of only externally related atoms (individuals, commodities) and who thus begin to think of the universe as a whole in much the same way, so that there appears to be no global purpose to which either cosmos or society are ordered. To this extent the unlocking of the secrets of nature also turns out to be a disenchantment of nature, so that having found his prize, the wizard's charms are at long last spent and Nature, having been rendered compliant to our will all at once loses the charm which lured us to court Her in the first place. Third, precisely because it describes the universe without recourse to a *telos*, which it regards as unnecessary and uneconomical, mathematical physics becomes part of the bourgeoisie's polemic against metaphysics and the *via dialectica* and its effort to ideologically disarm the working classes by undermining the foundations of moral discourse and leaving any possible critique of the market order radically ungrounded. These "ideological" dynamics, which govern the whole development of mathematical physics, do not mean that the discipline is incapable of truth. On the contrary, properly understood as rigorous descriptions of the local motion of physical systems the formalisms of mathematical physics can be quite useful. But recognition of the ideological function of mathematical physics allows us to dispel *its* charms and free us from its mystifications, so that we may once again engage the fundamental questions of meaning and value which it claimed to have settled once and for all.

THE SOCIAL BASIS OF MATHEMATICAL PHYSICS

Our first step must be to specify precisely the nature of the social structure of which are claiming mathematical physics is at once a reflex and an ideological agent. It is important in this regard to distinguish clearly between capitalism and the "petty commodity" societies of the ancient Mediterranean or the Middle Ages.[1] This distinction can be made either at the level of the productive forces (i.e., the level of technological development) or at the level of the relations of production (i.e., the structures which centralize and allocate resources for production). As we will see,

---

1. For a discussion of the various stages in capitalist development, see Marx 1867/1977, Mandel 1968, Amin 1979/1980, Mansueto 1997.

change at these two levels, while it does not move in lockstep, is closely correlated. Petty commodity societies presuppose the development of specialized agriculture and/or a highly sophisticated handicrafts production. This is for the simple reason that if there is to be trade there must be something worth trading, and if trade is to be more than a side-line for subsistence producers (large or small), then production must have become sufficiently specialized that many producers produce only or at least primarily for the market. In this sense specialized agriculture and crafts production go hand in hand with the sort of advanced social division of labor which makes the market possible, and which, in the absence of some conscious intervention which organizes production differently, also makes it almost inevitable. Initially, however, the process of marketization itself is driven primarily by the presence within the economic system of large-scale, nonmarket surplus extraction, generally by tributary states, which generate a market for the agricultural or crafts specialties. The resulting specialization in turn creates a further impetus to marketization, as specialized producers must purchase on the market the subsistence goods which they are no longer producing for themselves.

The earliest stage of capitalist development—what is generally called mercantilism—differs from petty commodity production primarily in that the marketplace itself begins to take the place of demand on the part of nonmarket producers as the principle economic regulator. The underlying technology—specialized agriculture and advanced handicrafts—remains the same, though there may be some significant extension of this technology. Thus French wine technology in the eighteenth century of the common era was far superior to Greek wine technology in the fifth century before the common era, but both are properly classed as specialized agricultural technologies. The clock, which represents in many ways the supreme achievement of medieval urban craftsmanship, opened up powerful new possibilities both for science and for the organization of production and social life generally, but it is still a product of handicrafts and not a properly industrial technology. What differs in mercantilism is that specialization has reached a certain critical mass so that forces of supply and demand begin to operate and direct the allocation of resources in a way which may still be influenced by state policies—taxation, public works, etc., but which is not wholly determined by it. Whether or not this stage was reached in the ancient world, for example at the economic height of the Roman Empire, remains an open question. It was the European conquest of Asia, Africa, and the Americas, with the resulting expansion of plantation agriculture, slavery, and trade which made mercantilism a reality in Europe by the seventeenth century at the latest.

In mercantilist, as in petty commodity societies, goods and services but not labor or capital have become commodities.

The further development of capitalism, however, depends on specifically industrial production processes. By industry we mean, on the one hand, the development of energy sources based on the decomposition of more complex forms of matter—combustion, fission, etc.—and, on the other hand a technical division of labor which subdivides the production process into minute tasks which can then be constantly organized and reorganized in order to increase efficiencies. This, in turn, involves the dispossession of producers who are increasingly separated from their skill and their tools, and who are forced to sell raw, unskilled labor power in order to survive. The result is the industrial capitalism analyzed so powerfully by Marx in which not only goods and services, but also labor-power itself has become a commodity subject to allocation by the forces of supply and demand. We should note that even very substantial progress in, for example, the nature of the underlying energy sources used by the system (from steam to electricity and internal combustion to nuclear power) does not fundamentally alter the overall economic structure.

Industrial capitalism, however, is still not complete capitalism. For this it is necessary for capital itself to become a commodity. Partly this is the result of economic processes: the gradual concentration of capital and the formation of a new stratum of *rentiers* on whom industrial entrepreneurs and managers are effectively dependent. But it also depends in significant measure on the development of technologies which allow rapid reallocation of capital from one activity to the next. The vastly improved transportation and communication networks which began to develop in the nineteenth century with the growth or the railroads and the telegraph and which continued in the first half of the twentieth century with the automobile, the airplane, the telephone, and the radio made possible some tentative progress in this direction, and had Lenin convinced that the imperialism or "finance capitalism" of his period represented the highest stage of capitalism. In reality, however, this finance capitalism was still radically incomplete and had to await the development of new electronic information technologies in the wake of the Second World War. The result is a pull towards a system in which all shares of all enterprises are publicly traded in perfectly competitive capital markets in which each investment is constantly and instantaneously re-evaluated against all other possible options and capital is constantly and instantaneously re-allocated to those options which promise the highest rate of return. This stage we call *infokatallaxis*. There are fundamental physical barriers to its complete realization[2] but it nonetheless represents the ideal of neoliberalism and the principal aim of most public policy at the end of the second millennium of the common era.

While capitalism is first and foremost an economic system, it is nonetheless has very definite political and ideological requirements—requirements which, however, change over the course of its development. We have already noted that the commodification of labor presupposes the dispossession of the laborer and the entrepreneur. No one who can work for himself or herself will willingly labor for another. Historically this has meant first the enclosure of common lands and the eviction of peasant producers, then the ruination of small craftsmen and artisans by competition from large industrial establishments employing ex-peasant labor, and the gradual proletarianization of the *intelligentsia*, understood broadly to include all those who earn their living from skilled labor based on mastery of the liberal arts, sciences, philosophy, and/or theology. In some cases this stage of proletarianization takes the form of a transformation into wage laborers of what were formerly independent professionals with a small capital in their skills—e.g., physicians, attorneys, architects, etc. In other cases it takes the form of a progressive subordination to market norms of the incomes and conditions of labor of salaried teachers, researchers, and officials whose position had formerly been protected by guild regulations and a customary respect for their social functions. In the final years of the twentieth century, however, it has become clear that in fact proletarianization extends ultimately to the figure who was, at one time, regarded as the paragon of capitalism and still figures centrally in capitalist mythology: the entrepreneur. As production becomes ever more capital intensive, so that the start-up capital in technologically advanced sectors vastly exceeds the savings potential of a journeyman engineer or manager, and capital itself becomes a commodity, the entrepreneur is reduced to the status of an agent of his investors, who must be assured

---

2. This is because, even if all factors of production are reduced to pure information, special relativity prohibits instantaneous signaling and thus instantaneous transfer of resources or indeed anything else.

that they are getting the highest possible return on their investments. The development of capitalism also presupposes the construction of unified markets sufficiently large to support the development of industry, and thus the dispossession of all sorts of local authorities which had previously been involved in economic regulation: village communities, guilds, municipalities, feudal entities, and eventually the nation state itself.

This dynamic of dispossession, economic and political, requires the development of a powerful and sophisticated repressive apparatus. So long as the principal target remains peasants, artisans, and the weaker strata of the intelligentsia, and so long as the development of industry requires markets unified only on a national scale, this repressive apparatus takes the form of the nation-state. During the stage of primitive accumulation in particular this state may retain significant pre-capitalist features, as in the case of the absolutist monarchies of the sixteenth through the eighteenth centuries (Anderson 1974b) or the military regimes which guaranteed primitive accumulation in Asia, Africa, and Latin America up through most of the twentieth century.

Two factors, however, have historically tempered this trend towards absolutism. First, capitalism by its very nature creates plural centers of wealth and power, each of which has its own unique portfolio of interests which may differ very significantly from each other. Adjudication of these differences requires the development of some format of representation where the interests of the various sectors of capital can be thrashed out and compromises reached which are compatible both with the balance of power among the various interests and with the overall economic stability of the whole system. In the long run, therefore, capitalism is incompatible with any sort of political system which invests power in one single individual, family or organization (e.g., the military, a political party, etc.). Second, in its struggle against the tributary landed elites which it displaced, the rising bourgeoisie needed allies, which it could only find among the very peasantry, artisanate, and intelligentsia which it was in the process of dispossessing. And the negotiation of an alliance, even among unequal partners, requires the creation of institutional contexts in which the terms of the alliance can be negotiated. As a result of these two dynamics, the period of the development of capitalism, and especially of industrial capitalism, is also the period of the democratic revolutions[3]

---

3. A similar process, of course, took place in Ancient Greece, and above all in Athens, where democracy was the leading weapon of the emerging bourgeoisie in its struggle

Within each national process of capitalist development the specifically bourgeois form of democracy—essentially, as Marx put it, an executive committee representing various sectors of the ruling class—, has vied with the revolutionary and popular democratic forms of the peasant, the artisan, and the intellectual[4] and in each case a different settlement has been reached, which can be understood only in the context of the specific national history in question. Generally speaking the North American and English model reflects the relatively greater weight of the bourgeoisie, which either (in the North American case) had no feudal landed elite to vanquish or (in the English case) was able to do so without much aid from the people, by actually transforming this elite into a fraction of the bourgeoisie, while the Latin model reflects the a much stronger popular-democratic tradition which at times has even vied for hegemony.

The growing strength of the popular classes within even the highly imperfect democratic regimes of the advanced capitalist countries constitutes a constraint on the unrestricted operation of market forces, as does, ultimately, the nation-state itself. In its most advanced, *infokatallactic* stage, therefore, capital increasingly attempts to weaken state structures generally and democratic formats of representation in particular. Partly this happens spontaneously as a result of technological advances which permit the formation of an authentic global market, and thus the reallocation of resources in a way which evades democratically sanctioned restrictions on the operation of market forces. But this spontaneous process is supplemented by the creation of new international bodies such as the International Monetary Fund and the World Bank which apply pressure to vulnerable economic actors so that they act in accord with the interests of capital, and by the transformation of one state structure,

---

against the dunasthV and arconthV, a battle in which it did not hesitate to enlist the support of the very peasants and artisans which it had historically exploited (Anderson 1974).

4. These are, specifically, the village community, which historically exercised democratic control over the land and periodically redistributed it to ensure a rough equality among families, as well as enforcing traditional legal norms and often functioning as a cultic community, and the guild structures of the artisan and intellectual, which exercised a similar functions in an urban setting. In a very real sense, the medieval commune represents one of the high points of an authentically popular democracy, although even here the bourgeoisie was already gaining strength, and the commune never really mounted a contest for sovereignty with the landed elite, but rather existed in the contradiction between the two great feudal powers: the Empire and the Church.

that of the United States, into a global *hegemon* which provides political-military support for capital.[5]

At the ideological level, the most marked requirement of capitalism is, as we have already suggested, the emancipation of the market from all moral constraints which might interfere with the free operation of market forces and the allocation of resources to those activities which promise the highest rate of return. Capitalism, in other words, requires agnosticism regarding questions of ultimate meaning and value. Thus, as we showed in the last chapter, the emergence of petty commodity production in Ancient Greece was accompanied by the development of a variety of skeptical doctrines, rationalistic or atomistic in origin, which undermined traditional religious norms in terms of which the market allocation of resources might have been contested. And the resistance to petty commodity production was led first and foremost by a group of philosophers who focused their attention on the task of regrounding a substantive doctrine of the Good, and of a physics and a metaphysics which could sustain such a doctrine. That metaphysics, precisely because it was adapted to the task of answering both the spontaneous skepticism generated by the market order and the conscious polemics of its defenders became the principal obstacle to the ideological legitimation of capitalism, and the principal target of the ideological struggle of the bourgeoisies.

It is necessary, however, to distinguish two distinct tactics within the larger ideological strategy of the bourgeoisie. Here Georg Lukacs' *The Destruction of Reason* (Lukacs 1953/1980) is especially helpful. According the Lukacs the bourgeoisie, during the period of its rise, when it could still present itself as a force for progress vis-à-vis the old feudal classes, employed a direct apologetic, arguing that capitalism is, in fact, a force for the development of human capacities. After about 1848, however, the de-

---

5. The United States is ideally suited to this task because the United States is not actually a nation-state in the ordinary sense (Dunbar-Ortiz 1974). Rather, it is an imperial entity formed by a coalition of capitalist interests, mostly but not exclusively of English origin, by means of conquest, genocide, and the importation of a foreign labor, some slave and some "free," to carry out the various asks involved in empire building. There is thus no *people* sharing a common history of struggle with which the U.S. state structure is identified. On the contrary, the state structure is identified with the capitalist project as such, and such common identity as exists is focused on the "American," i.e., capitalist way. It is thus relatively easy for this state to expand its sphere of operations to the planet as a whole, portraying itself all the while as the defender of freedom and opportunity.

veloping contradictions of capitalism and the emergence of the workers movement puts the bourgeoisie on the defensive. It became increasingly difficult to legitimate capitalism as a force for social progress, which was being constrained both by ever deeper economic crises and by bourgeois resistance to the economic and political demands of the working class. The result was the elaboration of an "indirect apologetic," which argued not so much that capitalism was just as that a just society is impossible—and that socialism was therefore an empty dream. By the end of the century, this indirect apologetic had taken on the additional task of legitimating imperialist war and expansion—something deeply in conflict with the ideals of the democratic revolutions, but also the only way a capitalist society could resolve its internal contradictions (Lukacs 1953/1980). The direct apologetic presented bourgeois skepticism and agnosticism as an emancipation from a metaphysics which ultimately legitimated the authority of a clerical hierarchy which was hostile to progress and innovation. The indirect polemic, on the other hand, mounted a rather more subtle attack, claiming sometimes that metaphysics is an obstacle to authentic spirituality (Kierkegaard 1840/1941) and sometimes that it is merely a cover for our underlying "will to power (Nietzsche 1889/1968)"—and sometimes both (Heidegger 1934/1989).

Lukacs' theory has extraordinary explanatory power, but it also has some limitations from the standpoint of our task. Lukacs misses, first of all the fact that the "direct apologetic" remains the preferred tactics of the bourgeoisie in periods of economic stabilization and growth, which did not come to an end after 1848, and is alive and well in contemporary neoliberalism. He also remains unable to measure the extent to which Marxism itself is affected by both of the dynamics which he identifies—something which is reflected in its rejection of a transcendental first principle and its ambivalence on cosmic teleology even as it struggles to uphold a realist epistemology and the objectivity of value. This is a subject to which we will return later in this book when we examine the status of the Marxist dialectics of nature. These reservations notwithstanding we will see shortly how these two tactics were deployed beginning in the late middle ages to undermine the edifice of dialectical metaphysics by attacking its foundation in Aristotelian science.

IDEOLOGY AND SCIENCE IN THE STRUGGLE FOR MATHEMATICAL PHYSICS

We have already suggested that the mathematical physics is articulated with the marketplace in three distinct ways: as a τεχνη essential to capitalist processes of production, as a spontaneous reflex of the market order, and as an element in conscious ideological polemics. We need now to examine each of these levels of articulation in more detail.

As we noted in the last chapter after the Hellenistic period the dialectical tradition had incorporated into itself a body of knowledge associated with what were known as the "Hermetic disciplines": astrology, alchemy the kaballah, and related arts, which claimed to possess the key to the "secrets of nature," knowledge of which would confer on the possessor effective control over the material world. There developed a whole literature of "books of secrets" (Eamon 1994) which contained what purported to be occult or esoteric knowledge, whether revealed by the god Hermes or taught secretly by Aristotle. In reality, these books were mostly compendia of techniques—what came to be known as "natural magic," and what we would call technology. They included recipes for medicines, paints, perfumes, and various metallic alloys which could be used for different purposes. Always, however, these texts stressed that before one could understand this esoterica one had to be trained in the ordinary, exoteric disciplines of the arts, sciences, and philosophy. In this way, the books of secrets and the empirical, technological knowledge they contained, served to legitimate, rather than to challenge the leading role of Aristotelian teleological physics and the metaphysics in which it terminated.[6]

---

6. The literature of the *secreta*, with its emphasis on protecting the secrets of nature so that they do not fall into the hands of the *vulgus* is disturbing to most people today, who find the tone elitist and to whom the whole idea notion of concealing knowledge runs counter to the project of promoting universal education which has become dominant since at least the time of the Enlightenment. But let us look at this question more closely. The rationale for secrecy is always the danger that the power conferred by technological knowledge will be misused. Only the philosopher who can judge rightly regarding ends should have access to knowledge of such potent means. And it is not, furthermore, from the ordinary peasant or craftsman (who were often the real source of the secrets in the first place) that the books of secrets at first purported to conceal, and later began systematically to divulge this knowledge, but rather to princes and to the emerging bourgeoisie. What the code of secrecy forbids is placing knowledge which confers power in the hands of people who will use it simply as an agency of empire or a means of personal profit.

Gradually, however, beginning in the later middle ages, due in no small part to the efforts of Roger Bacon and other Franciscan experimentalists, the sort of experimental knowledge represented by the *secreta* began to emancipate itself from the hegemony of the schools and to establish itself as an independent discipline. Partly this process was aided by the fact that many of the phenomena investigated by the experimental or Baconian sciences—electromagnetism, chemistry, etc.—had never had much of a role in the university in the first place, but were the province of craftsmen and artisans searching for more effective techniques. But even older disciplines which enjoyed a place of prestige in the university, such as astronomy and the fundamental sciences of motion were given new impetus by the progress of handicrafts in the late middle ages—e.g., the development of the clock and of the telescope, without which modern mathematical physics and astronomy would be impossible (Eamon 1994: 13-90).

The gradual transformation of the literature of the *secreta* from one of concealment to one of revelation is simply one aspect of a larger trend: the emancipation of technological knowledge from scientific and metaphysical direction and the gradual subordination of science to technology. There has, to be sure, long been a link between mathematical physics and technological development. The marking out of fields, the division of the harvest, the production and use of spears and hoes and plows and

---

Second, it should be pointed out that in our own time we have our own codes of secrecy. Valuable new technologies are made inaccessible to a public which might benefit from them by intellectual property laws, which allow innovators or their *rentier* patrons to exact monopoly rents from anyone who wishes to have legal access to these secrets. And the state apparatus has its own complex system of "classified" knowledge which is accessible only to those who have proven themselves trustworthy servants of capital. Indeed, employment at the highly prestigious national laboratories—one of the few places left where scientists can pursue basic research without concern for market imperatives—is at least partly restricted to those who are able to obtain the coveted "Q" clearance which allows access to weapons research. The difference is in the criteria used for selecting individuals to whom secret knowledge is to be entrusted. The Pseudo-Aristotelian author of the *Secretum Secretorum*, wanted to restrict knowledge of the secrets to those with philosophical and moral training and who thus can be presumed to have some love of the truth. When U.S. government agencies do background security checks on prospective employees, on the other hand, they routinely ask references whether, assuming the subject of the investigation were to betray his or her country, it would be for ideological principles, money, or sex. Those whose references say they would betray their country for principle are most likely to be turned down for employment. Those who would betray for sex have the best chance of eventually being cleared for employment.

wagons and dwellings all posed a multitude of mathematical and mechanical questions. On the one hand, space and time had to be marked out and measured, and the underlying properties of their organization understood. On the other hand the local motion of objects, moved by human, animal, wind, or waterpower had to be analyzed in order to permit the production of more efficient tools and the more effective utilization of limited energy resources. Of all the technological processes bound up with the development of mathematical physics, however, none was more important than agriculture. We are not inclined, today, to think of agriculture as a force for innovation in mathematical physics, but it was the cultivation of plants which first posed for humanity the problem which has driven research in theoretical physics up through the present period: i.e., the measurement and prediction of the motions of the heavenly bodies and thus the construction of an accurate and reliable calendar on the basis of which correct decisions may be made regarding planting, harvesting, etc.

Excellence in the measurement of local motion, be it terrestrial or celestial, has thus been valued in all human societies, as well it should be. Nearly all societies count among the objects of their worship or veneration "culture heroes" remembered for contributing various arts, many of which are distinctly mechanical in nature. Consider Prometheus or Vulcan, or the Hopi Katchinas. And astronomy was almost always treated as a sacred art, closely allied with the priesthood. The preparation of the calendar did not only determine the time of planting and harvesting but also the dates of the sacred festivals, which were an integral part of the agricultural cycle and necessary for agrarian fertility. The earliest observatories formed an integral part of temple complexes, and in communitarian societies sacred structures such as the Anasazi kivas often had specific astronomical functions.

Even so, neither the toolmaker nor even the astronomer ever pretended to have understood the secrets of the universe. Theirs were strictly subaltern arts, ordered to the life-giving activities of peasant, the priest—and, in tributary societies, the warrior—on whom the welfare of the society ultimately depended. The peasant, who cultivated the soil and thus shared in the creative activity of the gods who had brought forth humans from this same earth was, in a sense, nearer the gods and more priestly than the tool maker or astronomer who served him much as he served the priests. Even when the heavens came to be regarded as the abode of the gods, and when the gods themselves were called by astral names—Ishtar, Citalinincue—their activities were represented in ways which marked the centrality of activities other than observation and measurement. Ishtar (the name means star) was a goddess of love and fertility, the Aztec Citalinincue, whose name means star-skirt, created humanity by sending the *tecpatl*, or sacrificial obsidian knife-blade to earth (Brundage 1985).

The emancipation of the mathematical physicist from the (Aristotelian) scientist and the philosopher whom served was driven in part by the technological revolution of the middle ages. As William Eamon points out, there was a rather complex and ambiguous relationship between *ars* and *scientia* during the middle ages. On the one hand academics were avid collectors of *secreta*, many of which were the product of midwifery, village-based herbalism, empirical medicine, and crafts techniques of various sorts. On the other hand, their aim was always to *explain* why these techniques worked and to use the resulting explanations to legitimate their claims to superior authority and social status. The difficulty, of course, was that often this effort failed. Alchemy, for example, produced far more useful chemical techniques—techniques which found applications in fields as diverse as the distilling of alcoholic beverages, pharmacy, metalworking, painting, and jewelry production—than it did convincing chemical theories. In other fields, such as medicine, the divide was greater still. Academic theoretical medicine had little or nothing to do with the actual treatment of disease. The result was a shift in the relative social weight accorded theoretical and practical knowledge and a tendency to undermine the political position of medieval science, and thus the scientific foundations of metaphysics. This process was hurried along by the advent of printing, which created a mass market for "how-to manuals" which were often new editions of ancient and medieval *secreta*, but stripped of both their Aristotelian physical and metaphysical underpinnings and of their esoteric trappings (Eamon 1994: 38–133).

The second factor in the crisis of metaphysics and its Aristotelian physical foundation was the spontaneous action of the marketplace on the ideological sphere. We have already seen that societies regulated by markets tend spontaneously to appear to their members as systems of quantities (prices), or else as systems of only externally related atoms (individuals), and that this soon becomes the model on which people think about the universe as a whole. This, in turn, changes the whole meaning attached to the measurement and formalization of local motion. In earlier social formations, communitarian, archaic, or tributary, measurement of local motion was always regarded as useful, but only as useful, i.e., as a means to some higher end. The calendar was important because it told the people when to plant and the priests when to hold their feasts. Planting and presiding at the feasts were, however, the really important activities to which the calendar was ordered. In an emerging petty commodity society, such as that of Ancient Greece, however, numbers increasingly seem to govern the organization of human society. So many bushels of wheat and so many yards of indigo wool are somehow equivalent, somehow the same, in the eyes of the marketplace. Higher prices command increased levels of activity in the way no priest or warlord ever could, and declining prices send previously eager producers into a state of apathetic lassitude from which public liturgies suddenly seem incapable of rousing them. It is little wonder that the Pythagoreans, who began to penetrate the mysteries of number and quantity soon constituted themselves on the model of a mystical sect and considered themselves the true priesthood of the new era. The cult of the number is the spontaneous ideology of the marketplace, the natural religion of the bourgeoisie, and the mathematical physicist is its philosopher of first resort. Other philosophers, we will see, are admitted only in times of crisis. The psychologist, who pretends to a doctrine of the soul on the "scientific" model of mathematical physics, becomes the priest of his private chapel. It is to mathematical physics that the bourgeoisie looks for the technological innovations which catalyze social progress. It is to mathematical physics that the bourgeoisie looks for the tools by which his portfolio of investments is to be managed. And it is to mathematical physics that he looks for a judgment regarding the "fate of the universe." Where once the astronomer answered to the priest or to the dialectician, who alone knew what made the heavens move, rather than merely describing their motion, now the priest and dialectician alike are obliged to answer to the mathematical cosmologist and to "reinterpret" their doctrines in a way respects the unquestioned authority of the "standard model," in cosmology as in economics.

The third factor in the rise of mathematical physics is one which we have already begun to examine in the last chapter: i.e., the Augustinian reaction which began in the middle of the thirteenth century as the clerical hierarchy became increasingly threatened by the rise of Aristotelian physics to prominence in the medieval university. We will argue that—contrary to the progressivist mythology promoted by the bourgeoisie as part of its "direct apologetic" for capitalism, which depicts mathematical physicists such as Galileo as great heroes in the struggle against an obscurantist Church wedded to outmoded Aristotelian ideas—the triumph of mathematical physics was in fact the work of profoundly reactionary social forces and that it is Stephen Tempier, Bishop of Paris and one of the leaders of the Reaction, and not Copernicus, Kepler, Galileo, or Newton who should be regarded as the father of modern physics.

We have already seen how Aristotelian science and metaphysics merged with Jewish, Christian, and Islamic theology during the middle ages, at once helping to legitimate a clergy which claim to be the bearer of prophetic tradition, and tempering the other-worldly tendencies which had emerged within these traditions, especially Christianity. We have also seen how this synthesis tended to work to the advantage of the masters of arts, and the guilds generally, by showing that all creative activity is in fact a real participation in the life of God, thus calling at least partially into question the privileged position of the clergy and threatening to challenge frontally the hegemony of the warrior elite.

It should thus come as no surprise that the clergy and the aristocracy should mount a counter-offensive. What is striking, however, is the extent to which this counter-offense shaped the future development of physics. Prior to the victory of the Augustinians in 1277, there had been a developing consensus in favor of the Aristotelian view that the universe was in fact eternal, that it consisted of a nine finite concentrically nested spheres surrounded by an empyrean heaven outside space and time, and that there could be neither other worlds nor extracosmic void space. All motion or change was driven by the attractive power of the unmoved mover, mediated by the perfect spherical motion of the heavenly bodies, and gave rise in the sublunar regions to the various mineral, vegetable, animal, and rational forms which populate the earth. Accommodation with the prophetic tradition required a difficult effort to reconcile the eternity of the world with divine creation "*ex nihilo*" and with prophecies of an end of time, a process that was by no means complete when it was cut short by the Condemnations of 1277, but which had every chance of success. The result was what we have called the "Aristotelian space-time," in which place and motion had definite axiological coordinates and in which everything shared to some extent in the divine nature.

It was precisely this latter point which constituted the focus of the Augustinian offensive. If God and the universe were too nearly alike—

if God was merely a natural tendency of the universe itself, and end to which it tended quite of its own accord—then perhaps the ministrations of the clergy were unnecessary and the surplus they consumed wasted. Thus the assault on a whole range of Aristotelian theses which pulled in this direction. Among the propositions which were attacked and eventually condemned in 1277, the following stand out for their importance to physics:

- the eternity of the world,
- the role of intermediate causes in the production of individual species,
- the impossibility of other worlds,
- the impossibility of extracosmic void space, and
- the claim that God cannot move the universe rectilinearly. (Grant 1996: 53–56)

What the condemnation did was to undermine the Aristotelian understanding of the relationship between God and the universe as one of necessary teleological attraction and replace it with a focus on a divine creativity radically different from anything of which human beings would be capable.

But if the Condemnations of 1277 were theological in motive, they had profound implications for the development of properly physical reasoning. This impact was both methodological and substantive. At the methodological level, the Condemnations pushed physics away from deductive explanation and towards mathematical formalization. The Augustinian defense of divine sovereignty implied that what God does, including His creative activity in the natural world, being radically free, cannot be the object of deductive knowledge. If we are to understand God's handiwork we must observe it directly, and even so we may never fully penetrate its secrets and reduce it to a rationally comprehensible system (Duhem 1913–1959). This, in turn, implied, that if we are to know anything at all about the universe, we must engage in careful empirical observation and search for patterns in the "book of creation." It is only one small step toward the focus on mathematical formalization which became dominant in the seventeenth century, and the fourteenth century did, in fact, witness enormous progress in the application of mathematical methods to physical problems, something to which the Franciscan schools which developed at Oxford devoted itself.

At the substantive level, the impact was no less dramatic. This is because, in order to be fully consistent with each other, the propositions which the condemnations required Christians to affirm,—especially the possibility of other worlds and of extracosmic void space—effectively required the existence of something like Newtonian space-time—i.e., of an absolute void space independent of but capable of receiving bodies. Indeed, it was in part a belief in the impossibility of such a space which had kept Aristotle and his followers from allowing the possibility of other worlds—which in order to best imitate the divine perfection had to be spherical, and which would thus necessarily leave extracosmic void space in between them.

The road from Aristotelian to Newtonian space-time was, to be sure, a long and complex one. So powerful was the Aristotelian identification of space with corporeality that at first an extracosmic void space could be conceived only as "imaginary" and without extension. This was the position held by, among others Nicole Oresme, John Major, Thomas Bradwardine, Francisco Suarez, Thomas Compton-Carleton, and the Coimbra Jesuits. What such an unextended space might be was difficult to specify, but it was, in general, associated in some way with the divine immensity without actually being identified with God. Emanuel Maignan, for example, argued that spiritual substances occupy space differently than corporeal substances. Since spiritual substances are simple and without parts, the whole of the substance is fully present in each point of its space, which is proportional to the intensive perfection proper to the spirit in question. For God, of course, this perfection and the space associated with it, is infinite. This imaginary extracosmic void space provided a place where God could create other worlds should he choose to—though very few thinkers actually claimed that he had. From here it is only one very small step to add dimensionality and extension to the void, something which effectively brings into being Newton's absolute space. Indeed Newton and Spinoza did not hesitate to in some sense identify this space with God. For Newton it was the divine sensorium (Grant 1996: 171–85). For Spinoza it was, along with thought, one of the two divine attributes which we could know, there being an infinity of others not accessible to reason (Spinoza 1677/1955). In a certain sense, however, it is the immediately pre-Newtonian step that is more interesting. Don't we find in the notion of an imaginary space the intellectual antecedent of such abstract spaces as event-spaces or a phase-spaces which are so important to the formalization of physical problems, and also, perhaps of the space into which the "bubble-universes" of contemporary many-worlds cosmologists emerge?

What the requirement of other worlds did for space the concept of creation *ex nihilo*—coupled with the expectation that the world would, at some point, come to an end—did for that of time. A universe with a beginning and an end is at once constantly changing and irreducibly a-teleological. Why, after all, would God destroy a universe which was tending toward perfection? Time thus became, like space, something value-neutral, the measure of purely local rather than teleological and progressive motion. Change, similarly, was increasingly understood not as a necessary response of matter to a teleological attractor, but rather as something driven from the outside—i.e., as an essentially mechanical process. One Augustinian thinker, Robert Grosseteste, even developed an early form of the Big Bang theory, according to which the universe emerged from a point of light which expanded in all directions, giving rise to mathematical proportionality and corporeal dimensionality. This light was, in turn identified with the divine illumination that, according to Augustinian doctrine, is the basis of human knowledge of intelligibles (Wallace 1978: 95–96). If this was not enough, the doctrine of *rationes seminales*, which taught that God planted within the creation "seeds" of all possible forms, was calculated to minimize the role of secondary causation and of human participation in God's creative activity. Everything that comes to be already exists seminally in God's creative act. The most any creature can claim is to tend God's garden.

The forces of the Augustinian reaction were joined in their attack on Aristotelian science by unlikely allies. We have already noted in the last chapter that as the Augustinian reaction took hold in the late thirteenth and especially in the fourteenth centuries, the secular intelligentsia, concerned to protect its autonomy from the clergy, began to adopt and increasingly secularist stance. At first this was apparent only in political philosophy. Thus Marsiglio of Padua restricted the state to the role of *Defensor Pacis*, defender of the peace, rejecting the claims or earlier Averroists that it was responsible for the moral education of humanity. This was because assigning to the state such an educative role threatened to place it under the direction of the Church, which presumably could at least teach and quite possibly rule on moral questions. The effect, however, was to undermine the whole Aristotelian theory of the state and to set political theory on the road to liberalism, which saw the state less as an agent for the Common Good and more as an arbiter between competing individual interests (Goerner 1965).

Political theory, however, requires an adequate metaphysical foundation. Marsiglio's proto-liberal theory of the state was incompatible with the larger Aristotelian doctrine promoted by the Averroists generally. Political Averroism turns out not really to be Averroist at all. This is because, with in the context of a teleological cosmology and metaphysics, all systems are ordered not only to an end, but to the End as such, which is God. While this means that the secular arena has a dignity all its own, which it derives from the fact that it represents a real participation in the life of God, quite apart from the action of divine grace or the sacerdotal ministrations of the clergy, it cannot be accorded radical autonomy. Liberal politics would require a new scientific and metaphysical foundation.

The key transitional figure in this regard is someone not often regarded as being in the mainstream of European political thought: Benedict Spinoza. Spinoza's *Tractatus Theologico-Politicus* is, in many ways, very much in the tradition of *political* Averroism. Religion is an amalgam of moral truths presented in imaginative form which provides a useful means of social control and moral education for the masses, but its content can be properly understood only by the secular intelligentsia which comprehends the intelligible content of the images, something which it has, in any case, already arrived at on the basis of reason. But the underlying ethics, and the science and metaphysics which stands behind that ethics, is no longer Aristotelian. What these moral truths really amount to is simply a system of rules designed to help individual "modes" of the one Substance, which is Nature or God persist in being by understanding the laws of nature, the principles which govern the operation of the system as a whole. And this whole has been stripped of the last remnants of teleological organization. Ethics is reduced to enlightened self-interest because no system higher than the individual can really be said to be an end, and certainly not a higher order end. The universe as a whole takes precedence over the individual, who must bow to its laws, simply because of its supreme power. And what is behind the collapse of cosmic teleology? The displacement of Aristotelian by mathematical physics.

By undercutting cosmic teleology, mathematical physics undercuts the metaphysical foundations of those political doctrines which would subordinate the individual to such higher ends as the human civilizational project or God and thus serves to liberate the individual to makes his own way in a world which is, however, increasingly bereft of meaning.

The Augustinian reaction, by attacking the notion that we can comprehend the universe by means of a deductive science promotes the development of mathematical physics, which focuses instead on the formalization of local motion. Mathematical physics, in turn, promotes the development of liberalism, which paves the way for the development of capitalism and the political ascent of the bourgeoisie. In the process of course, by undermining any rational basis for believing in God, and thus in the possibility and reasonableness of revelation, both polemics ended up by undermining the authority of the very clergy which had set the process into motion.

In practice, these two polemics intertwined with each other and interacted with the technological and economic developments associated with the rise of capitalism in a complex and subtle way. Thus, William Eamon points out that the artisan who rejected university (Aristotelian) science in favor of the empirical techniques embodied in the books of secrets was also likely to reject Catholicism for Protestantism—or later for freethinking liberal doctrines. Often, he was a journeyman whose ascent to the status of master had been blocked by the guildmasters anxious to preserve their privileges, or a member of new trades not regulated by the guilds—and incidentally closely associated with the development of a whole new culture of practically oriented literacy, facilitated by the advent of the printing press. This turn was initially experienced as an emancipation, which in many ways it was. But liberty under conditions of the market order soon turns into an alibi for exploitation. Merchant entrepreneurs soon began to accumulate capital and to gain control of the means of production. Initially they contracted with workers in their individual workshops, paying them part-wages and piece rates; later they began to group them into manufactories. The "recipes" provided in the "books of secrets" allowed them to hire and train workers entirely outside the guild apparatus, who had the skills necessary to do what the market required but who had no protections and little in the way of the larger vision of the purpose of human society and their place within it which had been provided by the guild community. Thus the development of literacy, the cultivation of a new sort of technical knowledge among the working classes, and their emancipation from the hegemony of philosopher and priest became instruments of proletarianization and capitalist development (Eamon 1994).

THE FUNDAMENTAL CONCEPTS OF MATHEMATICAL PHYSICS

It should by now be apparent that the emergence of capitalism presupposed a radical transformation in what was meant by "science" and in the way science is done. Having analyzed in some detail the social basis of this transformation, we need now to state more rigorously and formally what it involved at the conceptual level. The material object of science—the universe with all its myriad phenomena—remains the same. What changes is the formal object and the sort of abstraction which is used to analyze this object. While both teleological and mathematical physics study change, the first understands change first and foremost in qualitative terms, and regards local motion as simply an aspect, and not a very interesting aspect, of the larger problem of how matter evolves towards ever higher degrees of organization. Mathematical physics, on the other hand, understands *all* change, even change which appears qualitative, as local motion, i.e., as the rearrangement of the parts of a thing into a more complex pattern. And rather than attempting to explain why this change takes place, mathematical physics simply describes it in rigorous formal terms. It follows that if we are to understand mathematical physics we need to understand, first of all, what is involved in the idea of local motion and, second, what it means to produce a formal mathematical description of a physical phenomenon.

The Concept of Local Motion

The retheorization of change as local motion arises naturally out of life in the market system and, in turn, fundamentally alters the meaning of such basic concepts as space and time, matter and energy, order and organization. This reduction is at first a product of spontaneous processes: a focus on certain fundamentally mechanical technologies and on the movement of commodities in the marketplace. On the technological side, the development of handicrafts and then the systematization of crafts techniques in the "books of secrets" entailed a focus on changes which could be brought about by processes of a purely mechanical nature—cutting, joining, bending, heating, cooling, etc. Systematization of these processes necessarily involved a growing focus on careful measurement and thus the quantification of processes which may earlier have been understood in purely qualitative terms. On the economic side, life in a market economy involves, as we have noted, participation in what is at once a real space in which commodities move, quite literally, from one place to another, at a definite cost in terms of human, animal, or other forms of energy, *and* in the ideal or abstract space of the market itself, which is a pure system of quantities (prices) which "move" metaphorically in response to the (strictly informational) "forces" of supply and demand. What begins as a spontaneous process, eventually becomes, as we have seen, the object of a conscious polemic which makes the organic ideology of the bourgeoisie into the governing thought-form of the society as a whole.

Now the concept of local motion logically presupposes a whole complex of more fundamental concepts, each of which must be defined if local motion is to be theorized. There is, first of all, the concept of *space*. Things which move must be someplace, pass through some place, and arrive at a destination. Second, in so far as they move at all, and are not simply in more than one place simultaneously, things which move do so over *time*. Once space and time have been defined, it is possible to define a whole complex of subordinate concepts which describe motion itself, such as distance, direction, trajectory, velocity, and acceleration.

As we have seen, the Augustinian polemic against Aristotelian science served to undermine Aristotle's teleological and axiological space-time. This, coupled with the spontaneous movement towards formalization generated by the market order itself constrains the way in which space and time can be theorized, but it does not, by itself, specify them. On the contrary, we will see that the absolute, neutral space of Newton structured by a Pythagorean metric determined by the fixed frame of the stars soon gives way to the more fluid structure of Maxwell's electromagnetic space, determined by the medium of the luminferous ether and eventually to the relativistic space-time of Einstein in which fixed frames have disappeared entirely. The way in which space and time are defined in turn determines what is meant by local motion as such. This is true both at the level of the underlying mathematical formalization and its physical interpretation. Thus Newtonian motion is formalized as a vector within a real-valued vector space and interpreted physically as a point-particle with mass moving through an absolute space over time; Einsteinian (special relativistic) motion is formalized as a vector in a Minkowski space and interpreted as signaling between two independent frames of reference. What all of these various space-times have in common, however is their underlying value-neutrality. There is no privileged standpoint, no place which in and of itself (like the celestial spheres of Aristotle or the higher *lokas* or *dhatus* of Hindu and Buddhist cosmology) indicates a higher degree of development or greater proximity to God. The same is true of time.

Mathematical physics theorizes time in many different and—we will argue—contradictory ways. Thus from the standpoint of dynamics, whether Newtonian or relativistic, Maxwellian or quantum-mechanical, time is reversible. While it is not strictly speaking accurate to say that time is "just another dimension," because all of these disciplines theorize in ways which makes it mathematically distinguishable from the purely spatial dimensions, the formalisms themselves contain no arrow of time, nothing which suggests that events in the past cause those in the future any more than those in the future cause those in the past (Prigogine 1984). Thermodynamics, on the other hand, does have such an arrow— that of entropy, or increasing disorder—and thus presents a vision of the universe which is not only a-teleological but actually antiteleological (von Helmholtz 1854/1961). And evolutionary theory, which might be read as once again endowing time with axiological significance, in fact for the most part rigorously eschews such readings of its results as hopelessly "metaphysic", arguing that evolution, if it has a "direction" at all, is tends simply towards greater diversity, or towards the more efficient exploitation of available niches (Mayr 1982).

Local motion implies that there is something which moves and something which is the cause of motion. Thus the persistence, albeit with very different meanings, in mathematical physics of two key concepts from Aristotle: matter and energy. It is interesting to note here, however, that the pair matter/energy represents a bit of semantic cross over. For Aristotle matter, or ὕλη was contrasted with form or μορφη. The matter/form pair was then effectively identified with the pair potency/act or δυναμεια/ενεργεια. Matter, for Aristotle, is the potential for form or organization, form is the actualization of that potential. Pairing matter with energy already changes the meaning of the terms by emphasizing passivity of the former and the activity of the latter. Matter is, for mathematical physics, simply what is moved or, to be more precisely, the otherwise utterly undefined receptacle of the various quantitative determinations which make motion possible—i.e., of various energies. Thus matter is defined as being capable of having, without being thereby being identified with, any of the following: mass, extension, velocity, acceleration, momentum, force, charge, etc. What mathematical physics actually turns out to be about—when it is not about the underlying structure of space-time—is, in fact energy and not matter. Even when, as chemistry, it thinks of itself as studying the structure of matter, what it is really looking at are the way in which energy structures interact, something which is further reducible to local motion or the potential for local motion in the form for example, of changes in the arrangement of electrons between two atoms. We will see that as mathematical physics develops, the very distinction between matter and energy disappears as relativistic formalizations render such concepts of mass and length dependent on frame on reference and thus ultimately on velocity and quantum formalizations make the particle/wave distinction obsolete. We will also see that, like the matter/form distinction in Aristotelian physics, the matter/energy distinction is entirely ideological in origin, and that the mode of its disappearance is, similarly, ideological rather than scientifically determined.

At the beginning of mathematical physics the repertoire of fundamental concepts is limited to these. Gradually, however, as mathematical physics begins to extend its domain into the realm of biology and sociology, an additional problem needs to be theorized: that of organization and evolution. At least initially analyzing the physiology of a bird or the development of life from simple one-celled forms up to humanity seems rather a different sort of activity than modeling the motions of heavenly bodies or the operation of a heat engine. The same is true of analyzing a kinship system or a social revolution. Among other things, biologists and social scientists have found it difficult to purge teleological concepts entirely from their day to day practice. At the same time, for the reasons we have already identified above, it is vitally important to Capital, that teleological thinking be purged, *especially* in the social sciences. The result is a reduction of the concept of organization to that of order or structure. This tendency first appears in the mid-nineteenth century with the appearance of the concept of entropy. Originally developed to measure irreducible inefficiencies in the operation of heat engines, as energy was dissipated and rendered in capable of doing work, the idea was soon restated as a measure of the order or disorder of a system. This is, in turn, identical with the information content of a system, which is nothing more or less than our ability to specify, using a simple rule, the position and state of each of its elements. This, in turn, makes it possible to develop information-theoretical definitions of life and intelligence, so that both can be described in terms of local motion (Tipler 1994). Information theory, in other words, is nothing more or less than the reduction of organization to a problem of local motion, making possible the completion of mathematical physics and the unification of all of the sciences under its domain. Indeed, Frank Tipler even proposes an information-theoretical definition of God! We will have occasion to examine these theories in great detail later in this book.

What is Formalization?

Having specified what we mean by local motion and the reduction of change to local motion, we need now to specify what we mean by formalization. In order to do this we need to consider the act of formalization and the status of the formalism, or mathematical object, itself. As we have noted briefly above, and at greater length elsewhere (Mansueto 2002b), the process used by mathematical physicists when they describe physical systems is one of three distinct degrees of abstraction:

1. totalization, which abstracts from the individual to the logical whole of which it is a part, arriving at a rudimentary and informal definition which is usually little more than a collection of distinctions,

2. formalization, which abstracts from the individual to its underlying structure, which it attempts to model, arriving at a rigorous definition from which conclusions may be drawn analytically, and

3. transcendental abstraction, which abstracts from the structure of a thing to its underlying organizing principle—the reason for its being and for its being the way it is.

Formalization grows naturally out of totalization, and begins simply enough, with in an effort to render our systems of classification reasonable and rigorous. We look to classify on the basis of similar differences and different similarities. The result is a system of ratios. The relation between felines and canines is the same as (or similar to) the relationship between bovines and caprines—i.e., both are "families" within larger taxonomic orders. The ratio can, furthermore, be expressed in formal terms

$$A:B::C:D$$

This, or any other ratio, gives us two of the three building blocks of formal systems: a *relation* which defines *elements* in a system. Further development of the taxonomy gives us the other building block: *operations*. Thus we can add *taxa* and thus ascend the taxonomic hierarchy from family to order to class to phylum, or multiply this classificatory scheme by another: e.g., the distinction between male and female, marine or terrestrial, etc. It is our contention that all formal abstraction arises out of such efforts to render classifications rigorous.

As Piaget points out (Piaget 1952, 1968), however, the operations involved in classification are still concrete, i.e., operations on things rather than operations on propositions themselves. In order to advance to authentic formalization we must take one further step back and ask about the rules governing operations. The simplest examples of such rules are the laws of arithmetic. Are there, for example, additive and/or multiplicative identities or inverses for the operations we are using? Are the operations commutative? distributive? associative? We must also ask about the system itself. Is it closed under the operations in question? i.e., if we perform the operation on one member of the system do we get another member of the system, in which case we say the system is closed, or do we get a result which is outside the system we were considering entirely? A system of elements, defined by their relationships with each other, in which defined operations have certain definite properties, is a *category* (Geroch 1985). As we advance from totalization to formalization of any given system, we are, in effect, defining a category in which certain operations are possible and others are not, and in which these operations have certain properties. The more operations are defined within a category, and the more law-like the behavior of those operations, the more *structure* exists within a given category.

Mathematical physics is fundamentally the art of using mathematical categories to model local motion, or to model changes in the state of systems which is being treated as if it was local motion. Any given category, such as a set, a group, a ring or a field, can be represented imaginatively as a space in which the elements of the category are points which are related to each other by operations which obey the rules which govern the category. If we are describing local motion in a real space, then each point represents a definite location or instant; from there it becomes possible to model direction, velocity, acceleration, etc. If we are describing changes in the physical, biological or social state of a system—e.g., changes in temperature, pressure, or volume, population, rate of reproduction, rate of death, and effectiveness of exploitation, or supply, demand, and price, then each dimension represents one of the quantities being measured and each point a definite combination of values of these various quantities. The "space" in question is, of course, abstract.

In the mathematics by which we half-unconsciously formalize our day to day experience, all of the arithmetic operations are commutative, associative, and distributive, and all have identities and inverses. Thus we can add groups of objects to each other and subtract from them, multiply them and divide them, and expect all the rules of arithmetic to hold. More complex activities, however, such as the measurement of fields, the construction of buildings, and the description of local motion, whether celestial or terrestrial, can be formalized only in terms of categories more complex than those we use to manipulate discrete groups of objects. Among other things, we must define distance, something which involves the notion of a *metric*, or distance function, and eventually such objects as *vectors*, which combine quantity with direction. This is sufficient structure to formalize most of the physics which developed up through the eighteenth century.

Certain kinds of physical systems, however, can be formalized only using categories with less or different structure than that used in the conscious or unconscious formalization of everyday experience. Thus, for example, formalization of gravity turns out to require the use of metrics or distance formulae different from the familiar Pythagorean Theorem, with the counter-intuitive result that space is curved. Quantum systems can be described only using noncommutative operators, i.e., operations which give different results depending on the order of the elements operated on, something which gives rise to such counter-intuitive results as the Heisenberg Uncertainty Principle. Other sorts of physical systems—e.g., dynamic and thermodynamic systems such as weather patterns, heat engines, and complex chemical interactions—can be represented formally only in "abstract" spaces in which each dimension corresponds to a different property: temperature, density, etc.

Some aspects of biological systems, such as the chemical processes which make life possible or the dynamics plant or animal populations, can be formalized using methods not too different from those used in the physical sciences. The same is true of certain aspects of social systems. The laws of the marketplace have the same form as some of the most fundamental laws of physics and, like those laws, are described using the calculus. Other aspects of biological and social organization have proven more resistant to formalization. Biological taxonomies, for example, seem to possess no structure more interesting than a simple additive classification. Recently, however, there has been an attempt to formalize aspects of social organization which were hitherto considered most resistant to this sort of treatment: language, kinship, myth and cultural "texts" in general. It is this activity which has led to the emergence of the "structuralist" trend. Structuralism is rooted in the notion that social systems, as much as any other systems have the basic properties which make formalization possible. Piaget does a particularly good job of defining these properties. Structures are, first of all, characterized by wholeness. The elements can be defined—indeed, exist—only in relationship to each other. That this is true for the signs in a language, for positions in a kinship system, or for the elements in a myth should be fairly obvious. Words are defined in terms of other words. The position "aunt" exists only in relation to the position "nephew" and vice versa. The meaning of various elements in a myth depends on their relations to each other. Thus the cross has a different significance in the context of Christianity, where it represents redemption through suffering, than it does in Hopi culture, where it simply stands for the four directions of the universe. Second, structures are systems of transformation. They consist, that is, in operations which map one element in the system to another. Thus syntactic rules allow the mapping or association of one signifier with another, kinship rules the mapping or association of one individual with another, myths the mapping or association of one symbol with another. This claim is less obvious if it is intended as a unique way of understanding these phenomena, or if it is claimed that everything that happens in the systems in question is formalizable in these terms. But there is little doubt that it is possible to discover formal rules of this kind. Finally, Piaget claims, authentic structures are "closed" much as the set of real numbers is closed for addition, subtraction, division, multiplication, and the taking of square roots or distances. This property he ascribes to sociological structures only in the looser sense that social systems are "self-regulating" or have ways of maintaining their stability.

It follows from Piaget's formulation that to the extent that we are able to formalize social systems at all, the process involves defining categories with their own distinctive operations and properties. We begin, in the social as in the physical and biological sciences, by observing and classifying. But as we attempt to arrive at more rigorous classifications, and to understand the relationships between various *taxa*, we inevitably pass over into formalization. What distinguishes the structuralist trend from other currents in the social sciences is simply the strength of the claims made on behalf of formalization, and especially the claim that it is in grasping the underlying structure of social systems that we best understand them. We will see later that there are good reasons to doubt this claim.

What about the status of the formalism itself—of the mathematical object which is the result of the act of formalization? This is, of course, the fundamental question in the philosophy of mathematics, and the way in which we resolve it does much to determine the way in which we understand the results of mathematical physics. If mathematical objects are in fact real, then in identifying the mathematical structure of the universe, mathematical physics does more than merely figure out how the universe works in order to better use its resources. Rather, it takes a step, at least, towards understanding the mind of God of which the underlying structure of space time and the laws governing local motion are taken to be a reflection. This is view, which traces its origin to Pythagoras and the Platonic tradition, seems to have been that of Kepler and Newton as well, and continues to be popular among relativistic physicists in the tradition of Einstein.

It is possible, however, that mathematical forms are an artifact of the human mind and not a fundamental feature of the universe, the real nature of which remains impenetrable to us. This was the position of Kant who regarded space and time as fundamental forms of the sensuous intuition. Apart from these forms, he argued, we could experience nothing. The difficulty, of course, was that he identified these forms with Euclidean geometry and classical arithmetic and in general understood space-time in Newtonian terms. Radical Kantians, known as "intuitionists" reject the validity of all mathematics which yields objects, such as actual infinities and exotic topologies, which cannot be imaginatively constructed. More moderate Kantians, known as formalists, yield on this point but still have difficulty explaining just why objects which are the product of the way in which the human mind is structured turn out to be so useful in describing the way the universe operates.

One might have thought that this would provoke a return to Pythagorean and "Platonizing" approaches to mathematics, and to some extent it has. The difficulty is that while mathematics generally is very useful in describing the universe, the mathematical structures used by various disciplines are, in fact, very different and not ultimately compatible with each other—a point which we will develop at greater length in a later chapter. God, it seems, is of many minds. This has strengthened the hand of radical nominalists and empiricists, who believe that mathematical forms were merely conventions—useful ways of organizing our perceptions of the universe dictated not by innate forms of intuition but rather by the rules of logic or, in more contemporary formulations, by the economy of information storage and processing itself. This was the view of Bertrand Russell and Alfred North Whitehead, and it is the view of information theoretical neoliberals such as F. A. Hayek (Hayek 1988) and Frank Tipler (Tipler 1994) in the present period. It might seem that this view would call into question the hegemony of mathematics in the epistemic field, but it has not. We will see that this sort of subjective idealism in fact leads back, by way of quantum mechanics and information theory, to still another way of mathematizing the divine and thus divinizing the mathematical.

Each of these approaches to the philosophy of mathematics reflects a definite stage in the development of the market order. Pythagorean and Platonizing approaches reflect the situation under petty commodity production and mercantilism in which there remains a "fixed frame" of nonmarket institutions in which the market operates, including, generally a monarchic state which organizes and directs the operation of market forces. Kantian approaches reflect the realities of industrial, competitive capitalism in which this fixed frame has disappear and not only goods and services but also labor have been commodified. As Lukaçs pointed out (Lukaçs 1922/1971), under conditions of generalized commodity production the market knows only the price and not the use-value of a thing. People begin to believe that they cannot penetrate to the thing in itself; we know only how things appear to the sensuous intuition and the categories of the understanding. But the rootedness of the economy in material projection, which is constantly increasing, helps conserve the belief that there is indeed a use-value, a thing in itself veiled under the price-form and the phenomenon. Subjective idealist approaches reflect the trend towards finance capitalism and *infokatallaxis* in which capital as well has become a commodity and economic activity, at least from the standpoint of the *rentier* elites has little to do with material production and everything to do with consumption—and thus with the way in which things are perceived. We will see in later chapters how the development of capitalism from one stage to the next affects the larger development of mathematical physics.

The one position which has not been popular in the period since the "scientific revolution" of the seventeenth century is that of Aristotle, which holds that mathematical forms are abstracted from matter and are in a certain sense proper to it. It is possible, to be sure, to infer from the forms thus abstracted still other forms, which do not exist in matter, but these have no being outside the mind. Immaterial being, furthermore, being simple and without number or extension, lacks quantitative determination and is thus not subject to mathematical investigation. What this approach does, of course, is to make room for mathematics by providing it with a proper formal object which exists outside the mind and knowledge of which tells us something important about the real world, without endowing mathematics with epistemic hegemony. It is this "moderate realist" position which, it seems to us, is best in accord with the account of the act of formalization we have given here. Mathematics, like all other knowledge, begins with observation and proceeds to the formation of images and to classification. Mathematical formalization is just a higher degree of abstraction, which allows us to grasp the structure of things, but which does not advance to first principles, much less grasp the "mind of God." This perspective as well reflects a definite social location: that of the worker engaged in productive labor in a social structure which does not generate ideological mystifications which conceal the teleological ordering of things or the role of human labor in advancing their development.

What we are claiming here is not that mathematical formalisms are "merely" ideological, that they are "just" the reflex of definite social structures and have nothing to do with the way the universe works. Rather, we are suggesting, the development of the market system reveals certain aspects of reality which were hitherto hidden, while rendering opaque other aspects which were formerly quite transparent, and that this dynamic can be, and in fact has been, harnessed for ideological purposes by the bourgeoisie. The task of the philosopher is to separate out the truth which formalization reveals from the mystification which arises spontaneously as a result of its epistemic hegemony.

One of the characteristics of formalization is that it permits us to move from forms to forms without reference to further experience. This movement of the intellect we call inference. Given a formalization, and given the rules of logic, we can manipulate a formalism to generate new formalisms which are logically consistent with the first. These inferences may, furthermore, themselves be more or less abstract. They may remain at the level of descriptions of some physical, biological, or social system, in which case we call them *predictions* either of some past or future state of the system or of some property implied by the formalism itself. Thus Kepler's laws predict the motion of the heavenly bodies, the logistic equation predicts the change in the size of a population over time, and Marx's reproduction equations predict a declining rate of profit as an economy becomes more technologically sophisticated.

It is also possible, however, simply to consider the formal category itself, and to ask what kinds of systems are consistent with its structure, or to begin with a given category and ask what other categories might be *constructed* which are at least logically possible—i.e., consistent with the rules of identity, contradiction, and (for most mathematicians) the excluded middle. The role of the last rule is of particular importance. By showing that the contrary of a proposition is self-contradictory, and appealing to the law of the excluded middle, we can prove propositions which would otherwise resist demonstration. This makes possible the construction of categories which are not intuitively imaginable—such as actual infinities, certain kind of topologies, etc.

Inference is essential to the dialectical project. The dialectic proceeds by drawing out the implications and contradictions of existing ideas and driving towards a higher synthesis. This is why Plato included mathematics among the disciplines which were preparatory to the mastery of the dialectic itself. At the same time we have already suggested that there are definite limits to what formalization can teach us. To put the matter simply, formalization tells us how things work, not why. It describes but does not explain. And the picture that it gives us of the universe, if it is not supplemented by the higher, transcendental abstraction, is of a system which is ordered by without purpose, a universe which is not merely mechanistic but actually less than a machine (since machines all have some transparent purpose).

This brings us, finally, to the teleological ordering of formalization and thus of mathematical physics itself. By revealing how the universe is structured, mathematical physics gives us the tools we need in order to reorganize physical, biological, and social systems and use them for our own purposes. In this sense it is first and foremost, as we noted earlier, a servant of *techne*, and thus of social progress. But formalization can also be a servant of science in the authentic, dialectical sense. By telling us how the universe is structured, it tells us just what, precisely, science has to explain. And in so doing it helps us along the ascent to the first principle. Formalization, and mathematical physics generally, are steps along the *via dialectica*.

This said, it must also be noted that not all τεχνη promotes authentic progress. Reorganizing physical, biological and social systems for limited human purposes can undermine the integrity of ecosystems and of the social fabric. This is especially true when technologies are organized by the operation of market forces, which have no access to information regarding the impact of various activities on human development or on the integrity of the ecosystem and the social fabric. In this sense, formalization can also become an instrument of profit, careless of the higher purpose it ought to be serving. And when it claims hegemony in the epistemic field, presenting a vision of the universe as less than a machine, it becomes the willing tool of Capital.

Having described the historical roots of mathematical physics and its rise to hegemony, and having specified its fundamental concepts, we need now to see how mathematical physics has actually developed and test our theses against the historical evidence.

3

The Development of Mathematical Physics

IF MATHEMATICAL PHYSICS IS, in large measure, a reflex and instrument of the capitalist system, then it follows that as capitalism develops and changes, so to will mathematical physics. Part of this development is bound up with the creation of new technologies, which at once depend on basic physical theory and provide one of the social sites at which that theory is produced. It is this link with technology which has guaranteed that, the theoretical limitations of the discipline notwithstanding, mathematical physics continues to make authentic contributions to our understanding of the universe. Theories which must prove themselves through technological applications can never become entirely disassociated with reality. But we have seen that the generation of technological innovations is only one of three ways in which mathematical physics serves—and is hegemonized by—Capital. Spontaneous ideological effects and conscious polemics also affect the development of the discipline, and here the internal contradictions of capitalism manifest themselves from the very beginning. Indeed, we will see that as the process of capitalist development unfolds, the basic theoretical structure of mathematical physics changes so radically that it is impossible to say that it retains the same formal object throughout. What is more, it is not just that physics develops a variety of theories which are not fully unified; on the contrary, the way in which each of the subdisciplines understands its formal object is logically incompatible with all of the others, so that the whole complex of ideas becomes inconsistent. What begins as an effort to develop rigorous mathematical formalizations of local motion is fractured into a complex of competing theoretical perspectives. Our aim in this chapter is to analyze the development of mathematical physics as a function of the larger process of capitalist development of which it forms an integral dimension. We will show in the process that while there is indeed a place for mathematical formalization in the study of the universe, and while mathematical physics has made real contributions to science, on the whole the ideological function of the discipline has dominated its development, helping to secure the hegemony of Capital even over movements which have attempted to contest it, such as the international communist movement. We will also demonstrate that the internal contradictions of mathematical physics cannot be resolved at the level of formalization itself, but require a move to transcendental abstraction which alone can generate a complete, consistent, explanatory theory of the universe.

Our discussion will be organized historically, with separate sections on each of the principal periods of capitalist development identified in the previous chapter, i.e.,

- mercantilism
- industrial/competitive capitalism, and
- pure finance capitalism or *infokatallaxis*.

It must be remembered, however, that these stages or periods are defined sociologically and not chronologically. The dynamic which leads to industrialization reaches back well into the mercantilist period, and industrial-capitalist tendencies persist in our own *infokatallactic* era. Scientific developments will be discussed in the section proper to the dynamic of which they are a part, and not in chronological order.

MERCANTILISM AND PRIMITIVE ACCUMULATION

The Social Context of the Scientific Revolution

We have already sketched out briefly the principal characteristics of the period of mercantilism and primitive accumulation, but before we can analyze the development of mathematical physics during this period, we need to specify these characteristics in more detail. At the technological level, as we have noted, specialized agriculture and handicrafts continue to dominate. This is the period during which large scale plantation agriculture becomes a driving economic force, as Europeans conquer and subject to the norms of the global market the peoples of Asia, Africa, and the Americas. But this is also the period during which the process of technological innovation which had been set in motion during the feudal era is completed, with the invention of the telescope and microscope, reliable chronometers, the printing press, etc.—inventions which at once depended on and made possible further development in mathematical physics.

At the economic level two key events combine to create the rudiments of a global market in which effective demand for the first time begins to compete significantly with state policy as a determinant of economic development. First the European conquest of Asia, Africa, and the Americas enormously enriches the European ruling classes creating sufficient effective demand to serve as a real motor of economic development. Second, the expropriation of the productive classes, which begins in earnest during this period, forces people who formerly produced what they consumed to produce instead for the market and to purchase there what they needed for their own subsistence. This market was far from perfect, nor was it in any sense a spontaneous organization or an autonomous force. On the contrary, large numbers of people—in some regions the great majority—remained outside of it, producing for subsistence. The market depended for its creation on the direct action or indirect support of the state apparatus, and it continued to be constrained on every side by state policies which organized and directed the flow of commodities, and thus constrained the operation of market forces. There remained, in other words, a "fixed frame" of reference against the background of which market forces operated and a sovereign power which seemed to have brought both the fixed frame of nonmarket institutions and the market itself into being, and to which both remained subject. At the same time market forces became for the first time a sufficiently important factor in shaping social life that sovereigns felt obliged to engage the services of "political economists" to investigate these forces and advise them on how best to manage them.

This raises, of course the question of the state apparatus itself. During the mercantilist period, the dominant form of political organization was the absolutist state. There has long been debate among dialectical sociologists regarding the class character of this state. Some have seen it as an instrument of the bourgeoisie during its period of primitive accumulation and global conquest; others have seen it as essentially feudal. This seems to us to be the wrong way to pose the problem, because it fails to take into consideration the inherent dynamism of the state itself as a social institution. It is certainly true that the action of the absolutist state was largely shaped by the interests of the feudal elites. While most absolutist states had an estates system which represented the bourgeoisie as well as the feudal landowners and the clergy, by the seventeenth century these bodies had yielded most of their power and the states themselves had either become dominated by the feudal classes or become a means by which members of the rising bourgeoisie could become "ennobled," so that members of the bourgeoisie who entered state service lost their bourgeois character. And as Perry Anderson (Anderson 1974b) has pointed out, the absolutist state was structured first and foremost for war, which had always been the principal means of economic expansion under feudalism. But it is also true that the absolutist state confronted an increasingly bourgeois world. Dependent on bankers for loans, subject to the influence of radical price fluctuations due to the impact of American bullion on the world market, forced to supplement conquest with trade if they were to have any hope of maintaining their revenues, the policy of the absolutist state was above all an attempt to cope with dynamics which would have been utterly unthinkable to even a large feudal lord in an advanced region of Europe in, say, the twelfth century. What sets the absolutist state apart, however, from either a purely feudal lordship focused on maintaining the revenues of a single lord, or such properly capitalist institutions as the marketplace itself, which is without global purpose, is the tendency to organize itself to pursue a global public welfare or common good, even if the way in which that welfare is understood is deformed by feudal class interests and even if the good is pursued in a context of social dynamics which remain largely outside the purview of state control. What the state does is to attempt to understand the laws which govern society and use that knowledge in order to regulate society for the common good.

This new form of organization generates its own distinctive sort of personnel, and in the process produces a new social class or class fraction. To the extent that the state actually becomes a state, and is not simply a revenue generating activity of a great feudal lord, personnel are recruited on the basis of their ability and exercise authority based on their expertise. They may come from the ranks of the feudal elite or from those of the petty bourgeoisie or even the peasantry or proletariat. Generally they possess university education; indeed the expansion of the universities in the late middle ages was driven in large part by a growing demand for court officials. In so far as they earn their revenue from their labor power, this new state intelligentsia is a fraction of the working class; in so far as they are an elite supported by taxation they are themselves a sort of semifeudal or semitributary aristocracy. What sets them apart from the officials of archaic or tributary states, however, is the sense of confronting a complex "private sector" which at once operates according to its own laws, which the official must master, and which is the object of state action and regulation.

The absolutist state and its personnel were, in other words, distinctly modern phenomena. Indeed, it would not be too much to say that the state which came into being under absolutism persists today, even if the format of class representation has changed, from a weak estates system to a stronger party-and-legislature system. It would also not be too much to say that state intelligentsia which came into being under absolutism is the same intelligentsia which attempted to declare independence from and even suppress the marketplace under socialism and which is now under attack by a global market which makes economic regulation increasingly difficult at the national level.

Understanding the character of the absolutist state and of the new state intelligentsia which it produced is of paramount importance for understanding the specific character and development of mathematical physics—not only under mercantilism, but up through the present period. It is precisely during this period that the state becomes, for the first time, one of the principal patrons of the arts and sciences, and develops new institutions through which to organize scientific activity: the royal societies and academies of sciences—institutions which have a profound impact on the way science is done. If, on the one hand, the academies of science and the whole emergence of the state intelligentsia represent a penetration of the petty-bourgeois and proletarian principle of meritocracy into the state apparatus, something which is carried farthest in Russia, where membership in this social category carried noble status after Peter the Great, and where status within the nobility was no longer determined by birth but rather by meritocratic rank (Konrad and Szelenyi 1979: 88–90), the new system also represented a loss of autonomy for the intelligentsia. Decisions about merit were no longer made by autonomous guilds but rather by the state apparatus itself, which remained under the control of the feudal elite and later the bourgeoisie. There were, furthermore, strict limits placed on the authority of intellectual functionaries. The aims of state policy were still fixed by the monarch or later by a legislature or party organization; what the state intelligentsia contributed was technical expertise. This, in turn, had important effects on the development of the arts, sciences, and philosophy. The whole enterprise of reasoning about ends becomes suspect. Philosophy loses prestige and power by comparison to the other disciplines, and begins to retreat from the whole enterprise of reasoning about ends. It ceases, in other words to be philosophy. Thus the powerful critiques of teleology mounted by rationalists[1] and empiricists beginning in the seventeenth century and continuing up through the present period. It is only with Hegel that teleological reasoning begins to reassert itself, and when it does so it is accompanied by a political doctrine which attempts to put the intelligentsia in a leading position within the state apparatus.[2] *Techne*, by comparison is highly valued, and the relative prestige of disciplines depends in large measure on the power of their *techne*. Thus the leading role of the mathematical physicist, and later his practical counterpart, the engineer, who is at once extremely useful, generating directly or indirectly countless technological advances, while keeping at arms length ethical questions which might undermine the authority of policy-makers. The "social sciences," which emerge during this period in the form of political economy and political arithmetic, must, by comparison, struggle for respectability and against the taint of subversion.

William Eaton has pointed out the profound shift in the ethos of the sciences which took place as the absolutist "academy" replaced the "*universitas*" as the principal locus of scientific research. The medieval "*universitas*" was a petty bourgeois institution *par excellence.* Organized as a union of guilds, individual scholars and scientists at once learned from each other and engaged in sharp, even raucous debate—debate which took place in the tavern as often as is the lecture hall. Insight and logical prowess were valued over civility and consensus. In the new social space of the academies, which Eaton argues were created by displaced

---

1. Leibniz presents an interesting exception in this regard, the partial and highly problematic character of which proves the rule. Leibniz—philosopher and advisor to monarchs, paragon of the state intelligentsia and an hereditary baron, was, above all, concerned with the problem of reconciling finalistic and mechanistic modes of thought. His doctrine, however, according to which autonomous monads all act harmoniously without ever really interacting, more nearly resembles Adam Smith's doctrine of the invisible hand than it does than it does anything in the dialectical tradition. Ordering to an end is without knowledge; the philosopher is superfluous.

2. I am referring, of course, to the way in which Hegel positions his "universal class" of bureaucrats, all trained in universities dominated by philosophers like himself, to play the leading role in shaping state policy (Hegel 1820/1942).

aristocrats seeking a new function in the context of the emerging bourgeois order, the emphasis instead was on replicability of experiments and the creation of a collegial atmosphere which tended towards consensus. Reasoning about ends was explicitly excluded (Eamon 1994). These basic dynamics, which first took shape under the absolutist state, continue to govern the operation of official state science of the sort that is practiced in government laboratories and in universities heavily dependent on state funding to this day, and has had a profound impact on the whole ethos of the university as well, where the "ability to work collegially" (i.e., a commitment not to rock the boat) and an acceptance of the principles of value-neutral scholarship (i.e., to not questioning the market order) have increasingly become the precondition for appointment to tenured professorships.

This institutional framework had a powerful impact on the way in which those who formed a part of it perceived the world. The state intellectual confronts society as a reality independent of the state, operating according to its own laws, which it is his responsibility to formalize so they can become tools of state regulation. In so far as these laws are increasingly those of the marketplace, they are first and foremost quantitative laws—the laws of supply and demand and the other quantitative relationships that govern the movement of commodities in the abstract space of the market. The result is a tendency to see the universe as a whole as a system of quantitative relations—and in this the whole project of mathematical physics is already given. Rationalist philosophy, which takes mathematical physics as its epistemic ideal, follows naturally.

It is important to point out, however, that not all science fit within this model. The royal societies and academies tended to take over and dominate the disciplines which had traditionally been part of the university curriculum. This meant the theoretical sciences—especially mathematics and mathematical physics more narrowly understood. This is, perhaps, because it was these disciplines which regulated the other sciences and which were therefore strategically the most significant. It was here that the battle against Aristotle was fought out. What have often been called the Baconian sciences, however—those which were more experimental in nature, such as alchemy and natural history, remained largely independent of the academy system, and tended to be the pursuit either of inventors or tinkerers who were engaged in some practical discipline, such as medicine, pharmacy, metallurgy, etc. or else by leisured independent aristocrats. In this environment a very different sort of scientific ethos developed—one which stressed systematic observation and experiment, and which put a premium on the capacity for empirical pattern recognition. It was this milieu which provided the context out of which chemistry developed, and later genetics and evolutionary biology. It also produced the empiricist strain in philosophy which became dominant in the nineteenth century, in the wake of the industrial and democratic revolutions, just as Newtonian physics was beginning to exhaust itself (Eaton 1994).

We need, finally, to say a word about the impact of other ideological struggles on the development of science in the mercantilist period. The most important ideological development in this period was, of course, the Reformation/Counter-Reformation. We have already seen in the previous chapter the role of the Augustinian reaction of the late thirteenth century in undermining the foundations of Aristotelian science and laying the foundations for the development of mathematical physics. We will recall as well that the struggle between the partisans of Aristotle and the partisans of Augustine was bound up with the struggle over the authority of the hierarchy. On the one hand, Aristotelian philosophy, by making all human activities a participation in the life of God, promised the clergy a wide field for possible action. At the same time, Aristotelian philosophy also threatened to so emphasize *natural* human participation in the life of God as to make revelation and sacrament—and thus the clerical hierarchy—unnecessary. Augustinian pessimism, by contrast, highlighted the necessity of grace and revelation, and left little scope for the secular intelligentsia which had been become the principal antagonist of the clergy. Depending on the details way in which Augustine was read, it could either make the clergy the sole source of legitimate political authority or else confine the clergy to a ministerial role and thus the undermine the basis for the magisterium and for clerical intervention in political affairs.

It was this latter potential of Augustinianism that was developed by the Reformation, though the Lutheran and Calvinist variants differ significantly. Lutheranism represents a return to classical Augustinian political theology, which makes a sharp distinction between law and gospel, the Kingdom of Justice and the Kingdom of Mercy, the realm of the state and that of the Church. The state exists to safeguard order in a world given over to sin; the Church is the community of those who have the grace of faith in the saving death of Jesus Christ. It is little wonder that this doctrine was attractive to feudal princes and wealthy burghers anxious to be free of clerical restrictions. Calvinism, on the other hand, built on the political Augustinianism of the middle ages in arguing that legitimate political authority could be exercised only by those who held their authority from Christ. All else was mere organized banditry. At the same time, Calvinism assigned this authority not to those who had been anointed by the vicar of Christ, but rather to those who showed evidence of actually having been saved, judgment regarding which was exercise by a dispersed local clergy, often with significant participation by lay elders drawn from the gentry or the bourgeoisie. Financially dependent on these lay elders, even those Calvinist divines who wanted to assert their authority over the public arena were unable to, as Jonathan Edwards learned to his dismay when he was dismissed from his pulpit in Northampton, Massachusetts for, among other things, defending the land rights of the indigenous communities.

Either way, the Augustinian theology which Rome had used against the Radical Aristotelians now threatened to put it out of business.

The result was a sharp turn on the part of Rome away from Augustinianism and back towards the Thomism which had been effectively rejected in the thirteenth and fourteenth centuries. The Thomism which was embraced, however, was not that of Thomas, deeply rooted in empirical inquiry in the natural sciences, and bound up with the dynamism of a new lay spirituality in the cities, a Thomism which was no stranger to the alchemist's laboratory and which was in dialogue, if not always in agreement, with Judaism and Islam, with Radical Aristotelianism and the cult of the *Magna Mater*. It was, rather, a Thomism that more or less self-consciously capitalized on the potential of Aristotelian philosophy to legitimate the authority of the hierarchy in an increasingly secularized and skeptical world, using Aristotelian methods to demonstrate the existence of God and the credibility of revelation, while interpreting revelation in a way which reflected significant Augustinian influence (Thibault 1971).

Both the Reformation and the Counter-Reformation had a significant impact on the development of mathematical physics. On the one hand, the Reformation created a political-theological space in Northern Europe in which it became not only possible but in fact all but mandatory to reject Aristotelian cosmology entirely. The axiological and teleological space-time of Aristotelian physics was, after all, incompatible with both the tendentially *infokatallactic* order of the marketplace and the ταξις of the absolutist state, which saw it self as imposing order on society from the outside. The tendency on the part of Luther and Calvin themselves was to reject natural theology altogether, something which freed physics of all responsibility to the religious authorities.[3] And when natural theology began to re-emerge in the seventeenth and eighteenth century, it did so either in the guise of the purely formal, almost mathematical ontological argument revived by Descartes[4] or in the form of design arguments such as those advanced by Newton and Paley which treated God as sort of celestial absolute monarch who fixed the laws of nature by decree, rather than simply embodying them as a rational necessity.

In the Catholic countries on the other hand, the theologians of the Counter-Reformation struggled to conserve as much as they could of Aristotelian cosmology not because of its explanatory power but rather because it provided the necessary scientific infrastructure for the metaphysics which in turn was necessary to papal power. This meant that they clung to specific contents of Aristotle's system, including geocentrism and the heaven/earth dualism—precisely those aspects of the system which were rapidly being discredited by new empirical evidence, and which had always played a politically reactionary role—rather than conserving a broadly Aristotelian scientific strategy while attempting to accommodate new evidence, something which would have involved expanding the concept of teleology to take into account the realities of chaos, contradiction, and disintegration. The result was that Aristotelianism was discredited,

---

3. This liberation from the religious authorities did, to be sure, often create room within the new mathematical physics for forms of spirituality which in the twelfth or thirteenth century would more likely have found a home in Aristotelian circles, but which in the sixteenth or seventeenth were more likely to express themselves in Platonic language. Perhaps the best example of this tendency was Kepler, who sought in his astronomic research the pure forms which would lead him to the mind of God, and who, incidentally had to defend his mother against charges of witchcraft. The reason for this shift is simple. The Augustinian reaction effectively drove the creative ferment associated with the resurgent cult of the *Magna Mater* underground and destroyed or marginalized the Radical Aristotelianism which was its organic philosophy. By the seventeenth century Aristotle had become merely a tool of the Catholic clergy and would thus hardly have been attractive to devotees of the Great Mother. The relative freedom of at least some of the Protestant lands, and the philosophical tools of the Platonic tradition, which the Augustinians had by this point abandoned in favor of nominalism, seemed far more attractive.

4. For an argument that the ontological argument is in fact an (incorrect) mathematical argument, dependent on the (apparently unprovable) Zorn's Lemma, see Mansueto 2002b.

regarded (though the term itself did not exist at the time) more as ideology, and clerical ideology at that, than as science.[5]

The Newtonian Space-Time

The Fundamental Theories

What these forces did was to combine to bring into being what we have called the "Newtonian space-time," the principal characteristics of which can be described as follows:

1. There is a fixed frame, given socially by the network of nonmarket institutions against the background of which exchange takes place and represented physically by the fixed stars, which were not yet known to move.

2. The basic qualitative and quantitative determinations of things are also regarded as both given and distinct from each other. By the basic qualitative determinations of things we mean shape, color, etc. The basic quantitative determinations of matter are mass and extension Indeed matter appears simply as a collection of point-particles with mass extended in space. The fixity and independence of the basic determinations of matter is a residue of the experience of price

---

5. It is interesting to note in this regard the epistemological innovation introduced during this period by Dominican commentators on the work of Thomas Aquinas. Thomas had distinguished only three degrees of abstraction, the *abstractio totius*, which abstracted from individuals to their essential nature or definition, after the manner of a scientist who, studying individual rabbits concludes to what a rabbit is, the *abstractio formae*, which abstracted from the matter of a thing to its form, after the manner of a mathematician, and the *separatio*, which abstracted from both matter and form to Being as such. The Dominican commentators grouped these three sorts of abstraction together under the title of *abstractio formalis*, to be distinguished from the *abstractio totalis*. Each of the different degrees of formal abstraction was characteristic of a distinct science, each of which had its own distinct formal object, while total abstraction was simply the sort of rough classification which we use in everyday life. The result of this innovation was to guarantee the scientific status of Aristotelian physics, which they believed to be characterized by the *abstractio totius*, *alongside* the new mathematical physics which was gaining such prominence, and thus to save the scientific infrastructure of Aristotelian-Thomistic metaphysics—and of Thomistic theology. If our reading of the social basis and political valence of the disciplines in question is correct, this marks a recognition that the bourgeoisie had to be allowed entry into the ideological arena, albeit under the condition that they continue to recognize the hegemony of the clergy, represented in this case by the ruling or architectonic role of metaphysics in relationship to the arts and sciences.

stability, and of a natural price which underlies the market price of commodities which, it is now recognized, may fluctuate wildly.

3. It is assumed that it is still possible to rise to a standpoint outside of and above the physical processes which take place in the universe, something which is given socially in the absolutist state, which stands above the marketplace. The activity of the universal sovereign, however, is increasingly understood to consist in the design of the system in accord with the rules of formal logic, a reflex of the objective constraints on sovereign power by the realities of the market order.

4. The formal object of "science," however, becomes simply the local motion of point particles with mass. The fact that the formal object of scientific inquiry is restricted in this way is a reflex of the growing importance of the movement of commodities in the marketplace, as opposed to the complex of nonmarket institutions, including the state, against the background of which that movement takes place in determining the real allocation of resources, and thus in determining what happens socially.

The development of mathematical physics during the mercantilist period is simply the logical working out of this program, which was laid out more or less explicitly by Galileo Galilei in his *Discourses Concerning Two New Sciences* (Galilei 1638/1914), and its application in so far as possible to every sphere of inquiry. Concretely this meant,

1. the development of a credible formal model of terrestrial motion
2. the development of a credible formal model of celestial motion,
3. the unification of terrestrial and celestial physics under uniform "mathematical principles of natural philosophy," and
4. the extension of the resulting mathematical model so that the whole universe could, at least in principle, be modeled using a single equation.

The first task fell to Galileo Galilei. While the story of his experiment at the Tower of Pisa is probably apocryphal (Feather 1959: 122–23), it was in Pisa during the years between 1589 and 1591, working with metal spheres and inclined planes rather than leaning towers that he carried out his most important research, arriving at one quantitative and two qualitative principles. The quantitative principle may be stated as follows:

> In free fall under gravity the distance traveled from rest is proportional to the square of the time of fall. (Feather 1959: 124)

or, alternatively,

> In free fall under gravity, velocity increases linearly with time. (Feather 1959: 124)

The result was isolation of the concept of acceleration.

Galileo also discovered the fact that the accelerations of falling bodies (or rather bodies rolling down an inclined plane) of different masses are in fact identical, the implication of which was the identification of the acceleration due to gravity as a fundamental geophysical constant (Feather 1959: 124). A second experiment in which "two inclined planes were set facing one another, forming a shallow V" led to the observation that, "under ideal conditions, a ball which had rolled down one plane would roll up the other losing speed, as it had previously gained speed in descent, until it came to rest, momentarily, at a height above the horizontal which was equal to the height from which it had started (Feather 1959: 124)." The result was the isolation of the concept of inertia.

The change wrought by Galileo in our understanding of space, time, and motion cannot be underestimated. Not only, in arriving at a correct formal description of terrestrial local motion, does he seem to vindicate the turn from explanation to formal description, but in showing that bodies of different mass fall at the same rate, he radically disassociated even the basic quantitative determinations of bodies from their motion with respect to other bodies. This means conceiving the universe as a system of externally related particles—precisely the universe people were already beginning to experience with the emergence of generalized commodity production. The quantitative determinations of these particles and the inter-relations between these quantitative determinations can be known only by observation and are expressed most adequately in formal, mathematical statements. And behind this new way of understanding the universe is an emerging conception of space and time. Space is (implicitly) conceived here as a boundless, immaterial medium in which motion can take place. Time is, similarly, absolute and independent of anything external to it.

What has happened here, of course, is that the fixed frame in the context of which change unfolded for Aristotelian physics has been conserved, but at the same time detached from the specific cosmology with which it was originally bound up and thus from the metaphysics and the axiological structure which that cosmology supported. Space still has a definite structure, but this structure has become independent of what is happening. Time is still the measure of motion, and is itself still measured against an absolute standard, but that standard is no longer the motion of the heavenly bodies. Sociologically the fixed frame is the complex of non-market institutions against which exchange takes place but the qualitative determinations of which can be increasingly ignored. Physically the fixed frame is that of stellar (if no longer planetary) motion, but this motion has lost its axiological determinations.

That the fixed frame of the stars lost the axiological significance which it had in the old Aristotelian system, as the second highest of the heavenly spheres is, of course, due in large part, to the development of a new astronomy which treated the stars as physical bodies no different than any others. There were, of course, a number of critical developments which led to these changes: the growing inability of Ptolemaic models to account for improved observations, the development of alternative heliocentric and geocentric models of the universe by Copernicus and Tycho Brahe. But it was Johannes Kepler who, in developing a correct formal description of planetary motion finally undermined the old system and set the stage for the development of a new one—and for a new conception of "space" which reflected the new social conditions. Philosophically committed to the idea that planetary motions were governed by the geometric relationships between the Platonic solids, he was ultimately forced to abandon this vision in favor of laws that were far less pleasing from the standpoint of Platonic aesthetics.

1. Each planet moves in an ellipse with the sun at one focus.

    $$1/r = 1/b^2 (a - \sqrt{a^2 - b^2} \cos \theta)$$

    where a is the semimajor axis, and b the semiminor axis of the orbit, r is the distance between the sun and the planet, and q the angle between r and the major axis.

2. For each planet the line from the sun to the planet sweeps out equal areas in equal times

$$dA = \lim_{\Delta t \to 0} \frac{1/2 r^2 Dq}{\Delta t} = 1/2\, r^2 \frac{dq}{dt} = 1/2\, r^2 \omega$$

3. The squares of the periodic times of the planets are as the cubes of their mean distances from the sun.

The abandonment of the perfect celestial spheres of the Aristotelian system required an entirely new approach the problem of just how and why the heavenly bodies moved in the first place. For Aristotle the stars were moved by knowledge and love. Guided by intelligences that understood better than we could ever hope to the nature of the first unmoved mover, the heavenly spheres moved in a way that imitated the perfection of the divine nature. But, as Kepler pointed out, anything that would move in an elliptical orbit could not possibly be moved by an angelic intellect, which would never have opted for so inelegant a form. The stars must be physical bodies just like those we encounter here on earth. This, in turn, opened the way for the unification of terrestrial and celestial physics, a task which Newton undertook in his *Philosophia Naturalis Principia Mathematica* (Newton 1687/1729). The new, Newtonian physics assumed, as we have noted:

a. an absolute space and time independent of matter
b. externally related particles or bodies with absolute mass (quantity of matter) and
c. absolute motion with respect to space over the course of time.

On the basis of these assumptions, Newton was able to generalize Kepler's so that they applied to all motion, terrestrial and celestial, without exception.

1. Every body perseveres in its state of rest, or of uniform motion in a straight line, except in so far as it is compelled to change that state by forces impressed on it.
2. The rate of change of momentum of a body is proportional to the moving force impressed on it, and is effective in the direction in which that force is impressed.

$$F = ma$$

where F is the force applied to the particle, m is its mass and a is its acceleration.

3. An action is always opposed by an equal reaction, or the mutual actions of two bodies are always equal and act in opposite directions.

Gravity then appears a special case of motion in general.

$$F_{gravity} = G(m_1 m_2 / r^2)$$

where F is the gravitational force exerted by two bodies on each other, G is the universal gravitational constant G = 6.6726 * 10^{-11} m^3/kg*s^2.

We should perhaps point out that while the development of mathematical physics proper, unlike that of the "Baconian sciences," was not directly bound up with technological innovation, Newton's physics was by no means without technological applications nor were its concepts entirely free from determination by technological process. On the contrary, the Newtonian system depended on experimental work using the clock and the telescope. And the Newtonian system is completed not by the concept of force, but rather by that of work, the mechanical-technological concept *par excellence*. The work done by a force is simply the distance which it moves a point particle with mass:

$$W = fs$$

where W is work, f is force and s distance. It should be noted this equation does not really tell us anything about *how* to get work done; rather it simply supplies a criterion for measuring what has been accomplished. In this sense it is an investor's tool and not really the instrument of an engineer, except in so far as the engineer is beholden to the investor. In Newton's time the production process still depended on the principal sources of motive power that had been developed earlier in the middle ages—animal power and water power. New innovations would not come until the end of the eighteenth century when the steam engine made it possible to harness the energy of combustion. And even then it would not be the mathematical physics that drove innovation forward, but rather innovation that required the development of new scientific disciplines.

Later, in the nineteenth century, after a long and complex struggle to generate the necessary mathematical tools—a refined Calculus which permitted the solution of differential equations—Newton's laws were further generalized allowing the complete description of the state of a system by a single equation—the Hamiltonian, which expresses the total energy of the system. Let $q_1 \ldots q_n$ be the coordinates of the various particles or elements in the system and $p_1 \ldots p_n$ the momenta of these particles. Together these are called the canonical variables. E is the kinetic energy of the system and V its potential energy. Then

$$H = E(p_1 \ldots p_n) + V(q_1 \ldots q_n).$$

The laws of classical dynamics may then be expressed in terms of Hamilton's equation.

$$dq_i/dt = \delta H/\delta p_i$$
$$dp_i/dy = \delta H/\delta q_i \text{ where } i = 1, 2, \ldots n$$

Let us pause for a moment to consider what has been accomplished here. The one hand, the perfect mathematical regularity that for the scientists and philosophers of petty commodity societies was always and only a characteristic of the heavens has been made universal. Heaven and earth are thus joined in a kind of harmony that is, furthermore, at least in principle perfectly intelligible. Perception of this harmony does, to be sure, require a higher degree of formal abstraction. The ordered motions of the heavenly bodies were visible to the naked eye, so that any careful observer might notice them and thus rediscover for himself the artistry of the creator. Now the perception of order requires a mastery of the calculus and differential equations. But it is no less real for being subtler. It is, furthermore, possible at least in principle, on the basis of Hamilton's equation, to describe the universe as a whole—to write an equation for everything, at least in so far as everything constitutes a dynamic system.

At the same time, Hamilton's achievement has begun to undermine the very foundations of the Newtonian project. If the universe constitutes a single dynamic system in which everything affects the behavior (position and momentum) of everything else, then the "fixed frame" against which movement can be measured has already begun to disintegrate. The stars themselves, the fixed positions of which provided the background against which Newtonian motion took place, must themselves be in motion, under the influence of gravitational tides which reach throughout the universe. Thus we see at the scientific level a reflex of the sociological process which is at work during this period. The penetration of market relations into every sphere of life gradually erodes the fixed frame of nonmarket institutions, so that the market itself becomes definitive framework of society. We will explore this process at greater length in the next section.

Heaven and earth are brought together, furthermore, at the expense of a description of the "earth" which is deeply on contradiction with our ordinary experience. While the order of the heavens might seem to be eternally changeless (we now, know, of course, that this perception is in error) "earth" is a place of constant transformation: of development and decay, of change which cannot be undone. All of the processes described by classical dynamics are, on the other hand completely reversible. Time ceases to be, as it was for Plato and Aristotle, the measure of decay and/or development and becomes just another dimension of the complex harmony of the universe. We will see that this introduces into mathematical physics a serious contradiction as it begins to try to formalize the processes associated with the technological revolution which it help set in motion at the end of the eighteenth century with the advent of the steam engine and industrialization.

Applications

Before we proceed to an examination of these phenomena, however, we need to look at least briefly at attempts to apply the basic strategy of mathematical physics to other disciplines, such as chemistry, biology, and the emerging science of political economy. In the case of chemistry, the key advances in this period were driven by a turn to careful measurement and a focus on quantitative pattern recognition—a sharp turn from the earlier alchemical focus on the qualitative determinations of matter. Thus Robert Boyle, observing the behavior of gases, was able to determine the quantitative relationship between pressure P and volume V:

$$PV = k$$

where k is a constant. Boyle's work also, however, reflected the very strong empirical strain which chemistry had inherited from the Baconian tradition. He thus mounted an assault on the Aristotelian theory of the four elements, arguing that any which cannot be broken down into simpler substances should be assumed to be elemental (Read 1957: 111–16).

The critical problem in chemistry in the eighteenth century was that of combustion—something vitally important to the development of the technologies that would drive the industrial revolution. At first assumed to be the result of an outflow of something called "phlogiston," combustion was recognized by the end of the century to be the result of the combination of the combustible with something called oxygen. Antoine Lavoisier, who along with Joseph Priestly finally discovered oxygen and explained combustion, also recognized the conservation of mass during in the course of chemical changes (Read 1957: 134–44).

Lavoisier's success inspired other chemists to extend his research program. In an environment dominated by Newtonian mathematical physics, it was only natural to think of the matter of chemical change, like the matter of local motion, as point particles—or at least particles—with mass. It thus followed that all of the elements were made of such particles with mass, or atoms, and that compounds were simply combinations of the atoms of different elements. And while it could not be ruled out that atoms of different elements had various qualitative determinations as well, experiment soon demonstrated that they could be distinguished most easily by their differing atomic mass. Chemistry was gradually being reduced to mechanics, a process that would be completed with quantum-mechanical description of the atom in the early twentieth century. Meanwhile, Lavoisier had also recognized that oxygen was vitally important to living things, and that life must involve a process not unlike combustion -an insight which helped pave the way for the reduction of biology to chemistry, and thus ultimately to physics.

Progress in biology and in the social sciences in this period is much less marked. On the one hand, the dominant paradigm excluded theorization of organization as such, i.e., ordering to an end, which is what defines biological and social organization. At the same time, chemistry, which is the link between mathematical physics and biology was still very primitive, so that there was not a great deal that could be said about living organisms as physical systems. A few points are, however, worth noting. First, it was during this period that the basic approach of modern biology was fixed. If the formal object of "science" is the local motion of point particles with mass, then any "scientific" biology *must* treat organisms as if they were machines. This basic outlook on life, set forth quite explicitly by Descartes, who claimed that animals are merely automatons, determines the whole program which biology has followed ever since: that of analyzing, at either the anatomical or biochemical level the way in which living machines work. It is, indeed, precisely this focus, which has made it nearly impossible for biologists to say what life is. In reality they simply study a particular class of machines the boundaries of which are defined more by convention than by anything else. At the same time, we should note, the persistence of a sites outside the market order, and especially the privileged site of the absolute monarch, creates the basis in experience for imagining a rational soul independent of the body and not subject to the laws of mechanics, which are after all simply a reflex of the laws of the marketplace. Thus psychology during this period is not yet subjected to the full rigors of the mechanistic program (Damasio 1994).

This same dualism is present in the principal fields of the social sciences that are opened up during this period: political economy and political theory. These two disciplines are, it should be noted, closely related and only begin to be differentiated from each other very gradually. Both derive from the tradition of the "books of secrets" which we discussed earlier in this work (Eamon 1994), a tradition that included books on the secrets of statesmanship. Here the classic work is, of course, Nicolo Machiavelli's *The Prince*. What is distinctive about this tradition, like that of the books of secrets in general, is the gradual disassociation of the esoteric material, which above all concerns technique, from the exoteric training in philosophy generally, and ethics in particular, which had historically been the precondition for admission to esoteric training.

In the case of the social sciences, this disassociation is most rapid in the field of political economy. Rulers during this period desperately needed advisors who could help them understand and manage the new economic system that was growing up around them, the continued political dominance of the aristocracy notwithstanding. What is striking about this discipline is the difficulty that was apparently involved in even defining its proper formal object: the movement of commodities in the marketplace. Throughout most of the mercantilist period, the fixed frame of nonmarket institutions dominates the vision even of political economists. Thus the persistence throughout most of this period of a sharp distinction between the "natural price" of a commodity and its market price. The former is regarded, as it was for the scholastics, as determined by "labor and charges," the latter by supply and demand. Wealth is still seen as originating in something objective: ultimately in labor, especially agricultural labor, or in some cases in the land itself, and immediately in a favorable balance of payments. Even as the period draws to a close and Adam Smith proclaims the virtues of free markets, the "invisible hand" of which guides individuals to serve the common good while pursuing their own interests, the labor theory of value reigns supreme, and there remains a powerful sense that the world of the marketplace is somehow ultimately unreal and subjective. It would not be until the third period of capitalist development, with the marginalist revolution, that the program of mathematical physics would be fully applied to the field of political economy.

Political theory, on the other hand, had already found its proper formal object—sovereignty—by the time of Macchiavelli. At the same time, this formal object could not, by its very nature, be adequately theorized in terms of the mathematical-physical research program. This is because sovereignty is not some thing the motion of which can be described; it is itself the cause of motion, it is energy, the capacity to do work. Political analysis is causal analysis—just precisely what Galileo had counseled physics to abandon. Sovereignty is what establishes the fixed frame against which commodities move; political analysis is the ideological reflex of the absolutist state rather than of the market with which it always exists in uneasy tension. In this sense the social sciences in a capitalist society are always characterized by an internal dualism between political economy, which has for its formal object the laws of the marketplace, and the many varieties of "political science" of which sociology is the most highly developed, which attempt to explain just how the market order emerged in the first place. What we do see in this period is a recognition, which is nothing short of revolutionary, of the fact that power is somehow embodied in social relations and can be created, squandered, and destroyed. This idea, already implicit in Macchiavelli, is formulated quite explicitly by Hobbes, who recognizes the sovereign as social product, i.e., as the result of a compact among the people—and thus as not really sovereign at all. This, in turn, paves the way for the displacement of the absolutist state by the democratic revolutions, which is heralded by the development of a full-blown social contract theory by Rousseau.

Closely associated with this focus on the idea of power is a recognition of the role of ideology generally, and religion in particular, in political life. This was, in a certain sense, nothing new. Ibn Rushd himself, in distinguishing between philosophy, theology, and religion had implicitly recognized that whatever their claim to truth, ideas also function as means of social control. The theologian, in the Averroist hermeneutic, is above all the ideological engineer. What is different in this period is that the Reformation presented princes with real options in the ideological field and made the ideological structure of society an object of political analysis—something which thinkers such as Hobbes and Spinoza (*Tractatus Theologicus-Politicus*) attempt in a systematic way—and which, just as political theory of Hobbes and Spinoza, prepares the way for the democratic revolutions, helped write the charter for the "cultural revolution" theorized by Rousseau in his discussion of "civil religion" and actually attempted by the French Revolutionaries. Both moves represent an attempt on the part of the intellectual advisors of the absolutist state to declare independence from the sovereigns they served and to claim sovereignty for themselves.

The reality of course is that sovereignty is an illusion. Precisely because the "fixed-frame" of nonmarket institutions, including the absolutist state, is not really fixed at all, but rather a social product, and because human society is embedded in a system far larger and more complex than itself, there simply are not any "commanding heights" from which the historical process can be organized and directed as if by God. This is the truth that is implicit in political economy and which Marx makes explicit during the second stage of capitalist development and which Lenin—himself a member of a mobilized service intelligentsia in the process of declaring independence form its sovereign—too easily forgot.

HIGH MODERN SCIENCE

Industrial/Competitive Capitalism

The transition from the first stage of capitalist development to the second involves changes at both the technological and the economic levels. On the one hand, the perfection of medieval mechanical technologies and their integration with a more sophisticated handling of combustion leads to the development of the steam engine, which vastly increased the energy available to the productive process. During the course of this period, the energy of combustion is harnessed every more effectively, a development which concludes with the development of internal combustion engines towards the end of the nineteenth century, and a new form of energy is accessed: that of electricity, the generation of which involves the use of combustion to turn turbines.

At the same time, the progress of primitive accumulation has separated a sufficient number of workers from the means of subsistence that labor power itself is effectively transformed into a commodity. These two developments combine to significantly undermine the "fixed frame" of nonmarket institutions against which commodities had hitherto moved. From this point onward the price of all commodities is determined in relationship to that of all other commodities. The environment fixed by the state increasingly appears as simply a formalization of the laws of the marketplace itself—the laws of property, contract, and torts—or as a medium through which commodities flow—the medium of money. At first, up through about the middle of the century, cyclical crises notwithstanding, this new system seemed unambiguously progressive, an engine of growth of unprecedented proportions. Then, suddenly, first in England, later in regions which had developed more slowly, the internal contradictions of the system began to be apparent and it began apparent that there were, in fact, real limits to growth, a recognition which, we will see, had profound implications for the development of the sciences during this period.

At the political level, this is the period of the democratic revolutions. Where the absolutist state administered the emerging market economy for the benefit of a feudal aristocracy which was gradually, with greater or lesser effectiveness, adapting itself to the new circumstances of the market order, the new democratic states represented, on the one hand, the need on the part of the bourgeoisie for a new format of representation which would allow conflicts between the various factions of capital to be sorted out through negotiations rather than destructive military conflicts and, on the other hand, the growing power of the intelligentsia, the petty bourgeoisie, the peasantry, and the proletariat which had discovered that the state could be an instrument for reorganizing human society and which were anxious to make use of this power for their own ends. During the first part of this period the bourgeoisie relied on support from the popular classes in its struggle against the aristocracy; later it turns sharply against its former allies as they move towards independent political action and begin to question the market order.

Participation in political life, which increases throughout this period has a contradictory impact at the ideological level. On the one hand, the illusion of sovereignty persists. Participation in political life is a participation in an ongoing debate about how society ought to be organized, something that creates the impression that we can, in fact, organize it just anyway we please. Thus the development in this period of a strong doctrine of *laissez-faire* among the most advanced representatives of the bourgeoisie, who fear that it might be reorganized by either emerging bourgeois groups or the subaltern social classes in a manner which undermined their hegemony. At the same time, the growing power of the marketplace, which is the real organizer, imposes constraints on what can actually be accomplished. This, we will, see, is reflected in the growing pessimism of bourgeois thought, as well as the effective demise of utopian socialism among the working classes.

At the ideological level, two dynamics dominate. On the one hand, the emergence of a fully capitalist social order, coupled with the technological, economic, and political advances of the period, make possible the development of what Lukacs calls a direct apologetic for capitalism. At the center of this polemic is the notion of "freedom." The free exchange of commodities in the marketplace is linked ideologically with the free participation of individuals in political life and with the free exchange of ideas. If human beings are free to innovate, and to profit from their innovations, without interference from backward clerics or meddlesome bureaucrats, the argument goes, then innovate they will. The ideas that work will be conserved, those that do not will be discarded. This ideological linkage between the marketplace and freedom was a powerful asset to the bourgeoisie in its effort to enlist popular support for its struggle against the clergy and the feudal aristocracy.

As the internal contradictions of capitalism become more apparent, and socialism becomes a threat, another, more complex and subtle ideological dynamic takes over—what Lukacs calls the indirect polemic. Here, rather than defending capitalism directly as a system which actually promotes human development, alternative systems are attacked as even worse and the contradictions of capitalism are attributed to the laws of nature physical, biological and, increasingly, psychological and social. The claim here is that socialism is either impossible or else not worth the effort because human misery is a result of the way the universe generally, and human beings in particular, are structured.

The interplay between the direct and indirect apologetic had, we will see, a profound impact on the development of science during this period. On the one hand, the period between the end of the eighteenth and the beginning of the twentieth century is, in may ways the golden age of scientific progress and what we might call scientific progressivism—the belief that progress in the sciences, understood as the extension of mathematical physics to all realms of inquiry, would lead to a complete explanation of the universe and would support the development of technologies which would realize humanity's highest aspirations lead to resolution of most if not all of the planet's problems. At the same time, it is precisely during this period that science begins to generate results—such as the second law of thermodynamics or Malthusian strictures on population growth—which suggest that the prospects for human progress are, in fact, quite limited. Let us examine the interplay of these two dynamics in more detail.

High Modern Science

The High Tide of Scientific Progress

The starting point for science during the period of competitive industrial capitalism was, precisely, Hamiltonian dynamics. This approach to formalizing physical systems not only represented the completion of the Newtonian project, but actually defined the form of equation in which quite different physical phenomena, such as electromagnetic radiation, would eventually be described. We have already seen how Hamiltonian dynamics reflected the transition from mercantilism to competitive capitalism. The transformation of labor power into a commodity represented a significant step towards the dissolution of the fixed frame of nonmarket institutions, so that now every commodity was, ultimately, defined in terms of every other, just as in the Hamiltonian function the position and momentum of every particle is a function of position and motion of every other.

Since the Hamiltonian simply formalized the relationships between particles, and said nothing about the nature of the underlying forces embodied in those relationships, it follows that changing the nature of the underlying forces in question should do nothing to alter the form of the equations. This, precisely, is what scientists analyzing the nature of electricity and magnetism discovered during the course of the first half of the nineteenth century. The Fundamental Laws of Electromagnetism, developed by Gauss, Coulomb, and Faraday, and finally unified by James Clerk Maxwell in 1864 are of essentially the same form as the Hamiltonian equation. Let E be the electrical field and B the magnetic field, ρ the charge, ε the permitivity constant, t time in seconds, and μ the permeability constant. Then

$$\nabla * E = \rho/\varepsilon_0$$
$$\nabla * B = 0$$
$$\nabla_x E = \partial B/\partial t$$
$$\nabla x B = \mu_0 \varepsilon_0 \partial E/\partial t + \mu_0 j_c$$

The first law states that like charges repel and unlike charges attract as the inverse square of their separation. The second law states that there are no magnetic monopoles—"north" and "south" poles always go together. The third law states that any change in a magnetic field produces an electrical field at right angles to the direction of the change. The fourth law, similarly, states that a changing electrical field produces a magnetic field at right angles to the changes (Lerner 1991: 171).

Discovery of these laws represented an enormous advance at both the scientific and the technological level. On the one hand, they showed that electrical and magnetic fields do not require a physical medium, but propagate in empty space like waves. The equations made it possible to calculate the speed of light and to show that electromagnetic changes propagate at precisely this speed, suggesting that light is in fact simply a form of electromagnetic radiation. On the other hand, the questions laid the groundwork for the development of new electrical technologies and explained more fully how those that had already been developed actually worked. By changing the current running through a magnetic field, for example, it turns out that it is possible to produce constantly changing magnetic fields, which in turn produce changing electrical fields, resulting in the emission of waves of electromagnetic radiation in which information can be encoded, something Heinrich Hertz would later use to produce radio waves.

As it turns out, similar mathematical relations describe other sorts of physical systems as well, such as the motion of fluids.

Rivaling in importance the developments in electromagnetism, were those in chemistry. We have already noted that during the mercantilist period the use of quantitative methods laid the groundwork for the development of a chemistry that would ultimately be unified with mathematical physics. It was during the period of competitive/industrial capitalism that this approach finally began to bear fruit. Once again, it was the application of the Newtonian paradigm which drove research forward—in this case the assumption that matter consists of particles with various quantitative determinations. This lead to a revival of the atomic theory first advanced by Democritus and further developed, incorporating Pythagorean influences by Plato. The key figure in this regard was John Dalton, an English schoolteacher, who in 1808 published *A New System of Chemical Philosophy*. Dalton had noticed that some elements form more than one compound, and that when they do the ratios of the masses of the second element that combine with a fixed mass of the first can always be reduced to a whole number ratio. This suggested to him that the elements were in fact composed of tiny atoms. While the atoms of any given element are all identical to each other, those of different elements differ in at least some fundamental ways. Chemical compounds are combinations of different elements and any given compound is always composed not only of the same proportion of elements by mass—a point already noted by Joseph Proust—but also of the same relative number of atoms. Chemical changes involve the recombination of atoms with each other in new ways; they do not involve changes in the atoms themselves.

Now the most obvious ways in which the elements differ from each other is in their manifest properties—their appearance, but also the ways in which they react to each other. But it had also become apparent as a result of the empirical work of the last century, that the elements also differed from each other in at least one key quantitative determination: their atomic mass. This made it possible to theorize chemical interactions as interactions between particles defined by their differences in mass and thus reduce the qualitative changes we observe to their underlying quantitative determinations. This reduction of qualitative to quantitative difference was embodied first of all in the periodic table of elements, which was one of the key scientific discoveries of this period.

It is the identification of patterns among empirical properties that allowed the great chemists of the last century to group the elements together into the periodic table, certainly one of the most important achievements of the scientific revolution. This process proceeded slowly, and in starts, and, like Kepler's discovery of the empirical laws of motion benefited from more than one mistake. At first it was only local patterns that were noted. Johann Dobereiner (1829/1895), for example, discovered that if one grouped certain elements in triads according similar but gradually changing properties, one found that the atomic weight of the middle member of the group was, in fact, very close to the arithmetic mean of the two extreme members. The critical step towards development of a global view, however, was taken by John Newlands (1863) who argued that the elements were arranged according to some as yet undiscovered musical harmonic, so that certain properties recurred with every eighth element. Newlands was unaware of the noble gases, the existence of which disturbs his pattern, and in the end chemical organization turns out to have no more to do with music than planetary motion with the Platonic solids, but as with Kepler, Newlands love of harmony disciplined his mind to see patterns, even if the real form of organization turned out to be rather different that the one he expected to find. But it was Dmitri Mendeleev (1861) who finally put it all together, in large part because, also like Kepler, he was respectful enough of the empirical data to keep rearranging his table so that it actually described the real world, but confident enough of the power of correct theory to boldly claim that where there were gaps in his table, elements would eventually be discovered to fill them. Legend has it that the table came to him in a dream, after he had been playing solitaire!

It was the formal description chemical and electrical processes together that drove the key technological advances of the nineteenth century—and indeed many of those of the twentieth. On the one hand, understanding how electricity works made possible the development of electrical motors and the whole range of machinery which is drive by electrical motors, electrical lighting, radio and television, the telephone, the phonograph, the tape recorder, and the X-ray. Advances in chemistry, meanwhile, drove the development of the internal combustion engine and thus the automobile, more advanced locomotives, the airplane, and the rocket, as well as the vast array of pharmaceuticals, plastics, etc. which have so significant expanded the scope and intensity of human activity during the course of the past 150 years. Indeed, the importance of newer (information) technologies dependent on quantum mechanics notwithstanding, most of the technology we use on a day-to-day basis is still based on nineteenth century science.

At the same time, even within these fields, which were the locus of such fantastic scientific progress, sharp contradictions remained. The development of the atomic theory and periodic table on the one hand and of electromagnetism on the other hand brought science right up to the brink of a unified theory of matter and energy. Chemical interactions, after all, turn out to be electromagnetic interactions . . . This advance, however, eluded even such brilliant scientists as Maxwell. The reason was simple. Matter and energy were radically distinct. Matter was particulate, energy wave-like. Matter was fundamentally inert; energy set matter in motion and was the cause of all change.

Behind this matter/energy dualism, which was, in reality simply a transformation of the earlier matter/form dualism which had crippled Aristotelian physics, was a deeper sociological dualism: that between capital on the one hand, and "land" or raw materials and labor on the other hand. Under competitive capitalism land and labor had been fully transformed into commodities—as had the products produced by labor. This was not, however, true for capital, which remained largely in the hands of individual families or privately held joint-stock companies. It was only with the transformation of capital into a commodity that the basis in experience would exist for development of a theory which unified matter and energy (quantum mechanics) and which, it turns out, is homologous with the pure theory of capital developed by the most advanced sectors of capital during the period of imperialism-finance capitalism (Hayek 1940, Tipler 1994).

Similarly, even though Maxwell's theory of electromagnetism had implicitly eliminated the need for any medium through which electromagnetic radiation might be propagated, and even thought experiments continuously failed to find any evidence, direct or indirect, for such a medium, physicists during this period clung stubbornly to the notion of the luminiferous ether. The luminiferous ether, lineal descendant of Aristotle's celestial ether or quintessence, was supposed to be a very fine, almost impalpable, and essentially unchanging (and therefore undetectable) but nonetheless material medium through which electromagnetic waves flowed. This ether was ultimately a reflex of the monetary system, understood as a fixed medium through which commodities flow without either affecting or being affected by them. The transformation of industrial into finance capital and the subordination of the monetary system to the global market in the coming period gradually undermined this idea, and created the basis for treating money as simply another commodity. This, in turn, created a basis in experience for rejection of the luminiferous ether in physical theory.

Emerging Contradictions

But if the period of competitive/industrial capitalism was the period during which humanity unleashed in new and powerful ways the energetic potential of matter, it was also a period in which we began to discover some of the fundamental limitations on the development of physical organization. Here developments in two closely related disciplines: thermodynamics and statistical mechanics are of particular importance. Thermodynamics emerged directly out of the struggle for technological innovation. Specifically, it was intimately bound up with the effort to improve the efficiency of heat engines and related technological problems.

The first law of thermodynamics states very simply that energy, like matter, can be neither created nor destroyed; it can only change form. This conclusion, which we now regard as almost obvious, presupposed a number of prior advances. It was necessary, first of all, to recognize that heat was not a substance, but rather something that pertained to the state of a particular form of matter, an advance which was made by Benjamin Thompson (Count Rumford) while boring cannon for the Bavarian government. Up until this time it had been thought that heat was a substance known as caloric. As a substance was ground up, as happens in the boring of a cannon, its capacity to retain caloric was thought to degrade, with the result that the water which was used to cool the object heated and boiled away. Rumford, however, recognized that the water boiled even when the tools became so dull that they no longer cut. This meant that heat was being produced simply by the mechanical action of the boring process. Heat, in other words, was simply a form of energy which could be transferred from one body to another.

This meant, however, that there was a kind of equivalence relationship between heat and other forms of energy. Demonstration of this point fell to James Joule. Now the sort of energy with which scientists were most concerned was, of course, mechanical energy, the capacity to do work. Work, we will remember, is defined as the product of the magnitude of the force F applied to a particle and the distance s which the particle moves.

$$W = Fs$$

Joule developed an apparatus in which falling weights turned paddles in water, gradually increasing its temperature, and showing that a given quantity of work would produce the same quantity of heat. Further experiment showed that it made no difference how the work was done or what sort of energy was involved in doing it.

At this point in history, however, there was a very specific sort of apparatus which was being used to do work: the steam engine in which heat was used to cause the expansion of the gas in a closed cylinder in order to move a piston. A simple system such as this can be described by the following state variables:

> Pressure p
>
> Volume V
>
> Temperature T

The work done by the expansion of the gas in such a system as a result of heat supplied by the environment can be described as

$$dW = Fds = pAds = pdV$$
$$W = \int dW = \int pdV$$

where A is the area of a cylinder or piston. Now, there are many different ways in which such a system can be taken from any given initial state to any given final state. We might, for example, heat it at constant pressure to a given temperature and then change the pressure (and volume) at constant temperature, or we might first lower the pressure (and increase the volume) and then gradually raise the temperature at constant pressure. Each path involves a different flow of heat in to the system and results in a different quantity of work. Regardless of the path, however, it turns out that the change in the internal energy of the system U is always equal to the heat added minus the work done. This relation we call the first law of thermodynamics.

$$\Delta U = Q - W$$

The aim of all this research, of course, was to develop the most efficient heat engines possible. And it was here, for the first time, that humanity began to run up against definite physical limits to technological progress. The earliest engines were terribly inefficient, transforming into work only a small part of the heat energy applied to them. And, as Sadi Carnot pointed out (Carnot 1824).

> In spite of labor of all sorts expended on the steam engine . . . its theory is very little advanced.

Carnot set out to describe just what a perfectly efficient engine would be like. He noticed that

> The production of motion in a steam engine is always accompanied by a circumstance which we should particularly notice. This

circumstance is the passage of caloric from one body where the temperature is more or less elevated to another where it is lower ...

The motive power of heat is independent of the agents employed to develop it; its quantity is determined solely by the temperature of the bodies between which, in the final result, the transfer of caloric occurs.

The efficiency of an engine e is defined as

$$e = W/Q_H = Q_H - Q_C/Q_H = 1 - Q_C/Q_H$$

where QH is the heat absorbed and QC is the heat delivered lost through exhaust. A perfectly efficient machine would be one in which all of the heat absorbed was transformed into work or mechanical energy. If such an engine could, furthermore, be coupled with one which ran in reverse, which would collect the heat created in the environment by the work done on it by the first engine, and transfer it back to the reservoir from which the first engine derived its energy, the result would be a machine which could do an infinite quantity of work with a finite about of energy.

What the second law of thermodynamics states is that it is in fact impossible to build an engine the efficiency of which is one. As Lord Kelvin put it

A transformation whose only final result is to transform into work heat extracted from a source that is at the same temperature throughout is impossible.

In the course of transforming heat into work, in other words, energy is inevitably dissipated, fixing a limit to the amount of work that can be done with any given quantity of energy.

We should note here that as in the case of Newtonian mechanics, thermodynamics does not actually provide tools for technological innovation. Rather it measures the gain from and limits to innovations which had already been achieved by others working in the practical sphere.

The law can also be stated in terms of another quantity, known as entropy. The change in the entropy S of a system is defined as

$$dS = dQ/T$$

or

$$dS = dE + pdV/T$$

Just what entropy is is not entirely clear and is a matter of ongoing debate. The earliest formulations, which derive from work on heat engines, suggest that it is a measure of the dissipation of energy. Later formulations, especially those associated with Boltzmann, suggest that it is a measure of disorder in the universe, something that has led many to speak of order as "negative entropy" or "negentropy." That there should be relationship between energy dissipation and disorder does, in any case, make sense at least intuitively. Order involves a definite arrangement of the various parts of a system. Creating order, and sustaining it against degradation from the environment requires energy. If at least part of the energy which we expend trying to do work is dissipated then there is a limit to the amount of work which can be done and thus to the level of order which can be created. If, furthermore, we apply these concepts to the universe as a whole, we come up with somber conclusions indeed. At least part of the energy which the universe expends to do work and create order is also dissipated, and over an arbitrarily long period of time all of the available energy will be so dissipated, so that the universe gradually runs down, like a heat engine which has expended its fuel and gradually settles into thermal equilibrium or heat death, a state which came to be identified with maximum entropy or randomness (Helmholtz 1854/1961).

The implications of this conclusion for the way in which people in the nineteenth century understood their world were earth shattering. Much as the new mathematical physics had undermined Aristotelian teleology and the intellectual road to God associated with it, there had been no scientific results that really excluded the existence of God. Indeed, as we have seen, most mathematical physicists were also natural theologians. And even those who, like Laplace, rejected God as an hypothesis of which they had no need, saw themselves as laying the groundwork for a process of collective material progress which they expected would achieve the same aim as religion—divinization—but by different means. The second law of thermodynamics, however, undermined both of these ideological strategies. On the one hand, it revealed what could only be regarded as a flaw in the design of the universe. What sort of God would create a universe that was doomed to end in a cosmic heat death and absolute randomness?[6] At the same time, the second law also undermined secular

---

6. As we have explained in previous chapters, there *are* theologies that are compatible with a high degree of cosmological pessimism, but they are not the theologies that were dominant during the early stages of capitalist development, in which inner worldly

progressivism. No matter how ingenious we become, it suggested, we will eventually run up against limits to growth and things will gradually begin to disintegrate until there is nothing of interest left at all.

This recognition of the limits to technological progress and the attendant turn toward cosmological pessimism comes at a suspicious time in the process of capitalist development. It was just precisely in the middle of the nineteenth century that the process of transforming labor power into a commodity reached the point of critical mass in England and other advanced capitalist countries and that the internal contradictions of capitalism which Marx would soon analyze would come to the fore. Thermodynamics is, in this sense, the industrial capitalist science par excellence, at once rooted in and contributing to technological progress, while at the same time revealing fixed and apparently intransigent limits to growth.

When we point this out of course, we have already moved into a realm that is quite different from that of dynamics. All of the interactions of dynamics are time-reversible: the processes that they describe can run forwards or backwards. Neither direction is privileged. Not so with thermodynamic processes. What the second law of thermodynamics implies is nothing less than an arrow of time. As work is done and energy dissipated irreversible changes in the structure of the universe take place. The supply of available energy is gradually depleted; the universe as a whole is gradually degraded. Unification of thermodynamics and dynamics thus turns out, as we will see, to be very difficult.

Thermodynamic limits were not, however, the only physical limits that were discovered during the nineteenth century. Two other results: the Poincaré Recurrence Theorem and the Markov Recurrence Theorem also had profound impact on the way in which people in mature capitalist societies understood the universe. As it turns out these results were in part at least a product of efforts to unify thermodynamics with Newtonian mechanics (or rather Hamiltonian dynamics) and thus to overcome the contradiction which we have just identified.

Thermodynamics describes physical systems macroscopically, in terms of abstract state variables: pressure, volume, temperature, heat,

---

activity was seen as an integral part of God's plan for the universe. Religion in the mid-nineteenth century thus begins a turn back to otherworldliness, a turn represented above all by Kierkegaard, and continued in our own century by theologians such as Barth and Rahner.

entropy, etc. From the standpoint of the established physical theory of the nineteenth century, however, all of these macroscopic concepts were, in principle, reducible to microscopic equivalents. Pressure, for example, is the average rate per unit area at which the molecules of a substance deliver momentum to the fluid of a manometer (pressure gauge) as they strike its service. Temperature is average kinetic energy of translation of the molecules of a substance. Heat is the total quantity of molecular motion. This means that it ought, in principle, be possible to translate the formalisms of thermodynamics into the "language" of mechanics. Since it is, of course impossible to measure and/or calculate the paths of the billions of molecules involved in even simple thermodynamic systems, these are represented in aggregate and treated using the methods of probability and statistics. Thus the term "statistical mechanics."

The principal protagonist in this struggle was Ludwig Boltzmann. Boltzmann's strategy was to identify a microscopic basis for the irreversibility of time. This meant, first of all, developing a microscopic equivalent for entropy. Reasoning that according to the second law of thermodynamics, the most probable distribution of particles was the equilibrium distribution—i.e., that with maximum entropy—he associated the relative probability of any given distribution of particles in a system with that systems entropy. Let P be the probability of a given distribution, N the number of particles in the system, and Ni the various possible distributions. Then

$$P = N! / N_1! N_2 \ldots$$

The entropy S is then defined as

$$S = k \log P$$

and the negative entropy or information content H as

$$H = \sum_k P(k,t,) \log P(k,t) / P_{eq}(k,t)$$

Now assume N objects distributed between two urns, labeled A and B respectively. At regular intervals one object is chosen at random from one urn and placed in the other. Before each transition there are k objects in urn A and N-k objects in urn B. After each transition, there are k+1 objects in urn A and N-(k+1) objects in urn B. The transition probabilities for this system are as follows:

The Development of Mathematical Physics

for transition k--->k-1: k/N

for transition k--->k+1: 1-k/N

These probabilities depend only on the state of the system at the time of the transition and are independent of its past history. The result is what is known as a Markov chain, which evolves in accord with the above equation to a point where

$$H = 0$$

or the entropy is maximized and information content minimized.

In this way, Boltzmann was able to define a real irreversibility, but it was based not on the laws of nature, but rather on a subjective attempt to use present knowledge to predict future states of the system to predict. If Boltzmann was right, further more, all processes should appear to be irreversible, which is not really true.

Recognizing these difficulties, Boltzmann (1872) tried a second approach. Assume a population of molecules. Consider the evolution of the velocity distortion function

$$f(v,t)$$

as the sum of two effects; the free motion of particles, calculated in terms of classical dynamics and collisions, the frequency of which is proportional to the number of molecules taking part in the collisions. We can then define the negative entropy of information content

$$H = \int f \log f \, dv$$

which, Boltzmann claimed, could be shown to decrease of time until it reached H=0. There are numerous numerical verifications for such a trend. Here irreversibility is no longer subjective; it has a real microcosmic basis.

This was not, however, the end of the debate. Poincaré (1893) and Zermelo (1896) pointed out that Boltzmann had missed one crucial fact. According to classical dynamics, collisions that lead to velocity reversals

$$v \rightarrow -v$$

imply a temporal reversibility

$$t \rightarrow -t$$

as well. Collisions of this sort occur within 10^{-6} seconds in even a dilute gas. New ensembles are formed, something like the earlier nonequilibrium configuration and H rises. Eventually Boltzmann was forced to conclude that the universe as a whole is *already* in thermal equilibrium and that only small regions depart from this state, gradually evolving back towards it. There are two arrows of time, one leading away from, the other back towards, equilibrium. The implication is, of course, that we live on a small island of order and complex organization in a sea of chaos that will soon wash us way. The pessimism of this conclusion, coupled with what he regarded as his own failure to unify physics, led Boltzmann to commit suicide in 1906.

Boltzmann's failure led many scientists to conclude that dynamics and thermodynamics were, in fact, simply incompatible—two radically distinct ways of looking at the universe. The effort to unify the disciplines had, however, demonstrated that the dynamic perspective is no more hopeful than the thermodynamic. This conclusion was implicit in Poincaré's refutation of Boltzmann. Assume the first law of thermodynamics: that energy can neither be created nor destroyed. Assume as well that the phase space available to any system is finite and bounded.[7] Then over an infinite period of time, the system will return infinitely often to states arbitrarily close to its initial state as well as to all of the other state through which it evolves (Tipler 1994: 90–95).

A similar result can be obtained by more purely probabilistic methods. Assume a system with three states (1, 2, 3) and a probability of 50 percent of making a transition from any one state to any other. There is thus a 50 percent chance that the system, when in state 1 will make the transition to state 2 and the same chance that it will make the transition to state 3. Let us assume that we transition to state 2. The second transition will then be either to 3 or to 1, with an equal chance of either. The chance that the system will return to state 1 after two transitions is 50 percent. The third transition must be back to some previously occupied state, though it need not be to 1. The chance that it will be is again 50 percent, so that the chance of returning to 1 after three transitions is 25 percent and after two or three transitions is 75 percent. With each succes-

---

7. The phase space of a system is a 6N-dimensional abstract space which describes the position and momentum of every particle in the system. To say that the phase space is finite and bounded is to say that there are a finite number of locations available to the particles in the system and that there is a limit to their momentum—assumptions that would seem to apply to the universe as a whole provided it is conceived as a finite system of particles.

sive transition the probability of returning to state 1 increases, and over an infinity of transitions it increases to 1. This sort of recurrence is called Markov recurrence (Tipler 1994: 95–97).

It is interesting to note that the sort of pessimism connected with these "eternal return" theorems is quite different from that associated with the discovery of the Second Law of Thermodynamics. The second law of thermodynamics represents a progressive impulse—that of building ever more efficient heat engines, and thus increasing infinitely the level of organization of the universe, running up against definite limits—limits which, we will see, were given cognitively by the structure of the social system—competitive capitalism—in the context of which the effort was taking place. Thermodynamics represents the position of a progressive industrial bourgeoisie running up against the limits of its own class nature. The outlook of the revolutionary intelligentsia and proletariat at this point in history turns out, as we will see, not to be too different after all. The eternal return theorems, on the other hand, represent a fundamental assault on the idea of progress altogether—essentially an argument that the idea itself is incoherent at a fundamental physical level. It is little wonder that these recurrence theorems were in fact anticipated by Nietzsche, whose doctrine of the eternal return is, in fact, cast in physical terms, and is in fact close to if not convertible with the recurrence theorems cited above.

> If the Universe may be conceived as a definite quantity of energy, as a definite number of centers of energy . . . it follows that the Universe must go through a calculable number of combinations in the great game of chance which constitutes its existence. In infinity, at some moment or other, every possible combination must once have been realized; not only this, but it must once have been realized an infinite number of times. (Nietzsche, 1889/1968: 1066)

This is the outlook not of an industrial but of a rentier bourgeoisie which has lost any illusion of being different or more progressive than preceding ruling classes—which has recognized that capitalism represents just another means of exploitation, and which has resigned itself to eventual extinction as another wave of predators replaces it.

If the period of competitive capitalism was the period during which the internal contradictions of mathematical physics began to become obvious, it was also the period during which not only the general methods but also the larger paradigm was extended to other fields of inquiry in such a way as to begin to generate a global view of the world and at least the outlines of a unified theory. The key links in this regard took place in the disciplines of biology and political economy. We need to consider each of these fields in turn.

The key developments in biology, of course, were the beginnings of genetics and the development of evolutionary theory, especially in its Darwinian form. Both of these theories by themselves already represent at least a loose application of the paradigm of mathematical physics—and, more to the point, the ideological impact of the market order. In order to understand this, it is necessary to recall just where biological science had been in the preceding period. The seventeenth and eighteenth century, we will recall, had witnessed the application of a broadly mechanistic perspective to living systems. There had also been some significant progress in anatomy, progress which, thanks to the development of the microscope, had begun to be extended to the microscopic level. Most of this work was, however, not only purely descriptive, but it fell well short of anything like mathematical formalization. The great "theoretical" achievement of the period was Linneaus' system of classification, but even Linneaus' work was still largely qualitative. What genetic theory does is to take the principal *qualitative* determinations of organisms, what came to be called their phenotypes, and reduce them to certain atomic "characters" called genes which are passed on from generation to generation, but due to the dynamics of sexual reproduction can become dissociated from each other and thus recombine in new and interesting ways. The level of formalization here is still very low:

1. the additive classification of Linneaus gives way to a multiplicative scheme in which describes the way in which alleles from two parent organisms can combine to form distinct genotypes and

2. there is a rudimentary distinction made between the outward, qualitative appearance of organisms (phenotype) and their underlying structure, which is capable of being specified quantitatively (genotype).

The groundwork, however, has been laid, once the genetic material itself has been isolated, for biology to be reduced to chemistry and thus ultimately to physics.

The relationship between evolutionary theory and mathematical physics is rather more complex, and can be understood only by way of the related discipline of political economy. On the one hand, evolutionary theory generally (as opposed to Darwinism in particular) reflects the ideological impact of the enormous technological progress represented by the industrial revolution and the social transformation wrought by the democratic uprisings in France and elsewhere. By living rapid progress for the first time in over five thousand years human beings became capable of seeing progress in the larger structure of the natural world. It should thus come as no surprise that it was in the years immediately following the French revolution that geologists began to understand the cataclysmic history of the Earth or that it was just precisely as skeletons were being dug out of the closets of the European "aristocracy" that the bones of other large predators whose time had passed were also finally unearthed.

Initially evolutionary theory took an unambiguously progressive, if not terribly sophisticated, form that had little or nothing to do with the larger paradigm of mathematical physics. Throughout the first two periods of capitalist development, and indeed right up to the discovery of DNA and thus of the chemical basis of life, a vitalist and teleological trend persisted in biology alongside the increasingly powerful mechanistic current. From the standpoint of this perspective, whatever might or might not be said about the teleological organization of the universe as a whole, it was precisely teleological ordering which defined living systems. Organisms were structured in such a way as to permit them to survive. As ecological conditions changed this required new behaviors, and new behaviors required new structures. Thus the claim, so often used to hold the early evolutionary theorists up to ridicule, that giraffes grew long necks because they had to reach high into the tree tops to find food. As we will see, this in fact the only way to explain *why* giraffes have long necks, and it necessarily involves teleological reasoning. Indeed, neo-Darwinists have difficulty avoiding such formulations themselves. The claim only becomes ridiculous when it is forced to become an account of the mechanism of evolution, i.e., to mimic the form of mechanistic theory and say that giraffes grew long necks *by* stretching them to reach food high in the treetops of the African savanna.

The critical link between this sort of evolutionary theory and Darwinism is the experience of the marketplace, and the development of a rudimentary theory of the market order. We have already seen that the first stage of capitalist development yielded the beginnings of a political economy that attempted to formalize mathematically the movement of commodities in the abstract space of the marketplace. We also noted that the persistence of a fixed frame of nonmarket relations meant that a sharp distinction remained between the market price, which was determined by supply and demand, and the natural price that was determined ultimately by labor. The period that we are now considering witnessed a contradictory development in the area of political economy as in the other domains of the sciences. On the one hand, labor is commodified and ceases to be part of the "fixed frame" of nonmarket institutions against the background of which commodities move. This makes it possible to develop a more nearly complete economic theory. There were, however, two ways in which this development might precede. One might focus on the actual process of production, a direction suggested by the enormous progress in the development of the forces of production wrought by the industrial revolution. Thus David Ricardo begins his *Principles of Political Economy* (1817) by claiming that

> The value of a commodity, or the quantity of any other commodity for which it will exchange, depends on the relative quantity of labor which is necessary for its production, and not on the greater or less compensation which is paid for that labor.

Recognition that it is labor that is the real source of all value eliminates the residual circularity that had marred the theory advanced by Adam Smith. The difficulty with this approach is that commodities do not in fact circulate at their values, but rather at prices that only roughly approximate their values, making it necessary to find some way to transform prices into values and vice-versa, a problem the solution of which eluded Ricardo. It was only Marx's theory of the equalization of the rate of profit and the development of the theory of prices of production that would show the way beyond this impasse—a way that involved recognition of the exploitative character of capitalism, the reality of class struggle, and its role in the determination of economic phenomena. Ricardo's approach represents the standpoint of the progressive bourgeoisie, actively engaged in the production process, but rapidly running up against its own contradictory class character.

The revolutionary implications of Ricardo's theory frightened the more backward elements of English capital—both the residual landowning classes, who met their definitive defeat during this period with the repeal of the Corn Laws and the establishment of free trade in grain, something which led to a collapse in ground rents, and the fully capitalist *rentier* strata which were only beginning to emerge. Thus, just as the progressive bourgeoisie begins to advance a nearly complete labor theory of value, its more backward representatives begin to attack the idea of social progress as such. The key figure in this regard was Thomas Malthus (Malthus 1798), a clergyman who had become interested in the problem of population, and advanced the now familiar thesis that whereas population grows geometrically, agricultural production grows only arithmetically. The implication was that the planet was headed for a major demographic crisis and that wages should be suppressed in order to hold down the tendency of the working classes to reproduce. At the same time, in order to avoid underconsumption tendencies, it was also necessary to increase the proportion of the national income devoted to luxury consumption on the part of the landed elite (Mandel 1968: 294–95). This argument on behalf of unproductive consumption was linked eclectically with the claim that the interest that rentiers received on their capital was compensation for their abstinence from earlier consumption that was taken to be the precondition for the accumulation of capital as such.

Darwinian evolutionary theory is simply a synthesis—or rather an internally unstable amalgam—of progressive evolutionary theory and the Malthusian concept of demographic pressure. Whatever its merits as an account of the dynamics of population growth and food production at the end of the eighteenth century, the basic insight that populations could grow so rapidly as to exhaust the ecological niches that they inhabit seemed to be valid. At the same time, it was clear that it was in fact possible to develop new strategies for survival that accommodate these ecological changes. What Darwin's theory suggests is that all organisms are constantly struggling to survive under conditions of scarcity. Those which are well adapted to their environments survive long enough to reproduce and pass their characteristics on to their descendants; those which are not die out, and their characteristics with them (Darwin 1859/1970).

This theory represents a key link in the generation of a unified theory on the basis of the general paradigm of mathematical physics. On the one hand, once Darwinian evolutionary theory was joined with genetics, and genetics reduced to molecular biology, the road was open for an explanation of even the most complex biological phenomena—i.e., the evolution of increasingly complex forms of living systems—in physical terms. Indeed, the concept of natural selection even informs properly physical theory. Physical and chemical processes, for example, tend to select for the lowest possible energy state, i.e., the state of thermodynamic equilibrium. On the other hand, Darwin provided a way in which bourgeois political economy could answer Marx without rejecting the notion of social progress altogether. What the market does is to provide an environment, a kind of social ecology, which selects for those practices that are most conducive to survival and prosperity, thus making it an agent of ongoing social progress (Hayek 1988). Complete development of such a theory, however, which reflects the standpoint of the investor deciding in which "practices" to invest, would have to await transformation of capital itself into a commodity something which was only beginning during this period.[8] The tendency, rather, was towards a crude "Social Darwinism" which saw society generally and the market in particular, as a mechanism for selecting fit individuals.

Even as it opened up the possibility of a unified theory, though, Darwinism introduced new contradictions. How, if the tendency of physical processes is towards equilibrium, does evolution take place at all? It is not sufficient here to point out that there is nothing in thermodynamic theory which says that local departures from equilibrium are impossible, as long as the total entropy of the universe increases; it is still necessary to *explain* those departures, and to do so without recourse to supernatural principles such as divine creation—though this was, in fact the answer of more than few nineteenth century scientists, and continues to be the default position of scientifically minded theologians. The problem is complicated by the fact that while many individual evolutionary steps which involve an increase in complexity and organization can in fact be shown to have enhanced survival, it remains true that very simple

8. What was needed, specifically, was something like the marginalist theory that abandoned the attempt to achieve an objective theory of value altogether and analyzed economic processes from the subjective standpoint of the investor. From this point of view, the "value of commodities is simply their "marginal utility," i.e., the intensity of the last fragment of desire not satisfied. The idea here is simply that the intensity of people's desires for particular commodities are reflected in their buy and sell decisions, which are then translated in aggregate into supply and demand. The supply and demand curves taken together then determine an "equilibrium price," i.e., the price at which exactly as much of a particular commodity will be produced as can be sold. In so far as labor power itself has been commodified, this same theory can be applied to wages and as capital was commodified, it could be applied to capital as well, making possible a unified mathematical theory of prices which described the operation of a pure market economy.

organisms such as viruses and bacteria have shown themselves far better able to survive and reproduce than complex systems like ourselves. Why, then, the global trend toward complexity? And what drives the process? It is one thing to point out that there is a natural selection for forms which have greater survival value; it is quite another thing to imagine that natural selection can actually innovate. Here the tendency is to fall back on random, purely mechanical interactions, something which recent studies have been shown fails to explain the frequency of innovations which contribute to survival.

As we will see, these contradictions were not resolved, but only compounded, in the next period.

Finally, before moving on to the period of imperialism and finance capitalism, it will be useful to say something about the development of dialectical and historical materialism, which first emerged in this period. In a very real sense, the scientific and philosophical work of Marx and Engels are every bit as much a reflection of the internal contradictions of competitive industrial capitalism as those of the bourgeois scientists we have been discussing. The difference is that whereas bourgeois science remains a prisoner of the marketplace and the categories which are its reflex, Marx is able to analyze the theoretical contradictions of bourgeois science—or at least of bourgeois economics—as a reflex of the underlying social contradictions of the system itself, and thus to point the way toward their resolution. Thus Marx's account of prices of production shows the way past the Kantian antinomies of Ricardo's theory and derives price from value.

$$P = (c + v) * (1 + r)$$

where P is the price of production, c constant capital (tools and raw materials), v variable capital (labor) and r the average rate of profit. Similarly, Marx's crisis theory shows the way beyond Malthusian pessimism regarding the future and demonstrates that the limits to progress are not demographic but rather economic and that reorganization of the economic system will once again unleash the forces of social progress. Since it is labor (v) which creates value, and thus surplus value (s), the rate of profit

$$r = \frac{s}{c + v}$$

tends to decline as a society becomes more technologically advanced, and fixed capital formation (c) a higher percentage of total investment costs. The result is disinvestment and economic decline. This in turn leads to the reallocation of resources to low, wage, low technology activities, holding back the development of human capacities and setting into motion underconsumption tendencies which also lead to crisis. Only a breach with the market order and thus a radical suppression of the law of value can open up the road to unlimited progress.

At the same time, it is quite remarkable given their ability to see past the contradictions of bourgeois political economy, that neither Marx nor Engels was unable to see the internal contradictions of bourgeois science generally. Where Marx looked beyond the mere formalization of the movement of commodities in the abstract space of the market to explain the genesis of the commodity form itself, neither he nor Engels was able to see beyond the strategy of mathematical formalization generally to the need for a genuinely explanatory theory of the universe. Indeed, Engels stood firmly by the results of bourgeois mathematical physics and against the Hegelian project of a higher "philosophy of nature" even though this made the task of developing a dialectics of nature far more difficult. Marx and Engels wanted to see themselves as opening up a new continent for "modern" (i.e., mathematical-physical) science, much as Newton and Priestly and Darwin had done before them, not as mounting a critique a critique of mathematical physics as such.

The reasons for this failure are to be found in the ideological strategy of the bourgeoisie. We have already suggested that mathematical physics played a central role in the ideological strategy of the bourgeoisie. By undermining natural theology, it undermined the metaphysical foundations for any substantive doctrine of the Good in terms of which the market allocation of resources might be judged and an alternative allocation legitimated. We have also seen that the secular intelligentsia, which had never really recovered from the its struggle with the Catholic hierarchy, had its own reasons to be attracted to atheism. If there is no God then the claims of the clergy to intellectual leadership are null and void and the secular intelligentsia can, at the very least, look forward to emancipation from its status as a "handmaid" to theology and at best can aspire to power itself. If there is no God, in other words, then the secular intelligentsia, or at least that section of it which has grasped the "line of march, conditions, and ultimate general result" of the human historical process, represents in fact nothing less that the global leadership of the universe. If Marx and Engels failed to see through the contradictions of bourgeois science, it was because this "science" supported their atheism, and their atheism supported their resistance to clerical hegemony and the aspirations of their own class-fraction to global leadership. In the process of course they yielded unwittingly to the strategy of the bourgeoisie and undermined any possible basis for grounding their own moral claims against the marketplace. One of the central tasks of the next chapter will be to show that our own critique of mathematical physics is, in fact, simply the completion of Marx's own critique of political economy—albeit a completion which had to await the completion of capitalism itself.

LATE MODERN SCIENCE

Imperialism and Finance Capitalism

The capitalism that Marx analyzed and of which he discovered the organizing principle was not yet a complete capitalism; the political economy that he criticized was still the formal theory of an incomplete system. Our task in this section is to show just how a mature or complete capitalism differs from the capitalism that Marx analyzed, to show what difference that makes in the way mathematical physics developed. As we will see, this has implications for the critique of political economy itself.

There have, to be sure, been many efforts to "update" Marx's analysis to take into account developments since the middle of the nineteenth century. The most fundamental of these was Lenin's theory of imperialism, which argued that during its highest stage, capitalism is characterized by

- a high level of concentration of capital, leading to the development of effective monopolies which dominate economic life,
- the fusion of banking capital with industrial capital to create "finance capital" and a financial oligarchy,
- the export of capital to regions where the organic composition of capital is lower and thus the average rate of profit is higher,
- the formation of international monopolies which divide the world among themselves, and
- an ongoing struggle among the principal capitalist powers over what has become a *de facto* division of the entire planet among themselves. (Lenin 1916/1971)

Lenin's analysis of imperialism was set in the context of a larger strategic analysis of the conditions for the transition to socialism. Lenin and the other Bolsheviks recognized, to an extent that Marx and the Marxists of the Second International did not, the alienating impact of market relations on the whole population, including the working classes, who were not, for the most part, able to rise spontaneously to socialist consciousness, but rather required the conscious leadership of the most advanced elements of their class, organized in the Communist Party. Bogdanov, Lenin's principal rival for leadership of the Bolsheviks, argued that the principal task of the party was educational, i.e., to actually raise the people to the level of socialist consciousness (Rowley 1987, Mansueto 1996). Lenin, on the other hand, took a more narrowly political approach, arguing that the party could seize power without actually raising the whole working class to the level of socialist consciousness by exercising leadership in the struggle against Imperialism. Imperialism, he pointed out, involved an alliance between international monopoly capital and semifeudal landed elites in the colonized countries—and by extension in the "weak links" of the imperialist chain" such as Russia, which held back the struggle for national liberation and national development in those countries. By standing as the most committed and effective advocates the democratic but not yet socialist aspirations of the masses of the colonized countries, communists could win their confidence and ultimately come to power at the head of a broad movement which they could then gradually lead in a socialist direction after they had seized the commanding heights of state power.

The power of Lenin's analysis is measured by its strategic effectiveness. Clearly Lenin understood something very important about what was happening in the world at the beginning of the twentieth century, indeed about what was going to be happening in the world throughout most of the twentieth century. But just as clearly he missed something about the long-term evolution of capitalism, which ultimately proved itself capable of resisting what initially seemed like a very powerful strategy. Where did he go wrong?

The problem, I would like to suggest, is that Lenin inherited Marx's still incomplete break with utopian socialism and "vulgar communism" which defined capitalism and socialism in terms of the ownership of the means of production. Marx's great contribution was to transcend this error and recognize that it was the operation of market forces, and not ownership patterns per se which defined capitalism and which were holding back the development of human capacities (Marx 1844/1978).[9] Even so, the only method of restricting the operation of market forces that was actually put forward was state ownership and management of the means of production. And there was a tendency to analyze changes in capitalism in terms of changes in ownership patterns (greater concentration, geographic shifts) rather than in terms of an increasing degree of marketization and commodification.

I would like to suggest, first of all, that the developments which Lenin identified were in fact simply phenomena of a deeper transition in capitalism, a transition which can hardly be said to be complete even today and which in fact cannot be completed for reasons which will become clear very shortly. Specifically, imperialism as Lenin understood it was simply a stage along the way to the construction of a unified global market in which capital, due to the development of electronic information processing and telecommunications, coupled with the destruction of all political and ideological barriers, has become (almost) instantly mobile and is (almost) instantly reallocated to the most profitable activities. The concentration of capital that Lenin observed and the fusion of industrial with financial capital to create a new amalgam were simply the first stages of the process that have led to the dispossession of the entrepreneur and the privately held company. The export of capital to low wage, low technology regions in order to take advantage of higher rates of profit is simply a reflection of the increased stringency with which market criteria are applied, coupled of course with the pressure of the rising organic composition of capital on the rate of profit in the advanced industrial countries. The division of the planet by the principal imperialist powers is simply the first step in the creation of a unified global market —including a unified global market in capital—a process which ultimately culminates

---

9. This is not to say that excessive concentration of ownership cannot by itself constitute an obstacle to human development. But if it was the sole obstacle, it would be difficult to see why redistribution of land and capital to open up more opportunities for the expansion of the petty bourgeoisie, would not merit consideration at least on par with more traditionally socialist approaches to the resolving the contradictions of capitalism. It is the fact that the marketplace systematically destroys the petty bourgeoisie—and eventually, we will argue, even the entrepreneurial capitalist—rendering them subservient to investors who evaluate their activities exclusively on the basis of profitability, which makes this option unworkable.

by exposing the fictitious nature of national sovereignty even in the imperialist centers.

This kind of pure finance capitalism, in which entrepreneurs, managers, and workers are all fully subordinated to investors, who in turn behave in perfectly market-rational fashion, we call *infokatallaxis*, from the Greek *katallaxis*, which means exchange. In such a system, innovations are excludable only to the extent that they have not yet been reverse engineered, and monopoly rents on skill and innovation thus vanish in a time that converges on zero. This is the kind of hypercapitalist utopia promoted explicitly by people like Frank Tipler in a way that, we shall see in the next chapter, shows the link between the market order and mathematical physics rather neatly (Tipler 1994).[10]

Second, the tendency that Leninist theory identified towards the gradual merger of capitalism with the state apparatus, and which was apparent throughout the twentieth century in various forms (fascism, the welfare state), also represents a transitional phenomenon, partly generated by the need to ameliorate the internal contradictions of capitalism, and partly a response to pressure from the working classes, which may be dealt with either by repression (fascism) or by accommodation (the welfare state). The last two decades of the twentieth century, however, represented at the very least a modification of this tendency. The emergence of a global market has increasingly rendered the nation-state a less and

---

10. It might seem that with my focus on the marketplace rather than ownership, my position is close to that of dependency and world systems theory (Frank 1975, Wallerstein 1974), which define capitalism in terms of production for the market rather than in terms of the means of surplus extraction at the point of production. Nothing could be further from the truth. By failing to recognize the difference between the nonmarket means of surplus extraction which characterized mercantilism and which still characterize some parts of the Third World, and marketized surplus extraction by means of the wage relation, dependency theory in fact advances a less nuanced account of capitalist development than did Lenin and than do their contemporary adversaries, the so-called "mode of production" theorists (Laclau 1974). As a result they tend to misunderstand, even more radically than did Lenin, the reason why most successful revolutionary movements took place in the Third World throughout most of the twentieth century, rather than in the advanced capitalist countries as Marx expected. This greater revolutionary valence is due not to the fact that the superexploited Third World is in a perpetual revolutionary situation due to capitalist exploitation, nor is it due to the fact that these countries constitute the weak links in the imperialist chain, but rather to the fact that the lower degree of commodification and marketization means a lower degree of alienation and a greater capacity to develop the moral distance from the market order necessary to mount a critique (Lancaster 1987, Mansueto 1995, 2002a).

less effective instrument of policy. This has created particular difficulties for working class organizations already undermined by the pressures of marketization. As workers are forced to sell more and more of their labor power, less and less is left over to invest in building and maintaining the structures of community life. Working class organizations of every kind begin to disintegrate, even as capital benefits from loose labor markets. Fewer and fewer workers learn to build and exercise power, and the prospect of organizing against capital becomes ever more difficult, as there are fewer and fewer existing networks and emerging leaders to work with. The dynamic of political disintegration has, however, also affected the bourgeoisie, which looks increasingly to international organizations insulated from democratic pressures, to serve as the principal instruments for its policy, and to the military power of the sole remaining global hegemon, the United States, to enforce its decrees, acting wherever possible under the cover of international sanctions in order to blunt criticism from opponents of such intervention on the home front.

Third, contrary to the expectations of most Leninist theorists, both the direct and the indirect apologetics for capitalism remain very much alive. As we noted above, Lukacs, who first advanced this theory, believed that the direct apologetic for capitalism was an artifact of the rising bourgeoisie and had given way to the indirect apologetic after 1848, something which eventually culminated in the fascist irrationalism. And this was, indeed, the way things would have looked, especially from Europe, during the first part of the century. There has, however, since at least 1980, been a significant resurgence of ideological forms which argue quite directly for the superiority of capitalism on positive grounds, claiming that it is in fact an effective agent for the promotion of creativity and innovation (Hayek 1988). As we will see, both the direct and the indirect apologetics are intimately bound up with the development of mathematical physics in the twentieth century.

The fact is that *infokatallaxis* is impossible, at least for human beings. First of all, so long as production actually involves the reorganization of physical, biological, and social matter, the instantaneous reallocation of capital is impossible. This is, of course, why finance capital aspires to the creation of a pure information economy, and attempts to retheorize all activities, from growing corn to making steel to cooking food, as forms of information processing. One would in fact have to be at Tipler's Omega point in order to construct anything like a pure *infokatallaxis*. But even so, special relativity places definite limits on the speed with which even electronic information can be transmitted. Nothing can move faster than the speed of light. So it appears that even at Omega perfect markets are impossible. One is tempted to call *infokatallaxis* an angelic capitalism—but then angels, already being perfectly what they are, don't consume.

But let us assume for a moment that such a system could be constructed. What would it be like? Far from being progressive, as Tipler and his allies contend, *infokatallaxis*, to the extent that it tends towards perfect equilibrium, in fact tends towards entropic death. When all capital has finally been allocated in an optimum fashion and the instantaneous exchange of all information has eliminated the possibility of monopoly rents on innovation, there will be no further reason to reallocate capital, and thus no investment in new research and development, and no further progress (Martens 1995). Our neoliberal visionaries in fact aspire to nothing more nor less than eternal death. When a society's vision of its own future becomes focused on paths that are physically impossible, and that, were they possible, would lead necessarily to the end of all interesting organization in the universe, then the structures that have organized the development of that society are clearly spent. Progress requires a break with those structures, and the creation of something radically new. In our case this means a break with the market system.

Late Modern Science

The transformation of capital itself into a commodity, coupled with the increasingly rapid penetration of market relations into every sphere of life that results from this, had a profound impact on the development of mathematical physics. Two changes are of particular importance. First, the "fixed frame" of nonmarket institutions against which commodities move has now largely disappeared, and with it the fixed frame against which local motion takes place. Second, there is a shift in focus on the part of capital from production to consumption. Capital during the period of industrial and competitive capitalism was above all productive capital, and focused primarily on extending productive capacity. Thus the persistence of labor theories of value. Thus the fact that even pessimistic theories, such as that of Malthus, focused on the question of whether or not production could keep up with population growth, mounting a very indirect argument for the allocation of resources to luxury consumption.

In the new period of finance capitalism, on the other hand, the standpoint of capital is above all that of the investor or *rentier* interested in final consumption. Value from this point of view is determined not by contribution to material production but rather by a subjective "utility function." These two developments together determined the two principal developments in fundamental physical theory during this period, i.e., relativity and quantum mechanics. We need now to consider each of these developments in turn.

Relativity

The principal motive behind the development of relativity was the recognition that there is in fact no "fixed frame" against which motion could be measured. First the earth, and then sun, and finally the fixed stars themselves had been shown to be themselves in motion, making the definition of a stable system of cosmic coordinates effectively impossible. For a time the frame of the fixed stars was replaced by the idea of the "luminiferous aether," which penetrated all "ponderable matter" and through which moved waves of light and other forms of electromagnetic radiation. But the Michelson-Morely experiment (1887)[11] showed that the speed of light is the same in direction of Earth's motion and perpendicular to it. This could not be true if there was some medium through which the light was moving. This meant that it would be necessary to reformulate the laws of mechanics in accord with what Henri Poincaré called the "Principle of Relativity." Uniform translatory motion possessed by a system as a whole cannot be detected by an observer looking at phenomena within that system; thus there is no way of determining absolute motion.

Einstein's theory of special relativity was essentially a response to this realization. What Einstein realized was that if there is no fixed frame of reference, and that if light travels at the same speed in all frames of reference, then the measurement of such basic physical quantities as distance, time, and even mass depend on one's frame of reference. This is because measurement depends on signaling and if the speed of light is

11. It is interesting to note, in this regard, that already in 1883 the positivist philosopher Ernst Mach had published an historical-critical analysis of mechanics in which he rejected the notion of absolute Newtonian space on the ground that it is not observable. The notion that what makes something real is its observability, which would become a fundamental principle of quantum mechanics, is a reflex of the growing weight of consumption over production in the capitalist system and is evidence for the primacy of ideological over scientific factors in shaping the development of mathematical physics.

finite and fixed then instantaneous signaling is impossible. What we see "now" actually happened in the past, when the signals we receive were generated. This makes relatively little difference at speeds that do not approach that of light, but as speed increases, so do relativistic effects.

One particularly useful way of illustrating this result was developed by Sir Edmund Whittaker (Whittaker 1949). Let there be two rigid rods AB and DE of equal length, moving relative to each other at a speed close to that of light and with observers at the midpoints C and F of each respectively. Assume that signals are emitted from the midpoints of the rods at a time when the two rods are coincident with each other—i.e., side by side. When the signals arrive at the endpoints of their respective rods, the rods will have moved with respect to each other. The signals will appear to arrive at the endpoints of their own rods simultaneously. That is, the signal emitted from C will appear to the observer at C to arrive at A and B simultaneously; the same is true for the signal emitted from F. But the signal emitted from F will appear to the observer at C to arrive one end of rod DE before it arrives at the other end for the simple reason that one end will be closer to C than the other and the light from that end will arrive before the light from the other end. But our perception of just how long it takes light to reach the ends of the rods in question is bound up with the distance the light in question has to travel. Because they are moving relative to AB at a speed close to that of light, the segments DF and FE appear to change in length, one getting shorter and the other longer. Similar transformations affect time—the so-called "temporal dilation phenomenon" by which the time elapsed for a cosmonaut traveling at near light speed will be less than that which elapses for her earth-bound comrades—and even mass.

The absence of a fixed frame does not, however, mean that it is impossible to know from one frame what is happening in another. Rather, the uniformity of the speed of light makes it possible to transform the coordinates of one frame of reference into those of another. This is the so-called Lorentz transformation. Assume two different coordinate systems (w, x, y, z) and (w', x', y', z') each applying to frames of reference moving relatively to each other, such as those of the rigid rods described above. Then the two systems are related to each other as

$$w' = \frac{w - vx/c^2}{\sqrt{1-(v^2/c^2)}} \qquad x' = \frac{x - vw}{\sqrt{1-(v^2/c^2)}}$$

$$y' = y$$

$$z' = z$$

The comparable transformation for mass is Einstein's familiar equation

$$E = mc^2.$$

What this means is that distance can no longer be calculated using the three dimensional Pythagorean metric:

$$r = \sqrt{x^2 + y^2 + z^2}$$

We must rather use the four-dimensional Minkowski metric:

$$s^2 = c^2d\tau^2 = c^2dt^2 - dx^2 - dy^2 - dz^2,$$

where s is the distance, c is the speed of light, τ is the proper time, t time, and x, y, and z distance along each of the "space-like" dimensions.

There have been numerous attempt to make sense out of these counter-intuitive results, and specifically to determine whether or not such time, length, and mass transformations are real or only apparent. Our approach to this question is governed by the social epistemology we outlined in the introduction to this work and that we have been employing throughout. What does it mean to say that a scientific theory developed as much as a result of transformations in the social structure—in this case the transformation of capital into a commodity—as of scientific research as such? What, specifically, does this mean in the case of special relativity? We are *not*, it must be remembered, claiming that special relativity or any other theory is *purely* ideological in the sense of being "nothing more than" a reflection of the social structure or "merely" an instrument of definite political interests. Rather, the underlying epistemology that we set forth at the beginning of this work suggests that what the structure of a society does is to make us connatural with certain forms, enabling us to abstract them from the data of the senses—while concealing other forms. While some vantage points may be superior, all convey real knowledge.

Special relativity, however, presents us with some very difficult problems in this regard. It is quite one thing to say, for example, that mercantilism made it possible to look at the universe as if was a system of only externally related point particles with mass moving through absolute space over time, but that in reality the universe is something more than this, something which mercantilism obscured from most observers at the time. It is quite different to say that finance capitalism enables us to see that rods that are moving relatively to each other change length and that relativistic space travelers experience time dilation, but that there is a deeper perspective from which these things are not true. Either the rods change length or they don't; either the relativistic space traveler ages less rapidly than her comrades at home or she doesn't.

The solution to this problem lies in recognizing that special relativity, and the other theories we will be considering in this section, do in fact know something more profound and fundamental about the structure of the universe than our imaginations can accommodate; thus the persistent tendency to generate paradoxes when we present the results of relativistic theory in nonmathematical—i.e., imaginative—terms. But this greater depth is along the single dimension of formal abstraction. Special relativity represents a more fundamental grasp of the formal, quantitative relations in terms of which the structure of the universe is most compactly described than do earlier theories. But it also begins to run up against the limits of formalization, at least in so far as it can be carried out by animal intellects who always and only abstract from and return to images. It may be that we simply cannot purge the paradox from special relativity, or the other theories of twentieth-century mathematical physics, because there is an underlying contradiction between our natural mode of knowing (which requires a turn to the image after abstraction) and the degree of formalization required by special relativity. An intellect that could resolve the paradox would not feel it in the first place because it would not know by abstraction from and return to images, but rather by direct intuition.

This solution may seem unsatisfying, especially if we focus on the problem of time dilation during relativistic space travel. Won't the paradox *have* to be resolved before we can engage in near-light speed travel? But it must be remembered that special relativity also tells us that such travel, if not impossible, is in fact extremely unlikely. This is because as a mass is accelerated to the speed of light the same relativistic effects that produce time dilation also make the mass go to infinity, increasing the amount of fuel necessary for acceleration. This is, in fact, the argument used by most physicists to rule out the possibility that UFOs are extraterrestrial spacecraft from distant stars, even prior to examination of the evidence. The underlying science raises serious questions about the possibility, or at least the practicality, of such spacecraft. In this sense, special relativity may not only signal the limits of formal theory as a means of answering questions posed by animal intellects regarding the universe in which they live; it may also signal the limits of technological development driven by formal theory and mathematical physics.[12]

This may seem like a very pessimistic conclusion, but this is true only if one assumes that formal theory and the technologies based on it represent our only or our best option—a conclusion that is entirely unwarranted. At the sociological level the equivalent attitude is despair because the problems of capitalism seem insuperable—and no option besides capitalism is even on the horizon. Resolution of the limitations and internal contradictions of mathematical physics and of the technological impasse that these limitations and contradictions have created, presupposes transcending *both* mathematical formalization and the form of social organization of which it is the organic ideology. Only a new science, which integrates transcendental as well as formal methods will be able to resolve the paradoxes within and the contradictions between the various theories of mathematical physics and to point the way to new technologies which do not flee matter for a purely informatic utopia, be that utopia angelic or demonic, but rather realize ever more fully its potential for complex, dynamic organization. And such a science, though we may plant its seeds, cannot mature in capitalist soil.

Special relativity created problems for the way in which physicists understood gravity, which presupposed an absolute space-time and the

---

12. It is interesting to note that the principal attempt to argue for infinite progress on the basis of the two fundamental theories in mathematical physics—relativity and quantum mechanics—namely Frank Tipler's Omega Point theory (Tipler 1994), presupposes what amounts to a jettisoning of the body of our animal nature in favor of a purely informatic existence. We will analyze his angelic—or rather demonic—vision of the future in the next chapter. More broadly, it seems likely that if the relativistic limits to near-light speed space travel should be overcome, the result would be transcendence of the limits of space and time so profound that quite apart from any "uploading" to a purely informatic existence, the meaning of body as locus and limit of material power would at the very least be utterly transformed, and the role of the imagination in knowing radically transcended.

instantaneous propagation of gravitational effects throughout the universe—both prohibited by Einstein's discoveries. The general theory of relativity is simply an attempt to revise Newton's theory of universal gravitation in the light of these difficulties. Einstein's key insight at the physical level was to recognize the equivalence of inertial and gravitational forces. Bodies behave in an accelerated frame of reference, that is, in just the same manner as they do in a rest frame that is subjected to gravitational forces (Harris 1964: 53). In order to explain this idea, Einstein suggested the following thought experiment. Imagine a passenger in an elevator moving vertically up and down a very tall tower. If the elevator is at rest or moving at a constant speed, the passenger will find that objects dropped fall to the earth with the usual gravitational acceleration, just as they do when s/he is on the surface of the earth. But should the elevator begin to accelerate, the behavior of gravitational forces begins to change. If the elevator accelerates upwards, the object will fall more rapidly; if the elevator accelerates downward, it will fall more slowly. Indeed, if the elevator enters free fall the object will appear to be entirely weightless. Now, let us assume that rather than dropping a ball to the floor, the passenger in the elevator (perhaps perturbed by the sudden changes in speed and direction, and by the fact that the lights have gone out as a result of Einstein's gravitational shenanigans), shines a flashlight horizontally (parallel to the floor) across the elevator to the opposite wall. To the passenger the path of the light will appear horizontal, but to an outside observer the path of the light will appear curved, because by the time it hits the far wall the elevator will have moved and spot on the wall of the elevator which is "horizontally" across from the flashlight will have moved and will be at a different point along the height of the tower. Indeed, it would be difficult for the outside observer not to conclude that the light had mass and was subject to gravitation.

What this suggested is that while locally, within a given frame of reference, space is flat and structured much as Euclid would have had us believe it was, on a larger global scale it is in fact curved. This curvature is introduced by the presence of various fields of force, such as acceleration or gravity. Gravity, in other words, is a feature of the geometry of space-time.

In order to see how this is formalized mathematically, we begin by describing motion in a Euclidean 3-space. The distance r between any two points is given by the Pythagorean metric

$$r = \sqrt{x^2 + y^2 + z^2}$$

and the shortest path between two points, called a geodesic, will be a straight line. Similarly, in a four-dimensional Minkowski space, the distance between two events will be given by

$$ds^2 = c^2 d\tau^2 = c^2 dt^2 - dx^2 - dy^2 - dz^2$$

and the geodesic will be a straight line. But imagine a curved space, such as the surface of a balloon. Within such a system the distance between two points will be affected by the curvature of the surface, making it necessary to introduce new term into the metric, the curvature parameter k. If we attempt to model the curvature of a three dimensional object such as a sphere or a hyperboloid in a four-dimensional Euclidean space, we find that the curvature K, called the Gaussian curvature, after the mathematician who first investigated the problem, is given by

$$K = k / R^2$$

where R is the distance between the center of the object and its surface (i.e., the radius in the case of a sphere), and k is a parameter with value +1, 0, or -1, corresponding to the cases of a three-sphere, a flat three dimensional space, and a three-hyperboloid respectively. Rewriting the metric equation to take this parameter into account (and using spherical rather than orthogonal coordinates), we get the so called Robertson-Walker metric:

$$ds^2 = c^2 dt^2 - S^2 \left(\frac{d\sigma^2}{1 - k\sigma^2} + \sigma^2 d\theta^2 + \sigma^2 \sin^2 d\phi^2 \right)$$

where S is the cosmic scale factor, which represents the change in the distance between supergalaxies, and s the dimensionless ration R/S.

Now, recognizing the curvature of space-time, Einstein developed an equation which describes the action of gravity as a set of generally covariant tensor equations.

$$G_{\mu\nu} = \frac{8\pi G}{c^4} T_{\mu\nu}$$

where G is the gravitational constant, $G_{\mu\nu}$ the force of gravity and $T_{\mu\nu}$ a tensor describing the energy density, the pressure or momentum per unit area, energy flows, momentum density, and shear.

The place of general relativity within the context of mathematical physics is rather ambiguous. In and of itself it represents a terribly important, but still very partial achievement. Specifically, it represent a very partial unification: i.e., of the geometry of space-time (special relativity) with the theory of universal gravitation. In this sense it simply repairs the internal tension introduced into physics by Einstein's theory of special relativity, itself the result of the disintegration of the Newtonian space-time. At the same time, the development of general relativity made it possible for the first time to develop a mathematical model of the universe as a whole, giving the impression that relativity is the general theory par excellence. Indeed, the whole discipline of physical cosmology has been built up largely on the foundation of general relativity.

The step from universal gravitation to physical cosmology, however, involved making a fundamental assumption about the nature of the universe: namely that it is a uniform gas without any significant internal structure. Making this assumption, it then became possible to solve Einstein's equations and develop a model of the universe as a whole. The result was quite startling. Assuming that general relativity and a homogenous and isotropic distribution of matter, it follows that the universe is finite but unbounded. This means that if one heads out in a given direction one never reaches a cosmic wall or terminus, but simply returns after a very long but finite interval to the point from which one began. This is a consequence of the notion that gravity is simply a curvature in the structure of space-time.

Einstein found the notion of a finite but unbounded universe aesthetically appealing. He did not like some of the other implications of his theory, however, namely that the universe is a dynamic system, subject to expansion or contraction. In order to avoid these conclusions, he introduced a "cosmological constant," which guaranteed that the universe would remain static. Soon, however, this assumption was discarded and the equations solved by the Russian mathematician Alexander Friedman (1921) for the case of an expanding universe:

$$\frac{\dot{S}^2 + kc^2}{S^2} = \frac{8\pi}{3} G\rho \quad \frac{2\ddot{S}}{S} + \frac{\dot{S}^2 + kc^2}{S^2} = \frac{8\pi}{c^2} Gp$$

Now it had long been known that the light from the so-called spiral nebulae was shifted slightly to the red end of the spectrum, and that the most likely explanation for this fact was that these nebulae were moving away from us, and that the light waves were thus subject to the same Doppler effect which made the whistle of a locomotive seem to get lower in pitch as its sped away. At roughly the same time, as a result of the work of Edwin Hubble, it became possible to measure accurately the distances to these nebulae, and it became apparent that they were outside our galaxy and most likely separate and distinct galaxies themselves. It also became apparent that the farther away they were, the more red shifted the light from their stars. The implication seemed unavoidable. These galaxies were rushing away from each other and the further away they were the more rapid their flight. From this it was concluded that the universe must indeed be expanding, as Friedman's solution to Einstein's equations suggested. A Belgian priest by the name of Georges-Henri Lemaître soon drew what seemed to him to be the obvious conclusion: that the universe had begun with the explosion of a primeval atom and was now expanding out into space, as both Freidman's equations and Hubble's observational evidence suggested. This line of argument gained support from James Jeans and Arthur Eddington, who attempted a synthesis of relativity and thermodynamics, arguing that entropy increased as matter was converted to energy and that the universe must therefore have had a definite beginning in time.

Lemaître's original formulation of what came to be known as the Big-Bang cosmology was encumbered by a number of rather obvious errors. He took cosmic rays to be radiation left over from the origin of the universe and he upheld an incorrect view of stellar evolution that involved the complete annihilation of matter. As a result the theory did not really gain much support beyond a narrow circle of general relativists until after the Second World War, when the development of nuclear fusion technology laid the groundwork for a more credible theory of stellar evolution—and provided a powerful analogy for the Big Bang itself. The destructive technologies of capitalism became a metaphor for cosmic creativity. Even so, the theory vied with the alternative steady state theory until the discovery of the cosmic microwave background in 1964 provided what most physicists still accept as empirical evidence for a primeval cosmic explosion. As a result, the Big Band theory became the accepted orthodoxy in physical cosmology and by the late 1970s it was essentially impossible to publish papers which called the theory into question.

We will have an opportunity to examine both the further development of this theory and some of the tremendous challenges it faces—both internal contradictions and countervailing evidence—after we have looked at the development of quantum mechanics, a basic understanding of which has become necessary to grasp the further evolution of physical cosmology. But it will be useful here to make at least a brief note regarding the basic assumption on which the whole edifice of the Big Bang theory, and indeed the whole enterprise of mathematical-physical cosmology has been based: i.e., the assumption of cosmic homogeneity and isotropy. While this assumption may well turn out to be true on the very largest scales, the history of astronomy over the past century has been the history of the discovery of structure at ever larger scales. When Einstein developed his first cosmological model in 1916 it was still assumed that stars were distributed evenly in space, though as early as the 1850s some astronomers had suggested that the spiral nebulae were in fact separate and distinct galaxies. Within a few short years after Einstein published his theory Hubble demonstrated that this was in fact true and that nearly all the stars in the universe are organized into together in these galaxies. More recently, since 1970, astronomers have discovered a whole hierarchy of structure above the galactic level. If it should turn out that the universe is not homogenous and isotropic at the largest scales, this would mean that Einstein's fundamental cosmological claim—that the universe is finite and unbounded—could turn out not to be true. The curvature of space cased by the presence of matter could be such that a universe which is spatially and/or temporally infinite (Lerner 1991: 130–31), a possibility which should not be ruled out.

What is the social basis and political valence of relativistic cosmology? This is a difficult question because there are at least two distinct ideological trends which have become associated with this cosmology, what we might called the Einsteinian and Lemaîtrian trends. The first trend is focused on the attempt to grasp the universe through the simplest and most elegant mathematical models possible. Strongly motivated by aesthetic considerations, this trend represents in many ways a prolongation of the earliest impulses of mathematical physics—impulses which date back to the Pythagoreans—into the present period. Generally speaking this trend has its base in state-funded scientific institutes—the academies of science or their nearest equivalents—which provide a section of the intelligentsia with a vantage point which is at least formally outside the framework of the marketplace, but within the context of a society in which everything has been transformed into a commodity and the "fixed frame" of nonmarket institutions has largely disappeared. The result is an attempt to model the universe "as if" from outside on the basis of the very theory that says that there is no fixed frame of reference from which to do this. The whole enterprise of developing mathematical models of the universe—or indeed of numerous hypothetical universes—and then leaving to others to see which, if any, actually correspond to reality makes sense in (and only in) such a milieu. The universes modeled are all in one way or another pure reflexes of a perfect market order—they are systems of mutually determining quantities. The theorist alone stands outside the system, assuming the place of God.

Authentic general relativists—like Einstein himself—have generally had a marked affinity for rationalism, especially rationalism of the Spinozist variety. They see their work as a search for cosmic order, but not necessarily for meaning or organization in a teleological sense. Indeed, the sense here is of having so transcended primitive anthropomorphism and the merely human standpoint that not only the ultimately meaningful universe of Aristotelian cosmology but also the cosmological pessimism of the nineteenth century seems ridiculous. General relativists are too developed, too enthralled by the pure mathematical beauty of their equations to be concerned with such petty issues as the fate of humanity, or even of life and intelligence generally, in the universe. Largely protected from the ravages of the market order, the general relativist can afford to ignore it.

At the same time, relativistic cosmology has attracted a whole periphery of thinkers—of whom Lemaître was the prototype—for whom the Big Bang provides the scientific infrastructure for an essentially creationist metaphysics (Jaki 1988). These thinkers are drawn largely from the clergy and its intellectual periphery. For these thinkers, the Big Bang makes it possible to reconcile science and religion, without, however, having to transcend cosmological pessimism. If the universe had a beginning in time, then that beginning must be explained. Such an explanation, by its very nature, reaches back behind the point at which physical theory becomes valid and must by its very nature be metaphysical. At the same time, a universe which is finite and which appears to be headed for entropic heat death cannot inspire our ultimate loyalty. Big Bang cosmologies thus do not run the risk of grounding a pantheistic or semipantheistic metaphysics in the way the old Aristotelian physics had. The Big Bang gives us God without an ultimately meaningful universe, a God on whom we are radically dependent and who is the only possible object of our ultimate hope and concern. Big Bang cosmology, in other words, is very nearly the ideal cosmology from the standpoint of the Augustinian reaction.

Quantum Theory

The ideological-critical and philosophical problems presented by the theory of relativity pale by comparison with those presented by quantum theory, to which we must now turn. Quantum theory first emerged out of an effort to deal with a very specific empirical problem. In attempting to model the radiation emitted by a solid body heated to incandescence, Max Plank found that, assuming that energy transfer was continuous, Maxwell's equations for electromagnetism, which otherwise worked so well, seemed to predict that the radiation levels would go to infinity as the wavelength of the radiation entered the ultraviolet range, something which they did not, in fact do. The only way to avoid this problem was to assume that, contrary to all expectation, energy transfer was in fact quantized. Energy was, in other words, transferred in discrete packets. Specifically energy transfer can be modeled as

$$\Delta E = nh\nu$$

where E is energy, n an integer, ν the frequency of the radiation, and h Planck's constant, which has a value of $6.626*10^{-34}$ J sec.

It was only a small step from the notion that energy transfer is quantized, to the idea that electromagnetic radiation itself is quantized, and consists in particles known as photons, the energy of which can be modeled as

$$E_{photon} = h\nu = \frac{hc}{\lambda}$$

where λ is the wavelength of the light in question. Since, according to the theory of special relativity, energy and matter are interchangeable

$$E = mc^2$$

it follows that photons necessarily have mass, which Louis de Broglie determined to be

$$m = \frac{h}{\lambda v}$$

All of these developments would have seemed to point more or less straightforwardly toward a radically atomistic theory of matter in which every thing is ultimately composed of irreducible elementary particles which, in some mysterious way, also function as energy packets. Indeed, it was precisely this set of breakthroughs that made possible the triumph of the atomic model of matter. Already, during the early years of the twentieth century, working within the framework of Maxwell's classic theory of electromagnetism, J. J. Thomson and Ernest Rutherford had determined that far from being irreducible bits of matter, Dalton's "atoms" were in fact composed of smaller particles: negatively charged electrons and a positively charged nucleus. But this model presented grave difficulties for classical theory. The idea was that it was the electromagnetic attraction between the positive nucleus and the negatively charged electrons held the atom together, while the energy of the electrons revolving around the nucleus kept them from falling into it. The difficulty is that accelerating particles radiate energy, and the revolving electron, since it constantly changes direction also constantly accelerates. Stable atoms should thus be impossible.

It was Niels Bohr who first attempted to resolve this contradiction. What Bohr did was to synthesize Rutherford's earlier model of a nuclear atom in which negatively charged electrons move around a positively charged nucleus with the principle that energy transfer is quantum or discrete. Drawing on both Planck's basic insight regarding energy transfer, and experimental evidence concerning the spectrum of the Hydrogen atom, which suggested that only certain electron energies were allowed, he suggested that the electron in hydrogen atom moves around the nucleus only in certain allowed circular orbits, or, what is the same thing, only at certain definite energy levels

$$E = -2.178 * 10^{-18} J(\frac{Z^2}{n^2})$$

where n is an integer indicating the size of the orbit and Z the charge of the nucleus or the number of protons. This model showed how the hydrogen atom, at least, could be stable.

The Bohr model, however, turned out not to work for atoms larger than hydrogen. And some of the results of early quantum theory could be read in a way which called atomic theory itself radically into question. De Broglie's equation, for example, could not only be solved to give the mass for a "particle" of light; it could also be solved to give the wavelength of what had previously considered to be purely particulate forms of matter such as the electron:

$$\lambda = \frac{h}{mv}$$

Similarly, quantum formalisms seemed to imply, as Werner Heisenberg demonstrated, that it is in fact impossible to know with precision both the position and the momentum of an elementary particle. Stated formally:

$$\Delta x * \Delta(mv) \geq \frac{h}{4\pi}$$

where x is the position of the particle and mv is its momentum. This so-called "uncertainty principle," initially just a result of the use of non-commutative operators in formalizing certain problems in quantum mechanics, soon found experimental support. Assume an electron or photon source, a wall with two tiny slits, and screen on to which the "particles," after passing through the slits, can be detected. Each "particle" may well pass through a particular slit and land in a particular place, but it is quite impossible to determine precisely the path of any given photon or electron. The overall distribution looks more like that of waves passing through interference.

What this suggested was that matter and energy could not, in fact be understood as either purely particulate or as purely wavelike. Rather, its state had to be described by a wave function φ, where φ is a function of spatial coordinates (x,y,z) and φ^2 is interpreted as the probability distribution for the particle—i.e., the relative probability of finding it in any given location. φ in turn is obtained by solving the Schrodinger equation—something which can be done with accuracy only for the hydrogen atom:

$$H\varphi = E\varphi$$

where H is the Hamiltonian operator expressing the total energy of the atom and E is the same quantity expressed in different terms, as the sum of electric potential of the atom (the electromagnetic relation between the nucleus and the electron) and the kinetic energy of the electron itself. Each φ which solves the equation is interpreted physically as one of the orbitals in which an electron might be located—or, more properly, which describes its state.

The result was a model which was at once extraordinarily powerful, capable of describing, and even of offering partial explanations for the ways in which we actually observe matter to behave and deeply troubling, as it seemed to both to contradict other formalisms which also worked, and to generate paradoxes at the metaphysical level which have defied solution ever since. This is, indeed, the problem with quantum theory as a whole, which is fundamental to much advanced electronic technology, and therefore must have something to do with reality, but which also generates predictions which are clearly contrary to empirical evidence, formalisms which are in contradiction with relativity, and philosophical paradoxes which have effectively put an end to the role of mathematical physics as a rationalizing enterprise. Clearly this problem merits further analysis.

Let us begin by considering some of the successes of quantum theory. Clearly the most important of these is in the field of chemistry where, together with thermodynamics, it makes possible at least a partial explanation of the appearance and behavior of the various chemical elements and their interactions with each other. The first step in applying quantum theory to chemical interactions is to solve the Schrodinger equation. When we do this for the hydrogen atom, we find many wave functions that satisfy it, each of which is described by definite quantum numbers.

1. The *principal quantum number n*, which has integral values 1, 2, 3, . . . ; describes the size and energy of the orbital in question. The higher the value of n, the higher the energy of the electron in ques-

tion. The maximum electron capacity of an energy level is given by $2n^2$.

2. The *azimuthal* or *angular momentum* quantum number l describes the shape of the orbital It may have integral values 0 . . . n-1. Differently shaped orbitals are often referred to as sublevels, and designated by letters derived from the spectroscopic techniques which were originally used to identify them.

   s: $l = 0$
   p: $l = 1$
   d: $l = 2$
   f: $l = 3$

3. The *magnetic quantum number* m describes the orientation of an orbital relative to other orbitals. The magnetic number may have integral values $-l \ldots 0 \ldots +l$

4. The *electron spin quantum number* s describes the behavior of the electron within its orbital. I has -1/2 or +1/2.

Now, an electron may not be in just any energy state. With a few exceptions, unless the electron is subject to some outside force that excites it, it will seek to occupy the lowest energy state possible. Put differently, as atoms get bigger, acquiring more protons and electrons, the electrons fill up the lowest energy states first. This is the *aufbau* or building up principle.

But what is the "lowest energy state possible?" In order to determine this we need to have reference to one additional result of quantum mechanics—the Pauli exclusion principle, which states that no two electrons within the same atom can have the same set of quantum numbers.[13]

---

13. Mathematically this principle is formalized using a structure known as a Fock vector space. We will recall that a vector space is a set V of elements called vectors v, together with rules which given two vectors v and v' assign a third vector v+v' called their sum, and which, given a vector v and a number (real, complex) assigns a new vector written av, and called the scalar product of v, subject to the following conditions:

V is an abelian group under addition

The Distributive Law holds.

The Associative Law holds for Multiplication

There is an identity, namely 1 for scalar multiplication. (1v=b).

A vector space, in other words, is a set on which one can add and scale by numbers, satisfying all of the properties one would expect of these operations.

The Development of Mathematical Physics

This in turn implies Hun's rule: the lowest energy configuration is the one having maximum number of unpaired electrons allowed by the Pauli exclusion principle in a particular set of degenerate orbitals. As the lower energy states, constrained by the Pauli exclusion principle, are filled up, electrons must move to the higher levels.

The theory which we have outlined thus far essentially gives us the full range of possible electron states in a hydrogen atom, i.e., a relatively simple system of one proton and one electron, and tells us how systems of more than one proton and electron are built up, by filling the lowest energy states first. But application to atoms other than hydrogen is complicated by effect of intervening electrons, making it impossible to solve the Schrodinger equation precisely. Instead we must treat each electron separately, compensating for the *electron correlation effect*. If we do this we will be able to determine with some precision a wide range of values which affect the basic properties of the elements in question, including ionization energy and electron affinity.

The ionization energy is the energy required to remove and electron from an atom, which is what happens when ionic bonds are formed, and also when an electric current is run through a substance. This energy is determined by a number of factors. The two most obvious are:

Z_{actual}: the positive charge of the nucleus, which is determined by the number of protons, and

n: the principle quantum number, which describes the energy level of the electron in question.

The greater the nuclear charge, the more difficult it is to extract and electron. The greater the energy of the electron, the less the additional energy which must be added to extract it. But if there is more than one

---

Now, vector spaces can be used to describe states of systems of identical, noninteracting particles, so that taking linear combinations of vectors corresponds to taking superpositions of quantum states. One does this by taking the tensor product of two vector spaces for a two particle system, three vector spaces for a three vector system, etc. The resulting product space is called a Fock vector space. Now, there are two ways to formalize superpositions of states, symmetrically and antisymmetrically. The first kind of superposition corresponds to the particles known as bosons (pi-mesons, photons, gravitons), the second to fermions (neutrinos, electrons). What this means is that the formalization for an antisymmetric two-particle system with both particles in the same state yields zero or "vanishes." It is thus impossible to have more than two particles in any given orbital.

proton and electron involved, there are additional factors which must be considered. The first is the fact that the electrons at the lower or "inner" energy levels tend to "shield" the outer or valence electrons from some of the nuclear charge, but repelling it from the nucleus, thus reducing the additional energy that is necessary in order extract it. Electrons do not generally provide effective shielding for other electrons at the same energy level so the strength of the shielding effect will be very largely determined by the number of electrons at lower energy levels than the one for which we are attempting to determine the ionization energy.

Second, because the electron is not a particle, but rather a relation, it is not really possible to speak of it being "at" a given energy level in any rigorous sense. The values of all of the quantum numbers express probabilities. This means that even an electron at a high energy level might at some point be "found" at lower or even zero energy. When electrons drop to these lower energy states they lose the benefit of the shielding effect appropriate to electrons of their state, and it thus becomes more difficult to extract them. This is called the penetration effect. The relative tendency of electrons to fall to lower states, or strength of the penetration effect is, furthermore, determined by the "shape" of the orbital in question, which is given by quantum number l. In general, penetration is greater in the more or less spherical s orbitals, and declines as one moves to p, d, and f orbitals that have an increasing number of nodal planes from which the electron is excluded.

Now, taking all of these factors together, it becomes possible to explain the differences in the ionization energies of the electrons in even very complex atoms, using the equation:

$$E = -2.18 * 10^{-18} J \left(\frac{Z_{eff}^2}{n^2} \right)$$

where

$$Z_{eff} = Z_{actual} - \text{(electron repulsion effects)}$$

We should also note that the penetration effect helps us to refine our prediction of just how the various energy levels of an atom will fill. If we know the ionization energy of an electron, as well as its energy level n, we can calculate Z_{eff}. We can then compare this with the value we obtain by subtracting the number of core electrons from the number of protons in the atom in question. For example, if we are considering the single valence electron of a sodium atom, we would expect Z_{eff} to be determined by the 11 protons and 10 core electrons, to give a value of 1; instead we find it to be 1.84. The additional attraction is the result of penetration by the valence electron in the 3s orbital. Similar calculations allow us to understand why the 4s orbital fills before the 3d orbital, etc.

This same body of theory also allows us to explain the differences in the ability of atoms of various elements to attract electrons. This is measured by the electron affinity, or the energy change associated with the addition of an electron to an atom, considered, for purposes of uniformity, to be in a gaseous state. In general, electron affinity increases—i.e., more energy is released with the addition of an electron, as atomic number increases within a period, due to increasing nuclear charge. But slight changes in electron configurations can lead to break in this pattern. Carbon, for example, can add an electron to form a stable C- ion, whereas Nitrogen cannot form a stable N- ion. This is because the Nitrogen would have to add the electron to a 2p orbital which already contains an electron, and the nuclear charge is insufficient to overcome the additional repulsion effects, whereas Carbon can add an electron to an unoccupied 2p orbital. By the time we get to Oxygen, the nuclear charge has grown enough to overcome the repulsion effects sufficiently to allow addition of one electron—though not the two that would be expected given the many stable oxide compounds which form. It is only the attractive effects of the metal ions in the latter compounds that permit the formation of the required oxide ions.

Similarly, we also expect that electron affinity will decrease as we go down a group, as the any electrons added will be at a greater distance from the positive charge of the nucleus. Generally this is the case, but there are exceptions. Fluorine, for example, has a lower electron affinity than Chlorine, something which is attributed to the small size of the 2p orbitals to which it adds electrons, increases repulsion effects. In the other halogens, on the contrary, with their larger orbitals, we find precisely the expected pattern.

We are now in a position to demonstrate the explanatory power of quantum theory with respect to the properties and interactions of chemical elements. It is, first of all, the quantum principle itself, i.e., the fact that energy exchange is quantized, which explains the fact that we have discrete elements and not a continuum of different forms of matter with a continuous transition in their properties. Since energy comes in little packets, such as electrons, any given atom can have only an integral number of electrons—1, 2, 3, etc. And it is the electrons that effectively determine the chemical properties of the elements. So there cannot be an element which is "between" Hydrogen and Helium in its properties because there cannot be an element with $1 < Z < 2$. But there is more. Knowing the ionization energies and electron affinity of a given element allows us to explain empirical properties such as reactivity, conductivity, and the ability to reflect light. When atoms react to form ionic compounds they give or receive electrons. Just how many electrons an atom is likely to give or receive in an ordinary chemical reaction is determined by the ionization energies of its electrons and by its electron affinity. Consider sodium, for example. Just why Sodium is able to give only one electron, and thus combine 1:1 with Chlorine, which can only receive one, is a mystery until we know that the ionization energy of its outermost, valence electron is 5.1 eV, whereas the ionization energy of the first core electron is 47.3 eV. The first is likely to come off in a chemical reaction, the others will require far more energy than is ordinarily available. Aluminum, on the other hand, has three electrons with relatively low ionization energies (6.0, 18.8, and 28.4 eV respectively), though its fourth ionization energy is a very high 120 eV. Aluminum will thus give up three electrons, and combine with Chlorine in a ration of 1:3. The different ionization energies of Aluminum's three valence, electrons, by the way, is determined by the fact that the first is in a 3p and the other two in a 3s orbital. The first electron in the 3s orbital probably comes off more easily because of repulsion effects.

Similarly the fact that Oxygen and Chlorine do not generally give up electrons, and instead receive them, is determined by their higher ionization energies and electron affinities. Chlorine receives one, and oxygen two electrons, because of the way in which their electrons are configured in the highest energy levels.

Conductivity and reflectivity are both also directly related to ionization energy. When an electric current is applied to a substance, electrons flow through it. This is facilitated if the electrons of the substance in question are relatively loose, so that the atoms become bathed in a moving sea electrons. Light, striking the surface of an element with a low ionization energy makes the electrons of that element vibrate in harmony with it, giving off electromagnetic energy at the same frequency. This is why metals are so shiny. More detailed analysis can show why, for example, gold is yellowish and silver . . . well, silver.

It would be possible to continue this discussion at still greater length, showing how quantum mechanics allows us to explain the various ways in which elements combine together into larger wholes called molecules with distinct properties, and why some of these molecules are prone to form still more complex combinations that eventually take on the properties of life. But this is not a text in chemistry and readers are referred to such texts for a more complete discussion.

Chemistry is not the only discipline in which the application of quantum theory has led to advances. Indeed, our whole understanding of the subatomic structure of matter itself, as well as our understanding of three of four principle forces of nature, depend on the application of quantum mechanics. Here we can only sketch out briefly the development of what has come to be called the "standard model." The first step in this process was the development of quantum electrodynamics, developed by Paul Dirac in 1928, which applied quantum theory to the problems of electromagnetism, while attempting to take into account some of the implications of special relativity. We do not need to explain the theory in detail here, but it is necessary to sketch out the basic approach. In order to accommodate the discovery that energy transfer is quantum, Dirac replaced Maxwell's wave theory of electromagnetism with model in which electromagnetism is understood as a field across which forces are carried by point particles. The theory works remarkably well, making accurate predictions and proving itself extraordinarily useful in a wide range of technologies, including most contemporary electronic technologies. The difficulty is that the basic assumptions of the theory generate serious irrationalities. Electrical energy increases as distance decreases. If the electron is a point particle this means that it is infinitely small and that it is thus possible to be come infinitely close, so that the electron's energy becomes infinite. This by itself contradicts observation, and it generates two other problems. Since like electrical charges repel, and there is nothing that we are aware of which could hold the electron together, it ought to explode. Second, since energy and mass are convertible, the electron should have infinite mass. But neither of these conclusions corresponds to observation. In order to contend with this problem, physicists developed the technique of "renormalization," which has been used in all subsequent quantum mechanical theories. Essentially the infinities generated by the formalism are subtracted from the equations and observed quantities added in their place. When this is done the equations provide a good model of real physical systems—though they lose something of their theoretical elegance (Lerner 1991: 349).

Even renormalization, however, cannot resolve the most fundamental problem with quantum electrodynamics. The theory predicts that what we had previously thought to be empty space or vacuum is in fact full of virtual particles that are continuously passing into and out of existence. The result is that the vacuum has an enormous energy density. But according to general relativity, energy, which is convertible with mass, curves space. If quantum electrodynamics is true, all of space should be curved into a sphere not more than a few kilometers across (Lerner 1991: 350).

The further development of the "standard model" is essentially a story of extending quantum strategies to the description of the other fundamental forces—the weak and strong nuclear interactions and, much less successfully, gravity—and the subsequent unification of the resulting theories. This process has only been partly driven by theoretical considerations. The development of particle accelerators as a result of efforts to test the resulting theories led to the "discovery" (or perhaps the manufacture) of a whole zoo of particles which themselves had to be explained. Thus, it was soon discovered that not only are the positively charged nuclei of atoms composed of varying numbers of protons and neutrons, but these protons and neutrons are themselves composed of still more fundamental particles known as quarks. These quarks are bound together in differing combinations by the strong nuclear force organized into eight "color" fields mediated by still another set of particles known as "gluons," the operation of which is described by a theory known as "quantum chromodynamics" because it deals with "color fields."

Quantum chromodynamics has problems similar to those of quantum electrodynamics. Among other things, it predicts that protons have a finite lifetime of 10^{30} years, which means that, given the probabilistic nature of processes governed, like this one, by quantum mechanics, it should be possible to detect the decay of at least a few of them into pions and positrons. The experimental evidence, however, shows that this does not happen.

Attempts to model the form of nuclear radiation known as β–decay, meanwhile, led to the discovery of still another force, the weak nuclear force, which was carried by neutrinos. This force is quite different from any of the others: its range is on the scale of the radius an atomic nucleus. The particle principle which it involves has a mass far smaller than the electron. Unification of the electromagnetic and weak interactions is made possible by posting the existence of still another sort of field: the Higgs field, filled with Higgs particles. In the absence of a Higgs field, electrons and neutrinos are identical; in the presence of such a field one or the other becomes massive, depending on the sort of Higgs particle that is present. As it happens electron Higgs fields dominate, something that is attributed to spontaneous (i.e., unexplained) symmetry breaking during the early stages of cosmic evolution.

The standard model integrates this electroweak theory with quantum chromodynamics. Back in the mid-1970s, when the generation of theoretical physicists who currently dominate the academy was trained, it was assumed that it was only a matter of time before a way was found to fully unify these two theories. All one had to do was to define a unified field in which the various properties of the particles could be derived from their interactions, just as the properties of electrons and neutrinos had been derived from their interactions in the Higgs field. What happened is not so much that no such theory was forthcoming, but that many were, and it became extraordinarily difficult to decide among them. None of these theories, furthermore, actually explained why the basic physical parameters, such as the ratio between gravitational and electromagnetic interactions or between proton and electron masses are fixed the way they are, at levels which turn out to be fine-tuned for a universe which is capable of producing stars and thus life. Indeed, there are fully 20 parameters that have to be set "by hand" as it were if the standard model is to conform to real physical systems. And none of the theories explain interactions at what quantum theory suggests is actually the most fundamental scale of the universe: the Plank scale of roughly 10–33 cm (Smolin 1997: 47–74).

These difficulties in turn led to the revival of an idea that had first emerged in the 1960s: string theory. String theory actually derives from an alternative to the standard model developed by Geoffrey Chew. Reasoning that it made no sense to continue looking for ever more fundamental particles, Chew developed a series of equations, the so called bootstrap equations, which attempted to model the properties of each particle in terms of its interactions with all the others. The result was a startling conclusion: these elementary particles were not actually particles (i.e., dimensionless points) but rather one-dimensional strings. The idea is that what physicists had been calling particles actually resulted from the vibrations of these cosmic strings. The early successes of the quark theory, coupled with the fact that the theory required a 25 dimensional space in order to be consistent with relativity and quantum mechanics meant that initially this idea was not very attractive to most physicists. But when it predicted yet another particle for which experimental evidence was eventually found, and when other attempts at unification began to break down, it started to attract new attention. It turned out, furthermore, than by fixing the length of the strings at precisely the Planck length, the theory could be made to generate a force with all the characteristics of gravity. The theory's prospects were further improved when the development of "supersymmetry," which eliminates the distinction between forces and particles in field theories and made it possible to reduce from 25 to 9 the number of dimensions necessary to make the theory consistent with relativity and quantum mechanics. This also generated a theory that specified almost uniquely the values of the basic physical parameters. Once again, mathematical physicists thought that they were on the verge of a final theory.

Once again they were disappointed. Attempts to reconcile the 9 dimensional space required by string theory and the three dimensional space we experience by curling up six of the dimensions so that the universe has a diameter of only the Planck length along these dimensions undermined the uniqueness of the theory. There turn out to be 10,000 different ways to do this, each of which results in a different set of basic physical laws. String theory, furthermore, for all its mathematical elegance, employs a concept of space that is more Newtonian than Einsteinian, so that it is not fully unified with special relativity, though this problem may eventually be solved.

The result is nothing short of a major crisis in fundamental physics. On the one hand, the underlying quantum mechanical theory on which the entire standard model and its string-theoretical modifications are based emerged as a response to real conflicts between theory and experiment, and has produced verifiable predictions, at least some partial explanations (in the field of chemistry) and numerous technologies on which much (if not most) of the economic progress of this century has been based. At the same time, it is very difficult to regard quantum mechanics as a fundamental theory of matter, which is what it pretends to be. How are we to understand this paradox?

It is not only at the mathematical-physical and scientific levels, however, that quantum theory generates contradictions. The most fundamental problems of the theory can only be called metaphysical, in that they go the very core of our sense of what is real. We will recall that according to basic quantum theory the state of any system may be represented as a wave function ϕ. The question is just what this wave function represents at the physical level. The most straightforward approach, and that advocated by Schrodinger himself, is simply that it represents the relative probability of find an electron, or whatever other particle is under consideration, in a given state. The difficulty is that this presupposes that we are dealing with particles, or at least some other irreducible entity, which serves as a kind of material substratum for various states, a presupposition which quantum theory itself has gradually undermined. It also leaves unexplained why the state of something like a particle should be susceptible of only probabilistic description.

Alternative strategies, however, are even less satisfactory. Heisenberg and Bohr, for example argued that the wave function is collapsed by the act of observation, so that the state of the system is actually determined by the observer. This approach, the so-called "Copenhagen Interpretation" presents insuperable problems. Among other things it fails to account for the fact that scientists working on the same experiment inevitably collapse the wave function in the same way. This, in turn, has led Archibald Wheeler and others to suggest that the wave function is in fact collapsed by the whole community of observers over the whole history of the universe. But what if the various members of this community make different observations? Isn't there a need for some Ultimate Observer who can coordinate all observations and reconcile them with each other? Here we have returned to Bishop Berkley, for whom the universe is ultimate just a system of ideas in the mind of God (Gardener 1978). At the physical level such an Ultimate Observer presupposes a closed universe terminating in a final singularity without any event horizons (Barrow and Tipler 1986: 458–72)—something even advocates of theory admit is unlikely.

What all of these approaches have in common is a subjective idealist metaphysics. What exists is what is observed. We will see shortly that this is no coincidence. Subjective idealism had a powerful influence in physics beginning with Mach in the late nineteenth century. Many of the founders of quantum theory, Heisenberg in particular, were drawn to extreme forms of subjectivism in the 1920s and 1930s (Lukacs 1953/1980). But this subjectivism is not just a philosophical preference imposed on the theory; it is intrinsic to the quantum problematic itself. This becomes apparent if we consider the principal alternative currently proposed to the Copenhagen Interpretation, namely the so-called Many Worlds theory (Everett 1957). According to this theory the wave function does not collapse at all and every one of the infinite number of possible quantum states of every possible system is in fact realized along an infinity of different world lines. Proponents of this view such as Frank Tipler argue that it does not violate the principle of economy (Occam's Razor) because it simply enlarges our ontology (by allowing other "universes" or world lines) rather than requiring hidden variables which are inaccessible to observation or a complex of new physical laws to explain how observers can collapse a quantum wave function as do the statistical and Copenhagen interpretations respectively (Barrow and Tipler 1986: 495–96). The question, of course, is in just what sense the other universes exist, and here the subjectivism that is intrinsic to the quantum problematic reasserts itself. Tipler suggests that while all logically possible universes exist "mathematically" only those that are structured in such a way as to permit the evolution of observers can be said to exist physically. And since, as we will see, Tipler believes that all universes complex enough to evolve observers necessarily terminate in an omniscient, omnipotent Omega Point, i.e., in an Ultimate Observer, Tipler's Many Worlds interpretation turns out to be indistinguishable from the Berkeleyan variant of the Copenhagen approach suggested by Gardener.

In point of fact both the scientific and the metaphysical difficulties surrounding quantum theory derive from a failure to distinguish adequately between mathematical physics, explanatory science, metaphysics—and ideology. What quantum theory demonstrates, if nothing else, is the simultaneous usefulness and limitations of mathematical modeling. The theory arose out of an attempt to adequately model electromagnetic radiation, something that it does quite adequately, permitting the development of powerful new electronic technologies. In the process, by showing that energy transfer is always quantized, it showed why there are discrete elements rather than a continuum of properties, and made it possible to model the atomic and subatomic structure of matter well enough to explain most chemical processes—though as our discussion of covalent bonding indicates this explanation is not really complete. Where the theory really begins to break down, however, is when it is either forced (as in the case of quantum electrodynamics) is consciously mobilized (as in the case of the electroweak theory, quantum chromodynamics, the standard model, and unified field theories) either to actually say what things are (a question for science or metaphysics, not for mathematics) or to model nonelectromagetic processes. Thus, the irrationalities in quantum electrodynamics arise from the fact that the electron is treated as a point particle. Renormalization in this case is simply a matter of adjusting the equations to fit observation, and is not unlike what Kepler did when he surrendered his perfect spheres embedded in Platonic solids for the rather less elegant ellipse. It turns out that electrons can't be modeled as points. The record of attempts to apply quantum mechanical approaches in other domains, however, is far less successful, and suggests that while certain basic principles may be applicable (e.g., the quantum nature of energy transfer), mathematical physics needs to be open to radically new approaches.

More to the point, it suggests that a final, unified theory of the universe may well be impossible, at least at the level of mathematical physics, for the simple reason that different physical interactions require incompatible formalizations. This should already be apparent from the fact that relativity and quantum mechanics are themselves incompatible, and not simply because the mathematicians have not yet figured out a way to formalize quantum processes which does not presuppose something like an absolute space. Rather, relativistic formalisms are continuous and quantum formalisms are discrete and to the extent that the theories are worth anything at all this suggests that the physical processes in question (gravity and electromagnetism) themselves actually work differently.

Beyond this, however, the paradoxes generated by quantum mechanics raise important questions about the whole enterprise of making inferences from mathematical formalisms to physical processes, even when these inferences seem to be confirmed by experiment. Quantum mechanics began as an effort to model physical processes (electromagnetism) actually encountered in nature. But when it moved beyond this sphere to begin unlocking the secrets of the atomic nucleus, it did so using powerful machines to carry out experiments that were themselves designed on the basis of quantum mechanical assumptions. We cannot rule out the possibility that the "particle zoo" which physicists now labor so hard to explain is in fact simply an artifact of the experimental process. It is, in other words one thing to say that protons can be broken down into quarks whose interactions with each other can be modeled as an exchange of gluons; it is quite another thing to say that protons are "made out of" quarks.

Perhaps the best way to understand quantum mechanics and indeed mathematical physics generally is the way Eudoxus, Ptolemy and his followers understood their own work. As it became necessary to posit an increasingly large number of spheres, eccentrics, and epicycles in order to model the motions of the heavenly bodies, they gave up any claim that they were modeling the structure of a physical system; rather they were providing peasants and navigators and priests and astrologers with a valuable tool for predicting the motions of the heavenly bodies, a tool which worked remarkably well. It was only those who attempted to turn Ptolemaic mathematical astronomy into an astrophysics who produced truly grotesque results.

This is, in fact, how most working physicists and engineers actually use quantum mechanics and indeed the whole body of mathematical-physical theory. But we must remember that mathematical physics is linked to capitalism in complex ways; it is not only a *techne* or *metatechne* but also a metaphysics, or rather an antimetaphysical ideology which at once arises spontaneously from the market order and becomes an instrument in the conscious ideological strategy of the bourgeoisie. Specifically, quantum theory is the ideological reflex of a society in which all values have become purely subjective. Capital, having been transformed into a commodity, now takes the form primarily of money or finance capital, which might be realized in any number of ways. The way in which it is used depends on the decisions of millions of consumers, mediated through complex market mechanisms. Capital isn't anything in particular; it is a bundle of possibilities that can become whatever the consumer wants it to become. In this way, quantum theory forms an integral part of the direct apologetic for capitalism by suggesting that the universe really is the way the capitalism leads us to spontaneously experience it to be.

But there is more. Eric Lerner (Lerner 1991), building on the work of Paul Forman (Forman 1971), has brilliantly demonstrated the links between emerging quantum theory and the irrationalist currents dominant in Weimar Germany. Heisenberg, it turns out, was a member of the rightist *Freicorps*, which helped put down the revolution of 1919 and made a conscious decision to stay in Germany and support Hitler during the Second World War. Radical subjective idealism of the sort he upheld was, as Lukacs (Lukacs 1953/1980) demonstrated, central to the development of NAZI ideology. And by seeming to ground subjectivist irrationalism in rational science, Heisenberg and his associates helped give the NAZI worldview scientific credibility.

The mobilization of quantum theory to support a rightist agenda continues today, as we will see when we examine the work of Frank Tipler, who we have already mentioned, in more detail. Before we do this, however, we need to examine at least briefly developments in the biological and social sciences during the period of finance capitalism. Our aim here is not a complete discussion of these disciplines, but rather a demonstration that they are coherent with, and in fact represent an extension of, developments in mathematical physics.

The Application of Late Modern Physics in the Biological and Social Sciences

The fact that mathematical physics is in crisis, and is very far from a unified theory of even purely physical systems, has not prevented it from fulfilling its ideological function, and specifically from creating the impression that we are only a few steps away from a unified theory of everything, biological and social systems included. We have already seen that the first steps in this direction were taken in the late eighteenth and nineteenth centuries, as it became increasingly apparent that biological processes could, at least in principle, be reduced to chemical interactions and chemical interactions to physical changes. This reductionist agenda was further advanced in the twentieth century by two developments. The first of these we have already discussed, namely the quantum mechanical reduction of chemistry to electromagnetic interactions. The second development did not come until the 1950s and in fact represents the only real advance in fundamental theory in the postwar period: the discovery of DNA and the genetic code. This discovery made possible the development of a whole field of molecular biology, which treats living organisms as physical systems and provides the key link in the reductionist agenda.

What the discovery of DNA does is to provide a physical substratum on which natural selection acts, so that even population biology and ecology can be unified with the underlying physical theory. Living organisms are theorized as simply complex machines for reproducing DNA. The behaviors of living organisms, including any complex relationships they may develop with each other and with the complex system that constitutes their physical and biological environment, are at once products of and strategies for the reproduction of the underlying genetic code. Selection is for those sequences that generate morphologies and behaviors that lead to successful reproduction.

From this standpoint economics becomes simply a highly specialized branch of ecology or population biology. Human technologies are simply the survival strategies of organisms with big brains, a high level of manual dexterity—and not much else that is worth anything for survival. Social institutions become ways of organizing resources for production, and ultimately for consumption and the reproduction of the underlying code. Sociology, in other words, including the sociology of culture, becomes merely a branch of economics, which is itself a branch of ecology, which is a branch of biology, which is a branch of chemistry, which is a branch of mathematical physics.

It is interesting to note that each of these disciplines was, in fact, already developing along lines that would pave the way for this unification long before all of the pieces necessary for its completion were in place. Thus, there was a science of genetics that spoke of atomic "genes" that encode and reproduce biomorphology long before any such thing had been isolated at the biochemical level. This discipline was easily unified with the theory of natural selection to create the Neo-Darwinian synthesis that has dominated evolutionary theory throughout most of this century. Political economy, similarly, responded to Marx's development of a complete and consistent labor theory of value, by retheorizing the discipline entirely, so that its formal object was no longer production, or the creation of wealth, but rather consumption—i.e., the survival and "utility" of the individual organism. Thus, according to the marginalist theory, capitalism is the optimal economic system not because it maximizes material production—Marx had already successfully shown that it does not do that—but rather because it allocates resources in the way that best satisfies (effective) demand. Prices are determined by the intensity of the last unsatisfied fragment of desire. Effective demand is, of course, rooted in the struggle of individual organisms to survive and reproduce. It becomes effective to the extent that the organisms in question have previously pursued effective strategies for survival and accumulated resources that they can bring to the marketplace in order to satisfy their (ever growing) desires.

It is no wonder that the formalisms that have been developed by marginalist economic theory turn out to look very much like those of mathematical physics, and indeed of quantum theory generally. Indeed, the marginalist concept of capital turns out to be homologous with the quantum theoretical understanding of the state of a physical system. Just as the notion of the quantum state of a system has nothing to do with actual organization, but rather with the possible ways the system might be subjectively perceived and relative probabilities associated with each of these possibilities, the marginalist concept of capital has nothing to do with an actual capacity to do anything, but rather with opportunities for consumption.

> The datum usually called the "supply of capital" can thus be adequately described only in terms of the totality of all the alternative income streams between which the existence of a certain stock of non-permanent resources (together with the expected flow of input) enables us to choose... Each of the constituent parts of the stick can be used in various ways, and in various combinations with other permanent and nonpermanent resources, to provide temporary income streams... What we sacrifice in order to obtain an income stream of a particular shape is always the parts of the potential income streams of other time shapes which we might have had instead.... (Hayek 1941: 147)
>
> ... the only adequate description of the "supply of capital" is a complete enumeration of the range of possible output streams of different time shapes that can be produced from the existing resources. (Hayek 1972: 222)

As Frank Tipler has pointed out, this notion of a list of possible income streams is essentially identical with the many-worlds interpretation of the quantum wave function as an enumeration of all of the possible quantum states of the universe.

The principal objection that might be raised against this notion of a unified theory that extends the underlying problematic of mathematical physics to the biological and social sciences is, of course, that it has difficulty accounting for the development within this period of a range of approaches to the social sciences which reject rather explicitly not only any attempt to reduce social organization to biology and physics, but which, in some cases, at least, even reject the possibility of a "nomothetic" science of human society which generates law-like predictive statements. Here it is necessary to distinguish between the various theoretical perspectives: dialectical and historical materialism, functionalism and structural-functionalism, interpretive sociology, psychoanalysis, etc. The first of these, which at least claims to break with the problematic of bourgeois science, we will hold to one side, and discuss it in the next chapter.

Two theses have been put forward to explain the relationship between "sociology" and the principal discipline of bourgeois social science, i.e., marginalist political economy. The first was put forward by Swedish social theorist Goran Therborn (Therborn 1976). Therborn argues that Weberian or interpretive sociology was, in fact an attempt to "complete" marginalist economics by explaining the subjective meaning complexes which govern individual utility functions. Among other things, Weber attempts to explain the evolution of the historically unusual orientation towards the accumulation of capital which made industrialization possible—an effort which gave rise to his Protestant Ethic thesis. The larger problematic of interpretive sociology can, however, in principle support research into other meaning orientations as well, including those which are localized in specific time periods or subcultures. Durkheimian functionalism, on the other hand, he reads as a sort of utopian socialism not too different from that advanced by the young Marx in advance of his epistemological rupture with Hegel.

The first of these claims has considerable merit. Weber was, in fact, trained as an economic historian and was influenced by marginalist economic theory. The logic of his early research does indeed make it appear to be an attempt to fill in a gap in existing social theory without calling into question the larger theoretical problematic. Therborn's analysis of Weber, however, misses the subtext which runs through all of Weber's work and which by the time of his late works, such as "Politics as a Vocation" have become dominant. For Weber social life was not fundamentally about consumption, but rather about power. Meaning orientations, or ideologies as we would call them, including in different ways both Protestant and secular ideologies of accumulation, and the ethic of consumption which seems to have replace both, serve to legitimate the rule of a particular social class; Marxism is an attempt to legitimate the struggle of a rising class for power. In one place, Weber even compares human society a kind of "war among the Gods," i.e., between competing ideologies that legitimate different social interests. This aspect of Weber's work cannot be theorized as an attempt to complete marginalist economic theory.

Therborn's second claim is more problematic. Durkheim was, indeed, a socialist, but his critique of capitalism and indeed his whole theoretical perspective is very different from that of even the young Marx. Durkheim's theory traces its roots not to Hegel but rather to Comte, and through him to French traditionalism, which treated all knowledge as a product of revelation, mediated through social institutions. What Durkheim does is to secularize this theory by making collective effervescence, the intense solidarity experience in moments of revolutionary upheaval, rather than revelation, the source of new ideas. This is at once a powerful insight that, with some modification, can make an important contribution to epistemology, and a dangerous idea rich with the potential for fomenting irrationalism.

It is for this reason that the second account of bourgeois sociology, namely that advanced by Lukacs in *The Destruction of Reason* (Lukacs 1953/1980), seems more adequate. For Lukacs, most bourgeois sociology is part of what he calls the indirect apologetic for capitalism. As we have suggested above, where the "direct apologetic," of which political economy forms and integral part, defends capitalism as the optimal way of organizing society, the indirect apologetic defends it by arguing that it is no worse than the alternatives. Thus, Weber absorbs Marx's insight that ideas are rooted in social reality and transforms it into an argument for a dark, radically relativistic vision in which social classes and other social actors struggle endlessly to legitimate their power. Within this context, however, authentic moral and metaphysical legitimation is impossible because ideas are *merely* instruments in the struggle for power. The claims of the proletariat are ultimately no more valid than those of the bourgeoisie; they are just different. And bourgeois democracy, at least, has developed ways of containing the struggle for legitimate within the civil boundaries of the parliamentary process. Other thinkers, such as Freud can be read in the same way. Sure, capitalism makes us miserable, but so would socialism, because all civilization forces us to repress the erotic and aggressive drives the complete fulfillment of which would alone make us happy.

From this standpoint Durkheim still appears to be politically ambivalent. On the one hand Durkheim was able to focus on the critical problem of anomie in capitalist society, and in this sense goes further than Marxists such as Lukacs in pointing toward the real ideological strategy of capital. Without a doctrine which explains the ultimately meaningfulness of the universe, as we have argued, it is impossible to adequate ground an ethics and thus to advance a critique of the market allocation of resources. At the same time, Durkheim never really breaks out of the relativistic epistemology characteristic of bourgeois sociology. He identifies the social location at which and the social process by which new meanings are generated, but does not show how these meanings might be something more than social constructs—how they might actually be a window, however partial and historically conditioned, on the truth. It is not surprising that in the present period Durkheimian sociology and its Parsonian offspring have served as the basis for the resurgent traditionalist doctrine known as communitarianism.

Ultimately it must be admitted, that in so far as bourgeois sociology represents a tactic of the indirect apologetic, and thus of capitalism on retreat, it is not surprising that it is not fully unified with the underlying problematic of mathematical physics, which is the ideology of a rising and expansive capitalism. The complete unification of sociology with mathematical physics had to await the postwar period and the development the new discipline of information theory. Originally a purely technical discipline dedicated to improving electronic information processing systems, information theory has developed into an architectonic discipline that attempts to unify all others—and transform them into branches of applied mathematical physics. In the following chapter we will see how information theoretical neoliberalism at once completes mathematical physics and brings it to an end. We will also see that attempts to resolve the crisis of mathematical physics at the level of a rationality which is still formal and which rejects teleological explanation can never work.

4

The End of Mathematical Physics

THE CONTRADICTIONS OF MATHEMATICAL PHYSICS

IT SHOULD BE APPARENT by now that mathematical physics, while it has certainly made significant contributions to our understanding of the universe and even greater contributions to technological development, has shown itself no better able than its Aristotelian predecessor to advance a unified theory of motion. On the contrary, the mathematical-physical description of the universe is characterized by three fundamental contradictions which no theory thus far proposed has been able to overcome, i.e., the contradictions between:

1. relativity and quantum mechanics,
2. dynamics generally and thermodynamics, and
3. thermodynamics and evolutionary theory.

The first of these contradictions derives fundamentally from a difference in the mathematical formalisms used by each discipline. Relativity, which as we have seen describes both the underlying structure of space-time and the behavior of gravitational interactions, assumes that change is continuous—i.e., that space and time are infinitely divisible and that objects can move (and energy thus be transferred) in arbitrarily small quantities. Because light moves at a finite speed and nothing moves faster, relativity forbids instantaneous signaling, while at the same time insisting that in order for one part of a system to affect another some sort of signal must be exchanged. Relativity, in other words, conserves a very strong concept of causation. At the same time, the recognition that light moves at a finite and constant speed implies that space-time has a dynamic structure which depends on the relative motion of observers and their proximity to massive bodies. Quantum mechanics, on the other hand, which was developed to describe electromagnetic interactions and which has been extended to describe the weak and strong nuclear interactions as well, treats the universe as a discrete order in which energy transfer and thus movement are quantized. While quantum formalisms are fully deterministic, some quantum phenomena seem to imply something other than a classical concept of causality. And quantum formalisms, in so far as they describe the evolution of systems in space over time conserve an essentially Newtonian understanding of space-time. Even sophisticated string-theoretical formalisms fail to resolve these difficulties.

Above and beyond these purely theoretical difficulties, the amalgam of relativity and quantum mechanics which dominates physical cosmology has run into increasing empirical difficulties. The application of relativity to cosmological problems, for example, has historically depended on the assumption of cosmic homogeneity, but observational has been building for some time which suggests that the universe is anything but homogenous, and may well be structured at the very largest scales.[1] Most cosmological models, furthermore, predict that the quantity of matter in the universe should be at least close the value necessary to eventually halt cosmological expansion. Current measurements, however, suggest that this is not the case, something which has led cosmologists to postulate the existing of invisible "dark matter," for which we have no direct evidence. Recent observations have, furthermore, led to the discovery of stars older than the universe itself is supposed to be. And big bang models consistently make incorrect predictions regarding the basic ratios of such elements as Deuterium, Helium, and Lithium (Lerner 1991).

These contradictions notwithstanding, relativity and quantum mechanics have far more in common than either does with thermodynamics. The first two disciplines describe processes which are reversible using formalisms which do not distinguish a well defined arrow of time; the second describes irreversible change. While it is not, strictly speaking, true to say that relativity treats time as "just another dimension" (the negative sign on the time term in the Minkowski metric means that the temporal dimension still behaves differently than the spatial dimensions),

---

1. If indeed there is a largest scale. It is the assumption of cosmological homogeneity, we will remember, which leads (via the solutions to Einstein's field equations) to the conclusion that the universe must be finite. But if it turns out that the universe is not infinite, then there is no largest scale, but only an ascending hierarchy of structured systems.

no purely mechanical formalism can adequately describe irreversible change. In order to understand this simply assume any simple system of point particles with mass—e.g., the solar system. Now assume, variously, Newtonian, Hamiltonian, relativistic, or quantum descriptions of that system—i.e., descriptions in terms of position, mass, velocity, spin, charge, etc.. Now allow that system to evolve over time, then pick to arbitrary states of the system. You will not be able to tell simply from observation which state came first and which second. This is not true in the case of thermodynamic descriptions. If someone showed you a picture of a warm house on a cold winter day with all of the doors and windows closed and an internal temperature of 20° C, while outside the reading was -20° C, and another with the doors open and the readings now nearly the same, you would be constrained to assume that either the first picture was taken before the second, or that there had been some outside intervention into the system—e.g., the family living in the house returned to find the doors open and the heat off and rectified the situation.

This is not to say that the question of time is not important for relativity and quantum mechanics, but the questions pursued by these disciplines are not questions which arise from our day to day experience, but rather questions which are generated by the formalisms themselves: questions such as time dilation and the possibility of time travel. Thermodynamic time, on the other hand, is the time we fight on a day to day basis, the time which, "like an ever-flowing stream bears all her sons away"[2] and which is a mark of the finitude of all material systems.

But if thermodynamics is able to theorize irreversible change, the change which it theorizes is always and only dissipation and disintegration, and the one of the principal discoveries of the past two hundred years is the reality of evolutionary change, of a development at least locally from lower to higher degrees of organization. Thermodynamics, which is our only theory of irreversible change at the fundamental physical level, says that this really ought not to be possible, being ruled out by such basic principles of thermodynamics as the Second Law and the Boltzmann Order Principle (Prigogine 1977, 1984). To say that the principle of self-organization is supplied by natural selection is not really adequate. Natural selection, as biologist Lynn Margulis puts it, plays the role of editor, not that of author, in the evolutionary process. In rigor-

---

2. The reference here is to Isaac Watts' hymn "O God Our Help in Ages Past."

ous formulations of the Neo-Darwinist theory, first of all, it is random variation and the recombination of genes, not natural selection, which is supposed to generate variety. And random variation turns out not to supply anything like the level of innovation necessary to explain evolutionary change. Complex systems theorist Ilya Prigogine has shown that

> the time necessary to produce a comparatively small protein chain of around 100 amino acids by *spontaneous* formation of structure is much longer than the age of the Earth. Hence, spontaneous formation of structure is ruled out . . . according to the modern theory of self-organizing systems, classical arguments concerning the "coincidental" realization of a complex living system cannot be employed. (Zimmerman 1991)

Molecular biologist Barry Hall, similarly, has found that the bacterium E. coli produces needed mutations at a rate roughly 100 million times greater than would be expected if they came about by chance. Nor can random variation and natural selection account for the fact that evolutionary changes often seem to occur rather suddenly, rather than in gradual increments, as the theory of natural selection would suggest. A retina or a cornea, after all, without the rest of the organ, would have no survival value by itself, and would be unlikely to be preserved in future generations.

None of this should be taken as requiring an external, supernatural principle to drive or direct evolution, but it does suggest that there are natural processes which are at work which we have not yet adequately theorized and which operate in ways that contradict thermodynamics.

Above and beyond these specific contradictions, there is a more fundamental difficulty which has begun to affect mathematical physics, an issue at which we have already hinted in some of our earlier discussions. This is the problem of cosmological fine-tuning: the fact that some twenty fundamental parameters, including the relative strengths of the four fundamental forces and the relative masses of the four stable particles, are fixed in just precisely the way that would be necessary in order to make possible the development of stars, and thus the heavy elements and hospitable habitats, required for the evolution of life and intelligence. Even slight variations would lead to a lifeless universe. This discovery runs counter to the dominant trend in mathematical physics, which has been to undermine the basis for any sort of teleological or design reasoning, something which has, as we have seen, been central to the ideological function of the discipline. A vision of a universe without meaning or purpose is at once the inevitable reflex of and an invaluable support for the market system, which itself knows no global meaning or purpose. It should thus come as no surprise that mathematical physics has become obsessed with the problem of cosmological fine-tuning, with some theorists opting for various forms of "anthropic reasoning," arguing that for one or another reason, ranging from observational selection, through mathematical necessity, to design or teleological ordering, the universe must be structured to make possible life and intelligence, and others struggling with all their might to either find an explanation for the fine tuning which does not conciliate teleology, or else to argue that it simply isn't real.

It is, of course, entirely possible, that there is no unified theory and that the problem of cosmological fine-tuning lies outside the scope of mathematical physics. There is no good reason why gravitational and electromagnetic interactions should be described by the same formalism of type of formalism. Dynamic and thermodynamic change are quite different processes; perhaps we should not expect dynamic and thermodynamic time to be equivalent. And why should evolution and disintegration—essentially opposing processes—be described by the same laws? Why should we expect mathematical physics to explain a profound mystery such as cosmological fine-tuning? Mathematical physics is about prediction and control, not the search for understanding.

This is, in fact, the attitude of most working scientists, who dream not of a final theory but only of understanding the infinitely diverse processes of the natural world, each of which presents yet another lure for their curiosity. And most working scientists, especially but not only in the biological and social sciences, do not hesitate to supplement mathematical formalisms with explanatory arguments. But we have seen that mathematical physics functions not only as a tool for science and technology (its appropriate functions) but also as an ideology of the market order. And its effectiveness as an ideology depends on its claim to do what Aristotle's theory—otherwise so much more satisfying—could not do, namely to generate a unified theory of motion. Thus the struggle within the ruling theoretical disciplines—relativity, quantum mechanics, thermodynamics, and evolutionary theory—to resolve the internal contradictions of mathematical physics and to generate a unified theory of motion, while at the same time undermining teleological strategies of explanation.

Our task in this chapter is to assess these attempts, looking carefully at their ability to actually resolve contradictions and thus produce a unified theory, dealing in one way or another with the problem of cosmological fine-tuning, and their ability to describe and/or explain observational evidence. Of critical importance here is the ability of attempts at unification to describe or explain something the separate theories do not by themselves. It is not enough simply to link theories together with more general formalisms which by themselves produce no new knowledge. But we will also need to look at the social basis and political valence of each the strategies for unification. Each, we will see, takes up a quite specific stance in relation to the market order, and each has definite political implications.

ATTEMPTS AT UNIFICATION

There are, broadly speaking, three trends in the debate around the unification of physical theory, each of which includes a number of diverse tendencies. The first trend, which is currently dominant in theoretical physics, includes all those theorists who believe that unification is possible within the context of existing theory, and for whom information theory and or quantum mechanics constitutes the real matrix for unification and the fundamental theory with which all other theories must be rendered consistent. Here we include both cosmological pessimists such as Hawking and Krause and "optimists" such as Tipler and Smolin. This trend we call "rightist" because, in spite of significant disagreement regarding fundamental questions, including the ultimate destiny of intelligent life in the universe, all its variant tendencies in one way or another serve to legitimate the market order. The second trend, which we call centrist, includes all of those who, while accepting the basic principles of mathematical physics either reject certain results or interpret them in such a way as to generate theories which no longer unambiguously legitimate the market order. This trend includes those who favor realistic hidden variables approaches to quantum theory (Bohm), and those who maintain the primacy of relativity (Gal-Or), thermodynamics (Prigogine), or some other discipline over quantum theory and who are skeptical about information-theoretical attempts at unification. It also includes those who argue see in the paradoxes of mathematical physics simply an example of the limitations of human reason which Kant identified a long time ago, or a great mystery which can only be resolved at an extra-rational level (Berry and Swimme). The third, or dialectical trend, includes all those tendencies, currently very much out of favor, which reject the claim of mathematical formalism to exhaust the possibilities of human reason, and thus contest the associated claim of mathematical physics to the status of a science. This trend includes the Thomistic, Hegelian, and Marxist philosophy or dialectics of nature. Let us now examine each of these approaches in turn.

Rightist Solutions

Central to what we are calling the rightist approach to unification is an option for quantum mechanics as the fundamental physical theory and the matrix for unification. This option turns out to be characteristic even of some theorists who, such as Tipler, were trained in global general relativity. Now we have already seen that the roots of quantum theory lie in the irrationalist currents which swept Europe in the years between the first and second world wars—the years which saw the rise of fascism and the preparation of the Shoah. Quantum theory alone, however, does not provide an adequate matrix for unification: it provides no way to describe organization, life, or evolution. This role is played by another theory which developed out of the violent struggles of the mid-twentieth century: information theory or, as it was originally called, the theory of communication, first developed by Shannon and Weaver in 1949 (Shannon and Weaver 1949). Like quantum mechanics itself, this theory was developed in response to real-world problems, in this case the problem of encoding and transmitting information electronically, over radio waves—something which had become vitally important to the conduct of modern warfare and which research into which thus received massive state support. The development of electronic computers in the postwar period provided a further impetus for the discipline, which in many ways represented the cutting edge of technological progress.

Information theory turned out to be a powerful resource for unification. The messages (or later the programs) which were the object of information theoretical investigation are generated by electronic devices the basic physical operation of which was described by quantum theory. And like quantum theory, most information theoretical formalisms (at least those describing digital as opposed to analog systems) are discrete rather than continuous. Unification with quantum mechanics, while an ongoing process, thus presents no fundamental difficulties. At the same time, information theory provided physicists with a way to theorize organization—or at least something like organization. It turns out that the information content of a message can be formalized as the negative entropy of the message and that information theoretical entropy and thermodynamic entropy behave in much the same way, thus partially unifying information theory with thermodynamics—or rather giving a new, information theoretical interpretation to the thermodynamic formalisms. Meanwhile, the discovery of DNA during essentially the same period opened up the possibility of a unification with biology. Living systems could be theorized as machines governed by a genetic program encoded in the DNA. Even if the "hardware" was somewhat different that of the silicon based machines which information engineers were busy building, it still depended on the same electromagnetic interactions, described by the same quantum mechanical laws. And theorizing intelligence as information processing came quite naturally. Indeed, even social systems could be theorized in information theoretical terms. The market became a system for accessing information about peoples' interests and capacities, as manifested in their buy and sell decisions and for processing this information into prices which then regulated their activities (Hayek 1988). The state, religion—indeed almost anything—could be interpreted "cybernetically."

Not all information theoretical attempts at unification were unambiguously reactionary. On the contrary, many early theories incorporated insights from biology, or from the very different tradition of Soviet systems theory, which had its roots in dialectical materialism, and at least recognized the role of systems other than the market in social organization. Indeed, the early name for the field, cybernetics, derives from the same Greek root as the word govern, and "social cybernetics" was intimately bound up with postwar efforts at economic regulation. It was simply taken for granted that like the electronic computer, the market system was an effective mechanism for carrying out its intended function (resource allocation) but that it needed direction from the outside. This outlook was a reflex of the social context in which information theory was born: the state-financed research laboratory which formed the theoretical core of the military industrial complex—intensely anticommunist, but hardly *laissez-faire*, and in this way not at all unlike the fascist milieu in which quantum theory first emerged. Indeed, the leading bourgeois social theorist of this period, Talcott Parsons (Parsons 1957), was indirectly influenced by the same irrationalist German philosophy which had been so attractive to Heisenberg and his associates. Parsons theorized human society as a system composed of various structures, each of which carried out a definite function: latent pattern maintenance, social integration, goal orientation, and adaptation to the environment. The way in which these structures carry out their functions is constrained on the one hand by energy uptake from the environment, and on the other hand by the way the society in question perceives "ultimate reality." This latter term derives from the theology of Paul Tillich (thus linking Parsons, by way of Tillich, with such irrationalists as Schelling and Heidegger) and has to do with the way one answers fundamental questions of meaning and value. Is there a God? If so, what is God like? If not, then what if anything organizes and directs the universe? Parsons even refers to these two directions of causation as "cybernetic relations."

Neither the internal logic of capitalist development, nor that of information theory, however, really supported this sort of accommodation. The state-financed military industrial complex itself played a central role in the creation of a unified global market, and in the extension of that market through the defeat of socialism, but in the context of such a market economic regulation became increasingly difficult and the nation state itself began to atrophy. The defeat of socialism, furthermore, undermined the political power of the working classes in the capitalist countries and made it ever more difficult to constrain the operation of market forces. While military-related national research laboratories have generally been the last refuge from market pressures, by the late 1980s growing numbers of theorists were leaving to sell their services to finance capital or to work at corporate financed research centers such as the Santa Fe Institute. At the same time, the very idea of a system receiving input from the outside meant that information theory was not yet complete. Ultimate reality or whatever took its place itself remained unexplained. Thus the trend, beginning in the 1980s towards theories in which organization emerges spontaneously from within the system itself, much as it is supposed to in Neo-Darwinian evolutionary theory and marginalist economics.

There are a number of approaches to unification which stress spontaneous organization. These theories could be distinguished from each other in any number of ways, but they distinguish themselves ideologically by the degree of hope they are willing to invest in a universe which is, on their account, in many ways simply a mirror image of the market order. Some theories, such as Frank Tipler's Omega Point Theory and certain other forms of anthropic cosmology, attempt to reconcile the notion of spontaneous self-organization with a claim that the universe is ultimately meaningful and in some sense ordered to God. We will argue that this trend reflects the renewed optimism of the bourgeoisie in the wake of the crisis of socialism and the global expansion of the 1980s and 1990s. At the opposite end of the spectrum lie theories which, mobilize the basic reductionist agenda outlined above and join them to a far more pessimistic cosmology. This is the position represented by theorists such as Lawrence Krause, who has recently advanced an argument against the survival of intelligent life into the far future of the universe. This trend, which still dominates among more sober mathematical physicists, reflects the recognition on the part of the most advanced sectors of the bourgeoisie, that their system, however buoyant it may be in the present period, is ultimately unworkable. In between lie theories such as cosmological natural selection, advanced by Lee Smolin, which are resolutely atheistic and reject anthropic reasoning, but which present a moderately hopeful picture of a future which is not limited to this universe, but extends beyond it to its countless daughter universes, born from black holes and formed by an evolutionary process which selects for universes which, in allowing black holes, also, purely coincidentally, allow for life and intelligence. Smolin's approach reflects the standpoint of the dissident intelligentsia which came of age in the 1960s and 1970s, marginalized by capitalism but unwilling to assume the discipline of socialism, which knows that it has no future under the present system, but which has decided to enjoy the ride nonetheless. We need to consider each of these approaches in turn.

Information Theoretical Transhumanism

Tipler takes as his starting point the idea that the universe is a vast information processing system. Matter is the "hardware" component of the system, the laws of nature the "software." Drawing on the information theory developed by Shannon and Weaver (1949), Tipler argues that the organization of a system is its negative entropy, or the quantity of information encoded within it. "Life" is simply information encoded in such a way that it is conserved by natural selection. A system is intelligent if it meets the "Turing test," i.e., if a human operator interrogating it cannot distinguish its responses from those of a human being (Turing 1950). Intelligent life continues forever if

1. information processing continues indefinitely along at least one worldline g all the way to the future c-boundary of the universe; that is, until the end of time.

2. the amount of information processed between now and this future c-boundary is infinite in the region of space-time with which the worldline g can communicate; that is the region inside the past light cone of g.

3. the amount of information stored at any given time t within this region diverges to infinity as t approaches its future limit (this future limit of t is finite in a closed universe, but infinite in an open one, if t is measured in what physicists call "proper time"). (Tipler 1994: 132–33)

The first condition simply states that there must be one cosmic history in which information processing continues forever. The second condition states that it must be possible for the results of all information processing to be communicated to world-line g. This means that the universe must be free of "event horizons," i.e., regions with which an observer on world line g cannot communicate. It also means that since an infinite amount of information is processed along this world line, an observer on this line will experience what amounts *subjectively* to eternal life. The third condition avoids the problem of an eternal return, i.e., an endless repetition of events as memory becomes saturated and new experience thus impossible.

Tipler then goes on to describe the physical conditions under which "eternal life" is possible. In accord with the as yet incompletely unified state of physics, he presents separate "classical" or "global general relativistic" and "quantum mechanical" theories. We take his "classical" theory first. Information processing is constrained by the first and second laws of thermodynamics. Specifically, the storage and processing of information requires the expenditure of energy, the amount required being inversely proportional to the temperature.

> it is possible to process and store an infinite amount of information between now and the final state of the universe only if the time integral of P/T is infinite, where P is the power used in the computation and T is the temperature. (Tipler 1994: 135)

Eternal life thus becomes essentially a problem of finding an adequate energy source. Tipler proposes finding this source in the "gravitational shear" created as the universe collapses at different rates in different directions. This imposes a very specific set of constraints on the process of cosmic evolution. Only a very special type of universe, the so-called "Taub" universe, named after mathematician Abraham Taub, collapses in just precisely the way required. And even most Taub universes tend to "right" themselves, returning to more nearly spherical form. For information processing to continue forever, life must gain control of the entire universe, and force it to continue its Taub collapse in the same direction far longer than it would spontaneously (Tipler 1994: 137). Thus the requirement that intelligent life gain control of the universe as a whole, and control the rate and direction of its collapse, so as to create the enormous energies necessary to guarantee eternal life.

Meeting the second and third conditions outlined above requires, furthermore, that the universe be closed, because "open universes expand so fast in the far future that it becomes impossible for structures to form of sufficiently larger and larger size to store a diverging amount of information" (1994: 140). It also requires that "the future c-boundary of the universe consist of a single point . . . the Omega Point" (1994: 142). Finally, in order to meet information storage requirements, "the density of particles must diverge to infinity as the energy goes to infinity, but nevertheless this density of states must diverge no faster than the cube of the energy" (1994: 146). Tipler identifies, in addition to these requirements, which he calls "weakly testable," a variety of other predictions which can be used to test his theory, including the requirement that the mass of the top quark be 185 +/- 20 GeV and that the mass of the Higgs boson must be 220 +/- 20GeV (1994: 146).

In order to understand Tipler's Quantum Omega Point Theory, it is necessary to understand some of the internal contradictions of current quantum cosmology. In general relativity the spatial metric h and the non-gravitational fields F are taken as given on the underlying three-dimensional manifold S. Cosmologists then attempt to find a four-dimensional manifold M with a Lorentz metric g (the gravitational field) and non-gravitational fields F such that M contains S as a submanifold, g restricted to S is the metric h, and K is the extrinsic curvature of S, or, to put the matter differently, K says how quickly h is changing along the fourth, "temporal" dimension (1994: 162). In quantum cosmology, on the other hand, the universe is represented by a wave function Ψ(h,F,S)—an application of the Schrodinger Equation which we discussed in the last chapter—which determines the values of h and F on S (1994: 174–75). One feature of the system, however, remains arbitrary: the selection of the fixed three-dimensional manifold S. Hartle and Hawking have proposed to eliminate this contingency by allowing the wave function to be a function of any three-dimensional manifold. According to this view, the domain of Ψ includes all possible values of h, F, and S (1994: 178). The Hartle-Hawking formulation, however, still requires h to be space-like on all three-dimensional manifolds S. This restriction brings the formulation into conflict with classical general relativity, which does not distinguish so sharply between space and time.

Tipler points out, however, that the requirement that h be space-like derives from a subjectivist interpretation of quantum mechanics, which interprets the wave function as a probability amplitude at a given time. This, obviously, requires times to be sharply distinguished from space. Tipler, however, favors a Many-Worlds interpretation of quantum mechanics, according to which all possible values of the wave function exist mathematically, and all those which permit the existence of observers exist physically. This removes the need to distinguish between space and time, and thus the requirement that h be always space-like. Tipler proposes instead to allow the domain of the wave function to include all four-dimensional manifolds which permit a Lorentz metric g. All such manifolds permit what is known as a foliation. They can, that is, be represented as a "stack" of three-dimensional manifolds S(t), each representing the topology of a possible universe at a different moment of time. Each foliation will have a metric h, which need not be space-like, as well as non-gravitational fields, induced by the enveloping spacetimes (M,g). Any (h,F,S) which cannot be represented this way has Ψ=0; it does not exist. Similarly, there will be many spacetimes which permit the same (h,F,S). Some of these may have a future c-boundary which is a single point—the Omega Point (1994: 174–181). Thus the "Omega Point Boundary condition" on the universal wave function:

> The wave function of the universe is that wave function for which all phase paths terminate in a (future) Omega Point, with life continuing into the future forever along every phase path in which it evolves all the way to the Omega Point. (1994: 181)

Now, the Four-Manifold Non-Classification Theorem states that there does not exist any algorithm which can list or classify all compact four-dimensional topological or differentiable manifolds without boundary, nor is it possible to tell if any two given manifolds are the same or different (1994: 190). This means that it is impossible to derive the system as a whole from any one of its elements—a situation which, following William James, Tipler identifies with radical, ontological indeterminism (1994: 187). This means that the existence of life and intelligence, and the *decision* on the part of intelligent life to guide the universe towards Omega, is in fact logically and ontologically prior the universal wave function itself (1994: 183): "The wave function is generated by the self-consistency requirement that the laws of physics and the decisions of the living agents acting in the universe force the universe to evolve into the Omega Point (1994: 203)." Indeed, in so far as the equations of both general relativity and quantum mechanics are reversible, there is no scientific reason to assume that causality runs only in one direction: from the past, through the present, into the future. It might just as well be seen as running from the future, through the present, into the past. From this point of view it is God, the Omega Point, which, existing necessarily, brings the entire universe into existence and draws it to himself.

> At the instant the Omega point is reached, life will have gained control of *all* matter and forces not only in a single universe, but in all universes whose existence is logically possible; life will have spread into *all* spatial regions in all universes which could logically exist, and will have stored an infinite amount of information, including *all* bits of knowledge which it is logically possible to know. And this is the end. (Barrow and Tipler 1986: 677)

The question arises, quite naturally, just how we are to reach Omega. The key link between actually existing carbon based life, and this nonmolecular intelligent living system are a "race" of intelligent, self-reproducing, interstellar probes (the so-called von Neumann probes). Tipler proposes launching a series of such interstellar probes in the expectation that as they evolve they will grasp the conditions for the long term survival of intelligent life in the cosmos, and eventually reorganize the universe on a cosmic scale in order to bring into being the nonmolecular life form(s) which can survive into the final stages of cosmic evolution.

Such probes would, of course, be extremely expensive. It thus becomes necessary to identify an optimum path of economic development.

It is interesting to note that both Barrow and Tipler make extensive reference to the neoliberal economist F. A. Hayek in their work. Hayek, like Barrow and Tipler, identifies complex organization with negative entropy, or with the quantity of information that a system can encode. An economy is simply an information processing system. No centralized planning agency or redistributional structure can grasp the complexity of a highly interdependent, rapidly developing human system, and any attempt on the part of such agencies to plan the society will inevitably result in a loss of complexity and will hold back growth and development.

> Certainly nobody has yet succeeded in deliberately arranging all the activities that go on in a complex society. If anyone did ever succeed in fully organizing such a society, it would no longer make use of many minds, but would be altogether dependent on one mind; it would certainly not be very complex but extremely primitive—and so would soon be the mind whose knowledge and will determined everything. The facts which could enter into the design of such an order could be only those which were known and digested by this mind; and as only he could decide on action and thus gain experience, there would be none of that interplay of many minds in which alone mind can grow. (Hayek 1973: 49)

What Hayek calls the "extended order" of the marketplace, on the other hand, is uniquely capable of accessing, processing, and communicating vast quantities of information.

> Much of the particular information which any individual possesses can be used only to the extent to which he himself can use it in his own decisions. Nobody can communicate to another all that he knows, because much of the information he can make use of he himself will elicit only in the process of making plans for action. Such information will be evoked as he works upon the particular task he has undertaken in the conditions in which he finds himself, such as the relative scarcity of various materials to which he has access. Only thus can the individual find out what to look for, and what helps him to do this in the market is the responses others make to what they find in their own environments. (Hayek 1988: 77)

> Information-gathering institutions such as the market enable us to use such dispersed and unsurveyable knowledge to form super-individual patterns. After institutions and traditions based on such patterns evolved it was no longer necessary for people to strive for

> agreement on a unitary purpose (as in a small band), for widely dispersed knowledge and skills could now readily be brought into play for diverse ends. (Hayek 1988: 15)

The market thus takes on for Hayek what he acknowledges to be a transcendent character, organizing interactions of a scale beyond the capacity of any single mind or organization—beyond even the mind of God.

> There is no ready English or even German word that precisely characterizes an extended order, or how its way of functioning contrasts with the rationalists' requirements. The only appropriate word, 'transcendent,' has been so misused that I hesitate to use it. In its literal meaning, however, it does concern that which *far surpasses the reach of our understanding, wishes and purposes, and our sense perceptions*, and that which incorporates and generates knowledge which no individual brain, or any single organization, could possess or invent. This is conspicuously so in its religious meaning, as we see, for example, in the Lord's Prayer, where it is asked that "*thy* will [i.e., not *mine*] be done on earth as it is in heaven . . ." But a more purely transcendent ordering, which also happens to be a purely naturalistic ordering (not derived from any supernatural power), as for example in evolution, abandons the animism still present in religion; the idea that a single brain or will (as for example that of an omniscient God) could control and order. (Hayek 1988: 72–73)

Barrow and Tipler draw on Hayek's reasoning to argue that in a market system the technological and economic development necessary to support the construction of interstellar von Neumann probes will take place spontaneously. They argue that insofar as

> the economic system is wholly concerned with generating and transferring information . . . the government should not interfere with the operation of the economic system . . . if it is argued . . . that the growth of scientific knowledge is maximized by information generation and flow being unimpeded by government intervention, does it not follow that the growth of economic services would be maximized if unimpeded by government intervention? (Barrow and Tipler 1986: 173)

Indeed, they argue that if the operation of the marketplace is left to run its course, the cost of energy and raw materials relative to wages will decline to the point that humanity will become capable not only of interstellar travel, but ultimately of reorganizing the structure of the cosmos on a macroscale—developments which are both critical for their meliorist physical eschatology.

> the price of raw materials and energy have, on the long term average, been decreasing exponentially over the past two centuries . . . (Barrow and Tipler 1986: 172)

The sort of interstellar probes which Barrow and Tipler believe are necessary in order to secure the destiny of intelligent life in the cosmos would currently cost between $3x10^{10}$ and $2x10^{14}$, depending on their speed.

> These costs . . . seem quite large to us, but there is evidence that they could not seem large to a member of a civilization greatly in advance of ours . . . the cost relative to wages of raw materials, including fuel, has been dropping exponentially with a time constant of 50 years for the past 150 years. If we assume this trend continues for the next 400 years . . . then to an inhabitant of our own civilization at this future date, the cost of a low velocity probe would be as difficult to raise as 10 million dollars today, and the cost of a high-velocity probe would be as difficult to raise as 70 billion dollars today. The former cost is easily within the ability of . . . at least 100,000 Americans . . . and the Space Telescope project budget exceeds $109. If the cost trend continues for the next 800 years, then the cost of a $3x1010 probe would be as difficult to raise as $4000 today. An interstellar probe would appear to cost as much then as a home computer does now . . . In such a society, *someone* would almost certainly build and launch a probe. (Barrow and Tipler 1986: 583)

Tipler's cosmology even has theological implications. Despite his frequent references to Aristotle and Aquinas, and his effort to show the compatibility of his theory with most of the principal religious traditions, these implications tend very clearly towards Calvinist Christianity. This is because of the centrality of what he calls "agent determinism." Realization of the Omega Point is, in one sense, inevitable; it is required by the very existence of the universe itself. But it presupposes the subordination of the interests of individual carbon-based organisms to a larger cosmic plan which involves the displacement of carbon based by machine, and eventually by nonmolecular intelligence. And in so far as this transition is best carried out through the unimpeded operation of rationally inscrutable market forces, it requires the submission of individual carbon based organisms to cosmic imperatives which they cannot understand, with which, at the very least, they cannot fully identify. Eternal life, furthermore, is not something the soul achieves, by becoming actually capable of infinite self-organizing activity, but rather something bestowed on it by the nearly omnipotent and omniscient beings near Omega, simply because it is in *their* self-interest. Tipler makes a game-theoretical argument (1994: 245–59) that these beings will resurrect us, and will bestow eternal life upon us, and that this will be a life of potentially infinite richness and joy—but ultimately the decision is theirs. We have here, in effect, an anthropic cosmological argument not only for Reaganomics but for a peculiar, high tech, Calvinism.

Tipler's cosmology has a number of attractive features which has made it the focus of an emerging "transhumanist" trend which looks forward anxiously to the day when we will eventually be "uploaded" to a "higher level of implementation." Clearly, Tipler comprehends the cosmos as an evolving system developing towards ever higher degrees of organization, and recognizes human civilization—or rather the social form of matter in general—as a key link in the cosmohistorical evolutionary process. And he argues that far from being a mere counterpoint to stronger forces of cosmic disintegration, the forces of complex organization will, in fact, triumph in the end. On the scientific level he has attempted, at least, to make his theory testable and thus opened the way towards experimental verification of the claim that life will survive and develop towards Omega, and thus eventually embrace the universe as a whole. And he has made some effort, at least, to draw out the philosophical and political-theological implications of his position.

At the same time, his work has serious limitations. Some of these are shared with other information-theoretical attempts at unification: the theorization of life and intelligence in information-theoretical terms, the theory evolution by random variation and natural selection, and the claim that the market order actually advances technological progress. We will reserve criticism of these claims until the end of this section. Other problems are, however, particular to Tipler's theory and need to be considered here. There is, first of all, the problem of Tipler's specific cosmological claims. As we have noted, Tipler makes a number of predictions which he says can be used to test his theory. While the evidence is not all in, the situation does not currently look good for the Omega Point. Fermilab, for example, recently measured the top quark at just a little bit below the mass range which Tipler's theory requires. More to the point, however, the currently favored cosmological models suggest that not only is the universe not closed, but that its long-term evolution is dominated by the so-called "cosmological constant," a repulsive force which derives from the positive energy density of the quantum vacuum, and which recent observations suggest may be causing the universe to expand at an ever increasing rate—an argument we will consider in detail shortly. If this is true, then Tipler's strategy for the cosmic expansion of life and intelligence, and the intelligent re-engineering of the universe, would appear to be doomed.

Quite apart from the adequacy of his particular model, however, Tipler's approach leaves a great deal to be desired as a strategy for unification. Even if one were to grant the theorization of life and intelligence in information theoretical terms, and evolution by random variation and natural selection, his theory does not really engage with the underlying contradiction in fundamental physics, namely that between relativity and quantum mechanics. On the contrary, like nearly all the theories we will consider, including several which make far more modest predictive claims, Tipler simply absorbs relativity into a more general, in this case quantum mechanical formalism, without really addressing the underlying incompatibility in the mathematics or the physical concepts (space, time, etc.). This would be less of a problem if he was simply dispensing with relativity entirely, as if to argue that gravitational forces are unnecessary to his argument. But this is not what he does: the whole basic design of his argument is relativistic; it is only superficially "quantized" by incorporation of the underlying metric into the quantum wave function Ψ as a variable.

Tipler's information-content theory of organization, furthermore, fails to adequately theorize complex organization, life, and intelligence. We have already noted that quantum theory calls radically into question the atomistic logic and ontology which has characterized European philosophy since the time of the scientific revolution, and suggests, rather, that matter is relational at the most fundamental levels of its being. Tipler, however, does not seem to have fully comprehended this development.

In order to illustrate this problem, it is useful to distinguish three meanings of the word "system." At the lowest level of integration, a "system" consists of various elements, the *behavior* of which is determined by their relationships with other members of the system. As von Bertalanffy points out, systems of this type can be described by a system of differential equations. If the system is dynamic, i.e., evolves over time, then we must use partial differential equations. And if we wish to make the state of the system depend on its past states, then we must use "integro-differential" equations (von Bertalanffy 1969: 55–56). Despite the difficulty involved in solving such systems of equations, mathematical formalization is, in principle at least, possible.

There are, however, two higher levels of systemic integration. At the second level, the very nature or essence of the elements is determined by their relationships with the other elements, and at the third, their existence is dependent on—or even constituted by—their relationships with the other elements. It is not clear that either of these two meanings of "system" can be formalized mathematically, since most mathematical formalizations of this sort ultimately rely on set theory, which itself presupposes groups of particulars which are related to each other only in an external manner (Harris 1987).

Now Tipler seems to understand systems only at the first level. From the simplest to the most complex levels, his cosmos continues to be constituted by irreducible particles which are externally related to each other, rather than by a system of relationships the nodes of which merely appear to be particular when we abstract them from the system as a whole. That his "elementary particles" are "bits"—units of information rather than of matter—does not really change anything. His understanding of complex organization, life, intelligence, and social evolution is governed by an ultimately atomistic paradigm in which individual particles (bits, organisms, human persons, von Neumann probes) are externally related to each other. If systems are nothing but aggregates of externally related particles, then organization is nothing more than the order that prevails among those particles—the negative entropy or information content of the system. But negentropic and information theoretical approaches to organization and complexity run into serious problems when we attempt to apply them to biological and social systems. IBM scientist Charles Bennett (1988) has recently pointed out that the negative entropy theory has limitations even at the physical level. The human body, for example, is intermediate in *negentropy* between a crystal and a gas, while being more highly *organized* than either. Similarly, organized objects, "because they are partially constrained and determined by the need to encode coherent function or meaning, contain less information than random sequences of the same length, and this information reflects not their organization but their residual randomness." He proposes instead to define organization as logical depth, "the work required to derive a" message "from a hypothetical cause involving no unnecessary ad hoc assumptions," or "the time required to compute this message from" its "minimal description." This definition bears an interesting resemblance to the Marxist labor theory of value, according to which the value of a commodity is equal to the average socially necessary labor time necessary to produce it (Marx 1849/1978: 203–17).

The limitations of the atomistic paradigm become even more apparent when we attempt to explain the evolution of systems towards higher levels of complexity and organization. Random variation, competition, and natural selection—the mainstays of the atomistic paradigm—do not seem adequate to the task of explaining the emergence and development of living—and especially social—systems. We have already noted that random variation could not possibly have produced even complex proteins on the time-scale of the earth's history nor can it account for the rate of genetic innovation in even simple bacteria.

Biologists have identified two distinct types of processes that they believe contribute to the development of increasingly complex forms of life. Molecular biologists have found that the genome operates as a complex interrelated totality, with some genes regulating the operation of others. Random mutations in some parts of the genome, where they threaten to undermine well-established life processes, are systematically corrected, while others, in areas where experimentation seems promising, are permitted. At the same time, small changes in one part of the genome can trigger fundamental structural changes in the system as a whole. This is why animal breeders, in the process of selecting for certain traits, so often produce undesired side effects. It also helps to explain how whole new structures, (such as the eye), with significant survival value, might have emerged all at once. Variation, furthermore, is constrained by the material out of which organisms are built. Genetic instructions to construct an elephant with legs as thin as those of an ant, Kevin Kelly points out, simply cannot be carried out. Matter, as potential organization, provides life with certain structural options, but systematically excludes others. This is another reason why structural leaps are more common than incremental changes. The genome must undergo considerable internal reorganization before it can produce a new form that is both structurally different and viable. This complex of phenomena has led some biologists to suggest that the genome contains algorithmic search instructions which help it to discover mechanically stable, biologically viable, ecologically progressive, new forms. Life, it appears, is at least incipiently creative and self-reorganizing.

At the same time there is growing evidence that cooperation plays an important role in the evolutionary process. Biologist Lynn Margulis, for example, has argued that nucleated cells, with their specialized organelles devoted to photosynthesis and respiration, and their genetic high command, came about through symbiosis, when membraned cells incorporated bacteria which had already developed these processes and the structures necessary to carry them out.

These new developments suggest that natural selection is only one of many processes which contribute to the emergence of new, increasingly complex, forms of life. And its contribution is largely negative. Natural selection, as biologist Lynn Margulis puts it, is the editor, not the author, of evolution. The creative self-reorganization of matter, and symbiosis, the cooperation between organisms, play the leading role (Waddington 1957, Lenat 1980, Sheldrake 1981 and 1989, Denton 1985, Wesson 1991, Margulis and Fester 1991, Kelly 1992).

If the evolution of biological systems involves more than random variation, competition, and natural selection, this is even truer of social systems. Even if one accepts the "information content theory of organization," it is clear that the marketplace has no access to information regarding the impact of various activities on the qualitative complexity of the ecosystem and the development of human social capacities. On the contrary, all the market "knows" is a quantitative expression of the existing capacities (supply) and current interests (demand) of individuals, as these are expressed in the form of price curves. It has no way to analyze latent capacities or optimum paths of development for either individuals or the system as a whole. It is market forces, after all, which draw people away from preparing themselves to be elementary school teachers, and towards selling crack cocaine.

Indeed, it is not clear that the information content theory of organization can even grasp the concept of the social form of matter. In so far as human beings are constituted and shaped as persons through their interaction with each other, the social form of matter necessarily involves mutual determination of the existence and essence, and not merely the behavior, of the elements in the system. The economic model that Tipler borrows from Hayek fails to understand this, and remains within the horizon of a universe in which human beings are irreducible atoms which interact with each other externally, but do not ever really influence, much less constitute, each other. A really profound understanding of the marketplace, for example, involves not merely writing a system of equations describing the mutual determination of a limited number of state variables, but an in-depth social-psychological analysis of the ways in which people's ideas and desires are shaped, e.g., by the socialization process, which constitutes them as producers, accumulators, consumers, by advertising, etc. But this kind of analysis involves looking not only at the behavior of individual consumers, but also at their psychological make up, including such factors as sexuality, which are manipulated by advertising campaigns. Once we look beyond the marketplace to family relations, the educational process, the organization of the workplace, the building and exercising of political power, the processes of artistic creation, scientific research, or philosophical reflection, of the complex operation of religious institutions, it becomes apparent that we can say almost nothing of interest so long as we confine ourselves to a model of externally related individuals, since all of these processes are in fact centered on the mutual determination of the existence and essence of the elements in the system. The atomism which relativity and quantum theory have made increasingly untenable at the physical level is in fact *prima facie* absurd at the social. The information content approach to complex organization has, furthermore, some potentially very dangerous policy implications. Working from very different tendencies within the dialectical materialist tradition, Ernest Mandel (1968, 1978) and the dependency and world systems theorists (Emmanuel 1972, Wallerstein 1974, Frank 1978, Amin 1980) have demonstrated that insertion into market relations in fact undermines a country's economic development, measured in value terms—i.e., in terms of the total quantity of socially necessary labor embodied in its products. On the one hand, as a system becomes more technologically developed and thus more capital intensive, the rate of profit declines, and capital is redeployed to low wage, low technology activities on the periphery of the world system, blocking capital formation and holding back technological development. At the same time, differences in productivity and/or the value of labor power lead to unequal exchange between developed and underdeveloped countries, draining the latter of a significant portion of the value they produce, and holding back their development. This, in turn, blocks the formation of demand for high technology goods and high skill services, constituting a further obstacle to social progress. Finally, in order to rectify the resulting tendency towards underconsumption, states attempt to "pump up" their economies through deficit spending on both income-transfer, demand supporting, and military technological programs. The resulting expansion of the public debt further strengthens *rentier* elements, raises interest rates, and leads to overconsumption of luxuries and a crisis in capital formation.

The market system is so destructive of social organization precisely because it treats human beings as individual atoms related to each other in a purely external fashion, and thus undermines the mutual determining relations by which social systems sustain and develop their complexity and that of their constitutive elements. The strategy for social and cosmic evolution proposed by Tipler, far from promoting the development of intelligent life towards an infinitely self-organizing Omega Point, would, in the short run, devastate the world economy by undermining investment in infrastructure, education, research, and development and, in the long run, replace complex, living, intelligent systems with a race of predatory machines which make some of the most frightening artifacts of science fiction, such as Star Trek's Borg (which at least assimilated, rather than completely destroying, other cultures) seem benign by comparison.

It is necessary, finally, to say something about Tipler's vision of eternal life as a kind of computer simulation run on the "hardware" of the Omega Point. Tipler's vision of the Omega point in fact seems to have more in common with a comfortable and even decadent retirement than with any project for the realization of the self-organizing activity of the cosmos in an infinitely creative, powerful, knowing, and loving future. The many minds which Hayek rightly points out are necessary for authentic social development, are here replaced by a single mind which spends eternity amusing itself with simulations of other minds which no longer exist—and which cannot therefore really challenge it to grow and develop in new ways. The neoliberal entrepreneur who boasts of his contributions to human historical—and even cosmic—development here shows his true colors. Behind the entrepreneurial cosmetic lies the decaying corpse of consumerist, *rentier* capitalism.

Evolutionary Cosmology

An alternative to Tipler's theory, and to anthropic reasoning which makes humanity, or at least intelligence generally, a condition of possibility of the universe, has recently been advanced by Lee Smolin, of Penn State University. Smolin, like the anthropic cosmologists, begins with the insight that so many fundamental physical constants, such as the relative strength of the gravitational and electromagnetic forces and the relative masses of the proton an electron, appear to be fine-tuned in such a way as to permit the evolution of life and intelligence.

Smolin begins with a far more adequate understanding of organization than does Tipler—one which reflects both a more profound grasp of the implications of relativity and quantum theory, and an authentic dialogue with at least some of the trends in complex system theory and evolutionary biology. The principal lesson of relativity and quantum mechanics, he argues, is the underlying relationality of the universe. All of the basic properties of elementary "particles," including both those theorized by relativity (mass, length, etc.) and those theorized by quantum mechanics (charge, spin, etc.) are defined in relation to other "particles" so that the term particle becomes little more than a relic of the atomistic history of the discipline. To this extent, Smolin is, as he claims, a true follower of Leibniz, who he takes as his philosophical mentor.

Smolin suggests that the complexity of a system be measured by its variety, i.e., by the quantity of information necessary to distinguish its parts from each other. The greater the variety, the less information required. This approach at least makes it possible to show how a living system is more complex than either a crystal or an ideal gas, which have entropies of 0 and one respectively, but which both require an enormous amount of information to navigate.

Working out of this understanding of cosmological fine-tuning, Smolin notes that there are a number of different ways in which cosmological fine-tuning might be explained. The approach most coherent with the history of mathematical physics would be the discovery of a unique unified theory which specified these parameters. The difficulty is that such a theory does not appear to be emerging. Even if the difficulties with string theory which we noted above are resolved and a credible theory of quantum gravity developed, it is unlikely that this theory will fix mathematically the basic physical constants. Rather, it will define a class, perhaps infinite, of mathematically possible universes of which ours is only one. Just why we live in the sort of universe we do—or rather why our universe is here for us to live in—will still need to be explained (Smolin 1997: 45-46). Above and beyond this, however, Smolin suggests that the search for a final theory reflects a failure to grasp the real lesson of relativity and quantum mechanics. If all properties are defined in relational terms, a final theory which understands the universe as if from the outside is in fact a contradiction in terms, and a relic of the metaphysical heritage.

The second strategy for explaining cosmological fine tuning is the anthropic principle. Smolin rejects the strong anthropic principle on the same grounds as the search for a final theory. It is a relic of teleological reasoning left over from the religious and metaphysical prehistory of science and rules it out of consideration. The weak anthropic principle, which holds that cosmological fine tuning is an effect of observational selection, he argues, is logically consistent, but impossible to test. According to this view there are many universes or regions of the universe in which the fundamental physical constants, or even the basic laws of physics, vary. We live in the one we do because it is the only one we could live in. The difficulty is that we have no way of knowing whether or not these other universes or regions of the universe exist because we cannot observe them (Smolin 1997: 202).[3]

If weak anthropic reasoning seems to violate the principle of economy (Occam's Razor), however, then Smolin's approach does no better. Smolin argues that in the early history of the universe, prior to the time when the universe became transparent to light, the fundamental physical constants were not yet fixed. They are a result of what amounts to a process of random variation. Drawing on a result of quantum mechanics which holds that there can be no true singularities, Smolin argues further

---

3. It should be pointed out that the fixing of fundamental physical constants by a unique unified theory would, in fact, also be a type of anthropic theory—specifically a variant of the strong, though not necessarily the final anthropic principle. It is strong because it requires the universe to be fine-tuned for life and intelligence. It becomes final only if it requires that the universe also be structured in such a way that once intelligent life comes into being it continues indefinitely. It becomes theistic only if it requires the universe to be structured in such a way that it presupposes divine intelligence. This step might be made by a design argument, or it might be made by showing, as Tipler attempts to do, that the universe must eventually evolve an intellect capable of knowing everything which it is logically possible to know.

The End of Mathematical Physics

that time does not come to an end in black holes, but rather that black holes are essentially the birth places of new universes, in each of which the fundamental physical constants vary at least a little bit. If this is true, he suggests, then those universes in which the fundamental physical constants are fixed in just such a way as to permit the creation of large numbers of black holes will, in effect, reproduce more efficiently. There will thus be a cosmological selection effect in favor of those parameters. Now it happens that the parameters that produce universes capable of generating large numbers of black holes are very similar to those which permit life and intelligence. Thus it is not surprising that we find ourselves in a universe "tuned" as it is.

Smolin goes on from here to argue that most of the promising solutions to the problem of unification in fact require that the universe be complex—specifically that it be a self-organizing, non-equilibrium system, i.e.,

> distinguishable collection of matter, with recognizable boundaries, which has a flow of energy, and possible matter, passing through it, while maintaining, for time scales long compared to the dynamical time scales of its internal processes stable configuration from thermodynamics equilibrium. (Smolin 1997: 155)

This is because complexity itself is a condition for the possibility of space and time. A universe at thermal equilibrium, he argues, could conceivably require more information to distinguish between its parts than could be stored in the universe itself, making it logically impossible in a relativistic space-time. And it is the development of the universe to higher degrees of organization which alone creates an arrow of time on which observers in different parts of the universe can agree (Smolin 1997: 220, 292).

This basic idea governs Smolin's approach to interpretation of quantum mechanics and his approach to reconciling it with relativity. Rather than associating a wave function Ψ with the universe as a whole, as do both the Copenhagen and Many Worlds theorists, Smolin, drawing on work by Louis Crane (Crane 1995, 1997b, 1997b, 1998, 2000) and Carlo Rovelli (Rovelli 1997a, 1997b, 1998, 1999, 2000) suggest using topological quantum field theory to partition the universe, with a boundary being drawn between each observer and the rest of the system. A distinct quantum wave function is associated with the possible knowledge each observer may have of the universe on the other side of the topological boundary. The laws which govern the universe are then inscribed not in the wave functions themselves, but rather in the relations between them, which must be such that all Ψ are consistent with each other (Smolin 1997: 272). This, in turn, requires a high degree of complexity. Space and time are generated out of the relationships between events at the quantum level, such as particle spin (Smolin 1997: 276–293), with the relative space-times observers coordinated by gravitational relations which render their observations ultimately consistent with each other.

What are we to make of this proposal? It must be said, to begin with, unlike Tipler, Smolin clearly has a good intuitive sense of what complex organization, life, and intelligence, are all about. Where Tipler theorizes the universe as a vast supercomputer, Smolin, search for a metaphor at the end of his book, chooses the city: an unplanned but highly coordinated system of relationships which constantly generates new possibilities. Indeed, even if Tipler's vision is, in a certain sense, more hopeful, promising resurrection and eternal life to all logically possible systems, one cannot help by feel pulled to choose mortality in a Smolin-universe over immortality at Tipler's Omega.

This said, the theory has two serious difficulties, both of which ultimately derive from Smolin's rejection of metaphysics and his apparent inability to engage in the sort of transcendental abstraction which the discipline requires. The first difficulty has to do with an issue we have already highlighted: the recourse to random variation as an explanation for the emergence and continued evolution of complex organization. This problem is especially serious in the case of Smolin's theory, because unlike the case of random variation in the genome, we know of no mechanism that would lead to such variation in the process of cosmogenesis, taking part as he supposes it does, behind the impenetrable veil of the black hole's event horizon. More broadly, however, Smolin falls into the trap set by neoliberal apologists of the market order such as Hayek, who distinguish only two ways in which organization can emerge: spontaneously, through random variation and natural selection, and through what Hayek (Hayek 1988) calls *taxis*, i.e., through rational centralized planning. Smolin, echoing the neoliberals, points out that planning leads not to complexity understood as variety, but rather to plainness and ugliness. Against the image of jagged coastline or a vibrant city of millions of individuals each pursuing their own agenda while remaining in intimate interaction with each other, Smolin conjures the specter of suburban tract housing and the "great monoliths of Soviet architecture" (Smolin 1997: 162).

In reality, however, this argument depends on a false dichotomy, as well as obvious historical error. There is a third way in which organization emerges: teleologically, in response to the attractive power of a common end which elicits distinct—indeed diverse—but harmonious responses from different centers of activity. This is, in fact, a far more accurate description of the way in which cities work, or even markets: diverse individuals pursuing a common end (survival, prosperity) in different but compatible ways. The fact is, however, that the market does not always lead to the highest level of variety. On the contrary, it was the market which was responsible for those suburban tract houses, not Joe Stalin. Truly beautiful cities—such those of the Anasazi, or those which grew up in medieval Europe—require ordering to some end higher than survival or prosperity, the sort of end which was presented to the people of Chaco by the myth of Thinking Woman or the citizens of Chartres and Köln by the Catholic doctrine of the beatific vision. Room for diverse responses to a common vision, and indeed for diverse visions of the Common Good are essential to this sort of organization, but so too is the conscious leadership of those with new and powerful ideas.

This same error is at the root of the more fundamental problem with Smolin's theory: its lack of economy. Like so many of his fellow physicists, Professor Smolin needs to pay a visit to Master William's Barber Shop for a good shave with Occam's Razor. The offense, of course, is "multiplying beings (in this case universes) unnecessarily." This is not to say that we ought not to greet with joy the possibility that black holes, far from being the endless pits of death and destruction which most physics up to now suggests they are, might actually be cosmic wombs out of which new universes are born. But we thus far have no independent evidence that this is the case, and to posit other universes in order to explain facts about ours which might be explained more simply is simply bad science. The cause of the offense is, as is so often the case, a failure to join Occam's Razor to Mansueto's Switchblade. The simplest or most economic explanation is not always the most reductive.

Behind this mistake, however, is the same error, now enlarged to cosmic scale, which Smolin made at the micro-level in his account of the way in which complex organization emerges. If centralized planning and spontaneous organization are the only options, then "anthropic" approaches to cosmological fine-tuning do indeed lead to something like a design argument. This in turn implies an observer, indeed a sort of cosmic engineer sitting outside the system, something which is abhorrent for logical, physical, and metaphysical reasons. Such a God, by observing and designing and creating, becomes part of the universe and thus cannot fully explain it. But cosmic teleology does not mean divine design. On the contrary, the whole motivation behind Aristotle's doctrine of the unmoved mover is to find some principle which, while outside the system and thus able to explain it, is itself defined in such a way as not to require any further explanation. God understood as a teleological attractor whose Beauty, Truth, Goodness and transcendental Unity draw all things into Being is the only principle which can meet this criterion. Smolin, by contrast, not only leaves the existence of the universe unexplained, but posits many more (an infinity?) which, even if their particular genesis is explained, still depend on a process the origins of which itself remain unaccounted for.

Metaphysics is not some sort physics practiced by a sovereign Newtonian engineer who designs universes the way one might design a watch, an engine, or a computer. It is not simply a matter of formalizing the data of experience and logically manipulating the resulting expressions. Rather, it requires the ability to abstract from structure to Being as such—a thought which does not even seem to have occurred to Smolin.

Smolin's error reflects the hegemony of neoliberalism over the dissident intelligentsia which emerged in the 1960s and 1970s, and which was too concerned with "doing its own thing" to think through the complex problems related to the dual crisis of both the capitalist and socialist systems. This hegemony is not exercised directly, but rather through a sort of soft postmodernism which does not hesitate to criticize the failures of the market (the mall, suburban tract housing) and which defends the independent existence of the material world, but which rejects the possibility of rising above one's own particular perspective to a ground from which might criticize the system as a whole. This "pluralist" postmodernism makes room for the particular interests and subcultural peculiarities of the intelligentsia while rendering them ultimately subservient to Capital.

But Smolin's perspective on his cosmology, as indeed he recognizes, is not the only one. If black holes are the cosmic wombs in which new universes are born, and if most if not all of them are likely to be structured in such a way as to make possible the development of life and intelligence, then ought we not create as many black holes as possible? Smolin is a aware of that his theory might be read in this way, but can offer only counsel that societies which have devoted themselves single-mindedly to an imagined future, such as the Aztecs or Stalinist Russia, have not survived for long. But then they need survive only long enough to lead this world up the steps of the pyramid to the altar of the sacrifice, where, beyond the pluralistic mask of soft postmodernism smirks the face of Tezcatlipoca, waiting to bring it to a violent end and make a new beginning. Might this not be the perspective of the great masses of humanity who are exploited by the global market and do not benefit from even the limited variety it makes possible—and who deprived of any sense of ultimate meaning and value in terms of which they might image a just society, opt for wanton destruction? Ultimately there is nothing that stands in the way of such an interpretation, nor is there any well-defined distinction between pluralist soft-postmodernism and the ontology of violence advocated by Nietzsche and Derrida . . .

The Irreducible Pessimism of Quantum Theoretical Approaches

Reading the work of theorists such as Tipler and Smolin one might get the impression that mathematical physics had, at least jettisoned the pessimism which has dominated since at least the middle of the nineteenth century. But this is not really true. While it is difficult to speak of a consensus regarding such a question in a field in which most researchers continue to be focused on more technical questions, it is clear that Tipler's work has not been well received, and Smolin is very careful to point out that his speculations are motivated in part by a failure to develop a mathematical theory which could win the approval of his colleagues. Indeed, there is every reason to believe that the long-range trend in mathematical physics will tend toward cosmological pessimism.

This pessimistic tendency has recently received new support with the discovery that the long-range history of the universe may well be dominated not by gravity but rather by the cosmological constant. The cosmological constant, we will recall, is a factor introduced by Einstein into his equations in order to compensate for the fact that they seemed to point to a dynamic universe in the process of expansion of contraction. Einstein and others soon discarded this constant, but recent calculations based on observation of supernovae are correct (Hogan, Kirschner, and Suntzeff 1999) the universe may well have a cosmological constant with positive value, meaning that it is not only expanding, but that the rate of expansion is accelerating.

Now an infinitely expanding universe may well seem to bode well for life, at least by comparison with a "big crunch." This is especially true since the same model which points towards accelerated expansion also suggests available matter, energy, and information, may well grow indefinitely. The difficulty, however, as Lawrence Krause and Glenn Starkman (Krause and Starkman 1999) have recently pointed out, is that in a universe which is expanding at an accelerating rate, it becomes increasingly difficult to access these resources.

> As the cosmos grows in size, the average density of ordinary sources of energy declines. Doubling the radius of the universe decreases the density of atoms eight-fold. For light waves, the decline is even more precipitous. Their energy density drops by a factor of 16 because the expansion stretches them and thereby saps their energy.

Krause and Starkman consider a number of strategies for coming to terms with this problem. Relying on gravity to bring resources to us won't work. Even in a universe in which the expansion eventually slows, after 10^{33} years all the matter in the universe becomes bound up in black holes and thus almost certainly inaccessible. In a universe in which expansion continues or accelerates matters are even worse. It may well be that our universe has currently reached the highest level of structure that it will ever achieve and that clusters of galaxies are the largest systems which can be bound gravitationally. Chasing down resources works no better. As the expansion accelerates, ever more resources must be used to maintain the speed necessary to access them, placing a fatal drain on the civilization in question.

Krause and Starkman note that there are certain forms of energy that do not become more dilute with cosmic expansion: namely cosmic strings (if they turn out to exist) and the quantum vacuum. It turns out, however, that if cosmic strings can be cut and leached, as it were, they will eventually disintegrate of their own accord. And the quantum vacuum cannot be mined, because this would require it to drop to a lower energy level. But it is already at the lowest energy level possible.

The apparent limits on the availability of useful resources have suggested to some physicists that the best strategy is to try to do more with less. This is the approach recommended by Freeman Dyson, who has devoted considerable effort to the problem of the long-term survival of life and intelligence (Dyson 1979). Concretely this means lowering our body temperatures, something which in turn presupposes transferring intelligence to something other than our current carbon based bodies. Dyson has shown that if intelligent systems can slow their metabolism as the universe cools, they can consume a finite amount of energy over an infinite period of time. A lower metabolism would mean slower information processing, but it would still be possible to process an infinite number of thoughts and thus enjoy subjective as well as objective immortality.

It turns out, however that there are a number of problems with this scenario. First of all, in order for metabolism to slow body temperature must drop, something which in turn requires the radiation of energy. But the efficiency of even optimal radiators decline as the cube of the temperature, i.e., even faster than the metabolic rate. This means that a point would eventually be reached when organisms would have to stop lowering their temperature and either start to heat up or lower their complexity instead.

Dyson proposed to counter this problem by having his intelligent systems spend most of their time in hibernation, allowing their metabolic rates to drop and permitting them to radiate energy. In effect, by sleeping more and more of the time they would still be able to survive indefinite and process an infinite quantity of information.

But this tactic also fails. Dyson assumed that the temperature of the universe would continue to drop indefinitely, providing a thermodynamic sink for his organisms. But if the universe has a cosmological constant, then there is an absolute floor to the temperature of the universe fixed by the Gibbons-Hawking radiation. Hibernation, furthermore, requires alarm clocks that operate reliably for longer and longer periods of time. But clocks depend ultimately on changes in the position and momentum of particles and the Heisenberg Uncertainty Principle imposes constraints on the accuracy with which both can be specified. Inaccuracies deriving from quantum constraints would thus eventually lead the clocks to fail.

It also turns out that there are fundamental physical limits to the computational process. While certain physical processes, such as Brownian motion and quantum fluctuations can be exploited to create a computer which does not expend a minimum amount of energy per operation, this requires the system to remain in thermal equilibrium with its environment and never to discard any information. If information is discarded, the computation becomes irreversible and irreversible processes by definition involve the dissipation of energy. But as the universe expands and the wavelength of light is stretched out systems have increasing difficulty emitting or absorbing the radiation they need in order to maintain thermal equilibrium with their surroundings. At the same time, with only a finite amount of matter available to them, the inability to discard information means that eventually the systems will begin to think the same thoughts over and over again.

Krause and Starkman acknowledge that their argument is not definitive. Dyson has recently suggested that if life is analog rather than digital, or if organisms it can grow radically in size or use a different sort of memory it may be possible to evade quantum limits on life. Others suggest escaping this universe through wormholes. From our standpoint, however, the whole tone of the debate is more important than the particulars. Even Dyson, the optimist, and for that matter Tipler, feel constrained by the logic of mathematical physics to resort to "extraordinary measures," either cutting back radically on consumption or engaging in a cosmic imperialism in search of new resources. Once cannot help but see this as a reflex of the internal contradictions of the market order, which imposes on Capital ever more extreme measures if it is to survive. Within this context Dyson's strategy of cutting back reflects the austerity of the 1970s and early 1980s when it was thought that the only future of capitalism was one of reduced consumption, hopefully accompanied by a higher "quality of life." Tipler represents the jingoistic capitalist expansionism of the 1980s—the (temporary) resolution of the contradictions of the system by global expansion. Smolin reflects the underlying awareness on the part of the intelligentsia that this system may not survive for ever, but that there is nothing which can be done but ride it out and hope that it gives birth to another with even more favorable parameters. Krause and Starkman remind us that the logic of the system argues against the long-term workability of any of these solutions. Capitalism, unlike other exploitative modes of social organization which simply lead to civilizational collapse, actually threatens permanent global destruction.

Centrist Solutions

Information theoretical neoliberalism is not the only voice, however, in current debates regarding the crisis in mathematical physics. There are, on the contrary, a range of perspectives which have emerged either out of attempts on the part of theorists trained in other disciplines to make sense out of the situation, out of minority views regarding the interpretation of quantum mechanics, or out of theoretical traditions less tied to the market order: relativity, complex systems theory, etc. Broadly speaking these approaches fall into three groups. The first, which is not currently very fashionable, we will call Kantian, because it regards the crisis of mathematical physics as an indication of the irreducible limits to human knowledge. While there are no major contemporary thinkers that I am aware of who argue this position, it represents an important logical alternative and must be assessed. The second position we will call "objective idealism by default." This position is reflected in the work of those who, such as Teilhard de Chardin or many in creation spirituality circles, sense at once the crisis in mathematical physics and the fact that it at once points towards and conceals a profound mystery—the mystery of an ultimately meaningful universe ordered to God. We call this position objective idealist because like Schelling, these theorists implicitly or explicitly regard mathematical physics itself as incapable of resolving its internal crisis and dissolving the mystery. It is objective idealism "by default" because these theorists are largely unaware of the element of mystification they are introducing, often simply as a result of intellectual sloppiness or poor training. Finally, there is a group of perspectives that we will call semi-dialectical, including the work of several important mathematical physicists such as David Bohm, Benjamin Gal-Or, and Ilya Prigogine. These scientists are working hard to develop a real solution to the crisis of mathematical physics and to extract from it an authentic doctrine of cosmohistorical progress.

We call all of these theories "centrist" because like the politically centrist positions they help indirectly to ground, they attempt to significantly ameliorate in a progressive way the contradictions of the system on which they operate, without, however, challenging the under lying structure of that system. We will see that while their work often generates interesting and important insights, it is as incapable of resolving the contradictions of mathematical physics as such centrist political positions as Social democracy and Social Christianity are of resolving the contradictions of the market system.

A Kantian Approach

Were mathematical physicists a bit better informed philosophically they would at the very least find that they have ample guidance available to them in understanding the box they have built for themselves. Kant's philosophy was centered on the task of assimilating the results of the scientific revolution and resolving the apparently irreducible contradictions into which the two main philosophies to which it had given birth (rationalism and empiricism) found themselves by the end of the eighteenth century.

Rationalism was born out of the success of thinkers such as Kepler, Galileo, and Newton in using mathematical formalisms to model physical systems. Mathematics provided for philosophers such as Descartes a model of "clear and distinct" ideas that they sought to emulate, avoiding the dialectical uncertainties that had always characterized the reasoning of medieval scholastics. Thus the attempt to ground epistemology and metaphysics on the basis of analytically self-evidence propositions such as the *cogito*, from which all other truths could then be deduced without reference to sense experience. The result was the development of internally consistent, often highly elaborate systems that, however, had difficulty establishing the reality of anything outside the mind. Descartes, for example, found himself forced to prove the existence of God, using a variant of the ontological proof, before he could prove the existence of the world!

Empiricism, on the other hand, emerged out of the success of the more empirically oriented Baconian sciences. Like the rationalists, the empiricists were impressed with the superior certainty which these new disciplines afford, and borrowed from them their epistemological criterion: that we know only what we can experience by means of the senses. While at first this seemed like a rather commonsensical approach, it soon led to grave difficulties. It turns out, as Hume demonstrated, that we do not actually experience causation, for example, but only the "constant conjunction" of facts and events that seem to be regularly associated with each other. And if the only things we can know exist are those which we experience, does this not mean (as Berkeley suggested) that reality is really immanent to the human mind, or at least to the mind of some Ultimate Observer who guarantees the permanence of things when we are not there to observe them?

Kant proposed to solve these quandaries by suggesting that in addition to the *a priori* analytic arguments favored by the rationalists and the *a posteriori* arguments favored by empiricists, there was a class of synthetic truths that could be known *a priori*. These are truths which we did not know by experience, but rather because they are the condition of any possible experience. Thus, space and time are fundamental forms of the sensuous intuition: we cannot imagine experiencing anything apart from spatial extension and temporal succession. Space and time in turn constitute the basis for geometry and arithmetic respective. Similarly, there are basic categories that the understanding uses to manipulate the data of the senses: quality, quantity, relation, and mode. Apart from these categories we can't really think about anything at all.

The result is that for Kant we see the world only as through a lens, never really getting at things in themselves—a notion that Lukacs (Lukacs 1922/1971) pointed out is a reflex of the market order. The market knows things only in their commodity-form; it cannot calculate regarding use-values. It also imposed strict limits on the use of speculative reason. The traditional arguments for the existence of God were invalid, for example, because they carried the understanding beyond its useful limit: the unification and organization of sense-experience. Similarly, there are certain fundamental physical questions that cannot be resolved because they are not susceptible to empirical test, and reasonable arguments can be advanced for either position. Thus we cannot know if the universe is finite or infinite or if matter is infinitely divisible or not.

Strict Kantianism (as opposed to the sort of Neo-Kantianism which shades into positivism) is unpopular in the physical sciences and in the philosophy of science because most mathematical physicists believe that the relativity and quantum mechanics falsify some of Kant's principal claims. Thus relativity presupposes geometries that are not based on the sensuous intuition of space, but are, in fact, radically counterintuitive. Relativity is taken to have shown that the universe is finite but unbounded and quantum mechanics to have demonstrated that matter is not infinitely divisible. We must remember, however, that relativity and quantum mechanics turn out to be in contradiction with each other. It is thus difficult to hold that they have solved the old Kantian antinomies without simply creating new ones. Indeed, the contradiction between continuous relativistic and discrete quantum formalisms is simply a form of the old Kantian antinomy regarding the infinite divisibility of matter. And many of the contradictions between the cosmological models based on general relativity and observational evidence derive from the assumption of cosmic homogeneity and isotropy, which in turn forces the conclusion that the universe is finite and unbounded.

It should be clear from the larger agenda of this work that I do not ultimately buy the Kantian position. But Kant may well have important lessons for us regarding the limits of what he calls the understanding and what we have called formal abstraction. All abstraction is ultimately dependent on experience, but formal abstraction depends on experience in a special way. It begins as an attempt to model experience in a way that allows us to make predictions. This is why certain Kantian philosophers of mathematics—the so-called intuitionists—have attempted to forbid formalisms that do not permit intuitive (i.e., imaginative) representation, such as those involving actual infinities. Perhaps as we reason mathematically in a way that takes into the realm of the unimaginable, as much mathematical physics does, we simply lose touch with reality. This doesn't mean that we cannot model physical systems, just that our models will always be partial, and internally contradictory and will never yield for us information regarding the ultimate nature of the universe. Where I will differ with Kant is in his conclusion that this makes such knowledge impossible. Rather, I will argue, it merely requires a higher, transcendental abstraction, which alone can takes us beyond the realm of what can be imagined and into the realm of the intelligible as such.

Objective Idealism by Default

There is, of course, another solution to the Kantian antinomies—the solution chosen by Schelling, who largely accepted the Kantian account of the understanding and its limits, but who argued that these limits could be transcended by an intuition (intellectual, aesthetic, religious) which was able to discover the Ground by which the disparate phenomena visible to the senses and related externally by the understanding could be unified and explained. Schelling developed several different systems that deployed this strategy in various ways; it would take us too far afield from our purposes to examine them in detail here. The general trend of his thought, however, was toward the idea that philosophy does not rise to demonstrate the existence of God, but rather presupposes it, as geometry presupposes the idea of space. God is the principle of any complete philosophical system, what makes it capable of unifying human experience.

In his later works Schelling increasingly tended toward the view that the universe itself came about through the self-limitation of God. Nature is nonbeing, that from which god contracts, but which is gradually drawn towards him in varying degrees, in ways manifested by the phenomena of gravity and of life, each of which in their own ways reflect a drive toward unity and completion. Humanity stands in a unique position in this regard, free in relation to both nature and God. When we use this freedom to activate the natural principle rather than subordinating it to God, nature falls and becomes opaque to us. This is the origin of evil. But even in this fallen condition we still seek unity. The state is an expression of this drive, but a radically inadequate one, unable to reconcile freedom and unity. Deprived of its proper force it cannot cope with the reality of evil in a fallen world; allowed to do its job it inevitably tends towards despotism. Redemption requires Revelation, and specifically the Incarnate Word, which mediates between God and humanity as humanity mediates between god and nature. The Church is a response to revelation and humanity's true hope for redemption.

It is not difficult to see why Lukacs and others have seen Schelling largely as an ideologue (albeit a brilliant one) of the Restoration. Schelling's philosophy attempts to mobilize the already significant alienation generated by the emerging market order in order to catalyze a global rejection of reason and to short-circuit the democratic revolution—moves which could not help but benefit his noble patrons. And indeed, after the end of the Restoration Era Schelling fell rapidly into disfavor—though he exercised a profound influence on Kierkegaard, Nietzsche, and through them on existentialism and postmodernism, and provides the real key to understanding the theology of Paul Tillich.

When we are speaking of an "objective idealism by default" among contemporary interpreters of developments in mathematical physics, we are not implying that they have either embraced or somehow reconstituted Schelling's system, or something homologous to it, in its entirety. On the contrary, while Schelling was an open apologist for authoritarianism and reaction, most of the thinkers we will discuss in this section see themselves as critics of authoritarianism in both the state and the church and advocates of a nonhierarchical, creation centered spirituality. What we mean, rather, is that the *method* used by these thinkers is objectively irrationalist, and by concluding to a doctrine of the ultimately meaningfulness of the universe and the existence of God on nonrational grounds they inadvertently reinstitute the ideological dynamic which led Schelling down the path to reaction in the first place. It would taken an entire book to discuss this trend in depth. For now it will suffice to look at a few examples.

The predecessor of this entire trend is, without question, Pierre Teilhard de Chardin, and his work already shows all of its major characteristics. There is, first, an authentic rootedness in the sciences. Teilhard was a paleontologist by training and profession, and had significant scientific achievements to his credit. There is, second, a profound intuition of the underlying unity and meaningfulness of the universe. For Teilhard this is apparent above all in the phenomenon of evolution—the development of increasingly complex forms of organization which, furthermore, because of their superior capacity to relate to each other, tend to draw the universe into an ever higher degree of unity, without, however, compromising the freedom of the individual elements in the system. This intuition is, in a very real sense, rooted in the results of the sciences: the drive towards complexity and organization revealed by evolutionary theory should be apparent to anyone whose objectivity has not already been compromised by the mechanistic ideology of mathematical physics. But it is not really demonstrated rationally on the basis of the sciences. There is no proof, either rational or empirical, that the trend towards the evolution of complexity is in fact the dominant trend in the cosmohistorical process. Third, there is a profound awareness that much "science" seems to weigh against the intuition of a cosmohistorical evolutionary dynamic and that many if not the majority of scientists would argue either that there is no global evolutionary trend or that it is in fact towards destruction and disintegration. For Teilhard this sort of science is represented above all by thermodynamics and by the concern that energy gradually dissipates making organization harder and harder to achieve and maintain. Finally, there is the solution typical to this trend—the suggestion that there is some force or energy not accessible to physics which explains just how it is that complex organization develops and why the universe is ultimately meaning, terminating in an Omega point of perfect unity and freedom, while at the same time evading a direct confrontation with the internal contradictions of mathematical physics. For Teilhard this force is radial or spiritual energy, which unlike tangential or material energy unifies without dissipation (Teilhard 1955/1961).

The End of Mathematical Physics

A more recent example of the same type of thinking is represented by Brian Swimme and Thomas Berry, whose *Universe Story* (Swimme and Berry 1992) is at once a great synthetic achievement and a dangerous example of objective idealism by default. It must be acknowledged to begin with that Swimme and Berry are not attempting science or philosophy; rather they are trying to remedy the failure of modern science to produce something comparable to the great cosmological myths of past civilizations, myths which make sense out of the universe and our place therein. At the same time, they insist that this story be based on mathematical physics and the disciplines to which it has given birth. What they do, in effect, is to tell the story of cosmic evolution according to the standard, big bang cosmology and current thinking regarding the origin and evolution of life, intelligence, and human civilization. And told in this way the story is indeed one of hope and progress—albeit not without struggles and setbacks. Above all they want to call attention to the dangers of the present period, especially the ecological crisis, and to instill in humanity a new respect for the universe which has given birth to us an on which we remain radically dependent.

> There is eventually only one story, the story of the universe. Every form of being is integral with this comprehensive story. Nothing is itself without everything else. Each member of the Earth community has its own proper role within the entire sequence of transformations that have given shape and identify to everything that exists.
>
> Until the present we have not been able to celebrate properly this larger story of the universe, yet this is the high achievement of our scientific inquiry . . .
>
> Without entrancement within this new context of existence it is unlikely that the human community will have the psychic energy needed for the renewal of the earth. (Swimme and Berry 1992: 268)

The difficulty is that in the process of spinning their story, Swimme and Berry gloss over all of the difficult questions, simply assuming answers to questions that have long defied solution by some of the greatest minds of the past two centuries. Consider, for example, this paragraph, near the very end of the book, regarding the degree of cosmological fine-tuning.

> A final integration of the Ecozoic era [the term Swimme and Berry use to describe the emerging era of ecological conscious-

> ness] within the larger pattern of the Universe Story such as we are narrating here has to do with the curvature of space-time. The nature of this curvature is bound up with the energy of the universe's primordial Flaring Forth. Had the curvature been a fraction larger the universe would have immediately collapsed down into a massive black hole; had it been a fraction smaller the universe would have explode into a scattering of lifeless particles. The universe is shaped in its larger dimensions form its earliest instant of emergence. The expansive original energy keeps the universe from collapsing, while the gravitational attraction holds the component parts together and enables the universe to blossom. Thus the curvature of the universe is sufficiently closed to maintain a coherence of its various components an sufficiently open to allow for a continued creativity. (Swimme and Berry 1992: 260)

Swimme and Berry simple *assume* a resolution to the most difficult question of contemporary cosmology: i.e., the question of the ultimate fate of the universe.

The difficulty here is not the vision that is presented—on the contrary it looks, at least in its general outlines, a great deal like what we will propose in the final part of this book—but rather the way in which Swimme and Berry, or for that matter Teilhard de Chardin, arrive at it. Rather than advancing an argument that the (still dominant) mechanistic or pessimistic interpretations of mathematical physics are incorrect, thinkers in this tendency simply counterpoise an intuitive, if admittedly rather convincing, look at the big picture.

> The important thing to appreciate is that the story of the universe as told here is not the story of a mechanistic, essentially meaningless universe but the story of a universe that has from the beginning had its mysterious self-organizing power that, if experienced in an serious manner, must evoke an even greater sense of awe than that of evoked in earlier times at the experience of the dawn breaking over the horizon, the lightning storms crashing over the hills, or the night sounds of the tropical rain forests, for it is out of this story that all of these phenomena have emerged. (Swimme and Berry 1992: 238)

What is the basis of this peculiar combination of irrationalism and a search for meaning and value? Most immediately, of course, the difficulty comes from an inability or an unwillingness to confront the internal contradictions of mathematical physics itself. This is not merely a result of the fact Swimme was trained as a mathematical physicist; most partisans of this trend are trained in theology or other humanistic disciplines. Rather, it is a mark of the enduring ideological power of mathematical physics: to challenge it head on is to risk one's intellectual respectability, so our mythogogues attempt to mobilize it service of an enterprise it cannot ultimately support.

At a deeper level, however, it is the alienation generated by the marketplace which makes it difficult for people to see their way clear to fully rational argument for the ultimate meaningfulness of the universe. Even so, this meaningfulness shines through, and as Swimme and Berry point out, and is in fact entirely accessible to anyone who considers the question in the right way. The result is a contradictory vision in which the antinomies of science are resolve in a higher, nonrational, mythic consciousness.

This sort of thinking has a definite social basis. This basis is, as our reading of Schelling has already suggested, the clergy—or rather those who exercise the priestly office whether or not they hold formally clerical status. It is the proper function of those who exercise the priestly office to lead humanity in its penetration of the authentic mysteries, i.e., those things which actually transcend the capacity of the finite human intellect. As we showed in *Restoring Reason* (Mansueto 2002b) this entails the cultivation of supernatural justice, i.e., in the capacity to order our actions to ends that transcend comprehension. In the cultivation of this virtue the traditional tools of the priest: ritual, pastoral counseling and spiritual direction, community building, etc., are essential. The priest also, of course, plays a role in the cultivation of natural virtue and thus natural wisdom, especially in communities where the religious institution is the principal locus of activity and access to formal education is limited. It is not, however, within the jurisdiction of the priest to mark out the limits of the mysterious and supernatural. On the contrary, this is the task of the prophet, who, by attaining an historically unprecedented degree of supernatural justice, actually discovers new supernatural truths, and the scientist and philosopher who, as human society becomes more complex, presses back the limits of what was hitherto mystery and render it intelligible.

Now there is a tendency for the clergy to see itself as in competition with the scientist and the philosopher, who tend to progressively constrain the sphere of priestly authority, though they ought to understand they can never negate it entirely. This problem has, furthermore, been exacerbated by certain trends in mathematical physics, which have attempted to argue that there is neither meaning nor mystery, and that the priesthood thus has no legitimate function whatsoever. Under these circumstances it is not surprising that priestly circles should generate their own special ideology. Not infrequently such ideologies represent truths which are authentically higher than those of mathematical physics or certain skeptical forms of philosophy, but which are nonetheless susceptible of rational demonstration, *as if* they were the result of some sort of special prophetic insight and thus properly the objects of infused contemplation or its equivalent in the particular tradition. By thus "discovering" new mysteries, the sphere of activity of the priest is expanded.

The danger is that in the process of defending its legitimate rights, the clergy—including even the progressive sectors of the clergy—will end up promoting an irrationalist and authoritarian agenda. Faith can indeed be shown to be a reasonable option and a necessary stage on the path of spiritual development—but only after the existence of an infinite, necessary, and perfect God who is the proper object of this faith has been rationally demonstrated, something which itself depends on a rational demonstration of the ultimate meaningfulness of the universe. To fail to engage these questions, and simply to insist on the mystery is to form humanity intellectually and morally for submission to impenetrable powers beyond their control. And in our society it is the marketplace that is the mysterious and uncontrollable power *par excellence*. In this sense, in spite of the fact that they explicitly advocate respect for ecosystem integrity and the promotion of the fully development of human capacities, thinkers like Teilhard, Swimme, and Berry inadvertently help to legitimate the market order. That the bourgeoisie maintains its hegemony over these sectors is apparent in the fact that while nearly everything they stand for presupposes a break with the market order, they are never explicit about this, their work is utterly innocent of any real class analysis, and they vigorously resist the development of the disciplined forms of political organization necessary to effectively contest the market order.

Semidialectical and Emergentist Approaches

The third "centrist" approach that we need to examine is by far the most progressive. It includes several leading physicists whose work points towards the underlying relationality of the universe and who mount sharp critiques of subjectivist quantum mechanics and information theoretical approaches to unification. At the same time, they fail to transcend an essentially centrist position because they are unable to see the limits of mathematical physics as such. They simultaneously fail to actually unify mathematical physics or to adopt a higher standpoint from which unification would actually be possible. The result is that their work continues to be susceptible to neoliberal or objective idealist interpretations.

Israeli theorist Benjamin Gal-Or is typical of this trend. He brings a "dialectical" understanding of the process of unification, as "a process of criticism wherein lies the path to the principle of all inquiries (Aristotle in Gal-Or 1987: 47)." This dialectic leads Gal-Or to the conclusion that it is necessary to unify theories of reversible and irreversible change first (i.e., dynamics and thermodynamics), before attempting to unify relativity and quantum mechanics (Gal-Or 1987: 29ff, 47–48). He rejects, furthermore, attempts at unification which give a leading role to quantum mechanics and to an information-theoretical understanding of organization. Quantum mechanics and information theory both treat the universe as first and foremost a statistical ensemble. Order and disorder are, in this context, fundamentally subjective concepts, and the expectation of an evolution towards maximum "entropy" or chaos is already given in the statistical underpinnings. Quantum mechanics, furthermore, cannot theorize even this sort of change, since it has an irreducibly reversible understanding of time, and can by made to yield time asymmetries only by imposing unexplained boundary conditions. Because of this, he argues, it must be treated strictly as a local theory describing the particular sorts of interactions it was developed to describe, and not as the matrix for unification (Gal-Or 1987: 47–48, 261–262, 374).

Gal-Or assigns priority instead to general relativity and to the gravitational processes which it describes. It is gravity which drives cosmic expansion and galaxy and star formation, and thus nucleosynthesis, and the emergence of chemistry, life, and intelligence (Gal-Or 1987: 41–46, 154). Once gravity driven phenomena are taken into account, furthermore, it becomes clear that the direction of evolution is not towards chaos, but rather towards even higher degrees of organization, understood as complexity (an increased diversity of elements) coupled with "centreity"— i.e., the closing of these elements in on themselves (Gal-Or 1987: 382). This is an inevitable consequence of the fact that beginning with even a small cosmic anisotropy, gravitational forces will cause matter to clump together into larger and larger systems. It is, furthermore, just precisely these gravitationally driven systems that lead to the formation of stars, planets, atmospheres, and oceans—i.e., to the matrix out of which living and thus intelligent systems emerge.

Gal-Or points out that there are grave doubts about the applicability of the concept of entropy on a cosmological scale. In order to apply entropy to the universe as a whole it is necessary for that it be an additive quantity: i.e., that the entropy of universe as a whole be equal to the sum of the entropies of all the local systems where entropy is observed and where it is at least arguably a meaningful concept. But it is not clear that this is true.

> Since only a finite quantity of information is required to specify (For us) a finite (albeit large) portion of the homogenous and isotropic world accessible to our observations, then, according to D. Layzer, the entropy per volume approaches zero as the volume increases indefinitely beyond the scale of supergalaxies. If such a conclusion is correct (which is far from certain) the very concept of additive entropy fails in describing very large isotropic systems. (Gal-Or 1987: 249)

Whether or not the concept of entropy can be rendered irrelevant for cosmology in this way, Gal-Or suggests that there are ways to retheorize thermodynamics which are free of this fundamentally subjectivist concept which, we will remember, is defined first in terms of our information about a system. Essentially this means a return the originally formulation of thermodynamics in terms of energy, heat and work, and results in a reformulation of the second law as follows: "The free energy of any isolated macroscopic system never increases" (Gal-Or 1987: 252).

The result is a progressivist cosmology centered on a recognition of the ultimate unity and organization of all things—what Gal-Or calls Hayavism, after the Hebrew word for the whole (Gal-Or 1987: 348ff.). Hayavism is, in effect, a radically historicized Spinozism, historicized primarily by incorporation of the insights of Einstein, who Gal-Or sees as the great completer of Spinoza's work (Gal-Or 1987: 400). Hayavism regards the universe as a radically interconnected whole in which each element can be defined or known only in relationship to all others, and in which the principle, though by not means the only, mediating interaction is gravitational. All things, including individuals and societies, struggle to persist in being for as long as they can. Their ability to do this is based largely on their ability to understand and thus control their environment, and thus on the progress of science and technology.

It should be noted that while Gal-Or's vision is hopeful and progressivist, he has no sympathy for the so-called "anthropic cosmology," nor is he really interested in the problem of cosmological fine-tuning.

The strengths of this approach notwithstanding, there are problems. First of all, while Gal-Or's critique of quantum mechanics is powerful, he does not show exactly what we should do with it. It is one thing to relegate it to the status of a special theory and quite another thing to unify that special theory with his larger relativistic and thermodynamic framework. Gal-Or's synthesis, furthermore, is dependent on the larger Big-Bang cosmology, the empirical problems of which he seems unaware, or at least chooses not to address. Gal-Or's understanding of organization, finally, is seriously constrained by his insistence on the priority of physical concepts. While gravity can produce an objective structuring, he does not show how it produces purposefulness, nor does he ever really settle the question of the ultimate purposefulness of the universe, remaining caught, as it were, between Aristotle, to whom he aspires, and Spinoza, with whom he is ultimately more comfortable.

This scientific and philosophical ambiguity is reflected in Gal-Or's politics. Political commentary is interspersed throughout the five hundred pages of his *Cosmology, Physics, and Philosophy* (Gal-Or 1987) but at no point does Gal-Or take a well defined stand *vis-à-vis* either capitalism or socialism. Rather, each come in for both sharp criticism and oblique statements of conditional support. On the one hand, he takes up the position of a defender of the West, and frames his criticisms in the context of this defense. On the other hand, the criticisms are harsh, especially in so far as they reflect on the failure of the West to develop a unified philosophical conception that might provide some larger meaning to its struggle with socialism. He is merciless in his critique of an academy driven by the struggle for state funds and thus subservient to its whims. On the one hand, "the history of dialectical materialism is to a large degree "a story of exaggerations and amusing naiveté's" (Gal-Or 1987: 463). On the other hand, most of the basic principles of dialectical materialism, Gal-Or seems to argue, have solid roots in the Western philosophical tradition, and seem to be supported by solid science. This does not, however, suggest to him, that we ought to take another look at socialism, but only that we must not surrender the basic principles of dialectical materialism to Soviet propaganda!

What is the social basis and political valence of Gal-Or's position? His criticism of big science not withstanding, we must locate him, like the whole rationalist, Einsteinian trend out of which he emerges, as a spokesperson for the state-funded research apparatus, descendant of the absolutist academies, which continues to be such a force in international physics. It is this vantage point outside of and in a certain sense above the marketplace which allows him to develop such cogent critiques of the current state of Western society—and more importantly of the pseudo-scientific ideologies which legitimate that society; it is the dependence of this vantage point on the bourgeois state which keeps him loyal and which prevents him from seeing clearly the limits of the market order and of mathematical physics as such.

This whole situation is summed up poignantly by Gal-Or's continuous references to the work of Karl Popper, whose ideas could not possibly be more different from his own, but whom he nonetheless quotes with respect, and who he constrained to write a Forward, in which Popper rejects Gal-Or's use of the term dialectics, because of its association with Hegel and Marx, rejects his interpretation of various philosophers, and in general rejects the book as a whole, all the while feigning respect and assuring the reader that Professor Gal-Or is undoubtedly correct wherever they disagree. It is precisely this sort of cow-towing to the established authorities of the academy, whose job it is to defend capital against the emergence of an authentically revolutionary intelligentsia, and make the world safe for the bourgeoisie, which undermines clear thinking and prevents even brilliant thinkers like Gal-Or from rising to a Truth which is well within their grasp.

The "semidialectical" approach to unification, holism, and emergent organization from within the physical sciences illustrates especially well how substantive rejection of key aspects of atomism and mechanism can exist side by side with an understanding of "unification" which remains wholly within the old paradigm. I would like to discuss two distinct examples of this approach: the work of David Bohm (Bohm 1980), and that of Ilya Prigogine and his students.

Bohm's starting point is a recognition that both of the great theoretical innovations in physical theory of this century, relativity and quantum mechanics, call into question the atomism which had dominated science since at least the time of Newton. Relativity calls this idea into question because the notion of rigid bodies and point particles implies signals faster than light, which relativity forbids; relativistic theory understands the cosmic order rather in terms of events and processes in a universe which must be regarded as an unbroken whole (Bohm 1980: 123–25). Quantum theory calls atomism into question with its concepts of particle-wave duality and nonlocality (Bohm 1980: 128–29). At the same time, he argues, *both* relativity and quantum mechanics fail to break decisively with atomism, mutually contradictory elements of which they conserve. The concept of signaling which is central to relativity implies an autonomy between events which quantum mechanics forbids; quantum theory, for its part, assumes the autonomy of quantum states prior to observation in a way which contradicts relativity. Behind this contradiction lies the underlying difference between discrete quantum and continuous relativistic orders (Bohm 1980: 136–137).

Bohm proposes to resolve these difficulties with the notion of an underlying implicate order, various aspects of which different theories "revelate" or make explicit, while concealing others, much as quantum measurement reveals position or momentum, but not both (Bohm 1980: 144ff.).

Prigogine, similarly, begins by acknowledging what he regards as the fundamental weakness of what he calls "classical" science, something which for him includes not only Newtonian mechanics and Hamiltonian dynamics, but also relativity and quantum mechanics—its inability to explain change (Stengers and Prigogine 1984: 58–73). This is because, as we have pointed out, all of the formalisms generated by these disciplines are time-reversible: there is no strong past or future. This situation was partly remedied by the development of thermodynamics and the introduction of the arrow of time provided by the second law. But the second law cannot explain the development of complex organization, nor has thermodynamics generally been adequately unified with dynamics, quantum mechanics, etc. It is these tasks which, as we have seen, motivated the work of Ludwig Boltzmann, and which frame the work which Prigogine has undertaken over the course of his long and fruitful career.

Prigogine's early work was centered on the first of these difficulties. he begins by pointing out that while the Boltzmann order principle, which shows that as temperature declines, the entropy term in thermodynamics relations gradually goes to zero, can be used to explain the development of low entropy structures such as crystals, it cannot possibly explain the development of dissipative systems far from equilibrium, and thus cannot account for the development of life. Consider the case which we discussed earlier of a single protein change of 100 amino acids, still far simpler than any real living system. Now the order of the amino acids matters for the functioning of protein chains. The number of permutations necessary to get any given order from an arbitrary starting point assuming that all orders are equally probable is on the scale of 10^{130}. Assuming that permutations occur every 10^{-8} seconds, it would take 10^{122} seconds to generate the protein chain we need. But earth is only 10^{17} seconds old. Spontaneous protein chain formation is thus an inadequate explanation for the origins of life on earth (Prigogine 1977: 23).

The only way to remedy this weakness is to extend thermodynamics far into the nonlinear, nonequilibrium region. In all isolated, closed, and linear systems, fluctuations may, as Boltzmann recognized, lead a system away from equilibrium, but they are invariably damped over time. When interactions become, nonlinear, however, the reverse is true. Far from being damped, fluctuations from equilibrium are reinforced and amplified, leading to the emergence of large scale organization in space and time (Prigogine 1977: 49–61, Prigogine and Stengers 1984: 140–141). Two points are in order here. First, this development is not driven by any thermodynamic potential, but rather depends on the global state of the system as a whole. Second, development of complex organization depends on ongoing exchange of matter and energy with the environment. This sets complex nonlinear systems, such as living organisms, apart from low-entropy structures such as crystals. Crystals form as a result of the properties of the molecules of which they are composed, through electromagnetic attraction and repulsion, and depend on the exchange of energy with the environment (cooling) but not matter. Living organisms, on the other hand, exchange both matter and energy with the environment and their organization is a function of the system as a whole and not simply of the chemical elements of which the body is composed—though these do, to be sure, make possible the chemical interactions on which the large scale interactions depend. While Prigogine has not been able to identify an single, universal law, which predicts when complex organization would emerge, the experimental evidence points strongly to a central role for catalytic loops (Stengers and Prigogine 1984: 144–45).

Prigogine's work has profound importance for understanding how life could have emerged from inorganic matter, as well as for the description of a wide range of inorganic and organic processes which have hitherto seemed at variance with physical theory. The chemical processes which make life possible, for example, involve just precisely the sort of catalytic loops which Prigogine says characterize complex organization generally—though complex inorganic systems tend to depend on simple molecules undergoing complex reactions, while organic systems involve complex molecules, themselves the product of a long evolutionary process, undergoing relatively simpler reactions (Stengers and Prigogine 1984: 1953). Thus DNA governs the formation of proteins, at least some of which then regulate DNA replication. Glycolisis, similarly, depends on a catalytic cycle involving ADP and ATP (Stengers and Prigogine 1984: 153–55). But Prigogine's ideas have applications at larger scale as well. He suggests, for example that there are morphogenetic fields defined by chemical gradients which govern the development of embryos and which at least help to explain why certain genes are activated in some cells, and other genes in others, so that cells containing the same genetic information can differentiate into eye cells, brain cells, stomach cells, etc. (Stengers and Prigogine 1984: 171–72). Even the succession of various populations of organisms, which is described by the logistic equation can be seen as a nonequilibrium system. Let N be the size of the population, r and m respective constants describing the rate of reproduction and of death, and K the carrying capacity of the ecosystem—which may be extended by more effective exploitation. Then

$$\frac{dN}{dT} = rN(K - N) - mN$$

or, in discrete form

$$N_{t+1} = N_t \left(1 + r\left[1 - N_t / K\right]\right)$$

Below r=2, the population approaches equilibrium uniformly. Where 2<r<2.444 the population fluctuates in a two year cycle, where 2.44<r<2.57 the population fluctuates in 4–8 year cycles. Where r > 2.5 the population varies chaotically. Organisms such as rabbits which attempt to survive by maximizing r are said to follow and r-strategy; those which survive by maximizing K by improving methods of exploiting the environment, are said to follow a K strategy. Now, in so far as economics is, in a certain sense, a branch of population biology, this suggests that nonequilibrium thermodynamics may also have something to teach economics. Indeed, in so far as an economy which follows an r strategy is essentially one which exploits people and then throws them away, the whole aim of a progressive economics could be theorized as identifying the conditions for the emergence of highly effective, sustainable new K strategies.

Prigogine's approach has also inspired the first real break with the hegemonic Big-Bang cosmology in several years. Hannes Alfvén and Eric Lerner (Lerner 1991) have argued that the facts of cosmic evolution are most economically explained by a universe infinite in space and time (so that any region, however large, has an environment with which it can exchange matter and energy) over the expanse of which fluctuations. Unlike Gal-Or, Alfven and Lerner argue that the first interactions were electromagnetic—specifically the formation of electromagnetic filaments in the uniform hydrogen plasma that they believe characterized the universe in the remote past. Because plasmas are unstable to fluctuations, these filaments could have emerged spontaneously, and gradually growing and attracting others. There are limits to the development of this sort of structure. As the vortices get larger, their rate of growth slows and they gradually begin to lose energy from synchroton radiation. But long before this becomes a problem, gravitational interactions within the agglomerations of matter created by the electromagnetic vortices take over, leading the formation of large scale structures, such as stars, galaxies, clusters, and superclusters. These gravitational interactions then give birth to nuclear reactions (in the stars), which leads to the formation of complex elements, and makes possible the emergence of chemistry and life. Alfven and Lerner paint a picture of a universe infinite in space and time, with a continuously increasing power density, ranging from 10^{-34} in the electromagnetic filaments which gave birth to complex organization, to 10^{31} in the plasma focusing devices which represent the most advanced human efforts to harness energy. Within the context of such a universe, which provides an infinite source of energy, life and intelligence might develop forever.

Prigogine's second task (Prigogine 1979) is to unify this expanded thermodynamics with dynamic theory using mathematical formalisms similar to those used in quantum mechanics. He does this by treating entropy and time as noncommuting operators, like position and momentum in quantum mechanics. The result is to unify dynamics and thermodynamics without reducing one to the other. The basic idea behind this approach can be illustrated using a something known as the Baker's Transformation. Imagine a square of dough or clay. Take the square and flatten it out into a rectangle and then fold it over to crate a new square. The surface is broken up and redistributed. More formally:

If $0 \leq x < 1/2$ then $(x;y)$—-> $(2x\ 1/2y)$ mod 1

If $1/2 \leq x < 1$ then $(x;y)$—-> $(2x-1;\ 1/2(y+1))$ mod 1

Now an internal operator time T is assigned to each partition or transformation of the system. This time depends on the global topology of the system. The eigenvalues of the system are the times t, which may extend from negative to positive infinity, and the eigenfunctions are the various spatial distributions. Looking into the future and the past of the system we find two Markov chains as the system tends toward equilibrium. This formalism makes possible two complementary descriptions of the system: a thermodynamic description in terms of operator time T or a dynamic description in terms of a well defined local trajectory. Both, however, are not possible at the same time (Prigogine 1979: 173–75, 269–73).

More recently Prigogine has used a similar strategy to introduce irreversibility into quantum mechanics itself, using superoperators which are both noncommuting and nondistributive (Prigogine and Petrosky 1988). While the specifics are quite different, and while Prigogine's approach is more conservative, the basic strategy for unification is not unlike Bohm's.

What are we to make of this approach to unification? It must be said, first of all, that Prigogine's work has gone a long way towards rendering thermodynamics compatible with the fact of evolution, defining rather precisely the conditions under which complex organization can emerge and showing that these are precisely the conditions which living organisms somehow manage to create and maintain. This is not, however, the same thing as *explaining* the emergence of complex organization. Prigogine shows that complex organization can emerge, and under what conditions, but he does not say *why* it emerges. On the contrary, if anything, Prigogine dispenses which the only explanation which has had any really currency among mathematical physics: i.e., that complex organization is the result of random variation leading to the formation of stable structures, something which Prigogine shows is extraordinarily unlikely.

The same is true for Prigogine's efforts to unify thermodynamics, dynamics, and quantum mechanics—and indeed of Bohm's efforts to unify relativity and quantum theory. That Bohm sees something fundamental when he talks about the "undivided" nature of the universe is unquestionable. Similarly, the fact that Prigogine has made critical contributions to our understanding of the universe, and more specifically to the defeat of cosmological pessimism and entropism, can hardly be doubted. Precisely because of these contributions, however, the limitations of their strategies stand out clearly. This is especially true of their basically common strategy for unification, which ultimately seems to have little in the way explanatory power. It replaces a larger number of more specific formalisms with a smaller number of more general ones, and even, in the more radical form advocated by Bohm, develops a metaformalism in which all possible formalisms can be embedded. It describes more with less. But Bohm cannot explain physically the relationship between the continuous and discrete orders "revelated" by relativity and quantum mechanics respectively, nor can he reconcile physically the apparent contradiction between the relativistic prohibition on faster than light signaling and quantum nonlocality. Similarly, Prigogine's formalisms do not really tell us how irreversible change emerges from reversible (in this Gal-Or is superior) nor do they show, contra Tipler, that *reversibility* is an illusion, or to be more precise, an artifact of a certain kind of formal abstraction.

But even at the substantive level there are problems. What *is* matter if it is not particles? Similarly, Prigogine's theory of self-organization is ultimately *descriptive* rather than explanatory. It tells us *how* complex organization is possible, and *how* it emerges, but not *why*. We never advance to a principle which can explain why the universe is, and is as it is, and not otherwise. Similarly, as with Gal-Or, we never get an argument regarding the ultimate meaningfulness of the universe. Clearly this is not because either scientist is hostile to the idea. On the contrary, both are clearly friends of progress, human and cosmic, and make it clear that they would welcome a convincing argument that our labors here are not in vain. Rather, it is a result of the limitations of mathematical physics itself, of the tyranny of the formalism and of what the Thomistic tradition calls formal abstraction, which allows us to grasp the structure or order of a system, without telling us *what* it is, something which depends of what

Aquinas called "total abstraction," or why, which depends on "separation" or what we prefer to call "transcendental abstraction (Aquinas, *In Boethius De Trinitate* Q5,6)." The concepts of essence and of final cause simply have no place within mathematical formalism. And only a scientific strategy which has room for these concepts can generate a complete explanation, telling us *what* things are and *why* as well as *how*, and only a such scientific strategy can approach in an open-ended way the question of the ultimate meaningfulness of the universe.

Mathematical Physics and the Dialectical Tradition

It should be clear from what has been said thus far that there is no way that the contradictions of mathematical physics can be resolved from *within* that discipline, for the simple reason that they are contradictions of formalization as such, and can be resolved only at the higher level of what we have called transcendental abstraction. Precisely to the extent that they accurately model particular physical systems, mathematical formalisms will always remain partial and disconnected from each other. Sophisticated attempts to link these formalisms up to each other result only in generalizations that produce no new knowledge. Indeed, even if mathematical physics were to arrive at a unique final theory, such a theory would only be descriptive and not explanatory.

The position that we are putting forward is not, to be sure, anything new. On the contrary, it was the position of Plato, of Aristotle, and of the medieval commentators and Thomas Aquinas, all of whom regarded mathematics as an art which, while certainly an important and powerful auxiliary to science, could never be the ideal of science itself. It was also the position of Hegel. Thus Plato make a sharp distinction, in establishing the hierarchy of the intellectual disciplines, between *dianoia*, or "thinking," which is proper to mathematics, and *noesis* or "intellection," which characterizes thinking about first principles. Where *dianoia* is forced to take its premises or hypotheses for granted and, using the rules of logic, to draw conclusions from them, *noesis* rises to a first principle which needs no explanation, and from this is able to derive the principles which mathematics takes for granted. Aristotle, similarly, distinguishes between mathematics, which studies only possible beings abstracted from the data of the senses, and both physics and metaphysics, which study real being—

the first material, the second immaterial. This same approach characterizes Thomas and the medieval commentators.

This hierarchization of the intellectual disciplines was, however, effectively overturned by the victory of mathematical physics in the struggles of the sixteenth and seventeenth centuries, when it was able to use its superior ability to account for new experimental evidence, and its superior adaptation to the ideological imperatives of the emerging market order, to displace Aristotelian science and undermine the leading role of dialectical metaphysics. As we have seen, those who continued to press the claims of Aristotelian science in the years following the publication of Newton's *Principia* were often throw-backs and dogmatists in the worst sense of the word. Nor can there be any real doubt about their own ideological function as apologists for a papacy in rapid decline.

Since that time, partisans of the *via dialectica*—both the older Platonic and Aristotelian dialectics, and the new historical dialectics advocated by Marx and Hegel—have followed one of two alternative strategies. The first of these strategies was charted by Kant. What it does, in effect, is to sign over the natural world to mathematical physics and its allied disciplines, while claiming for dialectics, or something like it, the newly discovered territory of *praxis*, of human history and human action. For some—and not only for Kantians—this choice has been principled, founded on the conviction that it is only the fundamentally intentional and rational character of human action which makes dialectical approaches appropriate in the social-historical sphere. Nature, as a realm of only external relations, cannot be approached in this manner. This is the position Lukacs and most so-called "Western Marxists," for whom Engels' *Dialectics of Nature* has always been an embarrassment. To be respectable, after all, one must respect the hegemony of mathematical physics in its own sphere. It is also the position of the Kantians within the "Thomist" camp, i.e., the so called "Transcendental Thomists," such as Rahner and Lonergan.

The same conclusion is reached by somewhat different means a second group of Thomists, the so called Historical or Gilsonian Thomists. Explicit discussion of the question within this school has been limited to a few scattered remarks to the effect that "science is best left to the scientists," but there is an underlying metaphysical and even theological reason why this school has been willing to jettison Aristotelian science and has shown so little interest in reviving anything like a philosophy of nature. For Gilson and his school Thomas was not merely an Aristotelian, or even the greatest of the Aristotelians. Rather he stands alone as the only thinker in the history of philosophy to grasp the concept of Being as such, which other philosophers confused with substance, essence, etc. This metaphysical achievement is, furthermore, rooted in the Christian doctrine of God as Creator *ex nihilo*. Aristotelian science, with its teleological research program, which terminates in an ascent to God as final cause, as first unmoved mover, merely distracts from the distinctiveness of Thomistic metaphysics.

This is not the place to enter into intra-Thomist disputes. Suffice it to say, however, that while Gilson is quite correct to point out the superiority of Thomas' doctrine of Being, this doctrine should by no means be pitted against the larger teleological strategy of the Aristotelian problematic. It is precisely the transcendental properties of Being—understood as the Beautiful, the True, the Good, and the One—which explain how it creates: i.e., by teleological attraction. The effect of the Gilsonian maneuver is to substitute for an intrinsically meaningful teleologically ordered universe one structured by divine decree, and to reinstate on a superficially Thomistic metaphysics most of Augustinian theology and spirituality.

Regardless of the specific argument by which dialecticians of a particular school arrive at it, the decision to let mathematical physics stand as the only theory of physical and biological organization has a definite social basis and a definite political valence. The key to this problem is to be found in the fact that this solution has been almost entirely hegemonic among dialecticians in Europe and North America, while the "dialectics of nature" found at least a modest constituency in the old Soviet bloc, and in socialist countries of the Third World. The unassailable hegemony of mathematical physics is a reflex of the apparently unassailable political hegemony of the bourgeoisie, which, whatever the gains the working classes might make in securing economic concessions, continues to occupy the commanding heights of state power and cultural control. The position of the bourgeoisie and the weight of the market order is, furthermore, felt as a kind of natural necessity, like that described in the laws of mathematical physics, inexorable but with out reason, inalterable but ultimately without explanation. The insistence on a dialectics of *praxis* and of human history, by comparison, ultimately amounts to little more than an existential protest, the bitter cry of an oppressed creature (the intellectual) confronting an alien universe (i.e., the market order), against which he is, however, ultimately unable to mount an effective challenge. That the standpoint of this dialectics may be put forward as the standpoint of the proletariat, and of totality, just marks the desperateness of the cry ...

The second strategy is that of the philosophy or dialectics of nature. It is the strategy put forward by Hegel, though it has been implemented by Thomists and Marxists as well. Speaking of the empirical sciences Hegel writes:

> In its own field this knowledge may at first give satisfaction; but in two ways it falls short. In the first place there is another realm of objects that it does not embrace—freedom, spirit, and God ...
>
> In the second place in point of *form* the subjective reason requires further satisfaction; this form is in general, necessity. The method of empirical science exhibits two defects. The first is that the universal contained in it—the genus, etc.—is, on its own account, indeterminate, external and accidental to the other; and it is the same with the particulars that are brought in to union: each is external and accidental to the others. The second defect is that the beginnings are in every case data and postulates, neither accounted for nor deduced. In both these points the form of necessity fails to get its due. Hence meta-thinking, whenever it sets itself to remedy these defects, becomes speculative thinking, strictly philosophical thinking. (Hegel, *Encyclopaedia of the Philosophical Sciences* 8)

Hegel's solution is to supplement the empirical sciences with a *Philosophy of Nature* which derives their categories from the Concept itself and which shows them to be part of its logically necessary unfolding. This philosophy of nature must

> be in agreement with our empirical knowledge of Nature, but the *origin* and *formation* of the Philosophy of Nature presupposes and is conditioned by empirical physics. However, the course of a science's origin and the preliminaries of its construction are one thing, while the science itself is another. In the latter, the former can no longer appear as the foundation of the science; here the foundation must be necessity of the Notion. (Hegel, *Encyclopaedia of the Philosophical Sciences*, 245 Remark)

There are, to be sure, significant differences among the various philosophers who have chosen this strategy. Hegel by far makes the strongest claims for the philosophy of nature. Dialectical materialism and Traditional or Dominican Thomism, the other two schools which have favored this approach, are more moderate by comparison. For Maritain and other Traditional Thomists, the philosophy of nature and mathematical physics should exist side by side, as they did in the middle ages. Mathematical physics represents a continuation of the *scientiae mediae* of that epoch, which used mathematical methods to describe physical systems, while the philosophy of nature represents an extension of the old Aristotelian physics. Unlike Hegel, Maritain makes no claims to derive the results of mathematical physics from some prior logical concept, nor does he actually continue to uphold anything like the whole system of Aristotelian physics, which is, after all, no longer tenable in anything like its original form. Indeed, he even denies that his philosophy of nature represents an exercise of the *separatio*, the traditional Thomistic term for what we have called transcendental abstraction. Rather, he suggests, it is an exercise of the *abstractio totius*, a type of formal abstraction that focuses not on the quantitative determinations of a system, but rather on what it is. This is, in effect, the sort of abstraction pursued by traditional natural history, and it is still common in the biological and social sciences. Such a philosophy of nature gives us a picture of the universe as a whole, as well as of its particular systems, and thus helps prepare us for the ascent to first principles. But it cannot be said to play anything like the role that Aristotelian physics played in the original Thomism of Thomas himself.

More modest still, from the point of view of its methodological claims, is Engels' *Dialectics of Nature*. Engels in fact denies that he is doing anything like Hegelian philosophy of nature. On the contrary, he insists that his

> recapitulation of mathematics and the natural sciences was undertaken in order to confirm to myself in detail—of which in general I was not in doubt—that amid the welter of innumerable changes taking place in nature, the same dialectical laws of motion are in operation as those which in history govern the apparent fortuitousness of events; the same laws as those which similarly form the thread running through the history of the development of human though and gradually rise to consciousness in the minds of man; the laws which Hegel first developed in all-embracing but mystical form, and which we made it our aim to strip of this mystic form and bring clearly before the mind in their complete simplicity and universality. It went without saying that the old natural philosophy—in spite of its real value and the many fruitful seeds it contains—was unable to satisfy us. (Engels 1878/1939)

The dialectics of nature, in other words, is simply natural science pure and simple, just as historical materialism, the application of the dialectical method to the study of human history and society, is social science. The old philosophy of nature, Engels claims, stands in the same relationship to the "dialectical natural science" as utopian socialism does to scientific.

We cannot, however, simply let Engels claims stand as an accurate account of either his method or his intent. The dialectics of nature is not, first of all, simply natural science; it is a discourse about the results of the natural sciences which attempts to demonstrate certain general theses regarding the laws which govern motion or change in general. In this sense, it is more like a philosophy of nature than it is like a natural science. Second, anyone who has read the introduction to the *Dialectics of Nature* cannot help but be recognize that Engels is concerned about more here than the applicability of dialectical principles to the natural world. The governing question of the opening passages of this book is nothing other than the question which governs this work: the ultimate meaningfulness of the universe, something which, for Engels, given his materialist orientation, is essentially convertible with the question of the long-term survival of life and intelligence. After a long passage in which he charts the evolution of matter towards ever higher levels of organization, culminating ultimately in communism, he runs up against the limits fixed for him by bourgeois science.

> Millions of years may elapse, hundreds of thousands of generations be born and die, but inexorably the time will come when the declining warmth of the sun will no longer suffice to melt the ice thrusting itself forward from the poles; when the human race, crowding more and more about the equator, will finally no longer find even there enough heat for life; when gradually even the last trace of organic life will vanish; and the earth, an extinct frozen glob like the moon, will circle in deepest darkness and in an ever narrower orbit about the equally extinct sun, and at last fall into it. Other planets will have preceded it and others will follow it; instead of the birth warm solar system with its harmonious arrangement of members, only a cold, dead sphere will still pursue its lonely path through universal space. And what will happen to our solar system will happen sooner or later to all other systems of our island universe; it will happen to all the other innumerable island universes, even to those the light of which will never reach the earth while there is a living human eye to receive it. (Engels 1880/1940: 20)

The End of Mathematical Physics

But then he pulls back from this somber conclusion and asserts that since matter **is** the drive towards organization, the entropic death of the universe will be followed with equal necessity by a rebirth, in a kind of eternal cycle.

> But however often and however relentlessly, this cycle is completed in time and space; however many millions of suns and earths may arise and pass away, however long it may last before in one solar system and only on *one* planet, the conditions for organic life develop; however innumerable the organic beings too, that have to arise and to pass away before animals with a brain capable of thought are developed from their midst, and for a short span of time find conditions suitable for life, only to be exterminated later without mercy—we have the certainty that matter remains eternally the same in all its transformations, that none of its attributes can ever be lost, and therefore, also, that with the same iron necessity that it will exterminate on earth its highest creation, the thinking mind, it must somewhere else and at another time again produce it. (Engels 1880/1940: 21, 25)

That mathematical physics, which was just coming to terms with the implications of the Second Law of Thermodynamics, could provide Engels with no more hope than this, more so than Marx's sociological critique of religion, is what ultimately committed dialectical materialism to an atheistic position, with all of the attendant difficulties.

The ambiguity inherent in Engels' position, claiming on the one hand to reject the philosophy of nature and to being nothing more than simply pointing out the essentially dialectical character of actually existing natural science, while on the other hand elaborating a metascientific discourse which understood the results of the sciences in a way very different from that put forward by most practicing sciences and which engaged what amount to properly metaphysical questions, was reflected in the later development of Soviet thinking on the natural sciences. Already before the revolution two distinct trends had developed: what would eventually become the "mechanistic" trend associated with Alexandr Bogdanov (though Bogdanov's ideas were, in fact, more complex than that of the other mechanists) and a "dialectical" trend associated with A. M. Deborin. Lenin himself, and later Stalin, sought a path between these two extremes, though it is by no means entirely clear that either actually succeed.

The "mechanist" trend was profoundly influenced by the ideas of the positivistic physicist and philosopher Ernst Mach. Mach argued that our ideas are merely economical ways of organizing our sense experience, and that no real, extramental existence should be attributed to even the ideas developed by scientists. Thus, he argued, there is no such thing as the atom; it is just that the idea of the atom turns out to be the most economical way to organize the data we have gathered regarding the structure of matter.

In the hands of Russian Marxists Mach's ideas played a dual role. On the one hand, they strengthened the impulse already present in the writings of Marx and Engels to see Marxism not as a new philosophical position, but as something that transcends and displaces philosophy. Specifically, what Marx had done was to extend the scientific revolution to the terrain of the social sciences. Indeed, many mechanists advanced what amounted to a Neo-Comtean history of ideologies, in which religion was the tool of the feudal landed elites, philosophy of the bourgeoisie, and science of the proletariat. At the same time, partly because of the mechanists' idolatry of mathematical physics, and partly because of their concern to find ever more economical ideas, there was a tendency to try to purge Marxism of its philosophical, and especially its Hegelian residues. Thus, where Marx regarded human history as the result of a dialectical interaction between the technological development (the forces of production) and economic structure (relations of production) Bogdanov argued that it reflected a drive towards ever higher degrees of organization—the notion of organization providing a more general context under which both technology (the organization of physical and biological matter) and economics, politics, and culture (organizing people) could be subsumed. Eventually this led to the transformation of Marxist social science into a kind of systems theory dedicated to maximizing technological development and social stability, and freed from "dialectical" categories that have no empirical referent.

This account of the history of mechanism, however, misses the internal tensions and drama which characterized the development of the tendency. Throughout the early period of Soviet history, it was the mechanists who were most concerned to advance the cause of militant atheism, and the mechanists attacked their "dialectical" adversaries as conciliators of religion. It was the mechanists, far more than Lenin, who shaped the official culture of Soviet atheism. But their great thinker,

Bogdanov, can hardly be regarded as a simple-minded atheist. Bogdanov was Lenin's only significant challenger for leadership of the Bolshevik faction during its early years, and an important thinker who developed a comprehensive vision with significant strategic implications. While he rejected philosophy, Bogdanov argued for the creation of a universal science of organization that would unify the special sciences and demonstrate the underlying material unity of the world. The result, which he called *Tektology* (Bogdanov 1928/1980), presented the universe as a complex, integrated system that develops towards ever-higher degrees of organization. Indeed, being itself is just another term for organization. The passage from capitalism to socialism was just another stage in this process. As such, he argued, it required the new ruling class, the proletariat, to develop its organizing capacity to the point that it was actually better able than the bourgeoisie to lead human society. Strategically this meant that unlike Lenin, who favored an appeal to workers and peasants on the basis of concrete transitional demands (bread, land, peace) which were accessible to the politically undeveloped but which the bourgeoisie could not meet under the concrete historical circumstances of Tsarist Russia, Bogdanov stressed the importance of in-depth political education. He was, furthermore, joined in this view by a group known as the "god-builders" because of their view that the cosmohistorical organizing process theorized by Bogdanov terminated in the creation of a perfect, infinite form of organization convertible with God. It should come as no surprise that Lenin denounced Bogdanov not so much for mechanism as for subjective idealism and conciliation with religion (albeit of a different kind that that of the dialecticians).

The "dialectical" tendency in Soviet Marxism stressed, against the mechanists, the Hegelian heritage of Marx and the enduring need for a distinct Marxist philosophy separate from the special sciences. Deborin, the leading dialectician, was a metal worker and a student of Plekhanov's who flirted briefly with Bolshevism but was drawn into the Menshevik fold by his mentor. He criticized Machism as the basis for Bolshevik voluntarism. After the revolution, his Menshevik history notwithstanding, he gained effective control over the philosophy section of the Institute of Red Professors and played the leading role in official Soviet philosophy until at least the "turn" of 1929.

What is interesting, however, is that Deborin in fact arrives at positions which sound suspiciously like Bogdanov's. Philosophy for Deborin is the "search for the universal connection of everything to everything" (in Joravsky 1961: 174). Like Bogdanov, Deborin rejected the simple-minded, atomistic understanding of matter promoted by some of the lesser mechanists. "Matter is the whole, infinite, connected aggregate of mediations," i.e., relationships, and the concrete scientific disciplines such as mathematics, physics, chemistry, biology, etc. deal with various forms and stages of the mediations of this same matter. Atoms are mere nodal points in this complex of inter-relationships. While higher levels of organizations emerge from lower, they cannot be reduced to them. Dialectics is the highest science, the universal ontology developed by Hegel but enriched enormously by the political experience of the working classes. In this sense, Deborin argues, philosophy must lead the natural sciences (Joravsky 1961: 174–76).

But the story becomes more complicated still. Deborin's position was dominant throughout the 1920s when the struggle against the party's left "Trotskyite" wing was in full force. After the left turn at the end of the 1920s, however, one of Deborin's leading students, M. B. Mitin, turned on him and charged him with separating theory from practice and conciliating religion. The result was Deborin's removal and the articulation of what became orthodox Soviet "diamat," which was essentially Deborin's "dialectics" reigned in by a more mechanistic conception of matter. The Communist Academy and Institute of Red Professors, which had been Deborin's political base—but where Bogdanov had also worked before his death in 1928—were closed and folded into the Academy of Sciences as part of its Institute of Philosophy. Leadership in philosophy was transferred to the Central Committee of the Communist Party.

The question of the social basis and political valence of each of these trends is extraordinarily complex. Throughout the course of the various struggles, the lines of political faction and philosophical trend seemed to cut across each other. Thus both Trotsky and Bukharin, arch-enemies during the struggles of the 1920s, held profoundly mechanistic views in philosophy. While Bogdanov began as a leftist, by the 1920s he was a firm advocate of moderation, as was, presumably, Deborin, who could not possibly have held the positions of leadership he occupied had he been, for example, a closet Trotskyite.

Notwithstanding this complex situation, the official verdict of the party was that mechanism had been an ideology of the right wing of the party, and had its social base among the *kulaks*, the rich peasants Stalin was bent on liquidating at the end of the 1920s, while Deborinism was a "Menshvizing idealism" which had its base among the ruined urban petty bourgeoisie and which provided ideological legitimation for the Trotskyite left. These conclusions are, perhaps, a bit less unfounded than they might seem at first. The mechanist position did, at least in its mature form, tend towards the transformation of Marxism into a systems theory which left little room for continuing the class struggle under socialism, and which, rather, like the Bukharinist right, counseled moderation and a focus on gradual, stable, economic and social development. Certainly the *kulaks* would have benefited from such a policy, though it is not at all clear they would have been the only ones. The dialectical trend, on the other hand, precisely because it did give a central place to the principle of contradiction, certainly could have provided a theoretical rationale for a more leftist orientation, while its emphasis on the leading role of philosophy might certainly have flattered the intelligentsia who Stalin counted among the "ruined urban petty bourgeoisie.

The real key to the social basis and political valence of the various tendencies in dialectical materialism lies not in the complex interactions of various peasant and petty bourgeois groups with the revolutionary process in Russia, but rather, on the one hand, in the inability of Marxism to actually transcend mathematical physics, and, on the other hand, on the emergence of the Soviet party apparatus as an independent social power which was threatened by the autonomy of the Communist Academy. Let us look at each of the factors in turn.

The truth is that neither Engels himself, nor his mechanistic and dialectical interpreters, ever really came to terms with the fact that mathematical physics paints a picture of the universe that is hardly favorable to the socialist project. The mechanist trend effectively subordinates socialism to the authority of the special sciences, so that in the end it is transformed into nothing more than a positivistic systems theory—or else, in the case of Bogdanov, makes the special sciences say something which they don't. The dialectical trend, on the other hand, as Mitin correctly pointed out, rapidly becomes cut off from the special sciences and ends up elaborating speculative philosophy of nature which is remote from empirical research. The inability of dialectical materialism to come to terms with mathematical physics is simply one dimension of the larger failure of socialism to come to terms with the market order, which it only partly transcended, overcoming the market in capital, but not the markets in labor power, goods, or services. Mathematical physics, as we have seen, forms an integral part of the ideological apparatus of the market order and one of the principal means of ideological hegemony of the bourgeoisie. Not to transcend mathematical physics is not to transcend capitalism itself.

At the same time, the socialist revolution witnesses the emergence of a new power—the revolutionary party. The reason both mechanism and dialectics had to be rejected by the party was the fact that they tended towards the creation of independent centers of authority which challenged the party's leading role in society. For the mechanists this center was in the special sciences. Letting loose this trend would have meant a turn towards technocratic leadership—a path which was in fact followed under Khrushchev and Gorbachev, with results which are now plain for all to see. For the dialecticians, this center was in philosophy. It is not at all clear where the hegemony of this trend would have led, nor is it clear that it would have been a bad thing.

What *is* clear is the fact that none of the dominant approaches to the relationship between dialectics and the physical and biological sciences are really adequate. This is because none of them actually transcend mathematical physics—they either subordinate themselves to it or leave it to one side and elaborate a philosophy of nature which is undoubtedly true in its general principles but which lacks credibility because it is not really engaged with reality and does not really produce any new knowledge. In this sense, at least, Engels' critique of the philosophy of nature is quite apt, and might be applied to the work of Deborin as well as that of Hegel.

What is required is an authentic extension of the work of Marx into the physical and biological sciences. Such a project has two stages: a critique of mathematical physics on the model of Marx's critique of political economy, and the development of a new dialectical science of physical and biological organization to complement Marx's science of human society. We have already largely completed the first stage of this project; it merely remains for us to show how Marx's critique of political economy is really just a special case of our critique of mathematical physics. In the final part of this book we will go on to outline the research program for a new dialectical science. In the process we will see that situating dialectical sociology in the context of a dialectical physics and biology alters some of its key concepts. We will also see that the resulting science grounds in a new way our ascent to first principles and thus opens up the possibility of providing what dialectical materialism lacked: an adequate metaphysical basis for its ethical imperatives.

THE CRITIQUE OF MATHEMATICAL PHYSICS

We have already seen, in he last chapter that mathematical physics is in itself in large measure a reflex of the emerging market economy; we have also seen that political economy, which is the market's own spontaneous self-understanding, not only tracks but often anticipates developments in mathematical physics. It should thus come as no surprise therefore if our critique of mathematical physics should turn out to be a generalization of Marx's earlier critique of political economy. In order to demonstrate our thesis rigorously, however, we need first to review briefly the main features of his argument regarding classical political economy. Scott Meikle's book, *Essentialism in the Thought of Karl Marx* (Meikle 1985) is particularly helpful in this regard. Meikle points out that many contemporary Marxists tend to focus on Marx's critique of the ahistorical character of classical political economy. Bourgeois economics analyzes the way in which the market works, they point out, but not how it came into being. This tendency, it might be added, is especially prominent among Third World Marxists and dependency and world systems theorists who reflect the interests of the national bourgeoisies or would be national bourgeoisies of the periphery, who (quite understandably) resent their position in the world market and are anxious to point out the history of conquest and exploitation on which the market system was built. It is also prominent among Leninists for whom dialectics means above all the principle of contradiction, and who counterpoise dialectics not to atomist empiricism or analytic rationalism but rather to "metaphysics." Marx himself, however, makes the distinction quite differently. The ahistorical character of classical political economy is a problem because it serves to obscure the real nature or inner essence of its object, i.e., the commodity, contenting itself instead with a description of the external relations between them. Marx's critique of political economy penetrated to the inner essence of the commodity. Bourgeois political economy, with its mathematical formalisms for determining price, etc., is a "necessary precondition for a genetic presentation" (Marx 1971: 500), but it leaves its categories themselves (commodity, money, capital, price, profit, etc.) unexplained.

> Classical political economy seeks to reduce the fixed and mutually alien forms of wealth to their inner unity by means of analysis and to strip away the form in which they exist independently alongside one another . . . it is not interested in elaborating how the various forms came into being, but seeks to reduce them to their unity by means of analysis, because it starts with them as given premises. (Marx 1971: 500)

This limitation he attributes to what he calls its "analytic method" (Marx 1963: 500). Bourgeois political economy takes its categories as given and then analyses their properties, reducing them ultimately to mathematical formalisms. The task of Marx's "critique of political economy" is to look behind these categories to the principle which alone can explain them:

> Now, however, we have to perform a task never even attempted by bourgeois economics. That is, we have to show the origin of this money-form, we have to trace the development of the expression of value contained in the value-relation of commodities from its simplest, almost imperceptible outline to the dazzling money-form. When this has been done, the mystery of money will immediately disappear. (Marx 1867/1976: 139)

Marx finds this principle in labor-power, which is the source of all value, and in terms of which alone the capitalist economy can be explained. What Marx does is to demonstrate that the underlying creative power of human labor, exercised in the context of a market order, manifests itself in the form of the commodity. From here the external relationships between commodities, which are crystallized in the form of the price, follow necessarily.

It should be noted that what Marx is doing here is nothing other than to ascend dialectically, i.e., by means of a critique of the internal contradictions and limitations of the existing ideas of political economy, to the first principle (labor) which governs a particular genus of systems—i.e., human economic systems. He is, in other words, laying the foundations of an Aristotelian deductive science of political economy. For once we have the conceptual key, it becomes possible to unlock the mystery. Marx himself, to be sure, laid only the foundation for this discipline, and certain of his specific conclusions may well have been wrong, but the explanatory power of Marx's economic theories, in spite of their less sophisticated mathematical apparatus is nothing short of extraordinary.

We should also note that Marx's achievement remains within the sphere of science; it does not advance to the level of properly metaphysical (or any other) wisdom. This is because he rises only to the first principle of a particular genus, i.e., human economic systems, and not to the first principle of all things. This may seem obvious, but failure to recognize this point may lead to the generalization of Marx's theory into an ersatz metaphysics that leads to serious error. Indeed, this is almost inevitable, since all intellectual disciplines require an implicit or explicit metaphysics and thus generate one even if they reject the possibility of metaphysical knowledge in principle. Among Marxists this has, generally speaking, happened in two ways. Those who reject the dialectics of nature simply take the first principle of economic systems, which Marx discovered, i.e., labor or the proletariat, and treat it as if it were the first principle of all things. This, fundamentally, is Lukacs' error, when he infers from the superior epistemological standpoint of the proletariat that this standpoint is in fact that of "totality," i.e., of God, and that the proletariat itself is the unique subject-object of human history. Similar errors are common among other European and North American Marxists, who substitute libidinous play (Marcuse) or communication (Habermas) for labor power in the position of first principle.

But this error is also committed by those who, in the tradition of Engels and Soviet Marxism, uphold the dialectics of nature. Here, the tendency is to abstract from Marx's historical dialectics certain general principles, such as Engels' famous three laws of the dialectic, verify their applicability to other sorts of systems (physical, biological) and then treat them as if they were in fact the first principle of all things. This is a bit ironic, given the fact that Engels' own designation for principles such as his three laws of the dialectic—i.e., general laws of the motion of matter—is far more apt and quite distinct from anything like a transcendental first principle. Indeed, a law of motion is a truth of what the Thomists would have called formal abstraction and Hegel the understanding. It tells us how something changes, not why. This error becomes especially problematic when one law is singled out and given prominence over all of the others. Thus a narrow focus on the spontaneous transformation of quantitative into qualitative changes, characteristic of the late Engels and of Social Democracy, leads at the strategic level, to reformism, while undue focus on the principle of contradiction characteristic of Leninism, leads to the notion that all progress comes out of struggle and violence and can quickly transform Marxism into a species of Nietzschean nihilism. I may perhaps be indulged a bias towards those who privilege the third law, which holds that all contradictions and struggles lead to a higher synthesis, for they at least highlight the teleological element in Marxism. But it is in terms of the *telos* itself, and not the teleological tendencies of particular systems, that a metaphysics must be constructed, science unified, and action ordered. Narrow focus on the third law, characteristic of both Bogdanov and Deborin, can also lead to strategic errors—specifically a tendency to ignore the importance of underlying technological development or political struggle in effecting social progress.

An authentic dialectical metaphysics presupposes a dialectical science, which Marx only began to build with his work in the vitally important but limited area of political economy.

We need now to show that our own critique of mathematical physics in fact builds on and extends Marx's critique. In order to do this it is not really necessary to do anything more than to summarize what we have demonstrated in this section of the book. We have shown, first of all that mathematical physics, like classical political economy, stops short at describing the external relations between phenomena, and does not actually explain them, something which require penetrating first to their inner essence or underlying structure and then concluding to the ground or cause of that structure. Second, we have shown that the formal objects of mathematical physics and of political economy are *formally* identical. Mathematical physics studies the motion of point particles with mass and/or other qualitative determinations in a real space-time; political economy studies the motion of commodities in the abstract space of the market. Indeed, we have shown that, on the one hand, the basic concepts of mathematical physics emerge as a reflex of the market order. They then determine the development of the other intellectual disciplines, serving as a model for the development of "sciences" of both specific types of physical systems (electromagnetic, chemical, nuclear) as well as biological and social systems.

Our single, remaining task is to advance to the underlying principle which lies behind the phenomena studied by mathematical physics—the principle which plays the same role in physics and biology as human labor plays in economics. Here, however, we must confess that our enterprise differs a bit from Marx's. Where Marx elaborated a critique of only one discipline, we have elaborated a critique of several, albeit formally identical disciplines. Even within physics itself, we have seen that dynamic and thermodynamics have different formal objects.

Our analysis has not, however, for all this, left us without clues. The burning question facing physics in the present period, the answer to which many physicists seem to believe, and with good reason, would resolve the problem of unification, is that of cosmological fine tuning. Any credible answer to this question would simultaneously explain why it is that the fundamental physical laws and constants are as they are, allowing, depending on the sort of principle proposed, a mathematical or some other deductive derivation. And what cosmological fine tuning means is that physical systems are structured in just such a way as to make possible the development of complex organization, life, and intelligence. Physics then, would seem to be the study of systems which are structured in such a way that, without themselves being organized, they make organization[4] possible. This understanding of the proper formal object of physics is remarkably coherent with the self-understanding of physics as a science of matter, provided we understand matter in the Aristotelian sense, as the potential for form or organization.

What about the relationship between physics, biology, and the social sciences? Living systems are, by comparison, those which are actually organized: i.e., those in which the relationships among the elements of the system are structured to serve some end or purpose, generally the reproduction of the system itself. Now, let us join this with Marx's insight that the underlying principle of human societies is labor. What is labor but the capacity to organize? If physics studies the conditions of possibility of organization, and biology actual organization, then sociology studies the development of human organizing capacities.

Does this mean that we have returned, by means of a circuitous route, to Bogdanov's *Tektology*? Not really. Bogdanov must, to be sure, be credited with discovering the unifying power of the concept of organization. But his theory was insufficiently differentiated, failing to distinguish between potential organization, actual organization, and organizing capacity. The most serious defect of Bogdanov's theory, however, is his rejection of dialectics in favor of a positivistic epistemology and metaphysics, which takes him further from, rather than closer to, an authentic

---

4. Organization, we will recall, involves a) system, i.e., radical, internal relatedness of the elements, b) some sort of order or structure, i.e., the determination of the relations among the elements by a general rule, and c) ordering to a purpose or end.

teleological principle. While the sciences themselves may be unified under the category of organization, or rather potential organization/actual organization/organizing capacity, the fact that organization is possible at all must still be explained. And for this, as Aristotle demonstrated long ago, nothing short of a teleological attractor will suffice. Otherwise, we descend into an infinite regress, or else leave everything ultimately unexplained, so that contingency becomes the principle of all things and science itself becomes impossible. But if science is simply an economic way of organizing our experience, then we cannot have recourse to principles which have no empirical referent . . .

This error has, furthermore, concrete strategic implications. Without recourse to a final cause, Bogdanov's theory really does lead to God-building. The drive towards organization terminates in nothing short of everything. While in some respects this may be seen as a hopeful rapprochement with religion, it also opens up the possibility of the worst sort of voluntarism, in which the drive toward organization degenerates into an individual or collective will to power which knows no bounds. Indeed, as various individuals or collectivities mount their own assaults on the gates of heaven, politics can descend into a real theomachy or war among the gods, something with (literally) unlimited potential for destruction. This may seem a harsh accusation to level at the gentle and brilliant physician who in many ways understood better than Lenin the conditions for actually building socialism. The question, however, is not one of character, but of ideology. Purposeful organization without purpose can only be a free expression of the will. Once again we are back to Nietzsche.

Bogdanov is not the only thinker who is subject to this caution. Much the same argument might be made regarding Deborin. It is only a transcendental principle which can offer an adequate explanation of the universe and which can properly order human action. Short of that all other systems reduce ultimately to nihilism. Let us turn, then to the reconstruction of the sciences on which the development of an authentic dialectical metaphysics depends.

5

The Principles of Scientific Explanation

WE HAVE DEMONSTRATED THE internal contradictions and limitations of mathematical physics, both as science and as a model of the way the universe works. We have also shown it to be at once the product of, and an ideological mechanism for reinforcing, the market order. But this takes us only part-way towards our aim. The more difficult task still remains: we must revalidate the use of teleological explanation in the sciences, sketch out a research program for a restored teleological physics, and make at least a preliminary argument for cosmic teleology. This chapter focuses on the first of these tasks, making a preliminary argument for the validity of teleological explanation in the sciences, and argument which will be deepened and enriched in subsequent chapters as we look more specifically at what a teleological physics, biology, and sociology might look like, and validate the usefulness of teleological strategies in each of these special sciences. This chapter will also, however, advance a general thesis regarding the organization of the universe, a thesis which will frame the research program which we are proposing and give specificity to our claim regarding the ultimate meaningfulness of the universe. We begin, however, by an argument regarding the aims of science, and its relationship to the other intellectual disciplines, since it is only in relation to an aim or purpose that the appropriateness or adequacy of a method or strategy can be assess.

ART, SCIENCE, AND WISDOM

The Changing Meanings of Science

In the contemporary university intellectual disciplines are divided into the arts and the sciences. This is a distinction which we have come to take almost for granted, and to associate with definite subject matters and distinctive approaches. The sciences concern those things which can be subjected to rigorous, value-free investigation which produces general laws or law-like principles which are universally valid with regard to some definite class of phenomena; the arts concern those things regarding which such laws or principles cannot be formulated and regarding which value-judgments of some sort are more or less unavoidable. The social "sciences," in this schema, constitute a kind of gray area between the two realms, with the possibility of value-free investigation and the production of law-like principles hotly debated.[1]

We have already seen that this schema is itself an integral part of the same ideological complex as mathematical physics itself—an ideological complex which reduces science to formal description and excludes from rational judgment all questions of fundamental meaning and value, so that the market allocation of resources is protected from critical scrutiny and the personal preferences of the bourgeoisie are transformed into a sacred individual right. In its original, Aristotelian form, however, the distinction between art and science had a quite different significance. Art or τεχνη meant excellence in making and along with prudence or φρονεσις—excellence in acting—it constituted the sphere of the practical intellect. The arts were further subdivided into the instrumental arts—those which made things which are useful, the fine arts, which made things which are ends in themselves,[2] and the liberal arts, which made arguments, and thus set us free from unquestioned authority and unexamined opinion, be it our own or that of others, and make us fit to serve as mature participants in the public arena. The liberal arts traditionally included both the *trivium* of grammar, rhetoric, and logic, and the *quadrivium* of arithmetic, geometric, music, and astronomy. Science or επιστεμε, on the other hand, along with νοεσις or understanding and σοφια or wisdom, were regarded as theoretical virtues. Understanding was excellence in grasping first principles. Science meant excellence in demonstration or explanation. Wisdom or metaphysics is a sort of special case of science which is able to rise to the first principle of explanation

---

1. This way of distinguishing between the arts and sciences is in fact relatively recent, the product of nineteenth century positivism on the one hand, and the German *Geistwissenschaft* movement on the other—a movement which, as Lukacs has shown, was deeply imbued with the very same irrationalism which eventually gave birth to Nazism (Lukacs 1953/1980).

2. Fine here comes from the Latin *fine* or end.

and of action—i.e., God—and thus produce a complete explanation of the universe.

The relationship between the various disciplines is reciprocal but not entirely symmetric. While in certain respects the theoretical disciplines may be said to serve the practical, as when science, by helping us to understand how certain forms of matter behave, helps advance technology, it is the theoretical disciplines which in the final analysis order and regulate the practical. Thus wisdom or metaphysics governs prudence by telling it what end it ought to serve. Science (e.g., psychology, sociology) governs prudence by telling it how human beings and human societies operate. Higher order disciplines, furthermore, govern lower order disciplines. Thus metaphysics, which alone knows Truth and Beauty, governs both science and the arts.

Now mathematics and mathematical physics (for which astronomy serves as a kind of representative in the older Greek and Latin schemae, being the only developed branch of mathematical physics) are not sciences, but rather liberal arts. They do not, properly, explain but rather make. In the case of pure mathematics, this means making arguments regarding what is logically possible.[3] In the case of mathematical physics this means making what amount to mathematical models (formalisms) and arguments regarding the relative merits of various formalisms in order to describe physical—and by extension biological and social—systems.

As liberal arts mathematics and mathematical physics always serve some other discipline—the question is which one. We have already seen that prior to the advent of generalized commodity production in the sixteenth and seventeenth century, the answer to this question would have been fairly straightforward, at least with respect to astronomy. Astronomy served a cluster of instrumental arts—agriculture, navigation, etc. But it also served the science of astrology, which attempted to explain sublunar phenomena in terms of the actions of the heavenly bodies, and the practical discipline of horoscope casting. Finally, it served science of physics, or more specifically cosmology, which it provided with a model of the large-scale structure of the universe which then served as a link in the larger explanatory chain, at once a principle of explanation and something which itself needed to be explained. And through physics or cosmology, astronomy served wisdom, in the form of metaphysics, by

---

3. One might argue that this means mathematics is *also* a science of possible beings, but this is not the connection in which it interests here.

helping to make possible the mind's ascent to the first principle, or God. Metaphysics, in turn, served theology—a higher wisdom—which at its outer reaches made possible the cultivation of authentic connaturality with God, something which results in "caritative wisdom" or infused contemplation.

What happened, as we have seen in earlier chapters, is that as a result of the Aristotelian renaissance of the twelfth century, metaphysics became an increasingly important adjunct to theology, something which threatened clerical elites who responded with what we have called the Augustinian reaction. Integral to this reaction was the claim that the universe is as it is because God, in His sovereign freedom, made it that way—not because of any rational necessity, as the Aristotelians claimed. This shifted the focus of scientific research from the attempt to rationally explain the universe to empirical investigation (since we could know what God created only by studying it directly) and formal description. Thus the prominence of such Franciscan thinkers as Grosseteste and Bacon in the early stages of the "scientific revolution." These early pioneers of mathematical physics—and indeed many of their successors, such as Kepler and Newton—imagined themselves still be in the service of theology, albeit more directly and less by mediation through metaphysics. But as mathematical physics—along with both the secular and clerical variants of the political theological critique—began to undermine metaphysics, mathematical physics was increasingly "emancipated" from this servitude, creating the appearance of an "autonomous" "science" which served no master but the Truth.

The reality, however, was quite different. From the thirteenth century on mathematical physics was an ideological instrument: first of clerical, and then of secular adversaries of metaphysics. And then, like the practitioners of less intellectual arts, the mathematical physicist found himself emancipated from the episcopal authorities who first chartered his guild only to end up bound to a more exacting master, whose terms were non-negotiable. I am referring, of course, to the marketplace. And the marketplace exercised its sovereignty not only through the spontaneous ideological mechanisms which we have already traced above, but also by direct economic leverage, by sponsoring those lines of investigation which promise to terminate in useful inventions, and neglecting those which do not. Mathematical physics, after all, is nothing if not a useful art –the basis of the new technologies which were already beginning to develop in the craft shops of the medieval Europe and which began to develop so rapidly after the seventeenth century. Far from being emancipated from science, metaphysics, and theology in order to become an "autonomous science" mathematical physics now serves technology, which in turn serves the marketplace.

Our aim in the foregoing critique has not been to argue that mathematical physics has no place among the intellectual disciplines, but rather to discipline this unruly member of the *universitas* and re-order it to its proper end, and one far more noble than that which it currently serves: the search for an explanation, as complete and logically consistent as possible, of the universe as we experience it, and ultimately for an answer to humanity's most pressing questions about meaning and value. This means serving science rather than technique, and through science serving wisdom in its various degrees.

Science Is Explanation

This said, we need now to specify just what it means to explain something, and just how the explanatory science we are proposing is related to wisdom proper, or metaphysics. In general, to explain something means to

a. say why some fact, event, or pattern of facts and events is as it is and not otherwise, to

b. say why something is what it is, and not something else, and/or to

c. say why something, or everything, or indeed anything at all, is in the first place.

We should note that these are three distinct levels or degrees of explanation. The first level of explanation is phenomenal and may or may not touch the nature of things. Thus, for example, if we say that the dam collapsed because it was too weak to bear the pressure which built up in the reservoir, that my stomach was settled because I took chamomile tea, or that the people of the steppes invaded the villages of the valley in order to claim a share in their greater wealth, we do indeed explain the event in question, but in a purely external way, without understanding the nature of the elements involved in the interaction or their interrelations. Explanation of this sort can be casual and incidental, or it can be the product of a systematic effort to accumulate and distill the results of many generations of human experience. In the latter case it forms the basis for what we have earlier called an empirical lore. By the same token, we can also attempt to explain phenomena in terms of some underlying structure, thereby looking behind the appearance to the essence. Thus, for example, we might explain the properties of gold in terms of its atomic structure, the different hunting behaviors of canines and felines in terms of the somewhat different niches for which they are adapted, and/or the way in which they have adapted to those niches, or an economic crisis in terms of the internal contradictions of a definite economic structure. In this case, though the explanation in question can only be arrived at by empirical investigation, this investigation terminates in a principle from which the phenomenon can be rationally derived, so that it is thus rendered authentically understood. It is this sort or deductive explanation which constitutes the first degree of authentic science.

It should be noted that at this first degree of explanation teleology can often be avoided, except in so far as purposeful organization or behavior or some sort is integral to the phenomenon being studied. Thus our explanation of the properties of gold in terms of its atomic structure need not be teleological, while the examples we have given from biology and sociology (hunting behavior and economic crisis) involve teleology only on the side of what is being explained, not on the side of the explanatory principle. Most of what is authentically science, and not merely mathematical model-building in contemporary mathematical physics and the disciplines inspired by it falls into this category. We should note, however, that in so far as the explanation refers to anything purely external, phenomenal, or contingent, such as the initial conditions or boundary conditions for some physical or chemical interaction, the explanation still retains elements of empirical lore. In so far as the initial conditions or boundary conditions are not actually observed, but merely inferred on the basis of theory, as is the case with much physical cosmology, they actually form an integral part of the mathematical model and are thus art and not science.

The second degree of scientific explanation is, by its very nature, more difficult. Here we ask not why gold has the properties that it does, but rather why the principles governing atomic structure are as they are and not otherwise—e.g., why is energy transfer quantum and not continuous? Why can't more than two electrons occupy the same energy state at the same time? etc. We ask not why cats and dogs hunt differently, but rather why there are these two different adaptive strategies in the first place, just how many possible adaptive strategies there are, why there are that number and not some other number, whether or not they are all realized, and why or why not, etc. And we ask that these question be answered not based on contingent data—i.e., in terms of a natural history of the planet, which operates on the level of a sophisticated empirical lore, but rather in terms of some rational principle from which structures or essences in question could be logically derived, if we understood the principle well enough and had the requisite intellectual power, and which in any case, even if we cannot advance to this level, helps us to "make sense out them," i.e., to render the structure of the universe and its subsystems meaningful.

The third degree of explanation attempts to answer a still more difficult question—i.e., not only why things are as they are, but why they are at all. Thus, if the first level of explanation might be called phenomenal, even when it explains in terms of some underlying structure or essence, and the second level might be called essential, the third level of explanation is existential. Here we attempt to grasp the mystery of beings and ultimately of Being itself.

Now while the first degree of explanation has, indeed, frequently been achieved by the mathematical physics and the various disciplines inspired by it, the limitations of the dominant paradigm notwithstanding, the second and third degrees of explanation generally have not. There are two reasons for this. First, the questions themselves have generally been ruled out of order as "not properly scientific." Here two factors are at work. On the one hand, the inability of intellectual disciplines operating under the dominant paradigm to answer the questions would call the paradigm itself into question, since the questions themselves are entirely reasonable. On the other hand, insofar as mathematical physics has functioned as a subaltern ideological agent of Capital, it has been necessary to rule out any line of inquiry which might render the universe meaningful and thus call into question the underlying nihilism of the market order. Second, the questions posed at the second and third degrees of explanation cannot be answered by empirical investigation, though any attempt to even pose the questions rigorously certainly presupposes a broad base of such investigation. This is because any explanation of the way things are, or of the fact that they are, in terms of some empirical data would amount to nothing more than an explanation in terms of the way things are and the fact that they are. It would either be incomplete, explaining one essence or structure, or the existence of one partial system, in terms of another, or else it would be tautological, explaining an essence or structure, or the existence of some partial system, in terms of itself. Nor could such explanations be the result of mathematical formalisms, which either formalize the results of empirical data, or model the shape such data might possible assume. Explaining why things are, and are the way they are at the most profound, structural level, require a research strategy which is distinctly non-empirical—which links observed phenomena and inferred essences together in a way which points towards a principle which itself is not observable and which is neither a formalization of observables or an imaginative construction, but which, once arrived at, can be known as real and rationally necessary.

What might such a principle look like? How does one explain the underlying structures of things which are themselves the most powerful principles of explanation we can wield in relation to concrete empirical phenomena? Here we must let the higher sciences, biology and sociology, take the lead in pointing us in the right direction. Biological and social structures—e.g., anatomical designs or economic structures—are generally explained as ways of achieving some definite end or purpose (minimally survival and reproduction) under definite material conditions. They are, in other words, generally explained teleologically. The same is true of many physical structures, even though there can be no implication of conscious intent or even unconscious striving. Thus the prevalence of some physical states over others is explained in terms of their superior energetic stability. The end aimed at is, furthermore, being—not yet Being as such, but certainly common being, understood as conserving the integrity of some structure, and possibly even expanding and reproducing it.

Science, it turns out, cannot resist teleological explanation even when it is foreign to the dominant paradigm. At most it can pretend that the explanations advanced are not teleological, and contain the ideological damage by using the most reductive language possible, and by resisting efforts to survey the results of the sciences across disciplines in order to identify general explanatory principles.

But there is more. Not only *are* explanations at the second and third degree teleological. They *must* be. The reason for this is not hard to understand. Our aim here is to be complete without being tautological. This means that we must ultimately arrive at some principle which is authentically self-explanatory, which acts on things without itself being acted upon (otherwise would, in turn have to explain what was acting on our principle, and would end up with an infinite regress). And, as Aristotle first demonstrated (Aristotle. *Metaphysics* XII.7) that which acts without being acted upon acts by teleological attraction, as its beauty, truth, goodness, and integrity (which can themselves be shown to be transcendental properties of Being) draw things from mere possibility into actuality, along a potential infinity of different paths of development.

From this standpoint the whole process of explanation appears as an integral whole. We begin with empirical pattern recognition, something which makes possible the accumulation of a rich and diverse empirical lore. We continue by penetrating beneath the phenomenon to the underlying structure—atomic configuration or anatomical complex, psychodynamics or economic system. And then we explain the structure itself in the one way possible: as a means of achieving the end of being or integrity, in whatever way that is possible at the level of organization in question, whether that means energetic stability, survival and reproduction, intellectual and moral development, or civilizational progress. As we do this an hypothesis emerges which is in one sense obvious, but which in the light of the past four centuries of science is also tremendously audacious: that in addition to all of the particular teleological attractors such as energetic stability, biological survival and reproduction, and civilizational progress, and spiritual development, there is also a "great attractor," Being itself, which accounts for all these finite participations in Being, as well as for some of the underlying structural features of the whole system which resist explanation as particular adaptive strategies, such as the fine tuning of basic cosmological constants, and the way in which certain physical laws are fixed (general and special relativity, the quantum principles identified above, etc.) Might not these fundamental structural features of the universe be "conditions of possibility" of material organization as such, and thus of finite participations in Being?

At this point, of course, this is only an hypothesis, and one which has not yet even been formulated rigorously. In order to do that we need to look in more depth at the actual process of doing science. Before we do that, however, we should note briefly that the sort of explanatory discipline we are proposing would by necessity include both the special sciences, or what Aristotle and Thomas called science proper, and wisdom or metaphysics. The boundary between the two is a fine one. Generally speaking, we call an explanation "science" if it remains within the boundaries of the first two degrees of explanation, and terminates only in an explanation of particular phenomena and structures. Thus extending the explanation of chemical properties in terms of atomic structure into an explanation of the principles governing atomic structure itself would still be science. Here it is still a matter of understanding some particular aspect of the world around us. When we cross over into the third degree of explanation, or put forward an hypothesis regarding the global ordering of the universe to a single end, we enter the realm of wisdom or metaphysics. Here the question concerns the existence and meaningfulness of the universe as a whole. Certain inquiries straddle the boundaries between these two disciplines. We might for, example want to understand cosmological fine tuning as a phenomenon in its own right, and thus approach the matter scientifically, but there is no way to avoid implications regarding the ultimate meaningfulness of the universe as a whole. Similarly, we might start out trying to explain the principles governing atomic structure but end up discovering that these principles flow directly from the requirement that the universe be structured in a certain way if it is to exist at all. Generally science, even a science open to teleological explanation, will take the end for granted and investigate just how the end is realized; metaphysics will attempt to understand the end itself in so far as that is possible. This in turn will point to differences in method which should become clear in the following section.

SCIENTIFIC METHOD

Method in Science

We have clarified the aims of science and of metaphysical wisdom; we need now to specify their methods. This is an important question, because since at least the seventeenth century, and to some extent since the late Middle Ages, there has been a tendency to define science first and foremost in terms of its method, without respect to the aims those methods were intended to serve. Under the influence of rationalist and empiricist epistemologies, there was a growing emphasis on some combination of controlled empirical research and mathematical modeling, driven by the belief that these methods and these methods alone could yield certain, or at least highly probable results.

The past century has seen the philosophy of science take a more humble turn, as the claims of the experimental method have been subjected to more careful scrutiny and the foundations of mathematics, once thought to be so firm, have proven themselves to rather difficult to establish. Thus empiricists and positivists, who in the seventeenth century might have spoken confidently of "experimental confirmation" of scientific hypotheses now speak more modestly—if also more awkwardly of "non-disconfirmation." All empirical research can do, it appears, is to show that an hypothesis cannot yet be ruled out. Similarly, the mathematical structures necessary to the formalization of physical systems, which Leibniz believed to be founded on the self-evident rules of logic, turn out to depend for their consistency and completeness on acts of transcendental abstraction or intellectual intuition—precisely the sorts of intellectual vagary the rationalist and empiricist programs had hoped to abolish from science.

The myth, however, that science offers certain answers, whereas history on the one hand and philosophy and theology on the other hand offer mere opinion, persists, and not only among the general public. One need only ask a working scientist his opinion of the humanities. From whence this conviction of methodological "hard-nosedness"? The answer, of course, lies in the largely unexamined aims of the "science" dominated by mathematical physics, which we identified above. Controlled experiment and mathematical formalization may not yield certain knowledge, but they do yield knowledge which is useful to the engineer and technician, whose products in turn are useful to Capital. The hard-nosed contempt of people in the mathematical disciplines for those in the humanities is the contempt of the businessman for the philosopher who, in the within the present social order, is impotent.[4]

The aims of the science we propose are quite different, and as a result the method must be different as well. Controlled experiment is an appropriate method for research which is directed, consciously or unconsciously, at developing technologies which can control or manipulate physical,

---

4. This is not to say, of course, that mathematical physics does not produce knowledge which, because useful to the engineer and technician, is *also* useful to humanity generally. But in a nonmarket (and nontributary) economy decisions about what is to be made are driven by philosophically informed public discourse. It is obvious that, useful and dignified as the work of the mathematical physicist is, that of the philosopher, because it helps to set the overall direction of development for the society, is more useful and dignified still. Thus the central importance of philosopher under the old Soviet Union, which made training in philosophy an integral part of its universal education system and which had more philosophers per capita than any other society on the planet.

biological, or social systems in a definite way. What this sort of research does, after all, is to identify a lever, subject to human control, which reliably produces a definite result. Mathematical modeling or formalization, similarly, is an appropriate tool for understanding the way the universe is constructed when our ultimate aim is reconstruct it in accord with our own aims. But if our purpose is not to control or reconstruct, but rather to understand—and in technological applications to tap into—the already existing dynamics of natural systems themselves, then these methods are not only inadequate, but actually suspect. Controlled experiments, for example, isolate one single factor and tell us how that factor affects the rest of the system being studied. But what if that factor operates differently when it is not isolated and subjected to manipulation? Mathematical formalization, similarly, at best identifies relationships between externally related phenomena. It is precisely attempts to formalize internal relationships which generate the paradoxes of relativity and quantum mechanics and transform mathematical physics from a hard-nosed attempt to bring nature under control into a discipline which has more in common with a mystery religion than an empirical science.

This is not to say that we reject the role of empirical investigation. On the contrary, the general theory of knowledge, which have already outlined in detail in an earlier work (Mansueto 2002b), makes it clear that all human knowledge begins with the senses. Science is no different. Indeed, if we are to break out of the stuck research programs and internal contradictions into which science in late capitalist society has fallen, and emancipate ourselves from the tyranny of the formalism, we need a science which has re-immersed itself in the data of the senses. The difference is that the emphasis of this empirical investigation must be *observation* rather than experiment, so that we begin to discover what nature is already doing herself, rather than merely what we can do to her.

This said, it must also be remembered that our cognitive faculties are hierarchically ordered, so that sensation is always already formed by intellect, and lower intellectual acts by higher. The teleological scientist is no more capable than the mathematical physicist of "pure" observation. This is why empirical research is always theory-laden, always formed by the questions we ask, which in turn reflect a definite theoretical stance. The observations we make—i.e., the raw sensory data we take in—are formed by the imaginative drive of the internal senses to form unified images and indeed a unified picture of the world around us. This imaginative activity is, in turn formed by the taxonomic schemes which are imbedded in language. The world around us, that is, turns out to be made up exclusively of "things" for which we have a name.[5] And when we discover something new, the very act of observation and image formation associated with the discovery is always accompanied by a properly intellectual act: the question "What is it?" Throughout this process we test our knowledge, constantly asking if we are seeing as well as we might, if our image really captures reality, if our way of naming a thing is really adequate or if, perhaps, it doesn't need to be modified or qualified in some way.

This is the level of cognitive activity typical of a child who is just learning language. The range of questions which govern our empirical explorations soon expand to include "how?" and "why." We naturally look for, and begin to identify patterns of relationships between things and between events and we begin search out among these relationships some which can be used to explain what is going on around us—both particular system and the imaginatively constructed whole we call the universe. Science and wisdom as we have defined them are nothing more or less than particularly rigorous and excellent ways of carrying out these natural human activities, and not some different activity with which ordinary humans have nothing to do.

In what does this rigor and excellence consist? It consists, first of all, in rendering the process conscious, and thus in focusing on each act so that we can do it well. This means, first of all, being clear about the question or questions which we are posing. Are we asking what? or how? or why? Are we classifying, modeling or formalizing relationships, or attempting to explain? And are we relating these questions to each other in a proper hierarchical ordering? Before we can model relationships we need to have some sense of what is being related to what, and thus an adequate taxonomy. Before we can explain we need to have a rigorous, formal definition of what is being explained. But each our taxonomies and formalisms must serve the effort to explain, since the search for meaning represents the highest order human function.

As science develops, it produces an accumulated body of theory which more and more begins to define what questions still need to be

---

5. This is true even if we think we don't know what something is. On seeing such an object we will still be able to classify it roughly in terms of shape, color, sound, smell, taste, texture, etc., if nothing else by setting off against things from which it seems to differ.

asked and what sort of answers are to be expected. Thus in a young science, research questions may be posed without pointing directly to some hypothesis to be tested. The hypothesis emerges only out of extensive empirical observation. In a mature science, on the other hand, the way the question is framed generally itself already implies an hypothesis. Excellence in science presupposes a grasp of this existing body of theory and the ability to work within it, but it also means the ability to identify those questions which represent not merely gaps which still need to be filled in, but real limitations of or contradictions in the dominant paradigm, and the ability to frame research questions which can either resolve these contradictions or point towards a new paradigm.

The second aspect of excellence in science is the capacity for systematic, authentically open-ended observation. This may involve a particular acuity in the senses, or it may involve the ability to design or use instruments which collect data which our senses cannot. But it always involves attention to such questions as representativeness and reliability. Is the data we are collecting really typical of the system we are studying? Will others see the same thing? If not, why not? More importantly, however, it involves an awareness of the complex interaction between theory and observation. To what extent is what I am seeing driven by what I expect to see? The scientist needs to discipline him/herself to be open to data which are authentically unexpected. Since the relationship between observation and theory is mediated by the imagination, this means above all disciplining the imagination to be open to unexpected possibilities. It is little wonder that really creative scientists are often enamored with scientifically improbable science fiction. Deeper training in the fine arts, actually learning to imagine and represent in painting, music, or literature life-worlds which conflict with existing theory, should form an integral dimension of scientific training.

Third, the scientist must excel at empirical pattern recognition. This is a subtle skill, which integrates imagination with the intellectual operations of totalization and elementary formalization. Patterns are always relationships of similarity and/or difference, which we have argued is the very essence of totalization or classification. But since empirical data are always fragmentary and incomplete, the recognition of a pattern involves the imaginative extension of data in order to construct a whole pattern. And since most patterns can, in fact, be characterized in multiple ways, we need to ask what is the best way to describe a pattern, something which points us very quickly towards formalization. We want our patterns, after all, to be characterized by systems of similar differences and different similarities, and this means a system of ratios which—implicitly or explicitly—quantifies our description.

Related to but distinct from excellence in empirical pattern recognition is the art of developing elegant formal descriptions. This involves looking beneath the empirical pattern for some principle or formalism which can describe it more elegantly or economically. Where the empirical pattern generally still embodies some element of contingency, the formal description is something which could, at least in principle, be derived from other formalisms as a sort of special case. Thus Tycho Brahe compiled empirical data on planetary motion and developed a preliminary model of that motion. Kepler reduced the data to a formalism which was later shown to be a special case of the more general Newtonian laws. Adam Smith identified general patterns in the behavior of markets; Ricardo reduced those patterns to formal laws which Marx then showed to be a special case of more general economic principles. It should be noted that while formal descriptions are often mathematical they need not be. Structural descriptions of the sort linguists give of syntagmatic rules or that anthropologists give of kinship rules are also formal. The criterion is simply that all the terms and their relations be sufficiently well defined that the proposition can be subjected to manipulation using the rules of formal logic.

Once the results of empirical observation have been formalized, then it is possible to seek an explanation. And it is here that teleological science requires certain habits of mind which differ radically from those cultivated by the mathematical physicist. What is required here is to infer from the structure of a system, and the way in which it relates to other systems, just what its end or purpose might be and thus why it is structured the way it is, and indeed why it exists at all. It must be stressed that we are not begging the question of teleology, local or cosmic, by insisting that the scientist attempt to conclude to the purpose of systems. First, we have already shown that any complete explanation will be teleological or at least involve teleological elements. Second, we are at this stage still identifying hypotheses which need to be tested. The scientific process remains formally open to the possibility that there is no purpose—and thus no explanation—for either some local system or for the universe generally.⁶

Inferring a purpose from a structure is an act of the intellect which we have earlier specified as transcendental abstraction. And as we noted above, the act of transcendental abstraction—the ability to see purpose—derives from living purposefully in a society which is well ordered towards the natural end of human life—the cultivation of the intellect and the will and the progress of human civilization. It is by creating beauty and by performing just acts that we are formed in such a way as to be able to discover the purpose of things and thus rise from the formally correct to the transcendentally True. In this sense aesthetic and moral discipline are as central to the formation of the scientist as properly intellectual discipline.⁷

---

6. It might be asked here why we do not take the road proposed by traditional Dominican Thomism, such as that of Garrigou-Lagrange (Garrigou-Lagrange 1932), which simply insists on the principle of "finality" as he calls it, as a logical consequence of the principle of identity and contradiction and the principle of sufficient reason, which implies that everything has a cause. Garrigou-Lagrange argues that it is only the principal of finality that can explain the fact of change without violating the principles of identity and contradiction. By showing that things are at once one thing (actually) and another (potentially) Aristotle overcame the contradiction between the correct but otherwise incompatible insights of Parmenides and Heraclitus and opened up the possibility of authentic scientific explanation.

The difficulty with this approach is that it takes as self-evident, or at least as following from principles which are self-evident, conclusions which are no longer self-evident to most people in our society. Partly this is simply a question of ideological strategy and tactics. People are not going to be convinced of the ultimate meaningfulness of the universe simply by being reminded that this conclusion follows from rules of logic for which they have little regard in the first place. It is hoped that a real engagement with mathematical physics and empirical scientific investigation will prove more convincing. At the same time, the development of formal logic over the course of the past century, especially as it has attempted to come to term with some of the paradoxes of mathematical physics, has called into question the self-evident character of the rules of logic. Similar issues are raised by the development of dialectical logics, which stress the role of contradiction as a principle of explanation something which, we will argue, must be incorporated into any teleological strategy if it is to accommodate the evidence of chaos and contradiction in the real world. Because of this, rather than regarding the rules of logic, and especially the principles of sufficient reason and finality as self-evident, we regard them as very high order abstractions based on experience, and thus as principles which must, like any other, be tested against experience.

7. It is little wonder that the popular imagination in capitalist societies has so easily embraced the image of the scientist as "mad" or "evil." Partly, of course, this may be simply a reflection of a general anti-intellectualism—though the humanistic intelligentsia is generally reviled as useless, lazy, or subversive rather than as positively destructive.

The Principles of Scientific Explanation

The final factor which defines excellence in science is the capacity to test and pass judgment on hypotheses developed through the foregoing process. Here there are two tests which must be applied. First, the hypothesis must be tested against the rules of logic. Is the hypothesis logically coherent or does it contain internal contradictions or conflict with established principles which we otherwise have no reason to discard? Second the hypothesis must be tested against the evidence. When we are talking about explanations, as opposed to mere mathematical models, this does not mean simply making predictions on the basis of the principle in question and then carrying out further observations to see whether or not the predictions are born out, though such activity might well form a part of a scientific test. Rather, we want the principle in question to *logically imply* what is being explained, i.e., the existence, structure, and/or behavior of the system in question, so that, knowing the principle we can conclude without further observation the system. Where this is not possible, because the system in question resists this level of comprehension, we want at the very least for our explanatory principle to *make sense out of* the system, so that when we understand the system in the light of the principle what previously seemed arbitrary and contingent now seems quite natural, because we have assimilated something of the nature of the system to ourselves and become conformed to it.[8] The closer the principle proposed

---

And the role of the science dominated by mathematical physics in the development of weapons of mass destruction, and the generally association of scientific research with the military sector, cannot help but accentuate the tendency to regard the scientist with some suspicion. But there is a deeper link between a science which refuses to ask questions of meaning and purpose and the image of the scientist as amoral or immoral. Since it is moral excellence—living a purposeful life well ordered to the Good—which enables us to see the purposes of things, it follows that someone who doesn't see purposes—indeed who stubbornly refuses to even ask about purposes—must somehow be morally defective. And even if this is not true, an intellectual formation which belittles questions of meaning and purpose can hardly be conducive to a purposeful and thus morally excellent life.

8. There are, generally speaking, two reasons why a system would resist complete comprehension. On the one hand, it might be more complex than we are, in which case it would be logically impossible for us to understand it, though we might specify at least some of its general characteristics. This is true of God and of what the philosophical tradition has historically called angels or separate substances. More common in science is the problem of systems which, because they are submerged in matter, are still more potential than actual and thus resist complete comprehension for the simple reason that the lines along which they will be formed, and thus become intelligible, has not yet been determined. Thus we can never complete comprehend dogs because there are so many ways

achieves the ideal of allowing us to derive from it the existence, structure, and behavior of the system or systems being explained, the greater its *explanatory power* and the more it is to be preferred over alternatives.

This is the positive criterion for judging proposed explanations. There is also a negative criterion, generally known as Occam's Razor. According to this principle, the simplest explanation, or that which makes the fewest unproven assumptions is, other things being equal, to be preferred. A word of caution is, however, in order. Occam's Razor is often invoked in a way which makes identifies economy in explanation with reductionism. Thus, it is assumed to be more economical to explain human or animal behavior by the combined action of any number of physical principles before teleological attraction is even considered. On the contrary, since the seventeenth century science has gone to ever greater lengths in order to defend reductionism against more obvious alternatives.[9] This is un-

---

to be a dog that the species cannot be reduced to a single logical principles from which all canine activity can be deduced. The same is true for all other material systems, physical, biological, and social. If certain physical systems give the impression of being more fully intelligible than say plants, animals, or societies this is because we have become used to a (mathematical) physics which abstracts certain very simple quantitative properties from the systems in question and then identifies the resulting mathematical model with the system itself. In reality the course of development of a cloud of interstellar gas is far less determined by principle than, say the development of an atom of carbon, a sprig of wheat, a donkey, the human intellect, or a human civilization. Each of these higher order systems, in so far as it remains what it is and is not reduced to its physical components, develops along a progressively narrower evolutionary pathway. Human beings, while far less predictable than a simple two-body gravitational system, are far more intelligible, at least once we have grasped the ends of human life and the structures through which we humans pursue those ends, as well as the material constraints under which we do so.

9. One of the best examples of this tendency is Freud's Oedipal theory—which also illustrates the transparent ideological functions of reductionism. Confronted by 18 patients, 12 women and 6 men who presented the unexplained physical symptoms (which might include anything from a persistent cough to paralysis) generally class as "hysteria" at the time, Freud began to interview them regarding their dreams. All reported images of sexual activity with adults when they themselves were still children. Freud reached the obvious conclusion: that the hysterical symptoms from which his patients suffered were there result of childhood trauma and in particular of sexual abuse. When the results were published in *The Aitiology of Hysteria*, however, the medical community reacted with outrage. Freud, after all, was accusing upstanding Vienna families of criminal sexual abuse and implicitly exposing the patriarchal structure of Austrian bourgeois society. His mentors took him aside and warned him that if he wanted a medical career he had best reconsider his conclusions. Soon an alternative explanation appeared, which ascribed the dream images to an unresolved desire on the part of his patients to have sex with their parents, something for which there was no independent evidence. This was the

The Principles of Scientific Explanation

warranted. Occam's Razor must be used in conjunction with "Mansueto's Switchblade":

> The most economical explanation is not always the most reductive.

In judging the adequacy of an explanation, or evaluating the relative merits of alternative explanations, the positive and negative criteria must be carefully balanced against each other. There is no general rule which can be used to rank order their priority. And it must, in any case, be kept carefully in mind that even when a scientific principle has been established as true, in the sense of providing a powerful and economic explanation of some natural system, this does not mean that it cannot or will not later be supplanted by some still more adequate explanation. Perfect science exists only in the mind of God, who knows not as we do, by observation and inference, or by logical analysis of Her own essence as the angels do, but rather as the cause of the things known, which flow from the divine nature.

Method in Metaphysics

We have, thus far, characterized the methods of science. What about the method of wisdom, or more specifically of metaphysical wisdom, which we have argued continues and completes the work science begins by arriving at last at a complete explanation of the universe and by providing an answer to humanity's deepest questions about ultimate meaning and

---

seed of what later became the Oedipal theory and the foundation of the whole discipline of psychoanalysis, which reduces humanity's great glories, work and love, to nothing more than (very imperfectly) sublimated sex and aggression. Humanity is at constant war with itself, forced to repress desires which are only natural but which conflict with our unusual survival strategy (civilization). It is this tension, and not exploitation which is the source of human misery, and efforts at social transformation are thus unwarranted. Women, furthermore, because of the less traumatic character of their Oedipal crises (they are "already castrated" and thus cannot be subjected to this threat, which apparently has such a salutary moral effect on men) are "less moral and more instinctual" than men, to whose supervision they must constantly be subordinated if their cynical manipulations are not to undermine human civilization (Freud 1927/1961, 1930/1961, 1931, 1961; Miller 1986).

The Oedipal theory is less economical because it posits a causal factor—the child's desire to have sex with its mother—for which we have no independent evidence in order to avoid a political problematic but far more straightforward explanation in terms of sexual abuse. It is more reductive because it reduces all human aspirations to expressions of sex and aggression. It is ideological because it tells us that human misery is a function not of capitalism but of the human condition as such.

value? As an intellectual discipline which like science aims at explanation, the methods of metaphysics are similar. But where science aims at explaining particular systems, or particular levels of organization, metaphysics aims at an explanation of the whole. In this sense it begins where the special sciences leave off, and takes their results, especially their most general results concerning, for example the very nature of physical, biological, and social organization, and the laws governing the large scale evolution of the universe, as its initial data. This is why we still use a name for this discipline—metaphysics—which to some extent arose accidentally, in virtue of the placement of Aristotle's treatment of these questions after his *Physics* when his works were compiled by editors. Because of this metaphysics does not engage in direct empirical investigation, but rather leaves this to the special sciences. Direct observation, imaginative construction, empirical pattern recognition, and formal model building are all outside the scope of metaphysical investigation. Where metaphysics overlaps with science is in the act of transcendental abstraction which infers from the structure of systems to their end or purpose. The difference is that where the special sciences engages in this sort of inference primarily in order to explain the structure of a particular system or the properties of a particular level of organization, metaphysics is interested in discovering whether or not there is an end or purpose and if so what that end or purpose is. Because of this the metaphysician will generally be interested in inferring the purpose of higher order rather than lower order systems: s/he will be more like to ask why basic physical constants are fixed as they are or why energy transfer is quantum rather than continuous than to ask why rabbits evolved in such a way as to derive much of the protein in their diets from bacteria in a special sort of fecal matter produced by an organ known as the cecum. The result of this process of transcendental abstraction is thus a general explanatory theory which unifies the sciences and which concludes to a single explanatory system in terms of which the whole universe can be shown to be rationally necessary.

Metaphysics does not, however, stop at this point, which might be described as the level of philosophical cosmology. Rather it continues its investigation by formalizing its description of the first principle as best it can and then using the methods of logical analysis in order to identify, in so far as possible, the properties of this first principle. Thus the argument that Being is convertible with Beauty, Truth, Good, and One or that the first principle must necessarily be infinite, necessary, and perfect, that it is omniscient, omnipotent, personal, etc. To the extent that the present work ventures into properly metaphysical territory, it will mostly confine itself to the first sort of investigation—i.e., to asking whether or not there is some first principle to which the universe as a whole is ordered and in terms of which it can be explained. Analysis of the nature of this principle will await a subsequent work.

The criteria for evaluating metaphysical hypotheses are not fundamentally different from those for evaluating hypotheses in science. Metaphysical theories must have explanatory power and they must meet the tests of logical coherence and economy. They must in other words, shed real light on the world as we experience it, helping us to make sense out of life even if they are not able to render the universe fully intelligible as a logical system. They must avoid internal contradiction. And they must attempt to do as much with as little apparatus as possible. These principles do, however, taken on a somewhat different sense in the context of metaphysics than in the context of the special sciences. Because of its distance from empirical investigation, there is a danger that metaphysicians will begin to spin vast systems which seems to make logical sense but which contain much which makes little or no difference in terms of the way in which we understand the world or live our lives. This is "speculation" in the worst sense and gives metaphysics a bad name. The metaphysician must resist the impulse to spin castles in the air and constantly ask what difference his/her work makes in practice.[10] Similarly, the metaphysician must keep in mind that when formalizing descriptions of systems more complex than ourselves, we only arrive at very general approximations. Attempts to then deduce from these formalizations complex statements regarding the divine nature, the nature of separate substances, etc., are profoundly misguided and represent the worst sort of intellectual arrogance. Perfectly logical deductions from premises which are always, because of the complexity of the principle they attempt to grasp, somewhat faulty, cannot lead us closer to the truth. What metaphysics does is to vindicate our natural faith in the ultimate meaningfulness of the universe

---

10. This is not to say that highly abstract metaphysical principles cannot make a practical difference. On the contrary, what may initially seem like very minor divergences in metaphysical theory can often yield, by way of their ethical implications, the most profound practical differences. Thus the very slight shift in emphasis between say Thomas and Dante towards understanding God more exclusively as final cause, leads to a shift in political allegiance from the papacy to the Holy Roman Empire.

and define the nature of that meaning in very broad outlines which permits us to complete science and ground ethics and to lay a foundation for human spiritual and civilizational progress. Baroque speculative systems are a distraction from the work at hand.

A GENERAL THESIS REGARDING THE ORGANIZATION OF THE UNIVERSE

Having specified the end or purpose of science and of metaphysics, and the methods by which one can arrive at those ends, it now remains for us to lay out the general thesis that will be defended in the final chapters of this work. We have already demonstrated in the opening part of this book and in foregoing sections of this chapter the principal constraints on this thesis. On the one hand, we have shown that any possible explanatory theory which is complete must also be teleological. On the other hand, we have seen that Aristotelian physics collapsed because of its inability to accommodate evidence of chaos and contradiction within the context of a unified theory of motion. What we need is a theory which can integrate teleological explanation with chaos and contradiction.

Aristotle's theory of the four causes (Aristotle. *Physics* 2.3, *Metaphysics* 1.7) already provides a basis for this move. According to Aristotle, any given system can be explained by

a. a material cause, or that out of which it is formed,

b. a formal cause, or what it is,

c. a final cause, or that for which it is, and

d. an efficient cause, or that by which it comes to be.

Now as we already noted in our discussion of Aristotle above efficient cause does not properly belong within this sequence, since it can often be identified with one of the other types of causes (Aristotle. *Physics* 2.7), and when it cannot (as in the case of a man who causes a javelin to fly to throwing it) this is a result of a different sort of analysis of causation, more historical and focused on contingent elements than scientific and aiming at necessary principles. This leaves us with three types of explanatory principles: matter, form, and end or *telos*.[11]

---

11. Aristotle sometimes suggests that the end or *telos* is nothing other than the perfection of the form, implying that formal and final cause may also be identified. While this is sometimes true (the mature form of the plant is, in a certain sense the end towards

Now in order to see the potential here for rectifying Aristotle's problem we need to remind ourselves of just what matter is in an Aristotelian context. Matter is simply the potential for form or organization; it is not in itself anything in particular. This point, often forgotten and perhaps never really understood by Aristotle and his followers means that the role of the material cause is not so much to provide an unchanging substratum to systems which otherwise undergo constant transformation, as some defenders of the principle of finality have argued (Garrigou-Lagrange 1932), but a reminder that while there may be one end towards which everything is ordered, which we have specified as Being itself, or the Good, the True, the Beautiful, and the One, there is also a potential infinity of ways of realizing this end. Teleological attraction operates with iron-clad necessity, but it does so against a background of infinite possibility.

As the *telos* reduces this potential to act matter becomes increasingly structured, formal, or organized. These forms or structures are ways of realizing the *telos*—of participating and persisting in Being or, what is the same thing, of becoming increasingly organized.[12] Note that under

---

which the vegetative processes of the plant are directed) it is not true absolutely. On the contrary, the structure of the mitochondrion has as its end not that structure itself, but the vegetative and animal functions of the organism of which it forms a part. And even the plant has an end beyond its own structure if it is considered in the context of a definite ecosystem, etc. Form or structure is an order, the end or *telos* is what the form or structure is ordered to.

12. That Being *is* organization should be obvious simply by considering the case of a system which lacked any organization at all. It simply wouldn't exist. Similarly, attacking the organizational integrity of a system destroys it, making it cease being what it is and reducing it in ontological grade. As something becomes more organized, integrating an ever greater diversity of elements in a more complex way to serve a common purpose, on the other hand, it participates ever more fully in Being. That which integrates all logically possible elements in perfect harmony is God or Being as such.

The convertibility of Being with its transcendental properties—the Beautiful, the True, the Good, and the One—follows immediately. When we say these terms are convertible with Being we mean that they refer to the same thing as Being, though they add some relation (Aquinas, *Summa Theologiae*, I, 5.1, 9.1, 16.3). It is this strategy precisely that we propose to use here. Consider, for example, the nature of beauty. By the beauty of a system, we mean simply its level of organization, understood as the object of (sensory or intellectual) perception. The greater the diversity of the elements organized, and the more perfect the harmony in which they are united, the more beautiful the system. This is true throughout the natural world, from simple harmonies of the night sky, through the more complex forms of the crystalline structures and living organisms to the rich, lush diversity of complex ecosystems and human societies. And it is true as well of great works of art, which are nothing if not a complex manifold of relations harmoniously

this formulation, teleology does not imply either or conscious intent of conscious design. Being an atom of gold is a way of being, or of participating in being, and thus of realizing the end or *telos*, and this in no sense requires to atom of gold to know what it is doing or why. Nor does it require that there is some cosmic architect who designed gold in a certain way in order to allow it to realize that end. Cognition and intelligence are emergent properties of material systems which appear only as they approach closer and closer to God.

Now form or structure actualizes the potential latent in matter, but it also limits or constrains, as Thomas was always at pains to point out. (Aquinas. *Being and Essence*). Becoming an atom of gold prevents one from being human, and vice versa. And herein lies the possibility—nay the inevitability—of contradiction and struggle and decay. Purely physical systems, which Aristotle would have characterized as mineral—i.e., capable of holding their form—do not undergo real growth and development. It seems that the higher levels of organization characteristic of living system require a certain amount of internal looseness or chaos in their structures, and indeed in their external environment, if they are to emerge in the first place and be capable of growth and development. What ever else we have learned in the past three hundred years it is that crystalline spheres represent not a higher but rather a lower degree of organization than we do—or indeed than a slug or witchity-grub. There is, furthermore, only so much growth and development which can take place with the scope of a given structure. And often even this limit cannot be reached. The formation of matter limits the way it can be used

---

arranged. Beauty itself, as Albertus Magnus and Thomas Aquinas taught long ago, is the capacity to bring things into being, and is thus convertible with Being itself, or God.

The truth value of a statement, a concept, or theory, similarly, is its capacity to organize large quantities of qualitatively diverse, and therefore highly complex experience. It is necessary in this connection to focus equal attention on the complexity of the experience organized and on the level of organization of the experience in question. Our experience is most highly organized when we identify highly compact "organizing principles," knowledge of which permits us to derive logically all the rich particularity of the experience on which the principle was based. It is this organizing capacity of theories which leads us to speak analogously of their "power." The most powerful theories are those which comprehend the full range of experience in unique compact statements which are themselves pregnant with rich experiential content.

The good, finally, is organization realized as something desirable, and thus as final cause. As final it is the object of our desire or appetite, whether sensual or intellectual, and as cause, it is the actual capacity to organize.

The Principles of Scientific Explanation

by other systems, so that supplies of useful energy and raw materials are often limited. While some finite systems are structured in such a way as to make possible harmonious co-existence or even symbiosis, others are not. Indeed, some systems are structured to realize the good by exploiting and even consuming others. Some forms may even be annihilated in the process. And all of this happens quite naturally in the course of matter's upward surge towards God.

Thus far our proposal may sound a bit like the liberal theories of evolution through random variation and natural selection which we criticized in the second part of this work, or the dialectical materialist "principle of contradiction" according to which every system has internal contradictions which accumulate until reorganization, which is often violent and destructive, is necessary, and a new, more complex structure takes its place. And there is indeed some common ground: the insight, which Aristotle lacked, that struggle and decay do not represent dead loss, but are real occasions for innovation. The difference is that for both the liberal and the dialectical materialist the process has no real meaning beyond itself, and the trend towards the development of higher degrees of organization goes unexplained.[13] From our point of view, on the other hand, it is precisely the attractive power of Being itself, whether realized as energetic stability, survival and reproduction, or intellect and will which draws things out of the pure potentiality of matter and into existence. Struggle and conflict are never merely that. They are driven by a contradiction between the drive towards the *telos* and structures which at once facilitate and hold back development. And as systems become more complex this evolutionary dynamism becomes more conscious and more complex. Animals use their complex sensory capacities to seek out new niches and then adapt to meet the challenges those niches pose. Human beings use their intellects to grasp the Good in ever more complete ways and then work to reorganize their societies in such a way as to make possible realization of these new aspirations.

The outlines of our thesis should thus be clear. Any material system can be explained with respect to three factors:

---

13. Why, for example, given the fact that bacteria and insects are far more successful at surviving and reproducing than are the higher birds and mammals, did these cumbersome and relatively inefficient forms development in the first place? Why should the crisis of capitalism lead to socialism rather than barbarism?

1. the material conditions under which it develops, which constrain the availability of various resources (raw materials, energy),
2. the dominant structure, which determines how these resources are used in the service of Being (system integrity), and
3. teleological attractors, both local and universal, appropriate to the level of organization in question.

At any given point existing structures at once facilitate and constrain development, so that the teleological drive towards higher degrees of organization, and thus a higher ontological grade, sometimes comes to conflict with the existing structure, which is then burst asunder and replaced by new forms more conducive to growth. This process takes very different forms at different levels of organization (physical, biological, and social). It is at once necessary, operating with iron-clad certainty towards the long term development of higher degrees of organization, and radically open, proceeding along lines which can never be completely predicted, constrained only by what is logically possible, and by certain general conditions, which are embodied in fundamental physical law, which are necessary to the existence of any sort of organization whatsoever. The process terminates only in a form of organization which is infinite, perfect, necessary, and thus divine—i.e., in Being itself, which is the attractor on which the process as a whole radically depends and from which it derives its ultimate meaning.

Having advanced this thesis, we need now to test it, seeing to what extent it can shed light on physical, biological, and social systems, and to what extent it makes possible definition of a promising research program. It is to these tasks that we now proceed.

6

Physical Organization

THE NATURE OF PHYSICAL ORGANIZATION

THE FIRST TASK OF any science is the definition of what must be explained. It is the definition of distinct formal objects which makes possible the division between the various special sciences, and a correct understanding of their relationship with each other, and with wisdom or metaphysics. Now from the standpoint of a science which is at least open to teleological explanation, and more especially from the standpoint of this inquiry, the most pressing question is that of organization, or ordering to an end. We want know whether or not the universe as a whole is organized, and if so how the category of organization can be used to explain, or at least shed light on, the behavior, the structure, and indeed the very existence of various physical systems.

Now when we consider natural systems from the standpoint of the category of organization, it immediately becomes apparent that some systems are at least locally organized: they are, that is, structured in such a way as to serve some end or purpose, namely that of their own survival and reproduction. It is these systems which we call living or biological. Of these biological systems some give little or no evidence of being able to represent these ends to themselves and thus become aware of them. These are the systems which Aristotle called vegetative, a category which includes not only what contemporary biologists call the Plant Kingdom, but also the fungi, protists, and other simple organisms. Some living systems on the other hand not only behave in a way that suggests purposeful behavior, by moving about in such a way as to better realize the ends in question, but also show evidence of definite structures—e.g., nervous systems of varying complexity—which allow them to encode information about their environments and organize their activity in such a way as to realize their ends. It is these systems which we call animals. Animals, in turn, may be divided based on whether or not they show evidence of pursuing abstract, universal ends, or merely definite goods accessible to the senses. Just precisely what sorts of behaviors indicate an advance to this level is a much disputed question. Language clearly meets the mark, as does tool making, but it is possible that primitive intellection occurs without these behaviors. Language and tool making, in any case, indicate passage to a grade of organization which is in excess of simple intellection; they involve not merely the maintenance and reproduction of a definite structure of organization, but also the construction of new forms of organization through conscious labor, whether the raw material in question is physical, biological or indeed social. This is the grade of organization at which we humans find ourselves and it is the highest grade for which we have direct empirical evidence, and indeed the highest grade for which such evidence may be possible. It is, however, possible to posit immaterial forms of organization, in particular various cosmic attractors, which are not merely organized or organizing, but which are the actual aims towards which organizing processes tend. If contingent such attractors would bear much in common with Thomistic angels; if necessary, such an attractor would, of course, be divine. The existence of such attractors, finite and infinite, while not empirically verifiable can, we will argue, be inferred from the empirical behavior of physical, biological, and social systems.

But what about those systems which have historically been studied by physics (and chemistry)? Is there any meaningful way in which the category of organization, and thus teleological explanation, can shed light on such systems? The question is extraordinarily important. After all, even on the most optimistic estimates, only a tiny fraction of the matter in the universe has achieved the level of living organization. An argument which can show the existence of purposeful organization and the usefulness of teleological explanation only at the level of biological and social systems may well make a case against the more extreme forms of physical reductionism, but it will hardly amount to an argument for cosmic teleology. At the same time, even the sort of unconsciously purposeful structure which we see in the simplest living organisms is not only absent in purely physical systems; it is the very absence of this sort of organization which makes us characterize them as "merely physical."

Perhaps it will be useful, in addressing this problem, to specify just what we *do* find at the level of "merely physical," and then to ask what bearing, if any, the category of organization or finality might have on what we find. Each of the characteristics we identify will bear further examination later on. For now we want merely to hint at an hypothesis. Physical systems, and indeed all material systems of whatever grade are, first of all, characterized by spatiotemporal extension. Just what this means remains a bit of a mystery. For now it suffices to say that there is something about the underlying structure of the universe which prevents everything from being in the same place or happening all at once—it allows difference, which is certainly not the same thing as organization, but it is clearly necessary to it. And indeed, if mathematical physicists are to be believed at all—and there is nothing in our critique that touches their conclusions in this matter—space-time has a definite structure that at least limits the way in which the elements in material systems can be related to each other. Indeed, a good bit of mathematical physics—general and special relativity, for example—has concerned itself with describing this structure in terms of its underlying topology or shape, its geometry, etc. What we will need to do is to see if we can explain it.

The second thing we notice about physical systems is that they appear, at least, as systems of interacting elements, though on closer inspection and analysis it is difficult to distinguish element from interaction, especially at smaller scales. What from one point of view appear to be massive particles undergoing gravitational interactions are, from another point of view, charged particles which are the means of some other sort of interaction. Indeed, it seems easier to define clearly what we mean by the elements in a system if we begin by describing the sort of interaction we are observing, than if we proceed in the other direction. And yet it seems nearly impossible to talk about a system without talking about the elements which, from one standpoint or another, make up those systems (elementary particles, atoms and molecules, massive bodies) as well as the means by which those elements interact. These elements are what mathematical physics has generally called matter, the interactions what mathematical physics has generally called energy. Because of our preference for the somewhat different Aristotelian meaning of the term matter, we will use the term "body" instead. While "matter" indicates simply the possibility for form or organization, "body" indicates a system which, while already "formed" to some degree, has definite spatiotemporal limits. The term "energy" however, in so far as it indicates a means of interaction and thus of the actualization of form, has similar valence in both Aristotelian and mathematical physics and will be used in both senses, with necessary qualification being supplied in context.

Now here too mathematical physics has supplied some description of the phenomena in question. Specifically, quantum mechanics, with its insistence on the quantum nature of energy transfer, is nothing if not an attempt to describe the subtle dialectic between bodies and the energies by which they interact. Indeed, as quanta of energy, elementary particles are by their very nature what we have defined as bodies even when they are also means of interaction and thus of the formation of systems. Mathematical physics has, furthermore, defined definite laws which describe the way in which different sorts of physical interactions (gravitation, electromagnetic, strong, and weak) work and the way in which the nature of these interactions both makes possible and limits the development of various types of organization. It is, for example, the quantum nature of energy transfer which defines the possibility of distinct chemical elements and the Pauli Exclusion Principle which limits atomic structure in a way which makes chemical interaction possible at all.

The third thing that we notice about physical systems is that they seem to operate under fairly rigid energetic constraints. Creating organization—doing work—requires energy, as does the conservation of organization which has already been built up. Left to themselves, the energy of physical systems tends to dissipate, to become useless and the integrity of the systems seems to degenerate. These are the phenomena described by thermodynamics, and especially by the Second Law of Thermodynamics which, as we have seen, has so often been used in arguments against cosmic teleology but which in fact will turn out to be among the basic conditions for the continued development of organized complexity in the universe. After all, if organization did not degrade over time, if there was not chaos and disintegration, organizational innovation would become progressively more difficult until all of the energy in the universe was tied up in existing forms of organization and further progress became impossible...

In addition to these law-like properties of material systems, described by relativity, quantum mechanics, and thermodynamics, it is also useful to note the apparent fine-tuning of numerous physical constants such as the relative strength of the strong and weak nuclear interactions, of gravity and electromagnetism, and of positive and negative electromagnetic charges, which appear to be fixed at just the levels necessary in order to permit the development of complex (biological and social) organization.

All of this suggests to us a general hypothesis regarding the nature of physical systems. While not themselves *organized* in the strict sense of being ordered to an end, physical systems have the structure necessary in order to make possible the emergence of more complex biological and social organization. Without the structure imposed by the laws of physics and by the fine-tuning of physical constants ordering to an end would be in conceivable. This is because such orderings by their very nature presuppose difference, discreteness, and the relative openness imposed by the constant disintegration of existing forms of organization in favor of new ones—though the presence of these conditions does not, by itself, imply or guarantee the emergence of properly teleological systems.

From this point of view the intuitive association between matter in the Aristotelian sense and the physical, while often the occasion of some confusion, is not entirely without sense. If matter is the possibility of form, and if physical systems are precisely those which make possible the development of complex organization, without themselves being so organized, then physical systems can, in fact, be identified with matter. Some caution is, however, in order. Physical matter cannot be regarded as prime matter, because it is already formed to some degree. It is governed by the structure of space-time, by the laws of quantum mechanics which require discrete energy transfer and which prohibit more than two elementary particles from occupying the same energy state, and by the laws of thermodynamics which impose limits on the development and conservation of structure. Prime matter, on the contrary, being wholly lacking in form, would be essentially nothing—or rather nothing in the presence of some Principle which can draw forth everything from nothing and thus render the universe possible.

It should be noted that our strategy offers an entirely new way of unifying physics. Rather than insisting on unification at the level of the mathematical formalisms which describe physical structures, we will show that these structures themselves—even if they cannot all be described by one single formalism—are in fact required by the common end to which they are ordered. The structures we encounter in the physical world are the condition of any possible organization and can be shown to be such.

Let us see what evidence we can adduce for this thesis, and what light it can shed on the problems we have identified.

THE ASPECTS OF PHYSICAL ORGANIZATION

Spatiotemporal Extension

Let us begin by analyzing what we mean by space, time, and extension. These terms are all ways of marking difference, and indeed they mark the lowest grade of difference which we can imagine—namely that of separation. In order for things to be really distinct they must be separated in one sense or another. Two objects occupying *exactly* the same region of space-time would not be really distinguishable: they would have the same shape, for the same period of time, and any other signals which they emitted would become hopelessly confused with each other. We could not experience one as orange and the other blue, for example—their colors would become blurred together. Nor could we experience one as loud and the other as silent, one as rough and the other smooth, one smelling and tasking of chili and the other of garlic. And the problem is not simply a result of our limited sensory apparatus. Were we to discover diverse signals emanating from a unique point is space time, our conclusion would not be that diverse objects occupied that point but rather that whatever occupied that point had a range of properties which we were experiencing through our senses.

Nor is it possible for there to be a material system which occupies only one point in space-time, at least so long as we give the term "point" its strict mathematical sense, as infinitesimal and lacking in any extension. Signals emanating from a single unique point would, in this sense, seem to be coming from nothing, and any mathematical formalisms which press us to think in this way should, whatever their other uses, leave us a bit skeptical about their ability to capture fully the structure of physical reality. Any real system will occupy a more or less definite set of points in space-time.

We humans experience spatial and temporal separation in somewhat different ways. We call spatial separations between things which we either can or could, were the range of our senses sufficiently extended, imagine experiencing simultaneously. Attempts to capture this difference more rigorously have, however, been less than successful, at least in so far as an attempt is made to restrict oneself to mechanical or dynamic considerations and thermodynamics, biology, and psychology are left to one side. This is because, as we have noted above, dynamic laws (such as those of relativity and quantum mechanics) are all time reversible. Thermodynamic, biological, and social processes are, on the other hand, irreversible by nature and provide the only rigorous basis for defining an arrow of time. And yet these disciplines bring in considerations which hardly seem intrinsic to the nature of spatiotemporal extension. It is important in this regard to distinguish between the question of the reality of temporal separation and the way in which it is experienced. The realist epistemology to which we are committed, on which this whole work is based, and the outlines of which we laid out in the Introduction requires that we acknowledge experienced difference as indicating real difference, but it does not require that we regard our raw experience as revealing the real nature of that difference. Thus events experienced as separated by time are in fact really so separated. But it may be simply the structure of our sensory apparatus, or the fact that we gain knowledge through the senses which makes us experience that separation as sequential rather than simultaneous. Eckhardt has argued for the first alternative, suggesting that evolution of a four dimensional imagination which could represent temporally separated events simultaneously, is extremely unlikely. But the problem may be more fundamental. If the special-relativistic ban on faster than light signally turns out to be correct, then separation and simultaneity are mutually exclusive for systems which draw their knowledge from sensation, as indeed any material system must. Indeed, the simultaneity of spatially separated events itself turns out to be only an approximation. This does not, of course, exclude the possibility that immaterial systems—the angels or God—might be able to know temporally separated events simultaneously. This would not, however, be "experience" as we understand it, but rather intellection. And of course we can intellectually understand temporally separate events simultaneously. We do so every time we think some temporal measure, such as a second or a year. It is only the intervention of the imagination, which is always present for us as the background to such intellectual knowledge, which reinforces the impression of nonsimultaneity.

Having established what we mean by spatiotemporal extension and why it is essential to material organization, we need now to see what light, if any, the principal physical theory of space-time—i.e., the theory of relativity—can shed on our problem, and what light our thesis can shed on this often enigmatic and counter-intuitive theory. We have already explained the genesis of the theory both historically and logically; here we need only summarize its principal claims. We will recall that the theory developed in response to the disappearance, as a result of our changing picture of the universe, of any fixed inertial frame against which to measure motion. First the earth, and then sun, and finally the fixed stars themselves had been shown to be themselves in motion, making the definition of a stable system of cosmic coordinates effectively impossible. For a time the frame of the fixed stars was replaced by the idea of the "luminferous aether," which penetrated all "ponderable matter" and through which moved waves of light and other forms of electromagnetic radiation. But the Michelson-Morely experiment showed that the speed of light is the same in direction of Earth's motion and perpendicular to it. This could not be true if there was some medium through which the light was moving. This meant that it would be necessary to reformulate the laws of mechanics in accord with what Henri Poincaré called the "Principle of Relativity." Uniform translatory motion possessed by a system as a whole cannot be detected by an observer looking at phenomena within that system; thus there no way of determining absolute motion. The result of this effort was Einstein's theory of special relativity.

What special relativity does is to represent motion in the context of a Minkowski space, a real four dimensional vector space in which distance is defined not by the standard Pythagorean metric, but rather by the Minkowski metric

$$\delta s^2 = -c^2 t^2 + \delta x^2 + \delta y^2 + \delta z^2$$

Because the sign of the time term, unlike that of the other terms, is negative, it is not strictly speaking correct to say that the Minkowski space simply adds a fourth, temporal dimension. The temporal component of distance works differently than the spatial components.

Given this larger geometrical structure it is them possible to define a linear transformation, called the Lorentz transformation

$$x'^2 = (x-vt)^2/(1-(v^2/c^2))$$

which relates spatiotemporal intervals as they are perceived in one inertial frame with the way they are perceived in another. An analogous relation makes it possible to transform measurements of energy into measurements of mass

$$E = mc^2.$$

These formalisms resolve a fundamental irrationality in earlier formulations of physical theory but, as we have seen, also generate some paradoxical implications. The notion of simultaneity becomes deeply problematic, as events separated spatially can no longer be perceived simultaneously. Distances and time intervals appear to be different to observers in different inertial frames. Even a quantity as fundamental as mass seems to undergo change as a result of acceleration. The structure of Minkowski space, furthermore, effectively divides the universe between those regions which are within the light-cone of any given event, and which may therefore be causally related to that event, and those which are outside the light cone and thus cannot be causally related.

Now the effect of these laws is to apply a definite structure to spatiotemporal extension. As counter-intuitive as the effects of assuming a constant speed of light in the absence of fixed inertial frames may be, in the absence of such a requirement the very notion of temporal separation would collapse. Instantaneous signaling would, in effect, mean that even if things took place in different locations, along however many different dimensions we might posit, they would in a certain sense be perceived, our at least could in principle be perceived, as taking place all at once. This is because instantaneous signaling, by its very nature, means that an event taking place at any point in an n-dimensional space could be registered, and thus affect, any system capable of receiving and/or being affected by it at any other point in the n-dimensional space. Simply specifying one of these dimensions as temporal and defining earlier and later directions without adding further structure does us no good. It is not merely that events taking place "later" could affect events which took place "earlier"; all points in the space-time would be affected equally and at once so that the "earlier" and "later" directions would be rendered meaningless. Everything would, in effect, happen at once, a result far more counter-intuitive than the paradoxes of special relativity.

This is not to suggest that there are no systems which are characterized by such an instantaneous structure. On the contrary, as we have already suggested, and as we will argue in greater depth later in this work, it is simply material or emergent systems that are so constrained—such constraints are precisely what we mean when we say they are material. An immaterial intellect, such as that of an angel or of God, could act simultaneously at as many different points in space time as its nature permitted, though this action would be of the nature of formal or final causation and as such would not be subject to direct empirical detection or reducible to physical interactions. It is something which we would have to infer from empirical data rather than observe directly. That there are such systems and that they do affect the material universe is suggested by a variety of phenomena which would otherwise require instantaneous signaling or which seem to involve causation where no physical mechanism can be identified, such as quantum nonlocality and the strong form of the "morphogenetic fields" thesis.[1]

Much is often made in this context of the possibility, which is not ruled out by special relativity, of faster than light particles, known as tachyons. And of course it would be possible to use the language of particle physics to describe phenomena which seem to involve faster than light signaling. But this smacks of efforts to physicalize phenomena which by their very nature defy the constraints which characterize what we ordinarily understand by the physical. It is rather like the attempts by Franciscan scientists during the thirteenth century (who are, as we have seen, the intellectual ancestors of today's mathematical physicists) to define a sort of "spiritual matter" out of which angels are composed. Doesn't it make more sense to allow that there are phenomena, even phenomena which we can at least partly understand, which stand outside the purely physical, and to find concepts which are appropriate to these phenomena, than to attempt to physicalize them at the cost of producing even more paradoxes than physics already contains?

---

1. Weaker forms of the morphogenetic fields thesis depend on chemical gradients within organisms which operate according to the laws of nonlinear thermodynamics in order to regulate the development of complex biological structures (Prigogine 1984). Advocates of stronger forms of the thesis (Sheldrake 1981, 1989) point to such phenomena as various chemicals "learning" to crystallize for the first time, and then subsequently beginning to crystallize all around the planet, something which seems to defy explanation by the more mechanistic forms of efficient causation. They also point out that while chemical gradients may well play an important intermediate role in morphogenesis, this does not explain what causes the chemical gradients themselves to form, or more generally the link between the information encoded in the genome, which merely codes for various proteins, and the formation of the larger organism, with certain genes being activated only at certain places in the body and at certain times.

But it is not only the fact spatiotemporal extension and the structure of space-time as described by special relativity which turn out to be necessary for the development of complex organization. It may well be that an ordered material universe is possible only in four dimensions. This, in any case, is the argument made by Errol Harris (Harris 1991: 49ff.) As Harris points out

> The existence and nature of all physical phenomena appear to depend on the propagation of classical and quantum waves, and the properties of wave equations are closely dependent on dimensionality. In less than three spatial dimensions, waves could propagate at arbitrary speeds, whereas in three they are restricted to one only (the velocity of light, c). Consequently, in a less number of dimensions signals radiated at different times could arrive at the same point simultaneously, and no sharply defined signals could be guaranteed. Further, it has been shown that reverberation-free impulses cannot be obtained in an even number of spatial dimensions, and that only in three can wave propagation be achieved without distortion. It has also been proved that three dimensions are essential for information processing of any kind, without which life processes, and in particular the functioning of the human brain, are not feasible . . .
>
> The above considerations are further consolidated by the demonstration that the fundamental natural units of the universe, constructed from the primary physical constants (G, h, and c) do not occur except in four dimensions, and upon these virtually all the known laws of physics depend. In a world of other than four dimensions, planetary orbits, whether determined by Newtonian or by Einsteinian laws, would be unstable, making the necessary conditions for the emergence of life impossible. Even more radical, only in four dimensions could the electronic orbits of the atom remain stable, so that matter as we know it can exist.
>
> Not surprisingly, therefore, Ehrnfest (in 1917) argued that all of the fundamental laws of physics depend upon the four-dimensionality of space-time . . . (Harris 1991: 49–50)

The significance of this fine-tuning will be considered later, along with that of fine-tuning in the strengths of various physical interactions. For now it will suffice to say that while not itself purposeful, the existence, structure, and apparently arbitrary dimensionality of space-time all turn out to be conditions of any possible purposeful organization.

The Nature of Physical Interactions

Gravitational Interactions

Having demonstrated the necessity of spatiotemporal extension and indeed of at least some elements of the specific structure described by special relativity for the development of complex organization, life, and intelligence, we are now in a position to look at the nature of physical interactions themselves and see what light, if any, a teleological approach can shed on the problem. Historically, mathematical physicists have identified four fundamental forces by which physical systems interact: gravitation, electromagnetism, and the strong and weak nuclear forces. The first of these forces was initially described by Newton's classical formalism

$$F = GM/r^2$$

and later by Einstein's general theory of relativity.

$$G_{\mu\nu} = 8\pi/c^4 \, (T_{\mu\nu})$$

We have already seen that like his special theory of relativity, Einstein's general theory leads to some results which are counter-intuitive at best. Space-time, it turns out, is a product of matter, and the presence of matter results in a curvature of space-time which is in turn leads to the interactions which we call gravitational. This solves some problems. Newton's formalism no longer made sense in the absence of a fixed frame, and led to serious difficulties should the universe turn out to be finite—i.e., the well known difficulty of what lies outside the boundary of the universe. If space-time is a product of matter the answer is simple: literally nothing. But Einstein's theory also creates difficulties, most of which have been exploited by the discipline of mathematical-physical cosmology in the service of the cosmological pessimism required by the ideological hegemony of Capital. Einstein's theory has usually been taken to rule out a universe which is infinitely extended. This is because, assuming that the universe is roughly homogenous, it will curve space-time around itself into a four-dimensional sphere, so that parallel lines, it they extend far enough, will ultimately meet. Einstein's equations, coupled with this assumption, known as the cosmological principle, together with a cosmological constant which Einstein introduced for aesthetic reasons, leads to the finite and static spherical universe which Einstein preferred. Without the cosmological constant, for which there was no empirical basis at the time, the equations lead directly to the "Friedman solution," and the Big Bang cosmology with all the difficulties we have hitherto identified.

This is not, however, the only way to read Einstein. We should point out first of all that at least certain implications of his theory are not only compatible with but are actually required by the line of reasoning which we have been developing. The most obvious point of contact, of course is the claim that space-time is a product of matter. Special relativity treats space-time as analytically distinct from matter; general relativity certifies that it is not itself a real underlying structure but rather a formal property of the way in which material systems interact. Another way of saying this is that the shape and size (the topology and geometry of the universe) is determined by what is going on there, and not the other way around. Higher order organization determines lower order organization. The structure of space time is determined by a universe in which there is indeed complex organization, life, and intelligence.

Eric Lerner (Lerner 1991: 130), furthermore, has pointed out that the assumption of cosmological homogeneity is not only unfounded, it actually contradicts empirical evidence, which points towards the existence of very significant large-scale nonhomogeneity, which cosmologies predicated on the cosmological principle have, not surprisingly been at pains to explain. Such a "clumpy" universe may well turn out to have a rather exotic geometry (though it is not at all clear we would ever experience that geometry as anything other than a texture of more or less expected gravitational fields); it need not be finite. And even if the universe should turn out to be finite in spatiotemporal extension, this need not imply that there is a limit to its level of complexity and development—a point Errol Harris, echoing Hegel, has made with some force (Harris 1965). Infinite complexity and infinite extension are not the same thing.

Above and beyond the specific laws which govern gravitational interaction, it is important to note the role of gravitational forces generally in promoting the development of complex organization. The boldest claims on this front are made by Benjamin Gal-Or, who regards gravity as the principal cause for the development of structure in the universe, including, at least indirectly, the emergence of irreversible thermodynamic process, and thus of geochemical and biological evolution. Among the contributions he cites are:

1. the expansion of the universe,
2. the break-up of the expanding, homogenous cosmological gas into individual clouds which then go on to form galactic clusters, galaxies, stars, etc.,
3. the production within stars through nuclear reactions ultimately driven by gravity of the heavy elements which in turn make possible life and intelligence, and the dispersion of these elements throughout the universe by means of supernovae.
4. the formation of planetary systems, and the long-term evolution of planets through gravitationally driven processes of differentiation (e.g., of molten minerals with different specific gravity) crystallization, and transformation (e.g., mountain-building, volcanic activity, pneumatiolytic and hydrothermal processes, etc.), which result in a chemical diverse and inhomogeneous planetary crust, and even
5. the development of life through the direct or indirect input of energy into geochemically "fertile" planetary environments (Gal-Or 1987: 354–61).

Of these claims, only the first, which is dependent on the big-bang cosmology, is really open to serious dispute. And even the alternative plasma cosmology, which tends to give priority to electromagnetic forces in the early stages of cosmic evolution, still reserves an important role for gravitational interactions.

Quite apart from phenomena of cosmic evolution, it is gravity which permits the coherence of systems which are not structured in such a way as to interact chemically (i.e., electromagnetically) with each other, and which are thus able to conserve their integrity. Were it not for gravitational interactions we could not walk on the earth without becoming chemically bound to the earth and thus cease to be what we are.

Non-Gravitational Interactions

In addition to the gravitational interactions which play such a central role in structuring space-time and in making possible the large-scale development of complex organization, there are three other sorts of interactions which have been identified by physicists: the strong and weak nuclear interactions and electromagnetism. The weak interaction is responsible for the decay of neutrons into protons and for neutrino interactions with matter. The strong nuclear interaction is what holds together similarly charged protons within the atomic nucleus. And electromagnetism, of course, is what makes possible the interactions of electrons with nuclei to form atoms, of atoms to form molecules, and of atoms and molecules with each other to form solids and liquids. The behavior of all three of these forces are, as we have seen, described by quantum field theories. Our focus here, as throughout this chapter, will not be on a detailed exposition of theories from mathematical physics, but rather on demonstrating the teleological significance of the underlying physical realities these theories formalize.

The first principle of quantum theory is, we will recalled, Planck's insight that energy transfer is not continuous, but rather quantum. One cannot transfer just any quantity of energy one wants, as those it was infinitely indivisible, but only packets, the size of which is described by the equation:

$$E_{photon} = hv = \frac{hc}{\lambda}$$

While originally developed to explain the behavior of light, this principle applies to all particles which carry energy. This means that elementary particles, whether bound within an atom or elsewhere cannot be just anywhere, or have just any amount of energy. Rather, they will occupy discrete levels and have discrete quantities of energy which they will gain or lose in "packets" as they become excite, or give of energy in the form of heat, light, etc.

The second principle of quantum mechanics states that elementary particles cannot be described precisely in terms of the position and velocity at the same time—the so-called Heisenberg Uncertainty Principle.

$$\Delta x * \Delta(mv) \geq hv = \frac{h}{4\pi}$$

Where Plank's discovery of the quantum nature of energy transfer forced us to think of things which we had formerly considered to be wave-like as instead being constituted by a flow of particles, the Heisenberg Uncertainty Principle then turns around and suggests that even things which we had thought of as particles really can't be rigorously described in this way. The notion that photon, electrons, and other elementary objects are both particles and waves, so that their location is smudged out across space and time, being more intensely present in some locations than others, is only a slight improvement. What sort of thing is it which is smudged out over space-time?

The solution becomes apparent if we follow the mathematical formalism—but do so with a philosopher's eye for systematic as well as quantitative relationships. Since the particle cannot be adequately described as a particle, with definite position and momentum (which is what it *means* to be a particle), physics generally describes it by a "quantum wave function" φ, where φ is a function of spatial coordinates (x,y,z) and φ^2 is interpreted as the probability distribution for the particle—i.e., the relative probability of finding it in any given location. Psi in turn is obtained by solving the Schrodinger equation—something which can be done with accuracy only for the simplest quantum systems, such as the hydrogen atom:

$$H\varphi = E\varphi$$

where H is the Hamiltonian operator expressing the total energy of the system and E is the same quantity expressed in different terms, as the sum of electric potential of the system and the kinetic energy of the its component parts. Each φ that solves the equation is interpreted physically, in the case of an atom, as one of the "orbitals" in which an electron might be located—or, more properly, which describes its state.

What this means is that all material systems constitute integral wholes the various elements of which are defined by their inter-relations, apart from which they cannot meaningfully be said to exist. Indeed, when we attempt to understand things as radically separate and distinct, on the model of classical atomism, we run into insuperable irrationalities, such as those imposed by the Heisenberg Uncertainty relation. As we continue the search for some authentically "elementary" particle, we find only ever smaller quanta of energy which mediate interactions between various types of physical systems. In this sense "matter" turns out to be nothing at all. Every real phenomenon is given by some formal relationship. And this radical interconnectedness is characteristic not only of microphysical systems of the sort ordinarily studied by quantum mechanics. The same quantum formulae can be used to described the universe as a whole, and phenomena such as quantum nonlocality suggest that even systems which extend over vast cosmic distances—distances at which the limit on the speed of signally makes communication between really distinct elements impossible—are actually interconnected at the quantum level.

At the same time these very ways of relating do define real differences—differences behind which there appear to be discrete *quanta* of energy but which we experience as *qualitative*. And without this real difference, material organization, understood as diverse elements ordered to an end, would be impossible. Imagine, for example a universe in which relationships did not define real difference. All that would be left would be a hierarchy of formalisms, each more general than the other, until one "ascended" to the supreme formalism within which all truth was embodied. Indeed, not only would the "diverse elements" disappear; the end to which they are ordered would cease to be an end in any meaningful sense because there would be nothing to be ordered to it. All that would be left would be a pure order, a system of only apparent differences with no meaning or purpose.

It is, further, necessary that the real differences defined by the relations governing physical interactions be discrete or quantum in nature. One of the most striking things discovered by the senses is the qualitative diversity of the various things which compose the world around us and the qualitatively diverse ways they interact and combine with each other. Some of these differences are visible to the naked eye. We experience gases, liquids and solid, as well as transitions between these states through freezing and melting, condensing and boiling. Some of the things we see around us have a shiny, silvery gray appearance; others are duller in texture but more colorful. Think of the yellow green of chlorine, the deep red of bromine, or the imperial violet of iodine. Some forms of matter (those we call metals, again) are good conductors of electricity, others are not. Most importantly, many of the forms of matter we find around us combine with each other in distinctive proportions, and it is possible to distinguish between elements—those forms of matter which are not the result of combinations of other forms—and compounds which are. We can also begin to group the elements together based on shared patterns of reactivity.

We now know, of course, that all of these many differences are due ultimately to differences in atomic structure which are, in turn, mandated as it were by the quantum nature of energy exchange. It is due to the quantum nature of energy exchange that Hydrogen and Helium are two distinct elements and not merely two points along a chemical continuum.

It is due to the quantum nature of energy exchange that gold is yellow and silver white. And it is due to the quantum nature of energy exchange that the universe contains the diverse elements which combine in the unique and complex ways which make possible the beauty of a precious stone such as lapis lazuli, long used by illuminators to make the brilliant blue pigment with which they adorn their manuscripts, or the carotenoids and anthocyanins which yield such magnificent reds and yellows just before the trees shed their leaves in autumn. It is due to the quantum nature of energy exchange that there are cats and dogs, men and women—and that we are all gloriously different, even if also ordered to a common end.

The Fine Tuning of Physical Interactions

This discussion of physical interactions should make clear that even if these interactions are not, by themselves, purposeful, they are wonderfully structured in such a way as to make the eventual emergence of purpose possible. But there is more at work here. As we have suggested numerous times above, not only are the various types of physical interactions themselves structured in such a way as to make possible complex organization, but the relative strengths of these interactions is also fixed well within what turns out to be a very narrow range compatible with the development of complex organization. It might be useful at this point to point out some of these incidences of fine tuning.

- Had the weak nuclear interaction been appreciably stronger than it is, then all of the hydrogen in the universe would have been very quickly burned into Helium; making it weaker would have prevented the formation of hydrogen because neutrons would never have decayed into protons (check for dependence on Big Bang. Leslie 1989:4)

- In order for carbon to form during stellar nucleosynthesis, the strong nuclear interaction has to be within roughly 1% of its current strength. Making it stronger would block the formation of protons, so that there would be no atoms, or bind them into diprotons, so that stars would burn too fast to ever generate life. Decreasing its strength on the other hand would unbind the deuteron, making stellar burning and thus the formation of heavier elements impossible.

- The ratio between the electromagnetic and gravitational interactions must be close to its actual value of 10^{40}. If electromagnetism were too much stronger, all stars would be red dwarfs; if it was too much weaker they would all be blue giants. Neither type of star is thought likely to produce planetary systems with life (Leslie 1989:4, Harris 1991: 51). This same ratio is important to the very possibility of planets, the size of which depends on the interaction between gravitation and the electron pressure generated by the effects of the Pauli Exclusion Principle, as well as electrostatic repulsion.

- The charges on protons and electrons, while opposite, are equal in spite of their mass. Were this not true, all atoms would either by positively or negatively charged, and would repel each other, with the result that no macroscopic bodies could be formed (Harris 1991: 49).

This evidence of fine tuning, just like that of the fine-tuning of spatio-temporal dimensionality, cannot help but suggest that physical order is in some sense ordered to the development of life and intelligence. We will consider later, in the conclusion to the chapter, in just what sense this can be said to be so, and will also answer some of the principal arguments against the teleological reading of cosmological fine-tuning generally—and for versions of the teleological reading which, believe, fail to do justice to the evidence or introduce unnecessary difficulties.

Thermodynamic Constraints

We come, finally, to that body of physical law that has most often been taken as evidence against cosmic teleology: the discipline of thermodynamics. From the very beginning thermodynamics has been bound up with the experience of human finitude. Born out of the effort to make a perfect heat engine, which would permanently recycle all of the energy it produced, so that it could do an infinite amount of work with a finite amount of energy, it thermodynamics, far more than any other scientific discipline, which finally sealed the fate of natural theology in the nineteenth century, with its somber predictions of a cosmic heat death. And it is the limitations imposed by thermodynamic laws which account for nearly all of the challenges and frustrations of day to day life, from the need to periodically clean our homes through the debilitating ailments of old age to the inevitability of death and decay.

For our purposes the significance of the laws of thermodynamics are best understood when considered in conjunction with one of the principles of classical mechanics, namely that energy is necessary in order to do work. In the context of classical mechanics work is formalized as the product of the force applied to a particle and the distance through which the particle moves.

$$W = Fs$$

or

$$W = mas$$

Work may also be expressed in terms of the pressure and volume of a gas acting on a piston

$$dW = p\, dV$$

where p is the pressure applied to the piston and V is the volume of the gas. The rather schematic character of these formalizations are the result of the fact that mathematical physics reduces all change to local motion. The basic point, however, remains valid—no change of any kind, and certainly no growth and development, can take place without an input of energy into the system the environment.

What the laws of thermodynamics do is, first of all, to drive home even more forcefully the energy requirements of complex organization and, second, to set strict limits to the ability of any system to make efficient use of its energy in order to create or conserve organization. These laws are, as we explained in an earlier chapter, as follows:

1. The change in the internal energy U of a system is equal the difference between the heat absorbed by the system and the work done by it.

$$dU = dQ - Dw$$

2. It is impossible to transform all of the heat extracted from a source which is at a constant temperature into useful energy or work, or, alternatively the entropy S of a system, where

$$dS = dQ/T$$

plus its environment can never decrease.

Physical Organization

Since most complex organized systems are far from an equilibrium state, this means that such systems require a constant input of energy not only in order to come into being in the first place, but also in order to conserve their integrity. Closed systems tend towards equilibrium, or what is the same thing, towards randomness and disorder.

Now it is easy to see why this discovery would have led to a certain pessimism. Depending on the details of one's cosmological model, it presents what are at the very least significant obstacles to the long-term survival of life and intelligence and may even imply inevitable cosmic death. Indeed, even though the prediction of cosmic heat death in its original form has been largely disproven, most cosmologists now envision the long-term future of the universe in a way which engages thermodynamic as well as quantum mechanical considerations to achieve an extremely pessimistic result.

Matters are not, however, nearly so simple. While it is true that thermodynamic law imposes real constraints on the development and conservation of complex organization, these same laws also turn out to be a condition of the possibility of such organization. Two points are in order here. It is necessary, first of all, to recall the distinction we have made between order and organization. Order is simply obedience to a rule which governs the location and/or behavior of the elements in a system or, alternatively, the information content of the system. The concept of organization includes that of order—organization is an ordering to an end. But the very element of teleology or finalism which is integral to the idea of organization seems to require a middling degree of order. Thus humans are, as physicist Charles Bennet points out, intermediate in order or information content, between a crystal or a gas, but are more organized than either. Systems which become too rigid, just like those which become too chaotic, are no longer able to realize their ends. Were it not for the thermodynamic tendency for systems to increase in entropy or disorder all of the matter in the universe might eventually become trapped in low entropy structures such as crystals, making the development of authentic organization impossible.

But there is more. The thermodynamic tendency towards disintegration requires that organized systems struggle to find ever more effective and efficient ways to capture energy and order their constituent elements towards their ends, and thus more effectively conserve their integrity. Did systems not have to innovate in this way, there is a danger that all of the matter in the universe would have become trapped in relatively low-echelon forms of organization which discover an easy route to conserving their integrity and reproducing their structures. In this sense, the Second Law of Thermodynamics is integral to any explanation of why there is evolution towards qualitatively higher degrees of organization when there are very simple structures which permit very successful survival and reproduction in a great many niches. Assuming that there is some movement towards organization in the first place—and we will establish that this is so, and that the movement is attributable to teleological attraction in the next chapter—what entropic disintegration does is to press life, and eventually intelligence, to search out ways of conserving and reproducing system integrity which are less and less vulnerable to entropic attack. In the process this conservation and reproduction becomes less and less focused on the individual organism and more and more focused on a wider and deeper meaning of the Good. Thus reproduction by cellular division, which produces exact clones, gives way to sexual reproduction which in turn enormously enriches the genetic diversity of the species and ultimately contributes to the development of new species. Concern for the purely biological integrity of individual or species is supplemented by concern for the new, higher order integrity of animal societies, and eventually for the integrity of cultural forms which survive even the civilizations which produce them.

Entropy, finally, is the condition for any authentic historical change. Even if, in an infinite universe, it might well be possible for authentic development to take place simply by expanding into new regions of space-time, this would still relegate "developed regions" to a stifling domination by the dead weight of the past. Ecological niches would fill up, entire continents and eventually entire planets would become hopelessly built up, positions of leadership would be taken up by impossibly ancient individuals whose experience and wisdom made their authority incontestable, locking out the new and the young for ever, established institutions and cultural forms would endure from age to age until the dead weight of tradition became such a crushing burden that intelligence died not of entropic disintegration but rather of regimented boredom.

The importance of entropy to the development of complex organization is most apparent in precisely the context that we find it most troubling, i.e., the context of our own lives—and of our own death. It is precisely the limited and transitory character of finite goods, which are all swept away by entropic disintegration which impels us to look for higher goods, which might be less obvious to us, but which, when we discover them, also prove more resistant to entropic attack. Thus, knowing that we will not survive for ever, we become interested in making some contribution that will, and thus begin to develop our latent potential for creative activity. And realizing the fragile character of even the greatest human achievements, we begin to discover that the self-organizing dynamic of the universe, while very real, and while authentically endowing our lives and struggle with meaning and direction, is nonetheless about something much larger than us. Without the necessity of struggle, failure, and even death imposed on us by the Second Law of Thermodynamics, we could know God only as *our* Good, and as such never know and thus love Her in Her own right—or indeed so know and love any system more complex than ourselves. It is knowledge of our finitude, which certainly carries with it the possibility, and indeed the effective inevitability of sin and failure, which reveals to us higher goods in their own right. This is the physical basis for the dark nights of the soul, which require us to put behind us the easy spirituality centered on the God of sunshine and autumn leaves and of our own success in favor of a confrontation with purposes larger than our own and never fully comprehensible by us. In this sense the universe as a whole is *naturally* structured in such a way as to order us to and make possible development of a *supernatural* spirituality, in the sense of a spirituality which transcends anything that we would, of our own accord, aspire to or achieve. Nature not only reveals God as her author and end; she also reveals God in Her own right in a majesty which, so far transcending our own finite knowledge and desire, cannot help but at first seem terribly austere but which, as we come to know it, draws us with a lure more powerful than any we could ever imagine. This is why John of the Cross was right to call the dark night—the night made possible and indeed inevitable by the laws of thermodynamics—"more loving than the rising sun," for it is this night which is the condition of the possibility of our own ordering to an infinite end, the means of our self-transcendence.

To what extent is this teleology Aristotelian? Christian? Marxist? Certainly the Aristotelian aim of understanding the universe, in so far as it is possible, through rationally necessary principles has been conserved, as has the sense that it is ultimately the final cause which is first and the sense that God acts eminently through teleological attraction. Indeed many Christians, and perhaps not a few followers of other religions of the book—those who follow Scotus and Halevi and al-Ghazali rather than Thomas and Maimonides and Ibn Rusd—will not doubt feel that we have produced just another physicalist system which leaves no room for freedom, human or divine. And many dialectical materialists will object that unnecessarily complicate our explanatory strategy by introducing immaterial teleological principles. But unlike Aristotle's teleology, which had such difficulty with violent motion and disintegration, our approach weaves struggle, contradiction, and even disintegration into the very fabric of teleological ordering and teleological organization, and in this sense we reap the lessons of the materialist dialectic, which is founded on the principle of contradiction. More to the point however, our doctrine supports a spirituality which, while deeply rooted in the *via dialectica* is more than Aristotelian, and which in fact resonates with the prophetic tradition which begins with Elijah and culminates in John of the Cross. Unlike classical paganism we do not regard the human situation as tragic—capable of discovering an order that transcends and is ultimately indifferent to human interests. And unlike much neo-paganism we do not attempt to dissolve that tragedy in platitudes about the unending cycle of life, death, and rebirth, whether that cycle is understood in individual in terms of the system as a whole. Rather, we find in the *via dialectica* at once confirmation of the ultimate meaningfulness of the universe and a confrontation with the fact that that meaning far transcends our limited natural capacities. The *via dialectica*, if followed through with rigor, sets us naturally on the mountain road, the *via negativa*, which leads out of the fertile valleys and into the dry uplands where the air is thin and cold, and the nights dark, but where alone, and only after a long period of acclimatization, we can come to see the stars. Indeed, because of its meditation on the centrality of death in spiritual development, our approach might even be called distinctly Christian—though Jews and Moslems and others surely have their own answers to the dark night. In any case, for this grace embedded in the darkest secrets of nature, we can only give thanks.

ON THE ORDERING OF PHYSICAL SYSTEMS TO HIGHER ENDS

The argument which we have been making regarding the ordering of physical systems to higher—biological and social—ends is, in effect, an extension of the argument which has a become commonplace in recent years regarding the fine-tuning of physical constants and other physical phenomena, an argument which has given birth to the controversy regarding the so-called "Anthropic Cosmological Principle."[2] We have, in effect, argued that not only certain key physical constants, but in fact the whole fabric of physical reality as we currently understand it is, in fact more or less finely tuned in such a way as to make the development of higher degrees of organization possible. Without the spatiotemporal extension, and indeed at least something very much like the actual structure of space-time theorized by special relativity, without the curvature of space defined by gravitational interactions and the complex dialectic between element and relation defined by the nongravitational reactions, indeed, even with out the degrading effect of thermodynamic constrains life and intelligence, and indeed any sort of *material* organization would, in fact be impossible. Having made at least a *prima facie* case that these physical structures are, in fact, required for complex material organization, we need now to engage the debate regarding the significance of such fine-tuning and show that a strongly teleological approach is, in fact, logical the most coherent and empirically the most economical.

There are several distinct positions which have emerged in this discussion.

- wholesale rejection of anthropic reasoning and of teleological explanations,
- what has come to be known as the Weak Anthropic Principle which limits fine-tuning to a selection effect,
- subjective idealist affirmations of anthropic reasoning such as that advanced by Frank Tipler
- objective idealist and "intelligent design" arguments,
- dialectical materialist readings of the evidence, such as that recently put forward by Eric Lerner, and
- the dialectical idealist position of Errol Harris.

2. We reject the term "anthropic principle" or "anthropic cosmology," as descriptions of our own position because it seems to us to imply that the universe is ordered to *humanity* specifically rather than to life and intelligence in general, and ultimately towards God. It also seems to us to be an attempt to evade use of the controversial and sometimes ambiguous term "teleology," even when this is, in fact what is actually being claimed. Because the term has come to dominate the debate however, we will us it when discussing the views of those participants in the debate who accept the term, while reserving the term "teleological principle" or "teleological cosmology" for our own position.

We need to consider each of these positions in turn.

The first position holds that the fine-tuning is in fact nothing but an extraordinary coincidence, and may, in any case, be rather over stated. In some cases this view is associated an expectation that the unification of physics will in fact show that many of the constants are in fact given by the mathematical formalisms which effect that unification. In other cases it is a result of a mind-set which not only takes the givenness and contingency of at least some phenomena for granted, but regards respect for givenness—i.e., for "data"—as the very foundation of scientific explanation.

The difficulty with this approach is that it leaves the fine-tuning entirely unexplained. This problem is all the more serious given our demonstration that it is not just a handful of physical constants, but the fundamental physical laws themselves which are fine-tuned. The effect is to leave the whole structure of the universe, itself so well-ordered, utterly ungrounded and contingent, something which undermines the whole logic of scientific explanation. The fact that this is not apparent to many trained "scientists" is due largely to the systematic intellectual rape which occurs in the course of their professional training which is designed to ensure that whatever else they become, the remain loyal ideological agents of the bourgeoisie, ever vigilant against the possibility that their research might uncover signs of meaning and purpose which could undermine the anarchic rule of the market order. Penetrating the mystery of cosmological fine-tuning is a difficult task indeed, and we must be cautious about facile solutions, but were there to be no solution there would, ultimately, simply be no science.

The second alternative, what has come to be called the Weak Anthropic Principle, holds that what appears to us to be cosmological fine-tuning is nothing more than an selection effect due to our observer status, and that there are vast regions of space-time where physical law and constants are different, whether this possibility is understood via the many-worlds interpretation of quantum mechanics or some other theory.

This approach is no better than the first. While there could, once again, be regions of space-time with different physical laws and constants, we have absolutely no reason, except for certain irrationalities and paradoxes generated by current physical theory, coupled with a desire to avoid any implication of ultimate meaning and value, to believe that there are. And to posit such regions in the absence of direct evidence constitutes

Physical Organization   331

an unproven assumption which renders the theory which depends on it singularly uneconomical. We can thus exclude this alternative as well.

This said, the question remains *in just what sense* physical systems can be said to be ordered to higher ends. The terms of the debate around this question have been set, in recent years, by Frank Tipler's subjective idealist Omega Point Theory. We have discussed the physical difficulties with this theory above. Here we focus on its adequacy as an explanation for cosmological fine-tuning. We begin by pointing out that while Tipler talk's freely about God and even about the resurrection of the body, his theory is, in fact an attempt to save mathematical-physical reductionism in the light of evidence of internal contradictions and countervailing evidence. The key link in his strategy is his identification of organization with information content and his theorization of the universe as a vast-information processing system. "Life" is simply information encoded in such a way that it is conserved by natural selection. A system is intelligent if it meets the "Turing test," i.e., if a human operator interrogating it cannot distinguish its responses from those of a human being (Turing 1950).

Now Tipler notes that the underlying mathematical formalisms of quantum and relativistic physical cosmology in fact allow a great many different sorts of universes, some of which might permit the development of intelligent life, but the vast majority of which do not. From this point of view the fine-tuning of our universe might appear to be simply a selection effect of our observer status, something which would reduce allow for only a weak anthropic principle. But Tipler argues that there is more at work here than meats the eye. A universe which did not allow for observers could not be observed. And yet observability is precisely what physicists generally mean by existence. He thus argues that while there are many possible universes, only those which allow for observers can be said to exist physically—and it turns out that such universes must look a great deal like ours. What begins as a weak-anthropic selection principle thus turns out to be a strong-anthropic constraint on physical possibility. In order to avoid the inelegance of multiple physical universes, Tipler then goes on to argue that all physically possible universes converge at the same end or Omega point, as a result of the organizing activities of intelligent systems on the structure of the universe as they take the measures necessary in order to ensure the indefinite continuation of intelligent information processing.

There are a number of difficulties here. First of all, Tipler's "solution" amounts to little more than a matter of definition. At no point does he *show* that existence and observability are the same thing and at no point does he answer the many criticisms which can be raised of this essentially Berkeley subjective idealism. Indeed, all he really shows is that *if* existence and observability are convertible terms, *then* physical universes must be structured to allow observers. Furthermore, if we assume his premise, and also the commonly accepted proposition that intelligent life evolved at a definite point in the history of the universe, so that there was a time when there was no intelligent life, and that the universe as it is today is a product of that earlier universe which had no intelligent life, we run up against an insuperable problem. By Tipler's criteria, the earlier universe, because it was not perceived, did not exist.[3] In this case the universe as we know it today is a product of nothing, which is impossible. If, on the other hand, we allow that the universe is caused by the action back through time of the infinitely intelligent system which exists at the Omega point—i.e., God—then we still need to ask how this is possible. As Tipler points out the reversible physical laws on which he relies (simply ignoring the problem of thermodynamic irreversibility) work as well back through time as forward into the future, but the causal mechanism itself still needs to be specified. Now what the Omega Point does is to process all logically possible information, so that it emulates the entire history of the universe (including us). But on this account it would be impossible to tell whether ours is the "original" (or one of the original) cosmohistories, or simply an emulation remembered by Omega. For Tipler this is not a problem—by the "identity of indistinguishable" the two are actually identical. But then the whole of physical reality is collapsed into an emulation on a cosmic supercomputer which appears to us to be the product of the future engineering feats of our descendants or those of other intelligent organisms but which in fact is all that actually exists—or what amounts to the same thing, into ideas in the mind of God. Now while this is a logically possible explanation for the world we see around us, it is hardly the most economical. Tipler "saves" mathematical physics by abandoning its principal aim: the economical formal description of physical phenomena. And he

---

3. There is, it is true, a slight difference between Tipler's criterion for existence (that the universe *allow for* observers) and the Berkeley *esse est percipi*. But there is no good reason for this difference; it is merely a conceptual slip that lets him dodge an obvious contradiction.

"restores" meaning to the universe by rendering the ground of that meaning—God—utterly trivial, little more than a cosmic masturbator who thinks us, with all our joys and hopes and all our struggles and suffering, simply for his own amusement.

Closer to Tipler's position than either of them would like to admit is that of Stanley Jaki (Jaki 1980), who takes the principal result of mathematical physics to be the dual recognition of the ordered nature and the radical contingency of the universe. Here the key conclusion is the Big Bang, which he takes as pointing towards creation *ex nihilo* and thus towards the existence of God. Cosmological fine-tuning, which he seems to understand primarily as the fixing of physical constants and other quantities at what in themselves are highly improbable values, simply highlights a contingent ordering which should already be apparent from the rest of physical theory (Jaki 1980: 11).

Jaki contrasts his position not only with a physical reductionism which simply fails to ask the larger question of what caused the universe but also with idealist or materialist pantheisms which attempt to mitigate the contingency of the universe, and thus of humanity, and their radical dependence on God in favor of doctrines which point towards self-organization (Jaki 1980: 15). Indeed, it is against the latter danger which he aims the main blow. Recognition of the beauty of the universe, he argues, leads to a temptation to see the order of the universe as somehow necessary on *a priori* grounds, but this enterprise is ultimately doomed by Godel's Theorem which showed that no nontrivial system of mathematical formalisms could have its proof in itself (Jaki 1980: 47–49). Physics, which he understands exclusively as mathematical physics, is simply a system of mathematical formalisms, and can never hope to prove the existence of God; this is a task for metaphysics (Jaki 1980: 102–3).

Jaki's position is, in effect, an application to the problems of contemporary cosmology of the larger philosophical-theological problematic of the Augustinian reaction. His principal concern is neither scientific or properly metaphysical, but rather ideological: he is concerned that the progress of science will undermine humanity's recognition of its dependence on God—and thus on His earthly representatives. And his principal concern here is not the nihilism and despair promoted by physical reductionism. On the contrary, he accepts the reductionist framework enthusiastically; he simply notes that they do not draw out the necessary *metaphysical* conclusions. Rather, his principal concern is with pantheism, which we showed in an earlier chapter to be the philosophical manifestation of the resurgent cult of the *Magna Mater* and always the principal competitor with the priestly hierarchy for the hearts and minds of the people. We will see shortly that there are difficulties with materialist and idealist pantheisms, but their errors are not nearly so grave as Jaki's.

What Jaki does, in effect, is to set up a straw-man, and then bludgeon it to death without ever really confronting his adversaries. Correctly pointing out that the order of the universe cannot be shown to be necessary *a priori*, he never addresses the possibility that it might be shown to be necessary, or at least to make eminently good sense in a way which suggests that it is probably rationally necessary by an *a posteriori* argument, as we have attempted to do. This failure indicates a failure to distinguish properly between formal and transcendental abstraction and to understand the intimate relationship, as well as the distinction, between science and metaphysics. Science shows the necessity of the cosmic order by concluding not formally and mathematically but transcendentally and dialectically to the end to which it is ordered and in the process demonstrates the existence of God; metaphysics then investigates the nature of God in so far as that can be understood by a finite intellect, showing, for example, the convertibility of the transcendentals, exploring the nature of the divine intellect and will, without ever comprehending the divine essence.[4] Mathematical physics makes the universe appear contingent because it is not really physics, not really science, but only an auxiliary to science which describes rigorously what must be explained, rather than even beginning to mount such an explanation.

The dialectical materialist approach to cosmological fine-tuning stands, in many ways, at the opposite end of the spectrum from Tipler's subjective idealism and Jaki's neo-Augustinianism. Where Tipler makes as much as possible of the mysterious paradoxes of mathematical physics, dialectical materialists such as Eric Lerner take these paradoxes as signs that, as we ourselves have argued, there are fundamental problems with dominant paradigm within the discipline itself. Indeed, Lerner sees himself as a critic of the whole trend towards anthropic explanations.

---

4. Jaki, who seems to think of himself as a Thomist, demonstrates the profoundly Augustinian character of much contemporary Thomism, especially that of the Gilsonian school. Authentic Thomism recognizes that Thomas was first and foremost an Aristotelian, and closer in spirit if not in letter to Hegel and Marx than to Augustine or Henry of Ghent.

Many supposed cosmic coincidences, he argues, are the result of errors in theory or fact. Thus the fine-tuning of ω, a quantity related to the mass of the universe and which determines whether it is open, closed, or flat, depends on the whole Big-Bang cosmology, which he has helped us to see is profoundly flawed. "Eliminate the Big-Bang and the incredible fine-tuning of omega is no longer needed" (Lerner 1991: 399). And the tuning of the ratio between the strength of gravitational and the electromagnetic interactions, he claims is not nearly so fine as Brandon Carter and others have claimed. "In fact the electrical force would have to be twice as strong or the force of gravity six thousand times stronger than it is before stars like the sun would be impossible" (Lerner 1991: 399).

These criticisms can, however, eliminate at most only some of the "cosmic coincidences" on which anthropic reasoning is based—they do not touch, for example, our larger claim that the whole fabric of physical law is fine-tuned for life and intelligence. Lerner's real objection to anthropic reasoning is that it is based on the notion that matter is inert and that the fact that it has taken on configurations which make possible, and in fact actually lead to life and intelligence is extremely improbable. This outlook, in turn, makes the actual course of cosmic evolution appear to be a great mystery, explicable only in terms of divine providence. Against this view he cites the growing recognition, due especially but not exclusively to the work of scientists such as Ilya Prigogine, of the self-organizing dynamic of matter itself.

> What all ignore, and what is emphasized in the new view of cosmology and thermodynamics, is the natural tendency of all matter, both animate and inanimate, to evolve continuously towards higher rates of energy flow, towards the capture of greater currents of energy. (Lerner 1991: 400)

Recognition of the self-organizing dynamism of matter, Lerner argues, renders recourse to immaterial teleological principles or to divine providence unnecessary—and indeed uneconomical. Both the pessimistic cosmology which mathematical physics tends to produce spontaneously, and the new anthropic mysticism are, he argues, reflexes of a capitalist society plunging deeper and deeper into crisis.

Now there is much to commend Lerner's position. Even if he rules out more incidences of cosmological fine-tuning than are really warranted, his diagnosis of the underlying contradictions of mathematical physics is right on the mark. The reduction of all change to local motion and of "science" to the formal description of local motion does indeed render matter dead and make the development of complex organization a mystery. And we have already argued in length that these reductions play an integral role in the ideological arsenal of Capital. The recognition of matter as a real potential for organization—as an authentic δψναμεια and not merely as dead stuff—furthermore, marks a break not only with capitalist but also with patriarchal-tributary ideological deformations which entered philosophy at the time of its birth.

This said, Lerner's concern to combat neo-Augustinian mystifications leads him into serious error. It is one thing to say that matter is self-organizing in the relative sense of always displaying a tendency to develop toward higher degrees of organization. It is quite another thing to attribute to anything finite an authentic power of self-movement. Indeed, the very logic of the claim that matter develops *towards* higher degrees of organization implies that it is moved, albeit only as final cause, by the higher principle towards which it tends. And in so far as matter never rests (and no good Marxist could claim that it does) this principle is not simply the next higher degree of organization (a claim which would bring a whole new cluster of problems with it—is the evolution of complexity a continuum, a quantum, or a purely qualitative phenomenon?) but rather organization as such, the synergistic integrity in which all beings participate but which is a transcendental property of Being itself. Far from being uneconomical, recourse to God is, as Aristotle demonstrated long ago, necessary for a complete explanation of material organization.

Second, Lerner's approach fails to explain why matter is dynamic and self-organizing—or indeed why there is matter in the first place. Recourse to the principle of the conservation of matter and arguments, no matter how convincing, for the eternity of the universe, do no good here. As numerous philosophers have demonstrated (Maimonides 1190/1963: 235–52, Aquinas. *Summa Theologiae* I.3), even an eternal universe, unless it is itself identified with God (Spinoza. *Ethics*) cannot be self-caused and thus requires some first principle outside itself for its explanation.

Lerner stands in the place of the old Radical Averroists: determined to combat the Augustinian reaction he ends up cutting the ground out from underneath of the very forces of progress he hopes to defend. As we have noted above and shown in detail elsewhere, this approach leads to a radical secularism which leaves the ethical claims of socialism unfounded.

Idealist dialectics in the Hegelian tradition takes one step forward from the dialectical materialist position, but also one step back. On the one hand, Hegelians such as Errol Harris (Harris 1991) are more than willing to grant the necessity of some logically prior organizing principle in terms of which the self-organizing dynamism of the universe, its tendency to develop towards increasingly complex forms of organization, can be explained. For Harris, this principle is nothing other than the logic of the whole itself, which specifies itself in successive finite forms, each of which gives it a more complex, more complete, and more adequate expression but each of which is superseded by still more complex, complete and adequate manifestations, until it gives rise to life, intelligence, and eventually to God.

> So regarded, the series of relationships, from mathematical to physical, and thence to organic, sentient, and cognitive, traverse a metaphysical spectrum which, being dialectical reveals the emergent conscious phase as the actualization of what is only implicit in its progenitors ...
>
> ... In the end ... it may well become apparent that the presence in the world of intelligent life at the level of human mentality does indicate a further extension of the dialectical scale and a final consummation in some conceivable necessary self-conscious supra-personality, no doubt beyond our capacity to envisage, but one which comprehends the ultimate whole, expressing itself in, and specifying the principle of its activity through, the phases of the dialectical scale.
>
> A consummation of this nature would correspond to Anselm's definition of God as "that than which a greater is inconceivable. (Harris 1991: 26–28)

In this context the cosmological fine-tuning discovered by mathematical physics is simply an initial and implicit expression of the drive towards life, intelligence, and indeed divinity that is implicit in the system from the very beginning.

Harris' position represents an advance with respect to dialectical materialism in the sense that, by acknowledging the existence of a logically prior organizing principle, a principle which is at least implicitly divine, Harris satisfies the principle of sufficient reason and does not leave the self-organizing dynamism of the universe unexplained. At the same time, by accepting so much of mathematical physics as a "sketch" of the organizing principle of the universe, Harris leaves himself open to the charge that he is attempting to show the rational necessity of the universe *a priori*, something which is ruled out by Godel's Theorem. He can escape this charge by claiming that he has recourse to a higher, dialectical logic which transcends the antinomies of mere formalism (Harris 1987), and much of his argument is, in fact saved by its authentically dialectical character. Harris fails, however, to see the link between the antinomies of formalism and the internal contradictions of mathematical physics. He thus ends up by accepting elements of physical theory which are deeply problematic, such as the Big Bang. And by making the universe essentially the necessary working out of a single logical principle, he makes it very difficult to account adequately for the very phenomena of failure, loss, death and disintegration which led to the crisis of Aristotelian physics in the first place. It is, to be sure, possible to argue that the forms which arise as a result of these phenomena are logically necessary for the completeness of the system, but this tends to make divine perfection into a sort of ruthless rationalist search algorithm, logically identifying and assuming every possible form for no good reason other than to be more complete than would otherwise be the case. The more classically Aristotelian approach which we have been developing on the other hand, makes failure an inevitable—but by no means logically deducible or predictable—result of the diverse ways finite systems respond to teleological attractors of varying strength under differing material conditions. The enormous burden of evil and the suffering which results from it is redeemed not because it is itself logically required for completeness, but because it helps to stretch finite systems to grow beyond their limited capacities—to become more than they are and thus grow towards God.

Our own approach to the problem of cosmological fine-tuning has already been laid out implicitly in the foregoing critiques. We affirm with Lerner and Harris and the whole dialectical tradition that the physical universe and its structure are by no means contingent or highly improbable. On the contrary, they can be shown *a posteriori* to be rationally necessary to any material organization whatsoever. Indeed, systems which lacked spatiotemporal extension, the subtle dialectic of element and interaction, particle and wave, matter and energy, and which were not subject to the constraints of thermodynamic disintegration would either not exist at all, or they would transcend the sort of emergent organization characteristic of material systems and enjoy an existence which could only be described as angelic, not so much tending toward particular perfections of form, but already actually being such perfections. Something which lacks spatiotemporal extension, which cannot undergo physical interactions either internally or with other system, and which is not subject to degradation or corruption is either nothing or else it is one of the ends towards which physical systems are ordered.

This said, physical systems are not logically necessary in the sense of being merely a preliminary specification of some organizing principle—e.g., the idea of Being. Rather they are really distinct participations in Being which as such have at least a limited beauty, intelligibility, goodness and integrity of their own. And this means that they can develop not, to be sure, along just any lines, but along any lines compatible with physical law and with the attractive power of Being which affects physical systems only as a tendency to conserve system integrity—i.e., a tendency to seek stable configurations. This introduces a real and radical contingency into the universe, since there are many ways to achieve such stability, not all of which are equally progressive from the standpoint of the larger dynamic of cosmic evolution. In this sense materiality is real limit on form in a way that idealist dialecticians such as Harris do not fully comprehend. This limitedness itself, to be sure, turns out to serve cosmic evolution, but not by something inherent in its own nature. Rather, it is by grace of the participation of limited systems in larger totalities that they are driven to becomes something more than themselves and offered the possibility at least of growing towards God.

Finally, we must acknowledge that we have not yet actually shown the necessity of physical matter and its structure, but only its necessity to higher degrees of material organization—e.g., life and intelligence. In order to complete our argument we need to show that life is in fact ordered to intelligence and intelligence to God. This will be the subject of the next three chapters. Only then, as we cross the boundary from science to metaphysics, will we be able to explore in what sense the universe as such is necessary and thus to resolve fully and completely its the question of its ultimate meaningfulness.

7

Biological Organization

THE NATURE OF LIFE

THE MOST DIFFICULT PART of our work is now done. We have shown how a teleological research strategy can be applied to the study of physical systems without contradicting established scientific results or negating entirely the value of mathematical formalization as an *instrument*, though not an ideal, of scientific research. We have seen that such a strategy offers us the possibility of making sense out of far more of the empirical data which we confront than does mathematical physics by itself. We now face the far easier task of showing how a teleological research strategy can be applied to biological and social systems—arenas from which teleology was never entirely banished.

Our first task is to define life, and thus the formal object of biological science. The currently favored approach to this problem is the information-theoretical strategy which we have already seen deployed in the context of Tipler's argument. According to this view, the organization of a system is its information content; living systems are those whose information is conserved by natural selection. We have already discussed the difficulties with this approach as a general theory of organization. Among other things it makes a crystal more highly organized than a living organism, and thus does not really capture what we mean by organization, as opposed to order. As a theory of biological systems it is even more problematic. Thus, according to Tipler's theory, an automobile is in fact a living thing. To be specific it is a sort of symbiotic parasite which has adapted itself to cooperation with humans who take care of its nutritional needs and reproduce it in return for the transportation services it provides. Even were it not for the underlying difficulties with the whole information theoretical approach, which carry over into its use as a theory of biological organization, this would render the theory useless. What we want is, precisely, a definition which at least attempts to distinguish between machines and living things, and gives up on this only if no real differences can be identified.

The difficulties of the mechanistic/information theoretical approach should not, however, lead us to embrace vitalism, which was the historical alternative. According to the old vitalist theories, living things were distinguished from nonliving by a distinct "life force." Now there are two principal difficulties with this theory. First of all, at a logical level, it is purely tautological. It is logically equivalent to saying that something is alive because it has—well, life. This gives us no criterion by which to distinguish between living and nonliving systems unless we believe we can directly perceive or intuit the presence of a life force. This leads to the second difficulty with the vitalist approach. It is, in most of its forms, simply the application to biology of a larger objective idealist agenda which we have already criticized at length in an earlier chapter. Correctly recognizing the inability of mathematical physics to account for the reality of complex organization, life, and intelligence, objective idealism incorrectly infers from this that discursive rationality generally is incapable of grasping these principles which are accessible only to an intellectual, aesthetic, or religious intuition. The ultimate object of this intuition is God, but at each level of organization there is some principle which reflects the organizing presence of the divine. Thus Teilhard's radial energy, the vitalists' life force—or the structural functionalist "ultimate reality."

Fortunately, there are, however, ample resources within the dialectical tradition to arrive at a definition of life which avoids both mechanist and vitalist errors. Our starting point here should be the definitions of the first great biologist, who was none other than Aristotle himself. What we call living systems include all but the lowest rung in Aristotle's hierarchy of forms. Mineral systems, we will recall, have the capacity to retain their forms. This does not qualify them as living. Vegetative systems, however, add the capacities for nutrition and reproduction. This is what sets them apart form mere crystals or machines. Animals add the capacity for sensation and locomotion, which will also attempt to explain as biological phenomena, and rational animals at the ability to know and will intelligibles, capacities which we will argue presuppose the existence of a properly social form of matter. This way of defining life may seem terribly simple minded, but it does correspond remarkably well to what we mean by life in our ordinary language, and thus offers a useful starting point. Aristotle would also seem to settle once and for all the question of whether or not machines—at least those we have created thus far—are living. In so far as they lack the capacity for nutrition and the ability to reproduce *themselves* they are not alive. This does not, of course, rule out the possibility that we will eventually create living machines, or even that some of the current artificial life researchers have not already done so, at least at a very simple level. But then we are no longer dealing with mere machines and technology will truly have entered a new epoch.

Aristotle is not, however, the only dialectical thinker to offer resources in helping us to arrive at a definition of life. Kant's third critique, the *Critique of Judgment*, by far his most dialectical work, as well as the work of Hegel, contain important insights which can help us to qualify further our definition (Naser 1995). For something to be alive, it must be a "natural purpose, "that is it must have an immanent teleological structure so that it is, at least in a proximate sense, "both cause and effect of itself" (Kant. *Critique of Judgment* 65). For this to be true, Kant argues, two conditions must be met.

> First, the possibility of its parts (as concerns both their existence and their form) must depend on their relation to the whole.
>
> A second requirement must be met if a thing that is a product of nature is yet to have, within itself and its inner possibility, reference to purposes, i.e., if it is to be possible only as a natural purpose, without the causality of concepts, which rational beings outside it have. This second requirement is that the parts of the thing combine into the unity of a whole because they are reciprocally cause and effect of their form. (Kant. *Critique of Judgment* 65)

Kant's criteria add two things to Aristotle's definition. First of all, they provide another way in which we can distinguish between a living organism and a machine which is structured to serve and end, and in that sense is also organized teleologically. Specifically, Kant insists that the teleology be immanent or internal so that it is apparent not only from the standpoint of the overall design or ordering of the parts, but also in the parts themselves. Thus a transistor or memory chip or electrical motor can be placed in any of a variety of machines, where it will serve similar proximate but very different ultimate purposes. A cell, however, has within itself the same ultimate purpose—to survive and reproduce, and thus participate in Being—as the organism as a whole, even if cells in different parts of the organism serve very different proximate purposes. Second, Kant's definition makes clearer than Aristotle's the role of the final cause in determining the structure of the organism. The end or τέλος is the organizing principle which ultimately determines even the inmost structure of the individual elements.

As Curt Naser points out (Naser 1995), drawing on both a careful exegesis of the *Phenomenology* and on Errol Harris' work in dialectical logic, Hegel's treatment of life builds on Kant's definition, while recasting it in a way which brings out more clearly the mutual determination of part and whole. What Hegel does is to recast Kant's criteria in terms of the dialectic of being in itself and being for itself.

> The demonstration of the unity of these determinations suggests that what an object (or a subject, i.e., a knowing consciousness or self-consciousness) is for itself, is only through another, or it has its being only through its relations to another
> ... each moment contains within itself both itself and its other. (Naser 1995: 14)

Naser is quite careful to point out that we ought not to be too quick to identify this radical, internal relationality with the storage of information regarding the structure of the organism in the genome. The genes code for proteins and nothing more.

> ... the process of ontogenesis is epigenetic, that is it constitutes its own conditions of development from out of itself. The developing system produces from out if the interactions of its parts information not present within any of these parts and this information is necessary for the proper development of the parts of the organism and their corresponding functions. Thus the genome alone is not a sufficient condition of development and cannot be said to contain in any positive way all the information necessary for the development and functioning of the organism. (Naser 1995: 12)

Hegel also adds to Kant's definition a dynamism which it lacks. Each individual organism, species, etc. is, for Hegel simply a more or less adequate expression of the underlying organizing principle of the universe as a whole, which he calls the Idea. In so far as it is finite, it is ultimately not adequate to its ground, and thus dies or experiences extinction and the Idea drives towards ever more perfect expression of itself.

> Universality, in the face of which the animal as a singularity is a finite existence, shows itself in the animal as the abstract power in the passing out of that which, in its preceding process, is itself abstract. The original disease of the animal, and the inborn germ of death, is its being inadequate to universality. (Hegel. *Encyclopaedia of the Philosophical Sciences* 37)

This insight, which is coherent with our discussion of entropy in the previous section, helps us to further explain how the ultimate meaningfulness of the universe is consistent with such unpleasant realities as suffering, death, and extinction.[1]

Thus the earlier Aristotelian and the later Kantian and Hegelian dialectics together allow us to advance clear definition of life. While physical systems are merely the possibility of organization, biological systems are actually organized. They are, that is, structured in such a way as to order the material conditions of their environment to a definite end, i.e., minimally but not only survival and reproduction, and thus their own participation in Being. This organization, while it emerges on the basis of a definite physical matrix, which alone makes it possible, and in response to some teleological attractor, is authentic *self-organization*: i.e., it is not the product of an external intelligence which has organized physical matter with some purpose in mind.[2] Precisely because of its teleological ordering

---

1. The finitude of the organism, and its ordering to higher ends, is also manifested in a more immediate way, in the phenomenon of excretion. The organism is finite in part because of its inability to perfectly assimilate to itself everything which it consumes, and is forced each day to give back to the universe part of what we have taken from Her, just as we are ultimately forced to give ourselves over wholly to Her in death. This is, perhaps, why we find the excretory act, and especially defecation, so humbling, but also, strangely, an occasion for reflection and even meditation. For it is only in recognition of our finitude that we can thematize our aspiration for the infinite and begin the search to act in a way which makes us connatural with God.

2. A brief note would note be out of place here regarding the relationships between mechanism, teleology, and "the argument from design." Contemporary scholars often confuse teleological and design reasoning, but in fact the two could not be more distinct, nor could the sorts of God to which they conclude be more different. Teleological explanation involves the discovery of an immanent purposefulness which is written into everything existing as the very condition of its existence and concludes to God always and only as a final cause, who draws things into Being by Her transcendental Beauty, Truth, Goodness, and Oneness, in which they participate to the degree of their organization. Design reasoning, on the other hand, is mechanistic at base, assuming that the only the intervention of an external intelligence could structure things in such a way as to give them the appearance of purpose. In this sense, design reasoning, while it always had a certain force in Augustinian circles, is most characteristic of the period between

to an end higher than itself, life is never content with any finite form. Thus the reality of death, but also of evolutionary development.

THE LIFE PROCESS

With this definition in hand, we are now in a position to show how a teleological research program can explain the phenomena associated with life. Specifically we need to show how such a program would approach

a. such fundamental life processes as nutrition and metabolism, reproduction and morphogenesis, sensation and locomotion,

b. the interaction of diverse organisms with each other and with their physical matrix in a definite ecosystem, and

c. the problem of evolution.

This means attempting to explain each phenomenon in terms of the underlying material conditions, structural factors, and teleological attractors. Clearly here we can, and need, offer no more than a brief sketch which will suggest the usefulness of the research program. The development of a teleological biology, like that of a teleological physics, depends on real empirical research.

In the case of the basic life processes the underlying material conditions are those given by physics generally, but most especially those given by nonequilibrium thermodynamics, which we had occasion to discuss earlier in this work. At the very most basic level, life involves the emergence out of the physical matrix of systems which are capable of exchanging matter and energy with the environment in such a way as to create, maintain, and reproduce teleological organization of the sort defined above. The sense in which this presupposes the basic characteristics of physical organization, such as spatiotemporal extension, gravitational and nongravitational interactions, etc. should be obvious to the reader of the last section. We have also discussed the role of entropy and other basic thermodynamic relations in the life process. Of more immediate

---

the ascent of mathematical physics in the seventeenth century and the discovery of the Second Law of Thermodynamics and the Poincaré Recurrence Theorem, which called into question the ultimate purposefulness of the universe, in the nineteenth. To distinguish between teleological and eutaxiological reasoning, as Barrow and Tipler (Barrow and Tipler 1986) do, while useful, does not resolve this problem. This distinction captures the difference between organization, or ordering to an end, and mere "good order," but not the difference between teleological and mechanical causation.

relevance, however is the problem of showing how it is possible, at least locally to resist the thermodynamic gradient and create organization. Here the results of Prigogine's early work (Prigogine 1977) are particularly important. In systems far from equilibrium, in which exchange of matter and energy with the environment is possible, fluctuations from equilibrium and thus more or less enduring structures, are not only maintained but actually intensified, so that, structures can become increasingly complex and better able to maintain their own integrity.

One of the most interesting questions here is just what sort of underlying chemistry makes biological organization possible. Is life bound to the carbon atom or not? On the one hand, there are a number of characteristics of carbon based chemistry which make the development of complex organization particularly easy—most notably the capacity of carbon to form a variety of very flexible covalent bonds with a wide range of other elements. But this does not mean that carbon based chemistry is the only one which is capable of giving rise to life.

It must be noted, however, that nonequilibrium thermodynamics, while showing how life is possible, does not really explain why it emerged. For this at least higher orders of explanation—structural and teleological—are necessary. It is above all the mutual determination of parts and whole which characterize the structure of living organisms. Clearly genetics has a great deal to do with this, in that in even the largest and most complex organism, information which is somehow associated with phenotypic traits is encoded in every single cell of the organism. But we have also noted the limits of genetic explanation. Genes code for proteins and nothing more. It is not clearly why some genes are expressed in some cells and other genes in other cells, nor is it clear just how the information in the genes which codes for proteins is associated with and perhaps translated into macrostructures during the process of morphogenesis. Here the insights of Kant and Hegel are especially useful, and are coherent with current thinking regarding morphogenetic fields (Sheldrake 1981, 1989). The idea here is that the organism as a whole constitutes, but is also in some as yet mysterious way constituted by, a morphogenetic field so that the position of a particular cell in the field determines which genes are activated and which are not, and thus which proteins are produced, where they go, etc.

The principal objection raised to this theory is that is unclear just in what these fields actually consist and how they work, i.e., in how they might be described in mathematical physical or mechanical terms. There is some evidence for the existence of purely chemical gradients within the body which might do some of the work and clearly this is an important area for further research. Such gradients could not, however, be at work between organisms separated by a considerable distance, nor between the inorganic chemicals which all seem to have "learned" to crystallize more or less simultaneously at different points around the planet, a point which to which Sheldrake attributes great significance. Fields of this sort might being exploiting quantum nonlocality, though this latter phenomenon is itself so poorly understood that we are very far from being able to even speculate how.

While research regarding the quantum mechanical and chemical basis for morphogenetic fields continues (properly part of the material conditions for life), it is important, however, not to become caught in a mechanistic reductionism—a reductionism which is deeper than that of mathematical physicists themselves. When quantum theorists find that a system is well described in field theoretical terms they do so without requiring that there be some *more fundamental* substratum out of which the field is constituted, even when they have not demonstrated that the interaction they are describing is itself fundamental. And if the exchange of information in the field requires "particles" then they posit them, figure out what properties they would have to have in order to carry out the function for which they were posited, and then ask the accelerator technicians to start looking for them. While I am hardly recommending such a procedure with respect to morphogenetic fields, I am suggesting that the fact that we do not yet understand what physical substratum these fields have and how information is exchanged across them does not mean that using the idea is somehow unscientific. We need only develop research plans in order to understand better how these fields work, how they interact with the genome, and indeed whether or not the genome and/or field approaches are really the most adequate ways to understand the structural determinants of the life process.

Nonequilibrium thermodynamics explains how life is possible; structural studies of organisms, including genetic and morphogenetic theory describe how life takes place. Neither, however actually explains why the possibility of life is actually realized, and why it is realized in the way that it is. For this it is necessary to have recourse to properly teleological explanation. The fact that purposeful organisms are possible and are structured in such and such a way does not by itself explain why they exist. In order to identify the teleological attractor we need only look for what actual living organization has over merely physical order, such as that of a crystal. And here the term of the argument can only be metaphysical, even if it points back to and helps explain a definite body of empirical evidence. What organisms have that crystals do not is a higher grade of or share in Being. Specifically, organisms can build themselves up rather than merely being built up by chemical processes in the environment. They can, within definite limits, sustain themselves against fluctuations in the physical environment. And they can, finally, reproduce themselves, so that their form, if not their particular physical substratum, endures (albeit with changes) over an arbitrarily long and possibly infinite period of time.

Once again, and even more so than the notion of morphogenetic fields, this idea requires a break with the mechanistic reductionism promoted by mathematical physics. What we are positing is, in effect, a properly ontological gradient which operates against the entropic tide even as it uses this tide to its own purposes in higher order biological processes, i.e., evolution. Life *can* emerge because of laws of nonequilibrium thermodynamics makes it possible. When it *does* emerge it takes on certain structural forms which appear to be encoded in both the parts of the organism (genetically) and in the whole (morphogenetically). But life emerges *because* of the presence of a teleological attractor, Being itself, which activates the latent potential of matter, catalyzing a dynamic yearning for organization, and draws it into actuality.

The metaphysical pole of this gradient may be immaterial (because it is fully actual), and thus not accessible to empirical observation. But its effects *are* empirically observable and show that the ontological gradient we are describing does in fact exist. There is no purely *physical* reason why chemical systems *have* to develop into organisms, but they *do*. This itself establishes the gradient's existence.

ECOSYSTEMS

Our very definition of life means that biological organization cannot be considered at the level of the individual organism alone. Life means, among other things, exchange of matter and energy with a physical substratum or with other organisms which are treated as (or which treat the organism in question as) a source of physical raw materials and energy. Thus any dialectical biology necessarily includes and presupposes an ecology, which explains the ways in which organisms interact with each other and with a physical environment. Such a biology, must, among other things, explain both the ways in which particular organisms exchange matter and energy with their environments, as well as the structure of the ecosystem as a whole.

The material conditions for an ecosystem include, first of all, a certain sort of material substratum. As in the case of individual organisms, one of the most interesting questions concerns just what sort of physical environments make life possible. This, in turn, of course, depends on what sort of chemical substrata can give rise to life. Is life possible on planets vastly different from earth or even in nonplanetary environments, such as the surfaces of neutron stars or in interstellar plasmas? Such questions are especially important in assessing the likely extent of life throughout the universe and the extent to which all matter is or can become animated.

In addition to a suitable physical environment, however, any stable ecosystem must be characterized by at least a minimal level of biodiversity. In the only ecosystem with which we are familiar, that of the Earth, this has come to mean one which includes both autotrophs and heterotrophs—and, among the heterotrophs, a sufficient diversity to include both predator and prey. Other ecosystems might, however, be organized very differently.

The question of biodiversity, however, already points beyond the material conditions for the existence of an ecosystem to its internal structure. This is because the various species which make an ecosystem diverse are differentiated first and foremost by the niches they occupy and by their strategies for survival. By a *strategy* here we mean a more or less consistent plan for (or in the case of subrational organisms, consistent, patterned way of) organizing, developing, and deploying resources in order to carry out the mission of the system in question, in this case, survival, reproduction, and any higher order purposes which may have emerged. We have already seen that population biologists distinguish between "r-strategies" centered on a high reproductive rate and low investment in the individual organism and "K-strategies" centered on highly efficient "exploitation" of the environment, something which usually also entails a higher investment in each individual, who must learn the techniques involved in so exploiting the environment. This is, however, only a very broad distinction. One of the most important aims of a teleological biology would be to characterize and explain the origin, development, and ultimate destiny of each of the multitude of survival strategies developed by all of the many species we encounter. Indeed, one way to distinguish among species is precisely on the basis of their survival strategies.[3]

Species-specific survival strategies, however, exist only in the context of the ecosystem as a whole, which is structured in such a way as to make certain strategies viable and others not. The ecosystem does this by making available certain definite *niches* or loci within the ecosystem's survival space, which are available for individual species to exploit. Biologists have already developed empirically based classifications of ecosystems, but these are largely descriptive and do not really grasp the underlying structures in question. One of the key tasks for a teleological biology will be to develop a "periodic table" of ecosystems based on a grasp of the underlying principles by which they are structured—something like either the periodic table of elements or the "periodic table" of modes of production developed by historical materialism. Only then will it become possible to explain ecosystems fully. Only after the structures have been defined will it become possible to explain how and why they develop.

Ecosystems, however, are not static. Indeed, ecosystems in the full sense—i.e., as including diverse organisms as well as a suitable physical environment—are by nature an emergent reality. The first organisms re-

---

3. There has been a tendency within biological taxonomy to polemicize against what is known as the "essentialist" understanding of species deriving from Aristotle, on the grounds that it ignores the diversity within populations and is ahistorical and thus incompatible with evolutionary theory. This tendency is most marked among advocates of what is called numerical phenetics, an approach to classification based on quantitative comparisons of observable (usually biochemical or morphological) characteristics, but it is also apparent among advocates of cladistics and evolutionary classification, who classify on the basis of genealogy, the first with, and the second without the assumption that evolutionary changes are dichotomous and involve the extinction of ancestral species (See Mayr 1982: 269–88). Definition of species in terms of their ecostrategies, however, is formally equivalent to the classification of social formations in terms of their modes of production. As Scott Meikle has shown (Meikle 1985) this involves grasping the inner, organizing principle or essence of a mode of production—something which is by no means static and which does not require negation of internal diversity within a society. By moving away from the focus on biochemical, morphological, and genealogical comparisons and towards a focus on ecostrategy (or rather relating the former to the latter), biologists should be able to elaborate a taxonomy which has the same sound epistemic status: grasping essence and not merely similarities in approach, while at the same time avoiding the dangers of stasis.

lated exclusively to physical matter for the simple reason that there were as yet no other organisms to which they could be related. These organisms, furthermore, both transformed the physical environment and, through an evolutionary process, gave birth the diverse forms of life which now exist. On the one hand, through their own metabolic interactions with the physical environment, primitive bacteria, and later early autotrophs, changed the chemical composition of that environment, giving rise, among other things, to the high-oxygen atmosphere which we enjoy to day. On the other hand, as this environment changed, new niches opened up and new species emerged to fill them, thereby creating still more niches for still other organisms. At the same time, certain niches which previously existed may be exhausted or destroyed by the accumulation of toxins which are the metabolic byproducts of emergent species.

Two points are in order here. First of all, there is clearly a drive within any ecosystem towards ever higher degrees of diversity and complexity. This is a trend which can not only be verified empirically but which can be shown to be a necessary result of the internal bio-logic which governs ecosystems as such. Second, this trend toward higher levels of diversity, while it appears as the result of a teleonomic "push" rather than a strictly teleological "pull"[4] (or at least can be explained without reference to such

---

4. The distinction is due to Roy Bashkar (Bashkar 1993). A teleonomic push is a drive toward a higher degree of organization which arises as a result of the working out of logical, physical, biological, social or other laws governing a system. A teleological pull is a drive towards higher degrees of organization which is a result of attraction to some material or immaterial principle outside the system. It is not surprising that at the level of the ecosystem we should see a teleonomic push rather than a teleological pull. The ecosystem itself, while in some sense a higher order reality than the individual organism or species, has no organ or faculty by which it can perceive a teleological attractor, i.e., a good outside itself. Rather, it is pushed toward such attractors by the structured interactions of individuals which do perceive such goods. We will see the same phenomenon at the level of human societies, which appear to be driven towards higher degrees of organization first and foremost by internal contractions of the sort identified by Marx and Engels—an example of teleonomic push. That such contradictions lead to higher levels of development however, rather than to disintegration or mere horizontal differentiation, is a result of the structured interactions between individuals who do perceive higher Goods. The discovery of teleonomic push represents an important scientific—and metaphysical—advance. It is a scientific advance because it permits the more complete and economical explanation of observed changes. It is an important metaphysical advance because it documents the latent and awakening dynamism of matter which is, to be sure, dependent in the last instance (but only in the last instance) on an immaterial attractor (i.e., God) but which always and everywhere participates actively in its own self-development.

a pull), never the less reflects the same ontological gradient which we noted at the level of the individual organism: i.e., a gradient towards a higher degree of participation in, and thus a larger share of, Being.

THE EVOLUTIONARY PROCESS

What this whole analysis suggests, of course, is that life is, by its very nature, a dynamic, evolutionary process for which self-preservation and self-transformation are one and the same thing. This much, at least, is not contested by the dominant mathematical physical paradigm which dominates most contemporary biology. Unfortunately, however, the easy agreement stops here. Neo-Darwinism, which we have shown represents the application of mathematical physics to the problem of evolution, is inadequate both in its characterization of the evolutionary process itself and in the explanation it offers. At the level of definition, the problem concerns the emergence of higher levels of organization. Early evolutionary theory, including Darwin's, and even much Neo-Darwinian thinking up through the mid to late twentieth century, simply took for granted that evolution involved the gradual emergence of increasingly complex, more highly organized species. Evolution, in other words, was seen as a progressive process. Indeed, Darwin himself was reportedly profoundly distressed when he learned of developments in thermodynamics which seemed to undercut the progressive cosmohistorical implications of his doctrine. More recently, however, evolutionary theorists—lead especially by Stephen Jay Gould—have begun to insist that while there is an evolutionary trend towards diversity, we cannot speak meaningfully of evolutionary progress. Species simply fan out to fill available niches—and become extinct when their niches are exhausted or destroyed.

Now this understanding of evolution *is* certainly more compatible with the internal logic of Neo-Darwinism, and even of classical Darwinism, than the progressivist position. If evolution is simply the result of random variation and natural selection for survival value then there is no reason to believe that there will be either a push or a pull towards higher degrees of organization. On the contrary, relatively simple forms, such as bacteria, have a better track record for survival than more complex organisms. There are, however, three distinct problems with this view. First of all, there is the simple fact that while much evolution may be merely horizontal differentiation, more complex organisms, defined in terms of higher order capacities, *do* in fact evolve. As we will see this fact creates problems for the whole logic of the Darwinist system. Second, horizontal differentiation, provided it is accompanied, as it always is, by higher degrees of integration, does mean higher degrees of organization at the level of the ecosystem. A 103 species ecosystem with complex lines of interdependence is, or at least has the potential to become, more highly organized than a ten species ecosystem. Finally, as we noted above, organisms do not simply adapt to their ecosystems. They adapt their ecosystems to themselves. And this is not only a characteristic of complex organisms pursuing K-strategies, like ourselves. It was, after all, primitive bacteria and archaic autotrophs which rendered the planet habitable for us in the first place. Now such transformation of the ecosystem certainly can be degrading, and we have no reason to believe that it will always be progressive. At the same time, the historical record is clearly toward increasing differentiation, punctuated to be sure by periods of crisis, as various ecological regimes ran up against structural limits and collapsed (Lerner 1991: 302–12). We should also note that even in the context of a market economy which orders all resources to a maximum return on investment, as people have become aware of environmental degradation there has been a real movement to halt it, so that humanity's net impact on its environment is progressive, contributing to rather than degrading diversity.

For these reasons a teleological biology must understand evolution as inherently progressive—as involving not only horizontal differentiation, but also the emergence of qualitatively more complex and highly organized forms of life, i.e., organisms with higher order capacities, which can do things which simpler organisms cannot. This means the development of sensation and locomotion and eventually of intellect and will. Evolution of this sort cannot be explained adequately in terms of random variation and natural selection. We have already noted that random variation does not produce useful innovations at either the rate we observe in nature, nor at a rate which would be sufficient to have given rise to even simple protein chains by this point in the earth's history. Molecular biologist Barry Hall, we will remember, has found that the bacterium E. coli produces needed mutations at a rate roughly 100 million times greater than would be expected if they came about by chance. Nor can random variation and natural selection account for the fact that such changes seem to occur rather suddenly, rather than in gradual increments, as the theory of natural selection would suggest. A retina or a cornea, after all, without the rest of the organ, would have no survival value by itself, and would be unlikely to be preserved in future generations.

We have also noted there is no reason to believe that random variation and natural selection for survival value would lead to the sort of progressive evolution we actually observe. We must, therefore, have recourse to an alternative theory.

This is an area in which there has been considerable work in recent years. Biologists have identified two distinct types of processes which they believe contribute to the development of increasingly complex forms of life. Molecular biologists have found that the genome operates as a complex interrelated totality, with some genes regulating the operation of others. Random mutations in some parts of the genome, where they threaten to undermine well established life processes, are systematically corrected, while others, in areas where experimentation seems promising, are permitted. At the same time, small changes in one part of the genome can trigger fundamental structural changes in the system as a whole. This is why animal breeders, in the process of selecting for certain traits, so often produce undesired side effects. It also helps to explain how whole new structures (such as the eye) with significant survival value, might have emerged all at once. Variation, furthermore, is constrained by the material out of which organisms are built. Genetic instructions to construct an elephant with legs as thin as those of an ant, Kevin Kelly points out, simply cannot be carried out. Matter, as potential organization, provides life with certain structural options, but systematically excludes others. This is another reason why structural leaps are more common than incremental changes. The genome must undergo considerable internal reorganization before it can produce a new form which is both structurally different and viable. This complex of phenomena has led some biologists to suggest that the genome contains algorithmic search instructions which help it to discover mechanically stable, biologically viable, ecologically progressive, new forms. Life, it appears, is at least incipiently creative and self-reorganizing. At the same time there is growing evidence that cooperation plays an important role in the evolutionary process. Biologist Lynn Margulis, for example, has argued that nucleated cells, with their specialized organelles devoted to photosynthesis and respiration, and their genetic high command, came about through symbiosis, when membraned cells incorporated bacteria which had already developed these processes and the structures necessary to carry them out. These new developments suggest that natural selection is only one of many processes which contribute to the emergence of new, increasingly complex, forms of life. And its contribution is largely negative. Natural selection, as biologist Lynn Margulis puts it, is the editor, not the author, of evolution. The creative self-reorganization of matter, and symbiosis, the cooperation between organisms, play the leading role (Waddington 1957, Lenat 1980, Sheldrake 1981 and 1989, Denton 1985, Wesson 1991, Margulis and Fester 1991, Kelly 1992).

Even these postdarwinian theories, however, have marked limitations. Essentially they focus on mechanisms for genetic or morphogenetic innovation and are not really comprehensive alternatives to Neo-Darwinism. How would a teleological biology approach this problem? We should note, first the fundamental importance of certain definite material conditions, which we have already noted earlier. For evolution to take place there must be both new, as yet unexploited ecological niches, or at least the possibility that existing organisms or larger geodynamic processes will create such niches, but there must also be certain definite thermodynamic conditions: both the nonequilibrium laws which make possible the development of more complex structures, and the entropic tendency towards disintegration which weeds out less effective organism. The first of these thermodynamic tendencies is what is ultimately behind the new mechanisms for innovation being developed by postdarwinian theorists; the second tendency is what is ultimately behind natural selection.

Second, evolution is governed by certain definite structural dynamics: i.e., dynamics which have to do with morphology, physiology, or, most importantly, with strategies for survival and reproduction. Some of these operate at the level of the individual organism. Thus postdarwinian theorists often point out the existence of selection factors quite distinct from "survival of the fittest." An organism with the body of an elephant and the legs of an ant simply can't be constructed and will not even be permitted to test itself in the contest for survival. The most important structural dynamics, however, are those which have to do with the emergence and exhaustion of ecological niches and ecostrategies. Eric Lerner has given a compelling account of the evolutionary process in just precisely these terms. The earliest prokaryotic organisms, he points out, derived their energy from fermentation. This is an inefficient process which produces waste products, namely alcohols, which themselves still contain quite a bit of energy. Eventually the accumulation of waste products seems to have provoked a sort of crisis and after about 2 billion years we see the emergence of primitive autotrophs—specifically cyanobacteria—which could engage in photosynthesis. Initially this helped rescue the prokaryotes, which fermented the food produced by the cyanobacteria. But eventually the build-up of oxygen began to poison them, leading to another crisis. One cell's poison, however, is another cell's pastry, and the high oxygen atmosphere made possible the development of organisms which engaged in respiration, i.e., the oxidation of their food, rather than in fermentation. Respiration, furthermore, returns to the atmosphere the carbon dioxide which autotrophs need for photosynthesis. Each step in this process, furthermore, involves an increase in energy flow and thus in the capacity of the organism in question. Subsequent stages in the evolutionary process—development of multicelled organisms, land organisms, reptiles capable of living away from large bodies of water, and eventually of warm-blooded bird and mammals—each overcome definite structural obstacles and led to the development of higher order capacities (Lerner 1991: 302–6).

The potential of this sort of analysis, particularly if joined to postdarwinian accounts of the sources of genetic and morphogenetic innovation, should not be underestimated. Lerner has sketched out for biology a theory not unlike the historical materialist account of social development, and one which merits further elaboration and empirical testing. At the same time, we must point out that evolution, at least the progressive evolution we actually observe, cannot be explained exclusively in terms of material conditions and structural dynamics. Together with postdarwinian accounts of the sources of innovations, Lerner's theory shows *how* progressive evolution occurs, but not *why*. It would, after all, have been possible for primitive prokaryotes to simply die out when they reached a crisis point, or to develop an ecostrategy which was different, and allowed them to get around ecological blockages without developing higher order capacities as measured, for example by efficiency of energy uptake. Here teleonomic push is insufficient. As with the problem of the emergence of life in the first place, the option for higher order development can only be explained in terms of what was gained, and thus in terms of a teleological attractor. By developing higher order capacities, organisms not only evade crises, whether externally imposed or written into their ecostrategies and thus of their own making; they also gain a greater share in Being.

Once again, we return to the ontological gradient. Life begins simply as a way in which complex systems conserve and reproduce their structure through exchange of matter and energy with the environment, but it rapidly becomes a way of acting on that environment in order to create new possibilities and new, ever more complex forms of organization. Life, in other words, is already incipiently labor and thus to the social form of matter, to which we must now turn.

8

Social Organization

WE NOW ARRIVE AT the highest form of material organization of which we are aware: i.e., the social form of matter. Here, as in the two preceding sections, our task remains that of sketching out what a teleological research program might look like, and showing why it is more promising than the alternatives, while laying the groundwork for an argument for the ultimate meaningfulness of the universe—something which must, at the very least, include an argument for the ultimate meaningfulness of human history. We have already analyzed in some detail the principal application of the hegemonic mathematical-physical paradigm to the study of human societies, i.e., classical and especially neoclassical political economy. We have also see that what appear to be "alternatives" to the formalisms of political economy, i.e., interpretive sociology and functionalism, turn out to be, on the one hand, simply attempts to complete it by explaining the origins of the preferences which govern consumer choice in the marketplace and, on the other hand, instruments of what Lukacs called the "indirect apologetic" for capitalism. Finally, we have shown that Marx's critique of political economy is in fact simply a special case of our own critique of mathematical physics. It would seem to follow from this that the social sciences founded by Marx, i.e., Marx's own dialectical political economy and historical materialism, his theory of human history and human society, would in fact represent just precisely the sort of approach to human society which our argument requires. Matters are not, however, quite so simple, and we have already hinted at why. Because of its failure to transcend the limitations of mathematical physics and develop and authentically dialectical science, dialectical materialism, leaves utterly ungrounded its claims for the ultimate meaningfulness of the universe, and thus of human history. And far from being simply a philosophical question (though it is certainly that) or even a question for physics, this failure has real implications for the way in which we understand the nature of value and development of human society. Let us examine this problem in greater detail.

We humans are complex beings, deeply rooted in material reality, but driven by profound spiritual aspirations. We are, on the one hand, animals, whose world is defined, at least to begin with, by what we know with our senses and who strive for ever more diverse and intense sensory experience. It is this desire for pleasurable sensation which motivates us to do what we need to in order to survive and reproduce and ensure the survival of the species. In this sense we are not too different from dogs, who charm us precisely because we share so much in common with them. Unlike dogs, however, we can abstract from the images we garner from the senses and rise to ever higher principles. We can ask what things are and what they mean and our sensations are thus always meaning laden—and all the more pleasurable or painful because of this. We want to know what the world means and to understand the significance of our place therein.[1]

These twin aspects of human nature—material and spiritual—come together in the one activity which appears to be uniquely human and which, were we to meet other species which engage in it, would define them as our close comrades in the cosmic hierarchy: the act of production or creativity. Unlike other animals, who merely reproduce, making more of their own kind, and unlike the angels of Catholic doctrine who contemplate God and manage God's creation, but do not themselves engage in material creation, we humans are constantly engaged in creating new and more complex forms of organization: new technologies, new relationships and social structures, new forms of art, science, and wisdom. The emergence of this new capacity is partly a result of our materiality

---

1. This formulation, which may seem reminiscent of Fromm (Fromm 1947), actually goes much further. For Fromm human spirituality is rooted in a disharmony in our existence. Unlike the other animals we are aware of our finitude and isolation and this gives rise to an existential anxiety which we seek to resolve by various means, some healthy (creative engagement with the world around us), and some not. While Fromm allows for a sort of nontheistic spirituality, he rejects the idea that we might actually be ordered to an end which transcends human development and civilizational progress. My own formulation, on the other hand, treats our animal capacities as the material basis for the development of higher order abilities which are not in conflict with them, but merely transcend them, and takes seriously the reality of the transcendental ends to which we aspire.

and finitude. The earth on which we evolved was already full of organisms which prosper simply by means of rapid reproduction, so that the death of large numbers of individuals is of little concern, and had its share as well of those which exploit narrowly defined niches on the basis of great physical prowess. We humans are neither rabbits nor lions. Big-brained weaklings that we are, we take too long too gestate and grow to maturity for what population biologists call an "r-strategy" centered on rapid reproduction to be realistic. And yet we could hardly hope to compete with the large carnivores, who best us in strength, speed, agility—and thus the ability to hunt. We *had* to learn how to make things.

But production is also, as we argued above, an intellectual act, and thus never purely material. It involves an understanding of both the raw material and some end or purpose. And even the most rudimentary ends—to help procure food, for example— have a profound spiritual dimension. We seek to escape our finitude and contingency, at least for a while, and to persist in Being. And once our more basic needs are taken care for, we quickly turn to the pursuit of more complex ends which, taken together, amount to civilizational progress and spiritual development. The development of humanity's productive capacities thus involves not only scientific progress, which helps us to understand better the matter on which we work, but also sapiential[2] progress: an ever deeper understanding of the end to which humanity, and the universe as a whole, are ordered. Civilizations are nothing more or less than the product of our efforts to achieve definite spiritual ends under definite material conditions, by means of definite social structures, and cannot be properly understood without reference to all three types of factors.

1. The *material* basis for the development of civilization is the human organism and the ecosystem or ecosystems it inhabits, which constrain profoundly the range of survival strategies which are open to it and thus the whole pattern of social development.

2. The *formal* cause of human civilization is social structure. Social structure includes:

---

2. I use the term sapiential to include all those disciplines which terminate or claim to terminate in wisdom or knowledge of first principles: religion, philosophy, theology, mysticism, etc. Sapiential progress is progress in wisdom; the sapiential authorities are those authorities whose legitimacy is based on their wisdom: religious leaders but also philosophers, theologians, mystics, and practitioners of connatural or caritative wisdom.

2.1 technological structures, i.e., particular ways of reorganizing physical and biological matter,

2.2 economic structures, i.e., particular ways of organizing human labor and centralizing and allocating resources,

2.3 political structures, i.e., particular ways of building and exercising power,

2.4 psycho-social structures, i.e., particular ways of organizing the human psyche to serve the aims of the society in question, and

2.5 ideological-cultural structures, i.e., particular ways of organizing our experience of the universe, including languages, natural and artificial.

3. The *final cause* of human civilization, as of everything else, is *Esse* or Being as such. But each civilization understands, and thus pursues, this cause differently. The way in which a civilization understands the end to which it is ordered we call its *Civilizational ideal*. Thus Chinese civilization historically understood itself as ordered to *Tian* or Heaven, Medieval India to the union of *Brahman* and *atman*.

The lines between material basis and social structure and social structure and teleological ordering are a bit ambiguous. Absolutely speaking the material basis is confined to the ecosystem. Technology and economics are just as much social products as politics and culture. Relatively speaking, however, the whole "built up" infrastructure of a society, including its technological apparatus and the social surplus it can generate, constitute the material foundation on the basis of which political and cultural realities develop. A religious ideology is, similarly, an integral part of the social structure, i.e., the way a particular society is organized, and not itself an end or *telos*, but the objects of which it speaks are such a *telos*. We gain access to the way a society understands its ends, however, by analyzing its ideological-cultural structure. The same is true of the relationship between the various instances of the social structure. Organizing labor and centralizing and allocating resources both involve building and exercising power. Building and exercising power, similarly, generally involves an appeal to fundamental principles and values. This is true even in predominantly secular societies. These categories should thus be used flexibly in a way which serves the purposes of the particular analysis which is being carried out.

As civilizations develop they leave a kind of deposit which is *material, structured* and *teleologically ordered*. This is often referred to simply as the "built environment," but this phrase fails to capture the extent to which the form of buildings and the structure of cities encodes a civilization's adaptation to its ecosystem, its way of organizing and centralizing resources and building and exercising power, and its way of understanding the end to which it is ordered. Phillip Bess (Bess 2006), who captures this reality better than other theorists I have read, uses the term "formal order" but in the philosophical context of this work this seems to ignore the materiality of the deposit involved. My preference is simply for the term *architectural* organization, both because of its reference to the discipline which studies and creates such global forms of organization, and because of its joining of a term for the end to which the built environment is ordered (*archi-*) to one for the act of building (*-tecture*), though the term must be understood to include the study and creation of entire urban and indeed rural landscapes and not simply single buildings.

The importance of the architectural organization of a civilization cannot be underestimated, because the accumulated architectural record constrains, in the way few other things can, the future direction of Civilizational development. However "secular" modern Europe may have become (and we have seen that this term is highly problematic) the presence, at the center of essentially every European city and village of a cathedral or parish church, marking a sacral center of meaning, constrains and orders human activity in a way which conserves elements of earlier Civilizational patterns. The same is true for the any other ancient civilization. Thus the Communist Parties of the Soviet Union and of China tried to hegemonize the sacred spaces at the center of their polities (St. Basil's and the Kremlin on the one hand, and the sacred complex formed by the Tian-an (Temple of Heaven), Tianamen, and the Forbidden City on the other hand, but were partially hegemonized by them.

But it is not only ancient structures which function in this way. Chicago, for example, is in many ways a high modern city *par excellence*, organized around a downtown of financial and corporate headquarters and high end shopping, with outlying districts built around factories of various types and sizes. But the people themselves altered this high modern space by placing at the center of their neighborhoods countless churches and synagogues which are the real centers of meaning in the city, and by creating shopping districts which serve the needs of distinct ethnoreligious communities (with dietary laws creating distinct economic niches). This Tocquevillian space, as Phillip Bess (Bess 2006) calls it, is perhaps unique to the industrial era cities of the United States. Dallas, on the other hand, understands itself as an intensely religious city. Dallas Theological Seminary is the intellectual headquarters of dispensational premillennialism. But the public spaces of Dallas are defined by office parks and shopping malls, with churches, no matter how grand, scattered unobtrusively through residential districts, so that they play essentially no role in the way the *meaning* of the city is ultimately defined. These architectural structures mean that it would be nearly impossible for a high modern "secularist" agenda to become hegemonic in Chicago or for a "Catholic" sense of sacramentality to become dominant in Dallas.

When approaching a civilization, it is possible to identify several different levels of analysis: metacivilizational, civilizational, structural, etc. Analysis at the metacivilizational level looks at clusters of civilizations with ideals which share common characteristics. A *metacivilizational project* is a cluster of civilizations which, while defined by different and even incompatible ideals, nonetheless share certain common characteristics. Broadly speaking it is possible to identify the following metacivilizational projects:

- Pre-Axial civilizations, such as the great agrarian sacral monarchic empires of the Bronze Age, regard meaning and unproblematic and are ordered to achieving divinization understood simply as *immortality*, generally only for the king or the aristocracy, by means of sacrificial rituals.

- Axial[3] civilizations accept the fact that meaning has become problematic, are characterized by religious rationalization and democra-

3. This represents, to be sure, a something of a redefinition of Jaspers' original characterization of the axial age (Jaspers 1953) and a departure from the way the term has been used in modern social science (Aronson et al. 2005), which emphasizes the beginning of a process of the disenchantment of the universe, a "disembedding" of the individual from society, the cosmos, and the divine (Taylor 2007: 146–58), and a shift in religious aims from worldly flourishing (to use Taylor's term) to salvation of some kind. Central to the thesis of this book is the idea that, at the deepest level, humanity's aim—and indeed that of the whole universe—has always remained the same. It is Being, or God. What changes is the way in which this end is understood and pursued. But simply survival or worldly flourishing, immortality, the union of *Brahman* and *atman*, *nirvana* or bodhisattvahood,

tization, and aim at regrounding meaning and at cultivating human capacities by means of rationalized spiritual disciplines. They generally understand human civilizational progress as a real participation in this process of spiritual development, but do not reduce spirituality to civilization building. The seek divinization by means of the cultivation of various spiritual capacities, though the capacities valued and cultivated often differ considerably.

- Modern civilizations claim that meaning can be rendered once again unproblematic by either revelation (in the case of the early modern ideal) or reason (scientific or philosophical) and aim at achieving divinity by inner worldly means (scientific and technological progress or revolutionary political practice).

Analysis at the *civilizational* level focuses on the complex interaction of material basis, social structure, and civilizational ideal. The ideals which constitute civilizations are constrained and shaped by the social conditions (both material basis and social structure) under which they develop. But social structures must be understood as ways of realizing definite civilizational ideals. And civilizational ideals also represent at least a partial grasp of the truth and can thus continue to motivate human action long after the conditions which gave birth to them have vanished. When this happens, the meaning of these ideals inevitably changes, though this may happen consciously, when the ideals constitute a living

---

the beatific vision, and the modern ideals of divinization through scientific-technological and revolutionary-political progress are all ways of understanding and seeking divinization. Indeed, Protestantism and certain forms of Asharite Islam are unusual in positing ends (a simple paradise for those who submit to God, or everlasting life for those who believe) which do not look much like divinization. In reality, however, these represent simply the carrying over of earlier, preaxial ideals of divinization into a context in which the idea of God itself has advanced in a way which prohibits humanity from actually seeking what God *is* –infinite power—for the simple reason that (unlike *Esse*) this cannot be shared and seeking it represents an assault on rather than worship of God.

This redefinition of what happens in the Axial Age implies that modernity does not continue and complete the axial revolution (as Taylor claims in the pages cited above) but rather represents a decisive break with it. Taylor is certainly correct that the axial revolutions were incomplete (Taylor 2007: 146, 43–439, 613–14). But this was not simply the result of an equilibrium in which the people pursued preaxial religious aims and virtuosi postaxial aims. Rather, the forms of popular religion themselves changed. The mystery cult, of which Christianity is the most successful, for example, was a classical example of a postaxial form which democratizes religious aims (divinization understood as immortality) and makes it accessible to the people. And modernity was not the completion of the axial revolution but rather its abandonment in favor of a new ideal.

tradition which values both continuity and change, or unconsciously, as fundamentalists reassert what they imagine to be ancient and unchanging truths but which (even when the words remain the same) are really innovations.

Structural analysis focuses on the way in which societies engage the material environment in order to realize a definite ideal. Several distinctive modes can be identified:

- *Band societies* are found in a variety of ecosystems, and generally have hunter-gatherer technology, a kinship system which only weakly influences the formation of actual groups, and a totemic religious structure which brings clans together for occasional religious festivals.

- *Tribal societies* are also found in a variety of ecosystems, but persist longest on open steppes or grasslands with large populations of ungulates. They have generally developed advanced hunter-gatherer or pastoral nomadic technologies which allow them to exploit these herds, sometimes supplemented with raiding or trading, and have strongly developed kinship systems which largely organize social life, and polytheistic religions often characterized by the emergence of male sky gods with warlike characteristics, such as the Aryan *Indra* or the Turkic *Tengri*.

- *Communitarian societies* are found in ecosystems which make the cultivation of food relatively easy, and have developed horticultural or agricultural technology. Land is generally owned by the clan or village and is often periodically redistributed. A strong kinship system is cross-cut by social forms which transcend kinship ties, such as the village itself and various religious societies. The polytheistic religions of communitarian societies are characterized by a strong emphasis on fertility rituals and are often dominated by a goddess of wisdom and fertility, such as the Keres *Sussistinako* or the universal Mediterranean goddess which forms the background of the cults of *Isis* and *Demeter*.

- *Archaic societies* are found especially but not exclusively in riverine ecosystems and have advanced horticultural or agricultural technologies. Surplus is centralized and reallocated by a temple complex, which may or may not form the center of an urban concentration. The polytheistic religious ideologies of archaic societies are characterized by the emergence of an increasingly well-defined high god concept, often associated with the sun. Evidence for such societies is scant; most were quickly absorbed into emerging tributary empires, but the Anasazi stage of the Puebloan civilization, the Mississippian civilization, and the societies which built Stonehenge and Avebury may all represent archaic structures.

- *Tributary societies* are often founded as nomadic raiders conquer communitarian or archaic riverine communities and impose rents, taxes, and forced labor, eventually building large urban centers and transforming the religious structure in a way which leads to a predominance of divine monarchs who integrate both warlike and priestly functions, such as the Egyptian *Ra* or the Babylonian *Marduk*.

- *Petty commodity* societies generally emerge in coastal or oasis ecosystems on the basis of specialized agricultural production. Resources are allocated by a market in goods and services, and political structures, which may vary from relatively democratic city state forms through large military empires, focus their attention on capturing as much surplus through trade as possible. Religious ideologies undergo a process of rationalization as myth gradually gives way to philosophy and new religious movements emerge with a greater focus on ethical conduct, social justice, and spiritual development. This is the Axial Age described by Karl Jaspers to which we referred above and which we will discuss in greater detail in the next chapter. These ideologies gradually assert ever increasing influence, both by hegemonizing state structures (Confucianism in Han or Sung China, *Dar-Al Islam*) or by building monastic or mendicant communities which become major economic and political as well as cultural actors (e.g., the *Mahayana Buddhist* monasteries of Sui and T'ang China or the Benedictine monasteries of Medieval Europe; the *Sufi* orders throughout *Dar-al Islam*, but especially Central Asia, and the Mendicant orders in late Medieval and Baroque Europe and in New Spain).

- *Capitalist societies* are defined by the development of industrial technologies, and markets in labor power and capital as well as goods and services. Political organization varies, but generally involves some sort of representative format except in transitional periods, but is strongly subordinated to the market, which it serves. Religious ideologies emphasize submission to a sovereign God who is a reflex of the mysterious imperatives of the market order, or else conceal themselves as secular doctrines which seek transcendence by technical and/or political means.

- In *Socialist societies* the state displaces the capital markets as the principal resource allocator, something which generally reflects a teleological ordering to civilizational progress rather than capital accumulation and luxury consumption, although the markets in goods and services, and in labor power, remain. Most socialist societies have insisted on an official atheism in order to guarantee that the drive of the population towards transcendence is focused exclusively on innerworldly means.

The way in which a particular society is structured in turn constitutes a definite complex of *social actors*. We distinguish between primary, secondary, and tertiary social actors. By primary social actors we mean groups defined by their position in the social structure. The most important of these are *social classes*, which are constituted first of all by position with respect to the economic structure, but which also develop their own characteristic forms of political organization and their own ideologies. These may be a refraction of the larger aims of the society as seen from their social location, but if the structure of the society is deeply in contradiction with either their survival or their development, oppressed social classes in particular may develop revolutionary ideologies which at least aim to become alternative civilizational ideals. Class struggles are thus never purely economic—even political-economic—in character. They are always, simultaneously, direct or indirect struggles around fundamental questions of meaning and value. *Peoples* are defined by their position with respect to political and cultural structures. They are groups of human beings which, generally speaking, share a common homeland and have a common history and culture. While they may have been incorporated into a larger civilizational complex, they often have distinctive beliefs and values which may be a variant on the dominant ideology of the civilization, but may also reflect an alternative civilizational ideal which has been subordinated to those of the dominant peoples in the civilization. When the oppressed classes and peoples of a civilization cannot resolve its internal contradictions, these contradictions are often resolved for them by invading peoples who impose an entirely new civilizational ideal. This was the role of the Germans and Arabs in the collapse of Roman Civilization. *Gender*, i.e., the meaning which a people or a civilization attaches to sexual difference, is defined by position with respect to the psychosocial structure of the society, its way of reproducing human social beings. This is expressed in the sexual division of labor, in power relations within the family, kinship, and larger social networks, and in the dominant ideology and culture, and can also form a line of demarcation along which fundamental social struggles unfold.

Primary social actors lie behind all social processes, but they are never, as it were, visible to the naked eye. They appear only when one scrutinizes social processes through the lens of social theory. Secondary social actors, on the other hand, are formed on the basis of primary social actors (or alliances of primary social actors) in order to act rationally in the public arena. These are groups which understand themselves as such and appear to others as concrete social actors. They include families, villages, corporations, organizations such as guilds or trade unions, political parties, educational, scientific, cultural, or religious organizations. Secondary social actors may represent the perspective of one primary social actor or they may articulate an alliance or coalition of such interests. Understanding how such coalitions are formed is one of the fundamental tasks of social analysis, as it provides the key to rendering intelligible otherwise opaque and apparently voluntaristic processes.

It is in this context that de Tocqueville's analysis of the "intermediate" institutions of civil society should be situated. Such institutions permit groups of individuals to pursue distinctive variants of the hegemonic Civilizational ideal, or even countervailing ideals by means of economic, political, and cultural activity. The scope which exists for such diversity within a society we call its degree of ideological pluralism. At the one extreme, we find *totalitarian* societies in which the institutions of civil society have been extinguished entirely or made instruments of the hegemonic tertiary (political theological) social actor. At the other extreme, we find societies in which the public arena is *constituted* by deliberation around fundamental questions of meaning and value and the civilization is constituted not so much by a single ideal as by an open and civil contest between ideals.

Tertiary or *political-theological* organizations are formed consciously and rationally to act on primary and secondary social actors in order to conserve or transform human civilizations. They may act at the level of civilizational ideal, social structure, or public policy, but at least implicitly have the capacity to act at all three levels. They may be informal –e.g., ruling class networks which negotiate aims and strategies through informal interactions in diverse social settings—or formal, like a religious order or political party. Generally speaking, however, informal networks have less capacity for common action that disciplined organizations, and generally represent efforts on the part of ruling classes to conserve the existing structure and manage change, rather than attempts at revolutionary reorganization.

Now human societies develop as human beings pursue the Good as they understand it, given the constraints imposed on their perceptions by the material conditions and social structures. They develop social structures in order to make possible the pursuit of the Good under those material conditions. When those structures begin to hold back their ability to pursue the Good they challenge and attempt to modify them, sometimes gradually and incrementally, sometimes through revolutionary upheavals. Particular ways of understanding our End or purpose (i.e., particular ideologies) can serve either as catalysts for change or as means of social control.

In analyzing the dynamics of human societies it is necessary to distinguish between civilizational, structural, periodic, and conjunctural crises.[4] A *civilizational crisis* takes place when, generally after a succession of structural crises, people actually lose faith in a civilizational ideal and stop pursuing it. A *structural crisis*, on the other hand, arises from a contradiction between the social structure or complex of structures by which the civilization organizes its activities on the one hand and the underlying material conditions (i.e., the ecosystem) and/or the real ends to which people aspire. Structural crises can be, but are not always, resolved by fundamental structural change. Anasazi-Pueblo civilization expanded beyond the carrying capacity of the ecological niche it inhabited and responded to the resulting crisis by decentralizing, abandoning large temple complexes of the sort we see at Chaco for the scattered villages which we now see among the Puebloan peoples, a shift which may also reflect changes at the religious level (Stuart 2001), but which also

---

4. These distinctions derive from Louis Althusser and his followers (Althusser and Balibar 1968/1970), but have been modified to reflect the larger approach to social theory outlined above.

reflects significant civilizational continuity. Roman civilization ran into a structural crisis because its basic strategy–using the surplus generated by chattel slavery to buy into the Silk Road trade— ran into insuperable limits. Logistic and ecological factors made further expansion impossible, bringing an end to the wars of conquest which provided a steady supply of slaves. The empire was forced to shift from the use of chattel slaves to the use of settled, dependent peasants, known as *coloni* and to significantly increase rates of exploitation. This exploitation was legitimated as service to the common good using Christian religious ideals, something which allowed the empire, but not, perhaps, Roman Civilization, to persist in parts of the East, where elements of the old structure served a new ideal. In the West and in the *Masreq* and the *Mahgreb*, this system lacked credibility and Roman Civilization was displaced by the religious civilizations of Christendom and *Dar-al-Islam,* both of which were inspired by ideals radically different from those which shaped Rome.

Both civilizational and structural crises are times of what Durkheim called *collective effervescence* when, unable to live in the old way, people interact more intensely and question more deeply than they other wise would. As we suggested above, it is out of such moments of collective effervescence that new insights into the mystery of Being, and thus new Civilizational ideals, ultimately emerge.

That the course of human history has been at least broadly progressive can be demonstrated in any number of ways. There is, first of all, the ecological success of humanity, evident in our growing numbers, as well as our very real technological progress, something which Eric Lerner has measured in terms of the rate of growth in energy use per annum (Lerner 1991: 316). This progress is also reflected in our ability to organize ever larger numbers of people in pursuit of a common purpose, something which has left us poised at the edge of a new era, ready to leave the cradle of the Earth and begin our journey out towards the stars. And behind this technological development is an ever deepening grasp of the organization of the universe, which alone makes it possible for us to *reorganize* physical, biological, and social systems in ever more complex ways.

At the same time, it should be apparent that social progress is by no means even or continuous. On the contrary, periods of progress give way to times of stagnation and even decline as the organizing potential of once progressive systems is exhausted or as fundamentally destructive systems such as slavery or capitalism take hold. This phenomenon is amply illustrated by the data collect by Lerner and Childe (Childe 1851), which shows a marked decline in the rate of technological innovation at precisely those times when exploitation appears to have been worst: the mid-late bronze age, the late years of the Roman Empire—and the present period. Indeed, the *per annum* rate of growth in energy use has been declining since the middle of the nineteenth century! And there have been no fundamental scientific innovations since the beginning of the twentieth century. The punctuated character of social progress supports our general thesis—i.e., that social structures sometimes develop which hold back progress and must be transformed if renewed growth and development is to be possible.

Clearly we stand at just such a crossroads. And if the foregoing analysis is correct, the crisis in the sciences is an integral dimension of a much larger social crisis which can only be resolved by transcending the market system. Of this much, of course, Marx himself was already aware—at just the moment, interestingly enough, when the long period of stagnation was to begin. What our analysis adds is a recognition that the internal contradictions of capitalism are not enough to push us forward. Systems can just stagnate, or even collapse and disintegrate, without giving birth to anything new. A real break with the market system presupposes transcendental principles of value in terms of which the market order can be judged, and from which criteria for resource allocation can be derived. And this, in turn presupposes a teleological cosmology on the basis of which alone it is possible to conclude to such principles of value. But there is more. The analysis set forth in this chapter also suggests that we need to break with the dominant technological regime, which is based on the mechanistic world-view fostered by mathematical physics, which breaks down physical, biological, and social systems in order to release their energy, and then rebuilds, as it were, from scratch. Industrial technologies are not only destructive of the environment; they also degrade the social fabric, or at least presuppose the degradation of the social fabric worked directly by the market system, in order to ensure a supply of unattached, deskilled workers. It was, in part, the failure of historic socialism to transcend this industrial regime which prevented it from realizing its full potential. And this break as well presupposes the development of a teleological physics, biology, and sociology, which can help us to grasp the potential latent in all forms of matter and develop new techniques which release and multiply this latent potential rather than simply exploiting it for the raw energy it embodies.

The overall implications of this transformation are not merely structural but civilizational. They point to a break not with the modern ideal of divinization by means of innerworldly civilizational progress. And such a break, in turn, presupposes at least the initial steps towards a new ideal.

Thus the importance of this book. Thus the importance of the next chapter, where we will, at long last, draw together the diverse threads of our argument, and show that the universe is, indeed, ultimately meaningful and lay the groundwork for a rational ascent to a first principle in terms of which the universe can be explained and action ordered.

Conclusion

STATEMENT OF THE PROBLEM

THE FORGOING CHAPTERS HAVE outlined a teleological research program, and suggested a general hypothesis regarding the organization of the universe, i.e., that the systems which we observe can best be explained in terms of the complex interaction of definite material conditions, which constrain the quantity and type of energy available for organization, the dynamics of existing structures which determine in large part how that energy will be used, and the action of teleological attractors which catalyze the development of still more complex structures, creating an internal tension between the underlying dynamism of matter and the constraints imposed by the present mode of organization. Gradually contradictions mount leading either to stagnation and decay or to a revolutionary transformation in which the old mode of organization is cast aside in favor of new, more complex forms, a process which, over the history of the universe, has lead to authentic progress in the sense of a development from lower to higher degrees of organization. It is one thing, however, to show that teleological explanation is legitimate and useful and that there is an empirical trend towards the development of higher levels of organization; it is quite another thing to show that the universe as a whole is ultimately meaningful. It is to this final and critical link in our argument that we must now turn.

We need to begin with some definitions. What, precisely, does it mean to say that the universe is meaningful or ultimately meaningful? Meaningfulness, as we have used the term throughout the course of this book, has to do fundamentally with organization, i.e., with ordering to an end. This presupposes system, or inter-relatedness, which may be either external (like the relationships between the particles of a perfect gas) or internal, i.e., determinative of essence, existence, or both. It also presupposes pattern, order, or structure, i.e., the arrangement of the elements across space-time in accord with some rule. Finally, it involves ordering to an end. This means that the structure can be fully comprehended only in terms of an end towards which the elements tend or strive.

We should note, however, that a number of different gradations of meaningfulness are possible, and that there are different ways in which things can be interconnected, ordered, and ordered to an end. We have already distinguished in earlier chapters between external and internal relatedness, and we have noted the varying degrees of structure which characterize different mathematical categories, e.g., sets, groups, rings, fields, etc. With regard to the question of ordering to an end it is possible to distinguish the following *degrees*:

1. a mere tendential direction (Bashkar 1993) in which, as a result of mechanisms which in themselves imply no intrinsic dynamic towards the development of higher degrees of organization, nonetheless lead to such developments over very long periods of cosmo-historical time,

2. orderings which do involve an intrinsically progressive dynamic but which do not act deterministically or coercively on each and every element, so that some elements remain outside the larger teleological or teleonomic scheme,

3. orderings which involve an intrinsically progressive dynamic and which, at least in the final instance, act deterministically on all elements so that "in the end" all things are optimally ordered to the Good, and

4. orderings in which the end logically implies all of the other elements and the whole course of the development, so that no result other than the optimum is even logically possible.

We should point out that mere tendential directions are possible if and only if the relations between elements are purely external. This is because internally related elements which tended towards an end would do so in accord with some principle or rule, and would thus, depending on the degree of structure involved, be ordered to an end in either the second, third, or fourth degrees.

It is also possible to distinguish between the various *ways* in which things can be ordered to an end. Generally a distinction is made between:

1. adaptive systems, which develop towards higher degrees of organization through purely external relationships, without reference either to either an immanent or transcendent principle,
2. teleonomic systems, which develop towards higher degrees of organization in accord with an immanent rule, which may be logical, as it is with Hegel, or material, as it is in the case of Marx and Engels, and
3. properly teleological systems, which develop towards higher degrees of organization under the influence of a transcendental principle.

There is clearly a relationship between mode and degree of ordering to an end. Systems which show only a tendential direction are most likely adaptive rather than teleonomic or teleological systems. Teleological ordering leaves the most room for some combination of intrinsic ordering to an end and nondeterministic development. A strictly teleonomic system will, by definition, be absolutely deterministic. There is, to be sure, no reason why the various modes of ordering might not be combined. A teleological attractor will tend to give rise to structures which are teleonomically ordered, and teleonomic rules may well involve some sort of adaptive mechanism, e.g., either a random or systematic search for the most stable structure. The thesis which we have advanced is of just precisely this variety. The motor force of cosmohistorical development is teleological, but the operation of both the ultimate and of local teleological attractors gives rise to various structures which have their own internal logic and, depending on the degree of structure, operate in a more or less deterministic fashion. Certain physical systems, being highly structured, behave deterministically; biological and social systems generally do not. There are, however, many (perhaps an infinity) of different ways that systems can be ordered to the End, and the choice of a particular pathway, while constrained by whatever structures have already developed, is initially radically open and contingent—though only those pathways which involve significant development toward higher degrees of organization will prove stable and viable. In this sense as in others, our approach integrates insights from both the Aristotelian-Thomistic and Hegelian-Marxist tradition, while allowing greater room for the operation of contingency than either.

The criterion of ultimacy requires that the end to which the universe is ordered be infinite, necessary, perfect, and thus divine. This is because if it was not infinitely valuable then it could not confer ultimate meaning on the cosmohistorical evolutionary process—some higher end would be possible which had not been attained. If the end is infinite, it is also perfect, since infinity is the absence of limit and something which is unlimited has all possible perfections. Finally, if it is infinite and without limit then there can be nothing outside of it, and it must, therefore, be necessary Being, *Esse* as such, having its cause in itself. Invoking the convertibility of the transcendentals, we can thus further conclude that the end, considered as an object of perception, is Beauty, that as an object of judgment, it is the Truth in terms of which all things can be explained, and that as an object of the appetites it is the Good, which draws all things to itself. Considered it itself, it is the perfect One, the transcendental integrity which, itself absolutely simple, holds all things in perfect unity. Showing the ultimate meaningfulness of the universe, in other words, involves proving the existence of God, and will thus involve us in a discussion of the teleological, cosmological and ontological arguments.[1]

Speaking about the ultimate meaningfulness *of the universe*, however, implies more than the existence of God and the ordering of the universe to God. It requires that the universe participate in some real way in the life of God, so that it really and truly makes a difference not only whether or not there is a God, but also whether or not there is a universe. Depending on just how we understand the meaningfulness of the universe, this may mean that the universe participates in bringing God into being (godbuilding), that the universe is in some sense a necessary manifestation of God (as in various forms of objective idealism), or both (as in the case of Hegel). Or it may mean that each finite system participates in a distinctive way, appropriate to its degree of organization, in the divine Being, while contributing to the development of ever higher degrees of organization over the course of the cosmohistorical process,

---

1. What does this imply about Buddhist cosmologies, at least some of which we classed as teleological in an earlier chapter, given the fact that Buddhism is generally atheistic? Here it is necessary to divide the question. Some early Buddhist cosmologies, which were essentially attempts to ground the basic Buddhist principles of suffering, impermanence, and liberation from rebirth, were *not* teleological. But the fully developed Mahayana cosmologies, which understand the infinite proliferation of universes as all ordered to the cultivation of enlightened beings, certainly *are* teleological. And most of these cosmologies treat the whole system of universes as the product of a primordial Buddha, Mahavairocana, who is, in effect, God. Other Buddhist cosmologies, including many later Theravada systems, stand somewhere in between.

as a free response to the attractive power of God. This final alternative, a radical historicization of traditional Thomism, is the option for which we will argue in this chapter.

ASSESSMENT OF THE PRINCIPAL HISTORIC ARGUMENTS

In so far as any argument for the ultimate meaningfulness of the universe involves demonstrating the existence of God, the most natural point of entry into this question is a consideration of the principal historic arguments for the existence of God. There have, historically, been four principal approaches to this problem. One of these, the transcendental approach, which includes most forms of the moral argument, we have already shown to be radically flawed and in any case irrelevant to the question at hand. Transcendental arguments, we will recall, attempt to show that what ever they are attempting to prove is in fact a "condition of the possibility" of something else, the existence of which is already established or at least uncontroversial. In the case of transcendental arguments for the existence of God, this generally means that the existence of God is regarded as a condition of the possibility of moral judgment (Kant's argument) or of our finite, everyday existential judgments (Rahner's approach). This approach is irrelevant to the question at hand, and in fact destructive of the main purposes of this book because it was developed precisely to evade the question of cosmic teleology and indeed any engagement with the sciences, the results of which were seen as weighing against the existence of God. As we pointed out in an earlier chapter, by attempting to show the existence of God without the ultimate meaningfulness of the universe, transcendental arguments conclude to a God who confers no intrinsic meaning on nature and history and thus to a spirituality which is otherworldly at best. The transcendental argument is, in any case, flawed because it fails to confront the possibility, raised by nihilist trend which has become so powerful in the present period, that neither science nor morality are possible, precisely because the condition of their possibility (God) either doesn't exist or cannot be adequately established.

This leaves us with the three traditional arguments for the existence of God, which have formed the mainstay of "rational metaphysics" since at least the time of Aristotle: i.e., the cosmological, teleological, and ontological arguments. Of these three, the ontological argument can also be ruled out as both flawed and hostile to the aims of this book, though we will see that an *a posteriori* version of this argument can, in fact, be salvaged and mobilized to demonstrate the logical necessity of both the existence of God and the ultimate meaningfulness of the universe, once these have been established by other means. The ontological argument, we will recall, begins from a definition of what it seeks to demonstrate, namely God. Thus for Anselm God is "that than which nothing greater can be thought" and for Descartes He is "perfect" being. The argument then goes on to show that existence is in fact included in this definition. Thus, if "that than which nothing greater can be thought" were not to exist, then we could imagine something greater still, which would contradict the premise, implying that God exists necessarily. Perfection, similarly, must include at least existence.

The difficulty with this approach is that, as Thomas pointed out, it begs the question, assuming what it claims to prove, namely that there is something "than which nothing greater can be thought" or something perfect. *Given this*, the argument works quite well, and in fact shows that such a being in fact exists necessarily. But the premise itself is a claim about the way the universe is structured. In the case of Anselm's formulation, it in fact implies that the universe has a very specific mathematical structure, namely that is a total order bounded from above by "that than which nothing greater can be thought." As I have argued elsewhere (Mansueto, 2002b), in order to make this version of the ontological argument work we would first have to show that the universe is indeed a total order, meaning that every element within it is either greater than, equal to or less than every other element, and then invoke Zorn's Lemma, which states that such total orders are necessarily bounded from above. That the universe is a total order can be shown easily, but only with respect to determinations which are not particularly important from the standpoint of its ultimate meaningfulness. We can for example, show that space-time is a total order, in the sense that smaller regions are ordered by inclusion to higher regions. The resulting God would, however, be greater than everything else only in size. When we attempt to compare higher order determinations we run into serious trouble. Is it really meaningful, for example to claim that a tiger is greater than, less than, or equal to a wolf? Zorn's Lemma, furthermore, while intuitively obvious, has never been adequately demonstrated (Geroch 1985). The nonquantitative language used in Descartes formulation offers some hope of evading the requirement that we show the universe to be a total order provided that we can arrive at some qualitative definition of perfection, but we must still show that such perfection exists *before* drawing any conclusions from it.

This leaves us with the two *a posteriori* approaches to the problem: the cosmological and teleological arguments. We will argue that these two approaches are on much firmer ground, but that when properly understood they are not really distinct from each other. First, however, we need to examine briefly the traditional forms of these arguments and some of the claims which have been raised against them.

The cosmological argument begins from two simple premises: first, that something exists, and second that the rules of logic, including at the very least the principle of sufficient reason or something very much like it, are valid.[2] From here the argument can be made in several different ways. What is often called the *kalam* (the word is Arabic for "rational") version of the argument, because of its popularity among certain Arabic philosophers, claims that the universe must have had a beginning in time, because otherwise an infinite number of years would have passed, so that it would have taken forever to arrive at the present, which means we would never have arrived here, which is obviously not true. Therefore the universe has a cause outside itself, which is God. This version of the argument depends either on an *a priori* argument regarding the impossibility of actual infinities, or on *a posteriori* results from mathematical physics, generally either the "standard" Big Bang cosmology or the Second Law of Thermodynamics. Versions of the proof which invoke the Second Law of Thermodynamics claim that since energy in the universe is gradually dissipating, so that the universe is "running down" as it were, it must at some point have been "wound up" by some supernatural power which is able to act against the direction of the second law. This approach is highly vulnerable to the arguments which we invoked in earlier chapters which question the applicability of the Second Law to the universe as a whole, as well as to the possibility that the universe might not have had a beginning in time (Lerner 1991) and/or that there are purely natural, electromagnetic (Lerner 1991) or gravitational (Gal Or 1987) process which might "wind up" at least significant regions of the universe over relatively long periods of time, whether or not this was sufficient to counteract long-term entropic tendencies. We have already noted above the significant difficulties faced by the dominant "Big Bang" cosmology. More to the point,

2. By the principle of sufficient reason we mean simply that fact that everything exists for a reason and that everything therefore has a cause of some kind.

however, the *a priori* variant of this argument at once depends on and contradicts the *a posteriori* variant. If actual infinities are impossible, then there must be *some* physical theory which describes the origin of universe in time. But the only such theory which we have, namely the Big Bang, depends on a mathematics in which the possibility of actual infinities is assumed. We should also point out that the *kalam* argument shares the political-theological difficulties of the *a priori* approaches to the existence of God—it shows the radical dependence of the universe on God, but not its intrinsic ordering to him, and thus points towards a spirituality of authority and submission.

The Aristotelian and Thomistic forms of the cosmological argument are on much stronger ground. Thomas identifies three variants: the proof from motion, the proof from causation, and the proof from necessary and possible being. The proof from motion derives from Aristotle's argument in *Metaphysics* 12.7. We observe motion[3] in the universe. Physics explains this motion (incompletely and without full unification in the case of Aristotle) in terms of the material substratum on which changes takes place, an ascending series of increasingly more complex forms, each of which confers higher order capacities, and (an also ascending series of) teleological attractors, which give rise to those forms. For Aristotle as for Thomas all sublunar motion is caused by the motion of the heavenly spheres, which act through various mechanisms, as we discussed in an earlier chapter. Each of the spheres has in turn its own mover, which is moved by a desire to emulate the next higher sphere, the attractive power of which draws it on. There cannot, however, be an infinite regress of movers, since this would be absurd. There is, therefore, a first unmoved mover which is the cause of all motion.

The proof from causation is similar to the proof from motion, except that it appeals directly to causation. In our everyday sense experience, as well as in science, we observe an order of efficient causation. None of the finite systems which we observe are, furthermore, their own causes. Therefore everything must have a cause. But there cannot be a infinite regress of causes, because if there were there would be no first cause, and thus no second, etc. and nothing would exist at all. Thus there is a first efficient cause which is God.

---

3. Motion is understood here to mean change, including growth and development, decay and disintegration, as well as local motion.

The proof from necessary and possible being is a bit more subtle. Thomas begins by pointing out that in the natural world the things which we observe are only possible beings. They come into being and pass away and thus do not have to exist. But if everything was like this, then at some point there would have been nothing.[4] And since nothing comes from nothing, there would be nothing now, which obviously isn't true. Therefore there must be something which exists by necessity, which is God.

All three versions of the proof have been subjected to criticism. This criticisms may be distinguished as epistemological, physical, and properly metaphysical. The most important epistemological critiques derive from Hume and Kant. Hume argues that the category of causality itself is problematic—that since all knowledge derives from the senses, and that since we do not actually observe causation as such, but only a constant conjunction of events, causal explanation itself must be called into question. Kant is more cautious, struggling to rehabilitate causation as a synthetic *a priori* category of the understanding, a condition of the possibility of experience itself, and thus a legitimate way of organizing our experience. But since its legitimacy derives from its usefulness in organizing experience, we cannot carry it beyond that realm into the supersensible. Thus arguments like the cosmological proof are invalid.

We have already responded to these arguments at length in *Restoring Reason* (Mansueto 2002b). If our inferences that one thing causes another were not legitimate (and not merely an illusion deriving from the constant conjunction of events, or a category of understanding in terms of which we organize our experience) then they would not prove so useful in our interactions with the physical, biological, and social universe. Since, furthermore, (as Hume correctly points out) causation is an inference and not a direct experience there is no reason why we cannot infer to things which are not themselves objects of possible experience. Indeed, science does this all the time when it postulates principles, such as the various elementary particles, which are not directly accessible to the senses but which are detectable only by experimental instruments which themselves embody the theory which they are supposed to test.

---

4. This is because over an infinite period of time all logically possible states will eventually be realized, including the state of nothingness. If the universe is finite in time, the proof does not work.

Physical critiques of the cosmological argument center have generally been mounted from two directions. Older versions of the critique do not really question the underlying principle of causation but rather argue that it is not necessary to resort to an immaterial principle in order to explain the existence of the universe. The most important and influential form of this argument was set forth by Engels in his *Dialectics of Nature* (Engels 1880/1940), and has recently been reprised by Eric Lerner (Lerner 1991). This argument begins from the fundamental physical principle of the conservation of matter—the notion that matter can neither be created nor destroyed. This principle then serves as a constraint on the development of physical cosmology, ruling out in advance the possibility that the universe had a beginning in time. But if the universe has always existed, then it is not necessary to explain how or why it came into being, but only how and why it changes, and in particular how and why it evolves from lower to higher degrees of organization—something which Engels believed the physical sciences were already doing, and which his three laws of the dialectic did in concise, summary form. Eric Lerner has, we have seen, used this same principle, coupled with sharp ideological critique of trends in contemporary mathematical physics, to call into question the dominant "big bang" cosmology, and has drawn on recent developments in plasma physics to suggest an alternative account of the cosmohistorical evolutionary process.

This argument is, however, valid only against the "kalam" version of the cosmological argument, which argues for a beginning of the universe in time. It misses the fact that even if the universe has always existed (a view towards which we are sympathetic) and matter itself uncreated and incorruptible, the fact that there is something rather than nothing and that there is growth and development as well as decay and disintegration must still be explained. To claim that matter itself has the power of being is to make matter self-caused and thus, from the standpoint of scholastic philosophy at least, fully divine. This was, in fact, the position of David of Dinant, a Latin Averroist of the early twelfth century, and certain comments of Siger of Brabant and Boethius of Dacia point in a similar direction. Indeed, as Helmut Dahm points out (Dahm 1988) there is a strong pull within dialectical materialism towards a materialist pantheism. It seems clear that this was where both of the two principal trends in Soviet philosophy after the revolution—the Tektology of Alexandr Bogdanov and the "dialectics" of A.M. Deborin, where headed before they were suppressed by party philosophers who saw in their work a "conciliation of religion" and the ideological basis for creating a critical center outside the party's central committee. According to this view, matter itself is the locus of infinite possibilities. It is the principle from which all things emerge, and to which they all return. The links to the cult of the Great Mother, which experienced a resurgence during the European middle ages, should be apparent.

This sort of materialist pantheism is itself open to criticism, or at least serious qualification. While it is true that matter contains infinite possibilities, it does so only because it is indeterminate and lacks specific limiting perfections of the sort which make it impossible to simultaneously become both a dog and a philosopher—except of course by intention. It is one thing to recognize with David of Dinant, Frederick Engels, and contemporary feminist philosophers such as Mary Daly that matter has an active "potency," and not merely a disposition to receive form; it is quite another to confuse potency with act. Any attempt to explain cosmogenesis exclusively in terms of material interactions, without reference to teleological attraction, leads inevitably back to an atomistic, mechanistic cosmology in which innovation takes place only by random variation and evolution by natural selection, and thus to the whole complex of problems we have analyzed in the forgoing chapters.[5] This said, it must be noted that materialist pantheism is not an atheism, and that by immanent critique the dialectical materialist position shows itself to be critical not so much of the cosmological argument as of a certain type of metaphysics which is sometimes associated with that argument, which puts too much emphasis on divine transcendence and creativity at the expense of divine immanence and the participation of finite systems in the life of God. From this stand point dialectical materialism can only be regarded as a constructive contribution to the ongoing debate and an authentic way towards wisdom.

5. Partisans of the cult of the *Magna Mater* need not feel that this relegates their way to secondary and subaltern status. The Goddess, we must remember, was not only Demeter/Persephone, but also Isis and Sophia, the cosmic librarian become Goddess of Wisdom. Some contemporary feminist theologians have tended to stress the "materialist" face of the Goddess at the expense of all others, something which leads to a spirituality centered on the biological life cycle and respect for the integrity of the ecosystem. Mary Daly, on the other hand, insists on both the active potency of matter and the reality of teleological attraction, sot that "biophilia" is realized in an intense intellectualism and an all-sided cultivation of human capacities (Daly 1984).

The same cannot be said of the other principal physical critique of the cosmological argument. This second critique emerges out of quantum mechanics and we have already noted its main outlines in earlier chapters. According to this view, quantum mechanics itself undermines or at least radically modifies the role of causal explanation in physical explanation and thus raises very serious questions about its appropriateness in metaphysical arguments. At issue here is the claim that, because of the Heisenberg Uncertainty Relation, elementary particles simply appear and disappear as the quantum state of the underlying cosmic vacuum fluctuates. According to this view whole universes can come into being out of nothing—and perhaps pass away without notice. But if something can indeed come from nothing, then the logic of the cosmological argument is defeated. The existence of the universe cannot (and indeed doesn't need to be) explained; science is restricted to formal description.

This critique can be answered in three ways. First, it is possible to call into question the physics on which the critique is based. Quite apart from the more fundamental critique of mathematical physics which we have offered above, we should point out that many physicists argue that quantum relations are, in fact, ultimately deterministic. This is true of most versions of the Many Histories approach to quantum mechanics, as well as certain others.[6] Second, if quantum theory *is* taken as a radical critique of causality, then it is self-defeating, since the very quantum processes which are being invoked to defeat causality in fact depend on a whole chain of scientific reasoning from which causal terms cannot be eliminated even by retroactive reformulation. The quantum nature of energy transfer is used, for example, to explain, and is thus said, in a sense, to cause (formally if not efficiently) the nature of the black body radiation and the fact that chemical elements form a discrete rather than continuous order. The Heisenberg Uncertainty Relation then arises out of an effort to describe mathematically the way in which quantum energy transfer works. If, on the other hand, quantum theory is taken only to qualify the concept of causality, ruling out some of the narrower, more mechanistic forms of causal reasoning, then the same issues which we raised with respect to the older, dialectical materialist form of the physical critique regain force. We must explain why it is that there is a universe in which things appear and disappear by means of quantum fluctuation.

---

6. For a more complete discussion, see Tipler 1994.

This certainly complicates the task of natural theology, but it does not render it impossible.

The final, political-theological critique of the cosmological argument has been advanced in both more radical, Augustinian, and more moderate semi-Thomist forms. The first, radical variant addresses the cosmological argument generally; the second, moderate form touches only the first version of the cosmological argument, the proof from motion. In both cases the problem raised concerns not so much the internal logic of the argument as its final term. Does the cosmological argument really conclude to God, or only to a purely physical first mover which acts (and only acts) as final cause. Augustinians, as we noted in an earlier chapter, suggest that the only way around this difficulty is by recourse to an *a priori* proof such as those offered by Augustine himself, Anselm, Duns Scotus, or Descartes. Gilsonian semi-Thomists, on the other hand, argue that second and especially the third variants of the cosmological argument, because they conclude directly to something which has in itself the power of Being, are in fact adequate.

We must begin by pointing out that this critique is not really a complete argument. It presupposes an entire theology that is then mobilized dogmatically to criticize the cosmological argument on the grounds that it poses spiritual dangers—in effect that it encourages pagan nature worship rather than Christian faith. In this sense the Augustinian and Gilsonian critique is simply the flip side of the critiques advanced by Latin Averroism, dialectical materialism, and certain forms of feminist theory.

The Augustinian and Gilsonian variants of this critique are best addressed separately, in that the first is radically flawed whereas the second errs because of a basic misconception, but nonetheless points towards an important truth. In so far as the alternative arguments advanced by Augustinian philosophy (especially the ontological argument) have shown themselves to be inadequate, the entire Augustinian edifice remains ungrounded. One cannot claim that an alternative argument is wrong simply because it points towards a different sort of spirituality than one advocates, unless on can first ground that spirituality and demonstrate rationally that it is superior. Indeed, as we noted above, the Augustinian and Gilsonian approaches themselves lead to highly problematic political and spiritual dynamics. In the absence of arguments which go to the value of the underlying claims of each perspective, the result is a stalemate at best, and (at worst) a philosophical mudslinging contest.

The issue raised by the Gilsonians is more substantial. Gilson was quite correct to point out that Thomas developed a far more adequate doctrine of Being than his Aristotelian predecessors, and that this owes a great deal to the Christian doctrine of creation—and ultimately to the Hebrew scriptures. At the same time, Gilson errs when he pits the power of Being against final causality and teleological attraction. Classical analyses of the nature of Being within the Thomistic tradition have identified it with the other transcendentals—Beauty, Truth, Goodness and Oneness, which are the teleological attractors *par excellence*. Thomas' first way, and Aristotle's argument in *Metaphysics* 12.7 even more so, in fact conclude to Being just precisely in the form of a teleological attractor which Aristotle himself, in *Metaphysics* 12.10, later identifies with the Good. We will address this issue at greater length in the final section of this chapter when we show that once Being is properly understood, the various forms of the cosmological argument and the (valid versions of) the teleological argument actually reduce to each other.

Before we can do this, however, we need to turn to the teleological argument itself. Broadly speaking, two variants of this argument have been made. The first and oldest, usually called the argument from design, begins with the fact that there are finite systems in the universe which appear to be ordered to an end or to show purposeful behavior, but which are not themselves intelligent. But, the argument runs, it is impossible for something to act for an end without intelligent direction. Thus the need for a governing intelligence which orders all things to their appropriate ends. This is, essentially, Thomas' Fifth Way (Aquinas. *Summa Theologiae* I.2.2.3). This argument is often restated in terms which make no reference to purposefulness at all, but point rather to the fact of order. In these cases the argument is called "eutaxiological." See, for example, Barrow and Tipler 1986.

A few points are in order here. First, it should be noted that this is not, by itself, an argument for cosmic teleology as we have defined it. On the contrary, it *begins from* local and limited teleologies, such as the ordering of the stomach to digestion, and then concludes to God as an explanation for this ordering. Second, the argument is very easy to defeat. As Kant pointed out, even if the existence of finite ordered or teleological systems is possible only in terms of a creative intelligence, there is no reason why the intelligence in question must be divine (infinite, necessary, and perfect) intelligence. On the contrary a finite intellect only infinitesimally superior to the highest created system would suffice. It is, furthermore, no longer clear that the development of ordered or even purposeful systems requires a designing or governing intellect. Boltzmann's order principle provides an adequate account of the way in which finite orders can emerge, and nonlinear thermodynamics coupled with post-Darwinian evolutionary theory promise to gradually make sense out of the development of complex organization, life, and intelligence. The design variant of the teleological argument by itself, therefore, is of little use to us.

The second variant of the teleological argument begins from a more difficult premise—namely that the universe as a whole is somehow meaningful and organized—and argues from this premise to the existence of God. An early form of this variant of the teleological argument is Thomas' Fourth Way, which it is worth examining in some detail.

> The fourth way is taken from the gradation to be found in things. Among beings there are some more and some less good, true noble and the like. But "more" and "less" are predicated of different things, according as they resemble in their different ways something which is the maximum, as a thing is said to be hotter according as it more nearly resembles what which is hottest. There is then, something which is truest, something best, something noblest, and, consequently, something which is most being; for those things that are greatest in truth are greatest in being, as it is written in the *Metaphysics*. Now the maximum in any genus is the cause of all in that genus; as fire, which is the maximum of heat, is the cause of all hot things as is said in the same book. Therefore there must be something which is to all being the cause of their being, goodness, and every other perfection. And this we call God. (Aquinas. *Summa Theologiae* I.2.2.3)

It may at first seem a bit peculiar to think of this argument as beginning from cosmic teleology. Most contemporary variants of the argument, as we will see, begin from cosmological fine-tuning and/or emergent evolution; Thomas' argument on the other hand presupposes a static cosmology in which, while particular organisms and individuals may grow towards their ends, gradually achieving the perfection appropriate to their forms, there is no global cosmohistorical evolutionary process. Once we control for this difference, however, the cosmic-teleological character of Thomas' argument becomes apparent. What Thomas is doing, in very concise summary form, is to begin with the results of the special sciences which reveal a cosmic hierarchy of forms: mineral, vegetable, animal, rational, etc., each of which has greater powers, and thus a higher degree of participation in being, than the one which precedes it. This implies, however, a principle of value in terms of which these capacities can be ordered. This principle is Being as such, which Thomas elsewhere shows to be convertible with the Good, the True, etc.

Thomas' formulation uses unfortunate quantitative language that makes the argument vulnerable to some of the same criticisms we lodged against Anselm's form of the ontological argument. Specifically, he claims that any ordered series must have a maximum element, i.e., must be bounded from above, thus invoking the as yet unproven Zorn's Lemma. This move is unnecessary and tends to draw attention away from the key link in the argument, which is that the ordered series must have a cause. A more detailed consideration of the hierarchized capacities which constitute the series would bring this out, for each of the capacities is itself an ordering to an end: thermodynamic stability in the case of minerals, nutrition and reproduction in the case of vegetables, food and mates in the case of animals, and intelligible goods in the case of rational animals and angels. As we have seen, in the context of Aristotelian science, it is the end which is ultimately the cause of the capacity which is ordered to it, a claim which has been reiterated by evolutionary theory, which suggests that it is emerging opportunities in new ecological niches, and the behaviors which they engender which form the context in which selection for structures which assist in these new behaviors takes place. But since all of these capacities are ways and degrees of participation in being, it is Being as such which is the real end they seek and which is the ultimate cause of their development. In this way the quantitative language, and thus the difficulties surrounding Zorn's Lemma, can be avoided.

Contemporary variants of the argument from cosmic teleology, we have noted, generally draw on the phenomena of cosmological fine tuning and emergent evolution. We have already considered at length the arguments surrounding cosmological fine-tuning in earlier chapters. Here we need only summarize and note how fine-tuning implies the existence of God. At issue here, we will recall, are a variety of physical constants which are fixed at just precisely the levels necessary for the emergence of life and intelligence. Thus, for example, the relative strength of the various fundamental physical forces (the strong and weak nuclear forces, electromagnetism, and gravity), the relative mass of the electron and proton, and a wide range of other, equally fundamental if somewhat more obscure, numbers must be within a very narrow range if stars are to evolve and complex chemistry is to be possible. Were gravity just a little bit stronger the universe would collapse on itself; were it just a little bit weaker gas would never condense to form stars. And stars make possible the formation of the heavy elements which are necessary for complex chemistry and thus for life. Similarly, given the existence of these complex elements, if electromagnetism were just a little stronger electrons would fall into their atomic nuclei; if it were just a little bit weaker they would never form part of atoms at all.

There are, we have seen, ways to answer the evidence for fine tuning in ways which do not imply cosmic teleology. The most popular of these involves positing the existence of "many worlds" with different physical laws, from which our own world has been selected randomly by the purely coincidental fact that it is the only kind of universe we could perceive (Leslie 1989). This approach is driven by the "many worlds" approach to quantum mechanics, which argues that all possible states of quantum states actually exist, so that at each instant the universe in fact diverges into an infinite number of world lines each corresponding to a possible quantum state of a single elementary particle. But this approach violates a fundamental principle of scientific explanation—what is known as Occam's Razor. Such theories "multiply beings unnecessarily," positing worlds for which there is otherwise no evidence in order to explain (or rather explain away) evidence of fine tuning which can be explained far more economically in teleological terms. The same is true of Smolin's (Smolin 1997) cosmological natural selection theory, which also fails to provide an adequate mechanism for innovation and depends, as we noted in our treatment of this theory, on a false dichotomy which considers no possible modes of cosmogenesis besides random variation and divine creation or intelligent design.

This said, we need to be clear about just what cosmological fine tuning contributes to an argument for cosmic teleology and the existence of God. In and of itself, it shows only that matter is, as Aristotle claims, the potential for form or organization, including complex, living, and intelligent organization. It in no sense makes the emergence of such organization physically necessary. It does not, in other words, imply a materialist pantheism. It does, however, suggest that the universe exists *for* complex organization, which must therefore exist necessarily. Now we know that the finite forms of complex organization which we observe are not necessary but rather possible. Therefore there must be some form of complex organization which does exist necessarily and which is the term towards which the material universe is ordered and which is the condition of its possibility. This is Being as such or God.

The second fact which is often mobilized in contemporary arguments for cosmic teleology is the phenomenon of emergent organization. By this we mean the fact that over time, we witness the development of ever more complex forms of organization, so that the universe itself seems to become more and more complex and highly organized. This suggests that the universe as a whole is evolving towards some end, and were the evolution to continue for a infinite period of time, all logically possible forms of organization would be realized, including a form which is infinite and perfect, i.e., God. But an infinite system is also a necessary system, since it there is nothing outside of it by which it can come into existence. An infinite universe characterized by progressive emergent evolution thus in some sense presupposes the existence of God, who is not merely a product of the cosmohistorical evolutionary process, as some Godbuilders would suggest but also its final cause.

Three main arguments are raised against this line of reasoning. First, some claim that evolution is not progressive but rather merely "horizontal," i.e., into new ecological niches. This claim is easily defeated when we note that some forms of organization include, and in some cases can even comprehend, the capacities of other forms of organization, which can thus be regarded as "lesser." One need not demonstrate the existence of a "total order" in order to make this point. Some systems may simply not be comparable.

Second, there is the question of whether or not cosmic evolution continues into infinity. This is a more difficult, and still controversial question, but our arguments in the foregoing chapters have gone a long way towards defeating the presumption in favor of pessimistic cosmologies, such as most forms of the Big Bang cosmology. We should note, furthermore, that any universe which produces intelligent systems capable of rising to the idea of God is, in some sense already ordered to God, at least as the term of its desire. Spiritual disciplines which allow one to become connatural with God by means of caritative wisdom, furthermore, make God really present within space and time quite apart from whether or not cosmohistorical evolution continues into infinity. This, coupled with the interpretation of cosmological fine-tuning cited above, is sufficient to demonstrate not only the existence of God, but also the ultimate meaningfulness of the universe. It might seem that such an approach would lead us to value individual self-cultivation above the struggle for social justice, but it must be remembered that a just society is, precisely, one which makes possible the full development of human capacities, including the cultivation of caritative wisdom. Such a cosmology thus validates the struggle for justice even if the structures created will not themselves persist into infinity or contribute to an ongoing systemic evolution which does.

The third objection arises from the claim that a teleological principle is not necessary in order to explain emergent evolution. We have already noted above that random variation and natural selection for variations which have survival value do not, by themselves, explain the emergence of life in the first place, or of the development of more complex living organisms. Nonlinear thermodynamics and post-Darwinian evolution do a better job of explaining how emergent evolution takes place, but they still do not explain why. Simpler structures, which require less energy input to build and maintain, are far more probable. And if survival value is measured in terms of population size, simpler organisms would, in general, seem to be by far the better adapted. And yet matter manifests this powerful drive towards complex organization. This uphill struggle of the universe against the energy gradient and against the laws of probability can be explained only in terms of some attractive principle which draws matter from potency to act, from mere possibility into the rich diversity of increasingly improbable and complex, high energy forms of organization which we observe in he contemporary universe. And since it is the diversity and increasing complexity of different forms of organization, and not simply the fact of the universe in general, which we are attempting to explain here, we must conclude that each form is ordered to, in fact exists because of, the attractive principle which draws it from potency to act. Such a principle, furthermore, must itself require no further principle of explanation—it must, as we noted in our discussion of the cosmological proof, be infinite, necessary, and perfect. i.e., divine.

AN ARGUMENT FOR THE EXISTENCE OF GOD AND THE ULTIMATE MEANINGFULNESS OF THE UNIVERSE

We are now in a position to draw together these strands of reasoning and demonstrate definitively the existence of God and the ultimate meaningfulness of the universe. Our first step will be to clarify a bit just what is actually assumed by the cosmological and the teleological arguments. We should point out, first of all, that we need not assume that the principle of sufficient reason (and thus the possibility of causal explanation) together with the other rules of logic are *a priori* truths. Rather, it is more useful to regard them as *a posteriori* results abstracted from experience. We know that A cannot be the same as not A because we never run into things which are, pure and simply, identical to their opposites. Similarly, the idea of causality emerges because we observe that there are in fact causal relationships between things. Initially, these ideas are merely insights on which the possibility of science, and indeed all practical activity depend. It is only once we have traveled the road of science, and shown that convincing causal explanations can in fact be developed, and that when we act on such causal explanations our action becomes more effective, that we can conclude that there are indeed such causal relations between things. In this sense, we will argue, the cosmological and teleological arguments are wholly *a posteriori*.

Second, we want to suggest that the substantive starting points of the cosmological and teleological proofs are, in fact convertible with each other. To assume the existence of the universe and to assume that it is organized are in fact to say the same thing. This is apparent from the analysis of the concept of Being pioneered by Alexandr Bogdanov (Bogdanov 1928/1980). Imagine for a minute something which is stripped of all organization: it has no purpose, no structure, and no relation, either internally or externally. Then the thing, quite simply, doesn't exist. For this reason Bogdanov concluded that being is in fact organization, and that the general theory of organization can take the place historically held by metaphysics.

Bogdanov's position needs to be qualified in some important ways—which, among other things, call in to question his negation of metaphysics. First, we should note that both "being" and "organization" are used in a variety of different ways. It is important, on the one hand, to distinguish between mere existence (what Thomas calls possible being) and *Esse* as such, the actual power of Being, which no finite system has in itself. On the other hand, it is important to distinguish between relation, form, order or structure, and organization. To be related is to be, but only in the limited sense of being an element of a larger whole. Any system which has a definite structure, however can be said to have its own distinctive identity, and thus to exist in the much stronger sense of being something of which other things can be predicated. "Organization," furthermore, may mean

a. being organized, in the sense of being ordered to an end,
b. having the capacity to organize, and thus create, or
c. being an end to which things are ordered.

When we say that "something exists" or "the universe exists," we are at the very least, assigning to it some degree of order, form, or structure, so that it is susceptible of being defined and being the subject of predicates. Most forms of the cosmological argument assume this but no more, though Aristotle's original version of the proof from motion rests on a larger teleological cosmology. The argument from design, which we have dismissed, assumes that there are local systems which are ordered to an end, which is obviously true. The argument from cosmic teleology, on the other hand, makes the larger claim that the universe as a whole is ordered to an end.

Matters look a bit different, however, when approached in the light of the teleological research program which we have laid out in the forgoing chapters. We have shown, first of all, that the universe is an ascending scale of different degrees of organization, and thus of participation in being. Specifically, it is possible to identify physical, biological, and social degrees of organization. Physical systems are not themselves organized in the full sense of possessing differentiated structures of the sort which we find in living organisms which carry out definite functions in the service of some global purpose. They are, however, structured, and in fact structured in just precisely the way necessary to make possible the emergence of complex organization, life, and intelligence. In this sense the physical universe as a whole can be said to be ordered to the higher end of complex organization, life, and intelligence. We have shown that even physical laws, such as entropy, which seem to work against the survival of particular complex systems, ultimate serve the cause of progressive cosmohistorical evolution. Some physical systems are, furthermore, structured in ways which permit them to conserve their form, which constitutes the higher degree of participation in being which Aristotle called the mineral soul. Such systems are also characterized by a chemical holism which means that they have distinctive properties which make them more than the sum of their parts in a way which is not true of mere mechanical ensembles. Biological systems, on the other hand are actually organized, i.e., structured in such a way as to promote an end, namely their own survival and reproduction. In maintaining themselves in hostile environments which would undermine many mineral species, and in reproducing themselves, living organisms achieve a higher degree of participation in Being than mere physical or mineral systems. Social systems finally, are not only organized but also have the capacity to organize, i.e., through labor to contribute to the creation of new and more complex forms of organization.

All of these various and sundry forms of organization are ordered to a common end, namely Being, which, however, they pursue in ways appropriate to their structure and under the form of specific goods which are accessible to them. For mineral species, and indeed physical systems in general, this good is the thermodynamic stability which allows them to persist in being. For living organisms the good is nutrition and reproduction—in the case of animals in the form of food and mates actively pursued and enjoyed. In the case of the social form of matter this good is creativity as such, which is known indirectly in the form of ordinary manual and intellectual labor, and directly when the intellect rises by transcendental abstraction or caritative wisdom to the knowledge of God.

It should be noted that everything, however humble, which participates in Being is, furthermore, itself a participation in the end or τέλος and thus in a very real sense a natural sacrament in which God is really present, and an authentic way to the divine. In this sense people in tribal and communitarian societies were not wrong to offer worship to animals, plants, and even minerals, even if in the light of philosophy and of the revelation of the divine name YHWH we recognize that what is actually to be worshipped is the power of Being in which these finite systems have a share and not the systems themselves.

Thus, when we say that "something exists" or that "the universe exists," in the light of our teleological research program, we in fact meant that it is a real participation in Being as such, to the knowledge of which we have already risen, if perhaps without fully realizing it, in traveling the road of the special sciences.

With this said, the outlines of a unified cosmoteleological argument for the existence of God, an argument which simultaneously proves the ultimate meaningfulness of the universe, emerges quite naturally. Not surprisingly, the argument ends up looking quite a bit like a radically historicized version of Aristotle's argument in *Metaphysics* 12.7. What a teleological science shows, even in its present undeveloped form, is an ascending scale of progressively higher forms of organization—higher in the sense that they constitute progressively superior forms of organization. Each of these forms of organization is, in a very real sense, a distinct form of the motion of matter, which is only potential being, towards Being as such (a way of putting things which also connects our formulation back to Engels' language and that of dialectical materialism). Their organization and their motion and the participation in Being are all one and the same. Now in the case of each individual system this organization, motion, and participation in being can be explained proximately in terms of the particular end to which the system is ordered: the possibility of there being any structure at all, thermodynamic stability, nutrition and reproduction, food and mates, or any of the myriad forms of organization which human beings and human societies labor to bring into being. But each of these particular ends or movers must (and in principle can) be explained in terms of further finite ends or movers at which they, in turn, aim. The whole ordered series, however, even if it is infinite in space and time, must itself be explained. There cannot, in other words, be an infinite logical regress even is there is an infinite physical regress and or progress in space and time. The series and each of its elements can, furthermore be shown to aim, albeit mediately, through the particular finite movers, at a common end which is *Esse* as such. This is the great Unmoved Mover which draws all things to itself and thus into the Being which is also Beauty, Truth, Goodness and Integrity.

When we have risen to this point, it furthermore becomes apparent that not only God, but also the universe itself, exists necessarily. That God exists necessarily is apparent. Being as such has within itself the power to be and thus depends on nothing outside itself for its existence. In this sense a sort of *a posteriori* version of the ontological argument becomes possible. The universe, as the ascending scale of different forms of organization which moves towards God, is not to be identified with God and is not a "necessary being." Given that God exists, however, the existence of the universe follows necessarily. This is because it is the attractive power of God which draws the universe into Being. Now God cannot cease to be God, and thus cannot help being attractive and drawing the universe into Being.

This, in turn, imposes definite constraints on physical cosmology. In order for the universe to exist at all, it must in *some sense* always exist, because God brings it into being necessarily. This does not necessarily rule out cosmologies which, like the Big Bang, may imply the finitude of the region of space time which we now identify with the universe, but it does imply that motion towards God is without beginning and with out end.

Our argument also bears on the question of individual immortality. Complete elaboration of this point would require a detailed consideration of the problem of personal identity, which is not possible in this context. Suffice it to say, however, that the human person cannot be identified with the matter which makes life possible, for we constantly exchange matter and energy with the environment and in this sense are by no means the same people we were even a few minutes ago. Nor can we lodge personal identity in the particular form or structure of either the body or the personality, since both of these also undergo constant change. Indeed, we cannot even ground identity in a particular unique purpose which individual serves, since we are constantly growing and coming to understand our aim or purpose in new and more profound ways. And each of these particular aims or purposes is nothing more than a participation in Being as such, the Common End which moves all things. Rather, our identity is lodged in a particular trajectory, shaped by definite material conditions and physiological, psychological, and social structures. What we are, each and every one of us, is a particular pathway towards God.

Now failure, decay, and death are real, but success, which is success in Being, is conserved. This is true for individual pathways as for civilizations. Even after the death of the body, and indeed of the personality, the pathway along which that body and that personality traveled remains open, at least in so far as it was successful. And everything which *is* succeeds in some degree, and is thus conserved in some degree, and being conserved continues its movement towards God over an infinite period of time. Other bodies, other personalities will take up that pathway and follow it towards God. Or rather, God, who is the cause of all things, will draw new matter towards Herself along that pathway, along *our* pathway, giving us new life so that over an infinite period of time, we eventually realize our full potential. In this sense not only the universe as a whole but every system within it is ordered to God and ultimately realizes its end. It does so, however, by the free exercise of its own powers, without any other compulsion than the attractive power of God, and with the ever present possibility of failure, death, and disintegration.

Beyond this, little more can be said. But it is enough. We have shown both that the universe is ordered to an infinite, necessary, and perfect principle Who brings it into being necessarily and which draws all things ineluctably to Herself, but also that our own individual efforts, and indeed every thing which happens in the universe, down to the very simplest physical event, make a real difference both in the sense that it affects the development of systems towards God and in the sense that it is conserved and compelled by its own attraction to God to rectify its errors and realize its latent potential for Being. This is enough because it provides a reason to believe and to hope and, at least implicitly, a standard by which to act: Create. Add to the level of organization of the universe, and assist all systems in so doing. In this way we become connatural with Being itself, and "once again able to see the stars" (Dante. *Commedia* XXXIII). We can engage productively the long discipline of life, which prepares us to rise and touch them, and drawn ineluctably forward, to come face to face with the wisdom and love and power which moves all things.

Bibliography

Abumasar. c. 850 CE/1994. *Introduction to the Science of Astrology*. Edited and translated by Charles Burnet, with technical and historical annotations by Charles Burnett, Graeme Tobyn, Geoffrey Cornelius and Vernon Wells. Brewster, MA: Arhat.
Alighieri, Dante. 1300–1318/1969. *De Monarchia*. Indianapolis: Bobbs-Merrill.
———. 1300–1318/1969. *Commedia*. Translated as *The Divine Comedy* and with commentary by John D. Sinclair. New York: Oxford University Press.
Althusser, Louis. 1965/1977. *For Marx*. London: Lane.
———. 1968/1970. *Reading Capital*. London: New Left.
———. 1966-1969/1971. *Lenin and Philosophy*. New York: Monthly Review. .
Amin, Samir. 1975 *El capitalismo y la question campesina*. Mexico: Nuevo Tiempo.
———. 1976. *Unequal Development*. New York: Monthly Review.
———. 1977. *Imperialism and Unequal Development*. New York: Monthly Review.
———. 1978a. *The Law of Value and Historical Materialism*. New York: Monthly Review.
———. 1976/1978b. *The Arab Nation*. New York: Zed.
———. 1979/1980. *Class and Nation, Historically and in the Current Crisis*. New York: Monthly Review.
———. 1981/1982a. *The Future of Maoism*. New York: Monthly Review.
———. 1982b. *Dynamics of Global Crisis*. New York: Monthly Review.
———. 1985. *Delinking*. New York: Monthly Review.
———. 1988/1989. *Eurocentrism*. New York: Monthly Review.
———. 1990. "The Future of Socialism." *Monthly Review* 42:3.
———. 1990. *Transforming the Revolution*. New York: Monthly Review.
Anderson, Perry. 1974a. *Passages from Antiquity to Feudalism*. London: New Left Review.
———. 1974b. *Lineages of the Absolutist State*. London: Verso.
Aquinas, Thomas. c. 1253/1968. *On Being and Essence*. Toronto: Pontifical Institute for Medieval Studies.
———. c. 1260/1963. *In Boethius De Trinitate*. In *The Division and Methods of the Sciences*, translated by Armand Maurer. Toronto: Pontifical Institute of Medieval Studies.
———. c. 1272/1952. *Summa Theologiae*, Chicago, Encyclopaedia Britannica.
Aristotle. c. 350 BCE/1946. *Politics*. Translated by Ernest Barker. Oxford: Clardendon Press.
———. c. 350 BCE/1952. *Metaphysics*. Translated by Richard Hope. New York: Columbia University Press.
———. c. 350 BCE/1973. *Physics*. In *Introduction to Aristotle*, translated by Richard McKeon. Chicago: University of Chicago Press.
———. c. 350 BCE/1973. *De Anima*. In *Introduction to Aristotle*, translated by Richard McKeon. Chicago: University of Chicago Press.

———. c. 350 BCE/1973. *Ethics*. In *Introduction to Aristotle*, translated by Richard McKeon. Chicago: University of Chicago Press.

Augustine. c. 386/1969. *Contra Academicos*. In *Medieval Philosophy*, edited by John Wippel and Alan Wolter. New York: Free.

———. c. 395/1969. *De libero arbitrio*. In *Medieval Philosophy*, edited by John Wippel and Alan Wolter. New York: Free.

———. c. 426/1972. *The City of God*. Translated by Henry Bettenson. New York: Penguin.

Balslev, Anindita Niyogi. 2005. "Cosmology and Hindu Thought," in *Zygon* 25:1.

Barrow, John, and Frank Tipler. 1986. *Anthropic Cosmological Principle*. Oxford: Oxford University Press.

Bennett, Charles. 1987. "Dissipation, Information, Complexity, and Organization." In *Emerging Syntheses in Science*, edited by David Pines. New York: Addison Wesley.

Berkeley, George. 1710. *Three Dialogues Between Hylas and Philnous*. London.

Bhaskar, Roy. 1989. *Reclaiming Reality*. London: Verso.

———. 1993. *Dialectic: The Pulse of Freedom*. London: Verso.

Bogdanov, Alexander. 1928/1980. *Tektology*. Intersystems Publishers.

Bohm, David. 1980. *Wholeness and the Implicate Order*. London: RKP.

Boltzmann, L. 1872. In *Sber. Akad. Wiss. Wien*, Part II, 66.

———. 1897. In *Ann Physik* 60.

Bonaventura. c. 1274/1970. *Quaestiones disputate de Scientia Christi*. In *A Scholastic Miscellany*, edited by Eugene Fairweather. New York: Macmillan.

Brundage, John. 1985. *The Fifth Sun*. Austin: University of Texas Press.

Bucher, Martin, Alfred Goldhaber, and Neil Turok. 1995. "Open Universe from Inflation." *Physical Review D* 52:6.

Bucher, Martin, and David Spergel. 1999. "Inflation in a Low-Density Universe." *Scientific American* 280:1.

Budiansky, Stephen. 1992. *The Covenant of the Wild*. New York: Morrow.

Burkhert, Walter. 1972. *Lore and Science in Ancient Pythagoreanism*. Cambridge: Harvard University Press.

———. 1985. *Greek Religion*. Oxford: Oxford University Press.

Cajetan. c. 1520. *In De Ente et Essentia*.

———. c. 1520. *De Nominium Analogia*.

Campbell, David. 1989. "Introduction to Nonlinear Phenomena." In *Lectures in the Sciences of Complexity*, edited by Erica Jen. New York: Addison-Wesley.

Caputo, John. 1982. *Heidegger and Aquinas: An Essay on Overcoming Metaphysics*. New York: Fordham.

Carnot, Sadi. 1824/1992. *Reflections on the Motive Power of Fire and on Machines Fitted to Develop that Power*. Translated by E. Mendoza. Glouster, MA: Peter Smith.

Chang Kwang-chi. 1963. *The Archeology of Ancient China*. New Haven, CT: Yale University Press.

Childe, V. Gordon. 1951. *Man Makes Himself*. New York: Mentor.

Cleary, John. 1995. *Aristotle and Mathematics: Aporetic Method in Cosmology and Metaphysics*. Leidin: Brill.

Collins, Randall. 1998. *The Sociology of Philosophies*. Cambridge, MA: Belknap.

Crane, L. 1995. "Clocks and Categories, is quantum gravity algebraic?" *J. Math. Phys.* 36.

———. 1997a. "A Proposal for the Quantum Theory of Gravity." Preprint available at xxx.lanl.gov/abs/gr-qc/9704057.

———. 1997b. "On the Interpretation of Relativistic Spin Networks and the Balanced State Sum, preprint available at xxx.lanl.gov/abs/gr-qc/9710108.
———. 1998. "An Octonionic Geometric (Balanced) state Sum Model." Preprint available at xxx.lanl.gov/abs/gr-qc/9806060.
———. 2000. "Hypergravity and Categorical Feynmanology." Preprint available at xxx.lanl.gov/abs/gr-qc/0004043.
Daly, Mary. 1984. *Pure Lust*. Boston: Beacon.
———. 1998. *Quintessence*. Boston: Beacon.
Dahm, Helmut. 1988. *Philosophical Sovietology: The Pursuit of A Science*, Dordrecht: Reidel.
Damasio, Antonio. 1994. *Descartes' Error*. New York: Grosset/Putnam.
Darwin, Charles. 1859/1970. *The Origin of the Species*. In *Darwin: A Norton Critical Edition*, edited by Philip Appleman. New York: Norton.
Dauben, Joseph W. 2007. "Chinese Mathematics." In *The Mathematics of Egypt, Mesopotamia, China, India, and Islam: A Sourcebook*, edited by Victor J. Katz. Princeton, NJ: Princeton University Press.
Davies, Paul. 1988. *The Cosmic Blueprint*. New York: Simon & Schuster.
———. 1992. *The Mind of God*. New York: Simon and Schuster.
———. 1994. *The Last Three Minutes*. New York: Basic Books.
Deborin, A. M. 1916. *Introduction to the Philosophy of Dialectical Materialism*. Petrograd.
———. 1930. *Dialectics and Natural Science*. Moscow.
Denton, Michael. 1985 *Evolution: A Theory in Crisis*. New York: Burnett.
Derrida, Jacques.1967/1978. "Violence and Metaphysics," and "From a Restricted to a General Economy: For an Hegelianism Without Reserve." In *Writing and Difference*. Chicago: University of Chicago Press.
Dobereiner, Johann. 1829/1895. *Die Anfänge des Natürlichen Systemes der chemischen Elemente*. Ostwald's Klassiker der Exakten Wiss. Leipzig: Wilhelm Engelmann.
Duhem, Pierre. 1909. *Etudes sure Léonard de Vinci*. Paris.
Dunbar-Ortiz, Roxanne. 1974. *Indians of the Americas*. London: Zed.
Duns Scotus, John . 1301/1965. *A Treatise on God as First Principle (De Primo Principio)*. Translated by Allan Wolter. Chicago: Franciscan Herald.
Durkheim, Emile. 1911. *Formes elementaires de la vie religieuse*. Paris.
Dussel, Enrique. 1998. *Etica de la liberación en la edad de globaización y exclusión*. México: Trotta.
Eamon, William. 1994. *Science and the Secrets of Nature*. Princeton: Princeton University Press.
Edwards, Jonathan. 1746/1957. *A Treatise Concerning Religious Affections*. In *Works*. New Haven, CT: Yale University Press.
Elkins, James. 1999. *What Painting Is*. London: Routledge.
Emmanuel, A. 1969/1971. *Unequal Exchange*. New York: Monthly Review.
Engels, Frederick. 1880/1940. *The Dialectics of Nature*. New York: International.
———. 1880/1978. *Socialism: Utopian and Scientific*. In *Marx–Engels Reader*. New York: Norton.
Everett, H. 1957. "The Many Worlds Interpretation of Quantum Mechanics." *Review of Modern Physics* 29.
Feather, Norman. 1959. *Mass, Length, and Time*. Baltimore: Penguin.

Forman, Paul. 1971. "Weimar Culture, Causality, and Quantum Theory, 1918–1927: Adaptation by German Physicists and Mathematicians to a Hostile Intellectual Environment." *Historical Studies in Physical Sciences* 3.
Feuerbach, Ludwig. 1841/1957. *The Essence of Christianity*. New York: Harper.
Foucault, Michel. 1966. *Les mots et les choses*. Paris: Gallimard.
Frank, Andre Gunder. 1975. *On Capitalist Under Development*. New York: Monthly Review.
Frend, W. 1957. *The Donatist Church*. Oxford: Clarendon.
Freud, Sigmund. 1927/1961. *The Future of An Illusion*. New York: Norton.
———. 1930/1961. *Civilization and its Discontents*. New York: Norton.
Friedman, A. 1922. "*Ueber die Krummung des Raumes*." *Ztschr. f. Physik* 10: 377ff.
Fromm, Erich. 1941. *Escape from Freedom*. New York: Holt Reinhart Winston.
———. 1947. *Man For Himself*. New York: Holt Reinhart Winston.
Fuller, Buckminster. 1975–1979. *Synergetics*. New York: MacMillan.
———. 1981. *Critical Path*. New York: St. Martin's.
———. 1992 *Cosmography*. New York: Macmillan.
Galilei, Galileo. 1638/1914. *Discourses Concerning Two New Sciences*. Translated by Henry Crew and Alfonso de Salvio. New York: Macmillan.
Gal-Or, Benjamin. 1987. *Cosmology: Physics and Philosophy*. New York: Springer.
Gamwell, Franklin. 1990. *The Divine Good*. New York: Harper.
Gardener, Martin. 1978. Untitled article. *New York Review of Books*, 23 November 1978.
Garrigou-Lagrange, Reginald. 1938. *Les trois ages de la vie interieure*. Paris: Cerf.
Gilson, Etienne. 1968. *Dante and Philosophy*. Glouster, MA: Peter Smith.
———. 1936. *The Spirit of Medieval Philosophy*. New York.
———. 1952. *Being and Some Philosophers*. Toronto: Pontifical Institute of Medieval Studies.
Geroch, Robert. 1985. *Mathematical Physics*. Chicago: University of Chicago.
Gilson, Etienne, Thomas Langman, and Armand Maurer. 1962. *Recent Philosophy*. New York: Random House.
Goerner, E.A. 1965. *Peter and Caesar*. New York: Herder & Herder.
Gottwald, Norman. 1979. *The Tribes of Yahweh*. Maryknoll: Orbis.
Gramsci, Antonio.1948 *Il materialismo storico e la filosofia di Benedetto Croce*. Torino: Einaudi.
———. 1949a. *Il Risorgimento*. Torino: Einaudi.
———. 1949b. *Note sul Macchiavelli, sulla politica, e sullo Stato Moderno*. Torino: Einaudi.
———. 1949c. *Gli intelletualli e l'organizzazione di cultura*. Torino: Einaudi.
———. 1950. *Letteratura e vita nazionale*. Torino: Einaudi.
———. 1951. *Passato e presente*. Torino: Einaudi.
———. 1954. *L'Ordine Nuovo*. Torino: Einaudi.
———. 1966. *La questione meridionale*. Roma: Riuniti.
Grant, Edward. 1978. "Cosmology." In *Science in the Middle Ages*, edited by David Lindberg. Chicago: University of Chicago Press.
———. 1996. *Planets, Stars, and Orbs: The Medieval Cosmos, 1200–1687*. Cambridge: Cambridge University Press, 1996.
Halliwell, Jonathan. 1991. "Quantum Cosmology and the Creation of the Universe." *Scientific American* 272:12.
Harris, Errol. 1965. *Foundations of Metaphysics in Science*. London: Allen & Unwin.
———. 1991. *Cosmos and Anthropos*. Atlantic Highlands, NJ: Humanities.

———. 1992. *Cosmos and Theos*. Atlantic Highlands, NJ: Humanities.
Hartle, J. B., and S. W. Hawking. 1983. "The Wave Function of the Universe." *Physical Review D* 28:12.
Hayashi, Takao. 2003. "Indian Mathematics." In *Companion Encyclopedia of the History and Philosophy of the Mathematical Sciences*, edited by Ivor Grattan-Guinness, 1:118–30. Baltimore: The Johns Hopkins University Press.
Hayek, F. A. 1973. *Law, Liberty, and Legislation, Volume One: Rules and Order*. Chicago: University of Chicago Press.
———. 1988. *The Fatal Conceit*. Chicago: University of Chicago Press.
Hegel, G. W. F. 1807/1967b. *Phenomenology of Mind*. Translated by J. B. Baillie. New York: Harper.
———. 1817/1990. *Encyclopaedia of the Philosophical Sciences (Outline)*. Translated by Steven Taubeneck. New York: Continuum.
———. 1830/1971. *Encyclopaedia of the Philosophical Sciences*. Translated by William Wallace. Oxford: Oxford University Press.
Heidegger, Martin. 1928/1968. *Being and Time*. New York: Harper & Row.
———. >1934/1989. *Beitrage sur Philosophie* ("Contributions to Philosophy"). Frakfurt-Main: Klosterman.
———. >1941/1979–1987. *Nietzsche*. San Francisco: Harper & Row.
Hickey, Isabel. 1992 . *Astrology—A Cosmic Science*. Sebastopol, CA: CRCS.
Hume, David. 1777/1886. *Enquiry Concerning Human Understanding*. London: Longmans, Green.
———. 1779. *Dialogues Concerning Natural Religion*. London: Longmans, Green.
Jaki, Stanley. 1980. *Cosmos and Creator*. Chicago: Regnery.
———. 1988. *The Savior of Science*. Washington: Gateway.
John Paul II. 1998. *Fides et Ratio*.
John of St. Thomas. *Ars Logica* .
Joravsky, David. 1961. *Soviet Marxism and Natural Science*. New York: Columbia.
Kant, Immanuel. 1755/1968. *Universal Natural History and Theory of the Heavens*. New York: Greenwood.
———. 1781/1969a. *Foundations of the Metaphysics of Morals*. Translated by Lewis White Beck. Indianapolis: Bobbs-Merrill.
———. 1781/1969b. *Critique of Pure Reason*. Translated by Lewis White Beck. Indianapolis: Bobbs-Merrill.
———. 1790/1987. *Critique of Judgment*. Indianapolis: Hackett.
Kelly, Kevin. 1992. "Deep Evolution: The Emergence of Postdarwinism." *Whole Earth Review* 76.
Kierkegaard, Soren. c. 1840/1941. *A Concluding Unscientific Postscript*. Translated by Walter Lowrie. Princeton: Princeton University Press.
Konrad, Gyorgy, and Ivan Szeleny. 1949. *Intellectuals on the Road to Class Power*. New York: Harcourt, Brace & Jovanovich.
Korner, Stephen. 1968. *Philosophy of Mathematics*. New York: Dover.
Krauss, Lawrence, and Glenn Starkman. 1999. "The Fate of Life in the Universe." *Scientific American* (November 1999).
———. Forthcoming. "Life, the Universe, and Nothing: Life and Death in an Ever-Expanding Universe." *Astrophysical Journal*. Available at xxx.lanl.gov/abs/astro-ph/9902189.
Laclau, Ernesto. 1977. *Politics and Ideology in Marxist Theory*. London: Verso.

Laclau, Ernesto, and Chantal Mouffe. 1985. *Hegemony and Socialist Strategy*. London: Verso.
Lancaster, Roger. 1988. *Thanks to God and the Revolution*. Berkeley: University of California Press.
Langton, Christopher. 1989. *Artificial Life: Proceedings of an Interdisciplinary Workshop on the Synthesis and Simulation of Living Systems*. New York: Addison-Wesley.
Laplace, Pierre Simon. 1819/1951. *A Philosophical Essay on Probabilities*. New York: Dover.
———. 1799–1825. *Treatise on Celestial Mechanics*. Paris.
Lasch, Christopher. 1977. *Haven in a Heartless World*. New York: Basic.
———. 1979. *The Culture of Narcissism*. New York: Norton.
———. 1990. *The True and Only Heaven*. New York: Norton.
Laudan, Rachel. 2000. "Birth of the Modern Diet," *Scientific American* 283:2.
Leibniz, Gottfried von. 1713/1992. *Monadology*. Amherst, NY: Prometheus.
Lenat, Douglas B. 1980. *The Heuristics of Nature*. Report HPP-80-27, Stanford Heuristic Programming Project.
Lenin, V. I. 1902/1929. *What is to Be Done?* New York: International.
———. 1908/1970. *Materialism and Empiriocriticism*. Moscow: Progress.
———. 1916/1976. *Philosophical Notebooks* (Volume 38 of the *Collected Works*). Moscow: Progress.
Lenski, Gerhard and Jean. 1982. *Human Societies*. New York: McGraw Hill.
Lerner, Eric. 1991. *The Big Bang Didn't Happen*. New York: Vintage.
Leslie, John. 1989. *Universes*. London: Routledge.
Levi-Strauss, Claude. 1949/1969. *The Elementary Forms of Kinship*. Boston: Beacon.
———. 1958/1963. *Structural Anthropology*. New York: Basic.
Levinas, Emmanuel. 1965. *Totalité et Infini: Essai sur extériorité*. The Hague: Nijhoff.
Lindberg, David. 1978. *Science in the Middle Ages*. Chicago: University of Chicago Press.
———. 1992. *The Beginnings of Western Science*. Chicago: University of Chicago Press.
Linde, Andrei. 1994. "The Self-Reproducing Inflationary Universe." *Scientific American* 275:11.
Locke, John. 1690/1967. *Two Treatises on Government*. London: Cambridge University Press.
Lukacs, Georgi. 1922/1971. *History and Class Consciousness*, Cambridge, MA: MIT Press.
———. 1953/1980. *The Destruction of Reason*. London: Merlin.
Luria, Aleksandr. 1973. *The Working Brain*. New York: Basic.
———. 1974/1976 *Cognitive Development*. Cambridge: Harvard University Press.
Lyotard, Jean Francois. 1979/1984. *The Postmodern Condition*: Minneapolis: University of Minnesota Press.
MacAleer, Graham. 1996. "Saint Anselm: An Ethics of *Caritas* for a Relativist Agent," in *American Catholic Philosophical Quarterly* LXX.
MacIntyre, Alisdair. 1980. *After Virtue*. South Bend: Notre Dame University Press.
Maimonides, Moses. 1190/1964. *Guide for the Perplexed*. Translated by S. Pines. Chicago: University of Chicago Press.
Mandel, Ernest. 1968. *Marxist Economic Theory*. New York: Monthly Review.
Mannheim, Karl. 1936. *Ideology and Utopia*. New York: Harcourt, Brace.
Mansueto, Anthony. 1995. *Towards Synergism: The Cosmic Significance of the Human Civilizational Project*. Lanham, MD: University Press of America.
———. 1996. "From Dialectic to Organization: Bogdanov's Contribution to Social Theory," *Studies in East European Thought* 48:1:37–61.

———. 2002a. *Religion and Dialectics*. Lanham, MD: University Press of America.
———. 2002b. *Knowing God: Restoring Reason in an Age of Doubt*. Aldershot: Ashgate.
———. 2005. *Against Philosophical Appeasement*. Lanham, MD: Lexington.
Mao Zedong. 1937/1971. "On Contradiction." In *Selected Works*. Peking: Foreign Languages.
Margulis, Lynn, and Rene Fester. 1991. *Symbiosis as a Source of Evolutionary Innovation*. Cambridge: MIT Press.
Marsilius of Padua. 1951. *Defensor Pacis*. Translated by A. Gewirth. New York: Columbia University Press.
Maritain, Jacques. 1937. *Degrees of Knowledge*. London: Bles.
Martens, Bertin. 1995. "Introduction to Complexity: A New Paradigm in Economics." Paper presented to the Symposium on the Emergence of Complexity, as part of the International Conference "Einstein Meets Magritte," Brussels, May 1995.
Marx, Karl. 1843/1978. "Contribution to the Critique of Hegel's Philosophy of Right: Introduction." In *Marx-Engels Reader*. New York: Norton.
———. 1844/1978. *Economic and Philosophical Manuscripts*. New York: Norton.
———. 1846/1978. *The German Ideology*. In *Marx-Engels Reader*. New York: Norton.
———. 1848/1978. *The Communist Manifesto*. In *Marx-Engels Reader*. New York: Norton.
———. 1849/1978. *Wage Labor and Capital*. In *Marx-Engels Reader*. New York: Norton.
———. 1859/1961. *Contribution to the Critique of Political Economy: Preface* in Erich Fromm, *Marx's Concept of Man*. New York: Continuum.
———. 1867/1977. *Capital*. Vol. 1. New York: Vintage.
———. 1881/1978. "Letter to Vera Zasulich." In *Marx-Engels Reader*. New York: Norton .
———. ?/1963. *Theories of Surplus Value: Part One*. Moscow: Progress.
———. ?/1971. *Theories of Surplus Value: Part Two*. Moscow: Progress.
Martzloff, Jean-Claude. 1996. *A History of Chinese Mathematics*. New York: Springer.
Matthews, Caitlin. 1991. *Sophia: The Goddess of Wisdom*. London: Mandala.
Maurer, Armand. 1963. "Introduction." In Thomas Aquinas, *The Division and Methods of the Sciences*. Toronto: Pontifical Institute of Medieval Studies.
———. 1993. "Thomists and Thomas Aquinas on the Foundation of Mathematics." *Review of Metaphysics* 47.
Mayr, Ernst. 1982. *The Growth of Biological Thought*. Cambridge, MA: Harvard University Press.
———. 1988. *Toward a New Philosophy of Biology*. Cambridge: Harvard University Press.
McCool, Gerald. 1977. *Catholic Theology in the Nineteenth Century*. New York: Seabury.
———. 1994. *The Neo-Thomists*. Milwaukee: Marquette University Press.
Meikle, Scott. 1985. *Essentialism in the Thought of Karl Marx*. London: Duckworth.
Mendeleev, Dmitri. 1869/1970. "On the Relationship of the Property of the Elements to their Atomic Weights." Originally published in *Zeitschrift für Chemie* 12 (1869) 405–6; republished in David M. Knight, ed., *Classical Scientific Papers: Chemistry, Second Series*. New York: Elsevier.
Milbank, John. 1990. *Theology and Social Theory*. London: Blackwell.
Mill, J. S. 1848/1965. *Utilitarianism*. Indianapolis: Bobbs-Merrill.
Miller, Alice. 1986. *Thou Shall Not Be Aware*. New York: Meridian.
Merton, Thomas. 1963. *Selected Poems*. New York: New Directions.
Miranda, José Porfirio. 1972. *Marx y la Biblia*. Salamanca: Sigueme.
———. 1973. *El se y el mesias*. Salamanca: Sigueme.

Morrison: Karl. 1975. "Where are the Prophets." Address to the 355th Convocation of the University of Chicago, 29 August 1975.

Multhauf, Robert P. 1978. "The Science of Matter." In *Science in the Middle Ages*, edited by David Lindberg. Chicago: University of Chicago Press.

Murdoch, John, and Edith Sylla. 1978. "The Science of Motion." In *Science in the Middle Ages*, David Lindberg. Chicago: University of Chicago Press.

Naess, Arne. 1989. *Ecology, Community, and Lifestyle*. Cambridge: Cambridge University Press.

Naser, Curt. 1995. "The Dialectics of Self-Organization and Nonlinear Systems." In *Dialectic, Cosmos, and Society* 7.

Newlands, John. 1863. "On the Relations Among the Equivalents." *Chemical News* 7.

Newton, Isaac. 1687/1999. *The Philosophical Principles of Natural Philosophy*. Translated by I. B. Cohen. Berkeley: University of California Press.

———. 1700. *The Reasonableness and Certainty of the Christian Religion*. London.

Niebuhr, Reinhold. 1941. *The Nature and Destiny of Man*. New York: Scribners.

Nietzsche, Friedreich. 1889/1968. *The Will to Power*. New York: Random House.

Owens, Joseph. 1980. *St. Thomas Aquinas on the Existence of God*. Albany: State Univeristy of New York Press.

Paley, William. 1802/1986. *Natural Theology*. Charlottesville, VA: Ibis.

Parsons, Talcott. 1957. *The Social System*. New York: Free Press.

Pawlikowski, John. 1982. *Christ in the Light of Jewish-Christian Dialogue*. New York: Paulist.

Peifer, John. 1964. *The Mystery of Knowledge*. New York: Magi.

Petras, James. 1997. "El Salvador Elections: Polarization in the Post-Peace Accord Period." *Z Magazine*.

Philo of Alexandria. c. 30 CE/1929–1953. *Works*. Edited and translated by F. H. Colson, 10 vols. Cambridge: Loeb Classical Library with 2 suppl. vols. of Ralph Marcus's Eng. renderings of works preserved in Armonian translation.

Piaget, Jean. 1952. *Logic and Psychology*. New York: Basic.

———. 1968. *Structuralism*. New York: Basic.

Pines, David, editor. 1987. *Emerging Syntheses in Science*, New York: Addison Wesley.

Pixley, Jorge. 1989. *Historia sagrada, historia popular: historia de Israel desde loes pobres 1220 a.C. a 135 d.C.*. San José de Costa Rica: Editorial DEI.

Plato. c. 385 BCE/1953. *Protagoras*. In *The Dialogues of Plato*, translated by Benjamin Jowett. New York: Clarendon.

———. c. 385 BCE/1953. *Gorgias*. In *The Dialogues of Plato*, translated by Benjamin Jowett. New York: Clarendon.

———. c. 385 BCE/1968. *Republic*. Translated by Alan Bloom. New York: Basic.

———. c. 385 BCE/1960. *Timaeus*. New York: Penguin.

———. c. 385 BCE/1953. *Statesman*. In *The Dialogues of Plato*, translated by Benjamin Jowett. New York: Clarendon.

———. c. 385 BCE/1953. *Laws*. In *The Dialogues of Plato*, translated by Benjamin Jowett. New York: Clarendon.

Pedersen, Olaf. 1978. "Astronomy." In *Science in the Middle Ages*, edited by David Lindberg. Chicago: University of Chicago Press.

Poincaré, Henri. 1893. *Revue de metaphysique et la moral* 1.

Prigogine, Ilya. 1977. *Self-Organization in Non-Equilibrium Systems*. With G. Nicolis. New York: Wiley.

———. 1979. *From Being to Becoming: Time and Complexity in the Physical Sciences.* New York: Freeman.
———. 1984. *Order Out of Chaos.* With I. Stengers. New York: Basic.
———. 1989. "An Alternative to Quantum Theory." With Tomio Petrosky. *Physica* 147A: 461–86.
Rahner, Karl. 1957/1968. *Spirit in the World.* New York: Herder.
———. 1976/1978. *Foundations of Christian Faith.* New York: Seabury.
Read, John. 1957. *From Alchemy to Chemistry.* London: Bell.
Ricardo, D. 1817/1933. *The Principles of Political Economy and Taxation.* London: Dent.
Roos, Matts. 1994. *Introduction to Cosmology.* New York: Wiley.
Reith, Herman. 1958. *The Metaphysics of St. Thomas Aquinas.* Milwaukee: Bruce.
Rousseau, Jean-Jacques. 1762/1962. *Le contrat social.* Paris: Freres.
Rovelli, Carlo. 1997a. "Loop Quantum Gravity." Preprint available at xxx.lanl.gov/abs/gr-qc/9710008.
———. 1997b. "A Note on the Formal Structure of Quantum Constrained Systems," preprint available at xxx.lanl.gov/abs/gr-qc/9711028.
———. 1998. Strings, loops and others: a critical survey of the present approaches to quantum gravity, Plenary lecture on quantum gravity at the GR15 conference, Pune, India.
———. 1999. "Quantum Spacetime: What Do We Know." To appear in: "Physics Meets Philosophy at the Planck scale," edited by C. Callender and N. Hugget. Cambridge University Press. Preprint available at xxx.lanl.gov/abs/gr-qc/9903045.
———. 2000. "The century of the incomplete revolution: searching for general relativistic quantum field theory." *J.Math.Phys.* 41 (2000) 3776–380.
Rowley, David. 1987. *Millenarian Bolshevism.* New York: Garland.
Ruether, Rosemary. 1974. *Faith and Fratricide.* New York: Harper.
———. 1992 *Gaia and God: An Ecofeminist Theology of Earth Healing.* San Francisco: Harper San Francisco.
Sacks, Oliver. 1985. *The Man Who Mistook His Wife for a Hat.* New York: HarperCollins.
Sadakara, Akira, and Haijime Nakamura. 1997. *Buddhist Cosmology.* Tokyo: Kosei.
Sartre, Jean Paul. 1943. *L'etre et le néant.* Paris.
———. 1960. *Critique de la raison dialectique.* Paris.
Scheler, Max. c. 1928/1961. *Man's Place in Nature.* Boston: Beacon.
Schelling, Friedrich. 1810/1994. *Stuttgardt Seminars.*
Schopenauer, Arthur. 1819. *The World as Will and Idea.*
Segundo, Juan Luis. 1985. *Theology and the Church.* New York: Harper & Row.
Seifert, Josef. 1981. *Back To Things in Themselves.* London: Routledge & Keagan Paul.
Seyvastyanov, V., A. Ursul, and Yu Shkolenko. 1979. *The Universe and Civilization.* Moscow: Progress.
Shannon, Claude, and Warren Weaver. 1949. *The Mathematical Theory of Communication.* Urbana: University of Illinois Press.
Sheldrake, Rupert. 1981. *The New Science of Life*, Los Angeles, CA: Tarcher.
———. 1989. *The Presence of the Past.* London: Fontana.
Silone, Ignazio. 1955. *Vino e pane.* Milano: Monadori.
Smolin, Lee. 1997. *The Life of the Universe.* Oxford: Oxford University Press.
Soloviev, Vladimir. 1878/1950. *Divine Humanity.*
Spinoza, Baruch. 1670/1951. *A Theological-Political Treatise.* New York: Dover.
———. 1677/1955. *Ethics.* New York: Dover.

Staal, Frits. 1999. "Greek and Vedic Geometry." *Journal of Indian Philosophy* 27 (1–2) 105–27. Online: http://dx.doi.org/10.1023/A:1004364417713.
Stone, Merlin. 1976. *When God Was A Woman*. London: Dorset.
Stumpf, Samuel Enoch. 1994. *Philosophy: History and Problems*. 5th ed. San Francisco: McGraw-Hill.
Therborn, Goran. 1976. *Science and Society*. London:Verso.
Thibault, Paul. 1972. *Savoir et pouvoir: philosophie thomiste et politique cléricale au XIXme siècle*. Quebec: Université de Laval.
Tillich, Paul. 1967. *Systematic Theology*. Chicago: University of Chicago Press.
Tipler, Frank. 1994 *The Physics of Immortality*. New York: Doubleday.
Tweeten, David. 1996. "Clearing a 'Way' for Aquinas: How the Proof from Motion Concludes to God." *American Catholic Philosophical Quarterly* LXX.
Turing, Alan. 1950. "Computing Machinery and Intelligence." *Mind* 59:433–62.
Turnbull, Herbert Westren. 1951/1956. "The Great Mathematicians." In *The World Of Mathematics*, 4 vols, edited by James R. Newman. New York: Simon & Schuster.
Tyler, Hamilton. 1964. *Pueblo Gods and Myths*. Norman: University of Oklahoma Press.
United Nations Development Program. 1990. *Human Development Report*. New York: Oxford.
Vatican I. 1870. *Dei Filius*.
Vatican II. 1966. *The Documents of Vatican II*. New York: Guild.
von Helmholtz, Hermann. 1854/1961. "On the Interaction of Natural Forces." In *Popular Scientific Lectures*, edited by Martin Kline. New York: Dover.
von Steenberghen, Fernand. 1980a. *Le probléme de l'existence de Dieu dans les écrits de s. Thomas d'Aquin*. Louvain-la-Neuve, Belgium.
———. 1980b. *Thomas Aquinas and Radical Aristotelianism*. Washington, DC: Catholic University of America Press.
Waddington, C. H. 1957. *The Strategy of the Genes*. London: Allen & Unwin.
Wallace, William. 1978. " The Philosophical Setting of Medieval Science." In *Science in the Middle Ages*, edited by David Lindberg. Chicago: University of Chicago Press.
Wallerstein, Immanuel. 1974. *The Modern World System*. New York: Academic.
Waters, Frank. 1963. *The Book of the Hopi*. New York: Viking Penguin.
Watt, Ian. 1996. *Myths of Modern Individualism: Faust, Don Quixote, Don Juan and Robinson Crusoe*. Cambridge: Cambridge University Press.
Weber, Max. 1920/1958. *The Protestant Ethic and the Spirit of Capitalism*. New York: Scribners.
———. 1921/1968. *Economy and Society*. New York: Bedminster.
Wesson, Robert. 1991. *Beyond Natural Selection*. Cambridge: MIT Press.
Wetter, Gustav. 1952/1958. *Dialectical Materialism*. New York: Praeger.
Whittaker, Edmund. 1949. *From Euclid to Eddington: A Study of Conceptions of the External World*. Cambridge: Cambridge University Press.
Wolf, Eric. 1969. *Peasant Wars of the Twentieth Century*. New York: Harper.
Woods, Richard. 1986. *Eckhart's Way*. Wilmington, DE: Michael Glazier.
Zermelo, E. 1896. *Ann. Physik* 57 and 59.
Zimmermann, R. E. 1991. "'The Anthropic Cosmological Principle' Philosophical Implications of Self-Reference." In *Beyond Belief: Randomness, Prediction, and Explanation in Science*, edited by John Casti and Anders Karlqvist. Boca Raton, FL: CRC.
Zurek, Wojcieck Hubert. 1990. *Complexity, Entropy, and the Physics of Information*. New York: Addison–Wesley.

www.ingramcontent.com/pod-product-compliance
Lightning Source LLC
Chambersburg PA
CBHW071226290426
44108CB00013B/1307